MW01252791

Stadium Worlds

Analysing football as a cultural practice, this book investigates the connection between the sport and its built environment. Five thematic sections bring together an international multidisciplinary range of perspectives on football's built environment, with particular focus on the stadium which often embodies the sport beyond its immediate performance.

Offering an analysis of the interplay of football and its sociocultural spaces, the chapters draw on examples from architectural design, politics and media studies to address a wide variety of issues: amongst others, migration, advertising, fandom, identity, emotions, gender and the sociology of space. Some contributors use the stadium to draw conclusions about contemporary economic, social and cultural developments; others, as a place to investigate particular themes: the transgression of social rules, the formation of communities, gender construction and the making of identities.

Texts and case-studies based on the editors' lecture series 'Stadium Worlds – Football as a Gateway to Society' are used to enhance this useful book for lecturers and researchers in sociology, cultural studies, geography, architecture, sport and environment as well as architects and urban or regional planners.

Sybille Frank and **Silke Steets** are sociologists working at the Darmstadt University of Technology, Germany.

THE ARCHI*TEXT* SERIES

Edited by Thomas A. Markus and Anthony D. King

Architectural discourse has traditionally represented buildings as art objects or technical objects. Yet buildings are also social objects in that they are invested with social meaning and shape social relations. Recognizing these assumptions, the Archi*text* series aims to bring together recent debates in social and cultural theory and the study and practice of architecture and urban design. Critical, comparative and interdisciplinary, the books in the series, by theorizing architecture, bring the space of the built environment centrally into the social sciences and humanities, as well as bringing the theoretical insights of the latter into the discourses of architecture and urban design. Particular attention is paid to issues of gender, race, sexuality and the body, to questions of identity and place, to the cultural politics of representation and language, and to the global and postcolonial contexts in which these are addressed.

Visualizing the City
Edited by Alan Marcus and
Dietrich Neumann

Re-Shaping Cities
How global mobility transforms
architecture and urban form
Edited by Michael Guggenheim and
Ola Söderström

Bauhaus Dream-house
Modernity and globalization
Katerina Rüedi-Ray

Stadium Worlds
Football, space and the built
environment
Edited by Sybille Frank and
Silke Steets

**Edited by Sybille Frank and
Silke Steets**

Stadium Worlds

Football, space and the built
environment

Routledge
Taylor & Francis Group

LONDON AND NEW YORK

First published 2010
by Routledge
2 Park Square, Milton Park, Abingdon, Oxon OX14 4RN

Simultaneously published in the USA and Canada
by Routledge
270 Madison Avenue, New York, NY 10016

Routledge is an imprint of the Taylor & Francis Group, an informa business

© 2010 Selection and editorial matter, Sybille Frank and Silke Steets; individual chapters, the contributors

Typeset in Frutiger by Wearset Ltd, Boldon, Tyne and Wear
Printed and bound in Great Britain by TJ International Ltd, Padstow, Cornwall

British Library Cataloguing in Publication Data
A catalogue record for this book is available from the British Library

Library of Congress Cataloging-in-Publication Data
Stadium worlds : football, space and the built environment / edited by Sybille Frank & Silke Steets.
p. cm. — (The architext series)
Includes biographical references and index.
1. Soccer fields. 2. Stadiums. 3. Architecture and society. 4. Soccer—Social aspects.
I. Frank, Sybille. II. Steets, Silke, 1973–
GV943.9.S63S73 2010
796.334–dc22

2009053033

ISBN13: 978-0-415-54903-5 (hbk)
ISBN13: 978-0-415-54904-2 (pbk)
ISBN13: 978-0-203-84856-2 (ebk)

Contents

Illustrations

Contributors

Bruno Arich-Gerz received his Ph.D from the University of Konstanz with a thesis on Thomas Pynchon's *Gravity's Rainbow* and reader response theory (2001) before he was appointed *Juniorprofessor* at the Darmstadt University of Technology in 2002 (until 2009). His publications include *Mittelbau-Dora. American and German Representations of a Nazi Concentration Camp* (2009) and *Namibias Postkolonialismen* (*Namibia's Postcolonialisms*, 2008), a collection of essays inspecting Southwest Africa-related literary and non-fiction texts through the prism of postcolonial theory, as well as *Mina – Medien – Allegorie* (*Mina – Media – Allegory*, 2004). Under the alias of Bruno Laberthier, he publishes regularly in *Der Tödliche Pass* (*The Lethal Pass*), a German football journal.

Corinna Assmann studied German and English literature at the University of Heidelberg. She started playing football at the age of six, mainly with friends in the street. In 2004, however, she followed her sisters Marlene and Valerie to join the women's team of BSV Al-Dersimspor, a club from the multicultural urban quarter Kreuzberg in the second Berlin district league. Together with Iranian director A. Najafi they conceived the documentary film *Football under Cover* about the first official women's football match in the I.R. Iran, which won two Teddy Awards at the 2008 Berlin Film Festival. She was a member of the organizing team for the friendly match in Tehran, and co-wrote and co-produced the documentary.

Christian Banse is Lecturer in Political Sociology, Sociological Theory and the Analysis of Social Structures at the Institute for Sociology at Göttingen University, Germany. He is currently working on his dissertation about national borders and transnational processes. His publications include a co-edited volume on *Nationale Grenzen in Europa* (with H. Stobbe, *National Borders in Europe*, 2004), as well as articles on TV addiction, anti-Semitism, sociological theory and national borders in general. Coming from a family that is literally crazy about sports, Christian seems to be equipped with a nothing short of manic data base knowledge of football. He will remain devoted to all sorts of ball games all his life, especially volleyball and, of course, football.

Christian Bromberger is Professor of Anthropology at the University of Provence at Aix-en-Provence, France. From 1988 to 2006 he directed the Institut d'Ethnologie Méditerranéenne et Comparative and from 2006 to 2008 the French Institute for Iranian Studies in Tehran. Since 1995 he has been Senior Member of the Institut Universitaire de France. He has published extensively on collective identities in Iran and in the Mediterranean. Among his publications devoted to the ethnography of football in France, Italy and Iran are *Le Match de Football. Ethnologie d'une passion partisane à Marseille, Naples et Turin* (*The Football Game. Ethnology of a partisan passion in Marseille, Naples and Turin*, 1995), *Football, La Bagatelle la Plus Sérieuse du Monde* (*Football, the Most Serious Bagatelle in the World*, 2004), and some English articles such as 'Cultures and Identities in Europe through the Looking Glass of Football', in M. Demossier (ed.) *The European Puzzle* (2007). He just finished a book on the meaning of hair Trichologiques. *Une Anthropologie des cheveux et des poils (Trichologics. An Anthropology of Hair, 2010)*.

Adam Brown is Director, Founding Member and Researcher for Substance, a social research cooperative that specializes in sport, youth inclusion and community regeneration, utilizing innovative approaches to research, monitoring and evaluation and reporting. He has a background in football and its fans but also has expertise in cultural industries and is currently leading a major research programme on the social and community benefits of angling. Adam is a board member of FC United of Manchester and was formerly Deputy Director and Senior Research Fellow at the Manchester Institute for Popular Culture, Manchester Metropolitan University. He is co-editor of *Football and Community in the Global Context* (2008), co-author of *Not For Sale: Manchester United, Murdoch and the defeat of BSkyB* (1999), and editor of *Fanatics!* (1998).

Tim Edensor teaches Cultural Geography at Manchester Metropolitan University. He is the author of *Industrial Ruins. Space, aesthetics and materiality* (2005), *National Identity, Popular Culture and Everyday Life* (2002) and *Tourists at the Taj* (1998), editor of *Geographies of Rhythm* (2010) and co-author of *Spaces of Vernacular Creativity: Rethinking the cultural economy* (with D. Leslie, S. Millington and N. Rantisi, 2009). He has written widely on theories of identity and space, globalization, leisure and tourism, urban ruination, and urban and rural cultures. He is currently pursuing projects about urban materiality and landscapes of illumination.

Sybille Frank is a Postdoctoral Research Fellow in the Research Area *Eigenlogik der Städte* (*Intrinsic Logic of Cities*) at Darmstadt University of Technology. She has worked at the Social Science Research Center Berlin (WZB), at UNESCO's World Heritage Centre in Paris, lectured at the Free University Berlin and held a position as researcher and lecturer at the Institute for

Sociology, Darmstadt University of Technology. Her doctoral thesis *Der Mauer um die Wette gedenken* (*Competing for the Best Wall Memorial*, 2009) reconstructs the Anglo-American scientific debate on the 'heritage industry' since the 1980s and confronts its results with the boom of communist heritage tourism at Checkpoint Charlie, Berlin. Sybille co-edited *Negotiating Urban Conflicts: Interaction, Space and Control* (2006) and published several book chapters on tourism, memory, heritage and urban development.

Gunter Gebauer is Professor of Philosophy and the Sociology of Sport at the Free University in Berlin. He has authored many books and articles on both topics, including *Poetik des Fußballs* (*Poetics of Football*, 2006), *Mimesis. Culture, Art, Society* (with Ch. Wulf, 1995), *Sport in der Gesellschaft des Spektakels* (*Sport in the Society of the Spectacle*, 2002), *Olympische Spiele, die andere Utopie der Moderne. Olympia zwischen Kult und Droge* (*The Olympic Games, Modernity's Other Utopia. Olympia between cult and drug*, 1996), and *Sport – Eros – Tod* (*Sport – Eros – Death*, 1986). He has also written an article about the architectural space of the Berlin Olympic Games 1936 (1986) and co-authored a book about the architecture of Ludwig Wittgenstein (1982). His latest publication is *Wittgensteins anthropologisches Denken* (*Wittgenstein's Anthropological Thinking*, 2009).

Silke Gülker is a Political Scientist and member of the Research Group on Science Policy Studies at the Social Science Research Center Berlin (WZB). Here, she concentrates on the problem of governance of science and on evaluation processes in particular. Silke has played football for around ten years and was involved in the founding process of the women's team at the club BSV AL-Dersimspor, a team from the multicultural urban quarter Kreuzberg in the second Berlin district league, in 2004. As one of the players she travelled to Tehran in the spring of 2006 for the friendly match against the Iranian women's national team, which is the subject of her co-authored chapter in this book.

Johannes John works as a Research Fellow at the Commission for Recent German Literature, Bavarian Academy of Sciences, preparing the historical-critical edition of the works and letters of Adalbert Stifter. He studied German philology, philosophy and drama in Munich and received his Ph.D from Munich University in 1987 for a thesis on Goethe's novels. Since 1987 he has taught a variety of German Literature courses at the Universities of Munich and Eichstätt. His numerous publications cover subjects from Goethe to Bob Dylan. Together with S. Erhardt and C. Melchior he publishes the quarterly journal *Der tödliche Pass. Magazin zur näheren Betrachtung des Fußballspiels* (*The Lethal Pass. Journal for close analyses of football*, 56 issues since 1995). He has played over 300 matches for Harla-chinger SV on numerous soccer pitches all over Munich, covering just about every position except goalkeeper.

Anthony King is a Professor of Sociology at the University of Exeter. He has published on the armed forces, football and social theory, including *The Structure of Social Theory* (2004), *The European Ritual: Football in the New Europe* (2003) and *The End of the Terraces: The transformation of English football in the 1990s* (1998). He just finished a monograph on the European military, entitled *From the Rhine to the Hindu Kush: The Transformation of Europe's Armed Forces* that will be published in 2010. In addition, he has appeared regularly in the media to discuss issues around football.

Bettina Kratzmüller is a freelance classical archaeologist from Vienna, Austria. Her research interests focus on ancient sports history and the comparison of ancient and modern sports phenomena. She has published on the issue of gender and ethnicities in ancient Greek vase-painting, authored the article 'Stadion und Politik in der Antike' ('Stadium and Politics in Classical Antiquity', 2005), in M. Marschik *et al.* (eds), *Stadion. Architektur, Politik, Ökonomie* (*The Stadium. Architecture, politics, economics*) and co-edited a 1000-page volume on *Sport and the Construction of Identities. Proceedings of the XIth international CESH-congress in Vienna 2006* (2007).

Steve Millington is Senior Lecturer in Human Geography at Manchester Metropolitan University. His research interests include urban regeneration, place management and branding, class and creativity. His recent publications are 'Illuminations, Class Identities and Contested Landscapes of Christmas' (with T. Edensor, *Sociology*, in press) and 'This is Our City: Branding, Football and the Myths of Locality' (with T. Edensor, *Global Networks*, 2008). He co-edited journal issues on *Mundane Mobilities* (*Social and Cultural Geography*, 2007), *Mundane Geographies* (*Environment and Planning A*, 2007) and a book on *Cosmopolitan Urbanism* (2006). Steve is a supporter of Manchester City and has regularly attended matches home and away since the mid-1970s.

Tiffany Muller Myrdahl is Assistant Professor for Women's Studies at the University of Lethbridge, Alberta, Canada. In 2008, she finished her dissertation thesis, entitled *Contested Spaces of Women's Sport*. Trained as a feminist urban geographer, her research interests include the cultural politics of leisure landscapes, uneven urban development, feminist and queer theorizations of identity politics, critical race and gender studies, and sport spaces. Her recent publications include ' "Lesbian Community" in WNBA Spaces' (*Social and Cultural Geography*, 2007) and 'Liberty for All? Contested Spaces of Women's Basketball' (*Gender, Place and Culture*, 2007). Tiffany grew up following the Minnesota Kicks and Minnesota Strikers of U.S. men's professional soccer. She watches women's soccer at any opportunity.

Jochen Roose is Assistant Professor for Sociology at the Free University Berlin. His main research areas are comparative research on Europe, cultural sociology and political sociology, his key publications are *Die Europäisierung von Umweltorganisationen* (*Europeanization of Environmental Organizations*, 2003), *Vergesellschaftung an Europas Binnengrenzen. Eine vergleichende Studie zu den Bedingungen sozialer Integration* (*Social Integration across EU Inner Borders. A comparative study*, 2010) and 'Die öffentliche Zuschreibung von Verantwortung' ('The Public Attribution of Responsibility', with J. Gerhards und A. Offerhaus, *Kölner Zeitschrift für Soziologie und Sozialpsychologie*, 2007). He co-edited *Fans. Soziologische Perspektiven* (with M.S. Schäfer and T. Schmidt-Lux, *Fans. Sociological perspectives*, 2010).

Mike S. Schäfer works as an Assistant Professor at the University of Hamburg. His main research areas are the sociology of media and communication, the sociology of fans, and social aspects of climate change. His key publications are *Die Herstellung einer öffentlichen Hegemonie* (with J. Gerhards, *The Establishment of Public Hegemony*, 2006), *Wissenschaft in den Medien* (*Science in the Media*, 2007), a book chapter on 'Die gesellschaftliche Bedeutung von Fußballbegeisterung' (with J. Roose, 'The Societal Impact of Football Enthusiasm', in G. Klein and M. Meuser (eds), *Fußball-Gemeinden* (*Football Communities*, 2008)) and the edited volume *Fans. Soziologische Perspektiven* (with J. Roose and T. Schmidt-Lux, *Fans. Sociological perspectives*, 2010).

Angelika Schnell is Professor for Architectural History and Theory at the Academy of Fine Arts in Vienna. She studied theatre science and architecture in Munich, Berlin and Delft. Between 1999 and 2009 she held teaching positions at the Berlin University of Technology, the Staatliche Akademie der Bildenden Künste (Academy of Fine Arts) Stuttgart, and at the University of Innsbruck. Her dissertation is entitled *The Construction of the Real. A systematic analysis of the historiographic position in the architectural theory of Aldo Rossi*. She has published numerous essays in magazines and books, focusing on the history and theory of modernism, on modern architecture and urban planning during the twentieth and twenty-first century, media and architecture, the notion of transparency, the relationship of postmodern architecture and theories to the arts, to literature, and psychoanalysis.

Hans-Jürgen Schulke is Professor for Sport- and Event-Management at Macromedia, College of Higher Education for Media, Hamburg. He has a long-standing research background in the development of big sport events and is a top manager in this area. In 2006, he was involved in the implementation of the big fan festivals with public viewing areas in the national administration of the FIFA World Cup. Prior to that, he conducted research and lectured at Bremen University for many years and was appointed to several offices in the area of sports and education in Hamburg. In recent years he co-edited the books *Der Zuschauer als Konsument* (*The Spectator as Consumer*, 2006), *Sport im Fernsehen* (*Sport on TV*, 2004) and *Nachhaltigkeit von Sportstätten* (*Sustainability of Sport Grounds*, 2003), and authored many journal and newspaper articles. He is a regular marathon runner.

Silke Steets is a Postdoctoral Research Fellow and Lecturer in Sociology at the Darmstadt University of Technology. She has published on space, art, popular culture, urban theory and the built environment, including 'The Russians are coming!' (2006), an article about football fandom in Russia, and *Living with Walter*, an essay about the way of living in and dealing with the architecture of the Bauhaus settlement Dessau-Törten (with K. Heinecke and R. Krehl, 2003). She also co-authored the textbook *Einführung in die Stadt- und Raumsoziologie* (*Introduction to Urban Sociology and the Sociology of Space*, 2007). Her dissertation theses *'Wir sind die Stadt!'* (*'We are the City!'*, 2008) deals with the production of alternative urban spaces through popular culture and independent art practices in Leipzig, Germany.

Michael Zinganel studied architecture, art and history. He is currently teaching at the Faculty of Architecture at Graz University of Technology. As an artist, curator and theoretician he has worked, exhibited and published on issues of deviance and security in art, architecture and urban planning, on sports and leisure architecture and most recently on migration and transnational cultural change in the tourism industry. His recent publications include *Stadion. Architektur, Politik, Ökonomie* (*The Stadium. Architecture, politics, economics*, 2005), co-edited with M. Marschik, R. Müllner and G. Spitaler, *Backstage Tours. Reisen in den touristischen Raum* (*Backstage Tours. Journeys in touristic space*, 2004), co-edited with P. Spillmann, and *Real Crime. Architektur, Stadt und Verbrechen* (*Real Crime. Architecture, the city and crime*, 2003).

Preface and Acknowledgements

Sybille Frank and Silke Steets

are you ready to forget
your family and your job
world cup oh oh
football round the clock
(woog riots, 2006)

The idea for this book arose from an interdisciplinary lecture series, which we organized in the summer of 2006 at the Institute for Sociology, Darmstadt University of Technology parallel to the World Cup football competition in Germany. The focus of the lecture series was the football stadium. This is not only the scintillating venue of the match, but also the place where violence, community, the joy of the crowd and the sorrow of football fans is experienced. The stadium has also increasingly become a location-supporting representational building, a multifunctional arena for different events, and a much envied global advertising opportunity and site.

The response to the lecture series was as impressive and gratifying as the quality of the speakers' lectures. They spoke as fans as well as academics. In contributing to the Archi*text* series – the result of a serendipitous coincidence – we wanted to transfer the spirit of the lecture series into the more permanent pages of a book and, reinforced by a few additional authors, make the outcome available to an international readership.

Our thanks go to the authors for their commitment, their expertise and their ability to relate the results of their research to other disciplines and new contexts. For constructive and targeted comments as well as their sympathetic ear, we are grateful to the editors of the Archi*text* series, Tony King and Tom Markus. We also thank Georgina Johnson-Cook for her always friendly and understanding supervision of this project.

For infrastructural and personnel support, we must thank Martina Löw, Institute for Sociology, and the LOEWE Research Area 'The Intrinsic Logic of Cities' at the Darmstadt University of Technology. Lora Seel and Merle Schulte were extremely helpful in researching image rights and during the formal revision of the manuscript. This book would also not have been possible without the financial support of the 'Promotion of Women' programme of the Department of Social and Historical Studies at our university. We thank Carolyn Kelly for the professional translation of many chapters, for her flexibility and her humour. Our partners, Hans Jakel and Reinhard Krehl, always showed great solidarity, and we would like to thank them for their caring support of this project. Not least, this book is an expression of solid female friendship.

We hope that the enthusiasm in engaging with the social and built space of the football stadium, present in each contribution to this volume, will be conveyed to the reader.

ILLUSTRATION CREDITS

Cover image: Silke Steets

1.1   Photograph taken from: www.stadiumguide.com/index.htm
1.2   Photograph: John Peters/Manchester United via Getty Images
1.3   Mixmotive/Fotolia.com
1.4   Photograph: Luis Ferreira Alves
1.5   FC Schalke 04
1.6   Photograph: Sybille Frank
1.7   Allianz Arena, Photograph: B. Ducke
2.1   Illustration taken from: J.H. Krause (1841) *Die Gymnastik und Agonistik der Hellenen*, vol. I, Leipzig: J.A. Barth
2.2   Illustration taken from: J.H. Krause (1841) *Die Gymnastik und Agonistik der Hellenen*, vol. I, Leipzig: J.A. Barth
2.3   Kunsthistorisches Museum, Vienna (Antikensammlung inventory number IV 3604)
2.4   Kunsthistorisches Museum, Vienna (Antikensammlung inventory number IV 769)
2.5   Kunsthistorisches Museum, Vienna (Münzkabinett inventory number 15.506)
2.6   Kunsthistorisches Museum, Vienna (Münzkabinett inventory number 7.042)
2.7   Kunsthistorisches Museum, Vienna (Antikensammlung inventory number V 49)
2.8   Illustration taken from: M. Vogt (1926) 'Der Sport im Mittelalter', in G.A.E. Bogeng (ed.) *Geschichte des Sports aller Völker und Zeiten*, vol. I, Leipzig: E.A. Seemann.
3.1   Stadtarchiv Dortmund
3.2   Photograph: Silke Steets
3.3   münchen.tv
3.4   Stadionwelt
4.1a   Quote taken from M.A. Leeds (2005) 'Sieger und Verlierer im Spiel der Stadien', in M. Marschik, R. Müllner, G. Spitaler and M. Zinganel (eds) *Das Stadion. Geschichte, Architektur, Politik, Ökonomie*, Vienna: Turia + Kant.

4.1b   Quote taken from M.A. Leeds (2005) 'Sieger und Verlierer im Spiel der Stadien', in M. Marschik, R. Müllner, G. Spitaler and M. Zinganel (eds) *Das Stadion. Geschichte, Architektur, Politik, Ökonomie*, Vienna: Turia + Kant.

4.2   Plan: Hans H. Albers/Michael Zinganel

4.3   Plan: Hans H. Albers/Michael Zinganel

4.4a   ACTS, Photograph: Norbert Jalitsch

4.4b   ACTS, Photograph: Daniel Raunig

4.4c   ACTS, Photograph: Norbert Jalitsch

4.4d   ACTS, Photograph: Bernhard Horst

4.5   Plan: Hans H. Albers/Michael Zinganel

4.6   Plan: Hans H. Albers/Michael Zinganel

4.7   FC Schalke 04

5.1   Drawing: Angelika Schnell

5.2   360-berlin.de, Photograph: Jens Knappe

5.3   Photograph: Angelika Schnell

5.4   Photograph: Silke Steets

5.5   FLC/VG Bild-Kunst, Bonn 2009

7.1   kavcic@arcor.de/Fotolia.com

8.1   Painting reprinted with kind permission of: Professional Footballers' Association (PFA)

9.1a/b   Photographs: Adam Brown

9.2   Photograph: Andy Barker, andy@fcutdphotos.co.uk

10.1   Photograph: Christian Bromberger

10.2   Photograph: Christian Bromberger

10.3   Photograph: Christian Bromberger

10.4   Photograph: Christian Bromberger

11.1   PUMA AG, Photograph: Stuart Ramson

11.2   Maryland SoccerPlex, Germantown, MD

12.1   Marlene and Corinna Assmann, Photograph: Gelareh Kiazand

12.2   Marlene and Corinna Assmann, Photograph: Gelareh Kiazand

13.1   Photograph reprinted with kind permission of Reinaldo Coddou H., www.fussballtempel.com

13.2   Photograph reprinted with kind permission of Thomas Franke, www.von-athen-nach-althen.de

13.3   Photograph reprinted with kind permission of Thomas Franke, www.von-athen-nach-althen.de

14.1a   McDonald's Corporation, Photograph: Mirja Huber

14.1b   Photograph: Richard Villalon/Fotolia.com

15.1   Photograph: Billy Stickland/Stringer/Getty Images

15.2   Photograph: Gabriel Bouys/AFP/Getty Images

15.3   PUMA AG

16.1   Bildarchiv Foto

16.2   Illustration taken from: W. Kemp (1783) 'Das Bild der Menge', *Städel Jahrbuch*, NF, 4, Munich

16.3   Photograph: Friman, License: Creative Commons by-nc-sa 3.0

While the authors, editors and publisher have made every effort to contact copyright holders of material used in this volume, they would be grateful to hear from any they were unable to contact.

Introduction

Football, Space and the Built Environment

Sybille Frank and Silke Steets

The objective of this book is to highlight association football as a space-constituting, sociocultural practice, and to investigate the connection between this practice, its spaces and the built environment, that is, the stadium. In doing so, we aim to connect the space of the built environment with the theoretical insights of the social sciences and humanities in order to establish fruitful perspectives for both sides.

The book focuses on the diversity of 'Stadium Worlds'. On the one hand, it sketches continuities regarding the development, built structure, use and worldwide spread of stadia, which have, since the days of antiquity, enjoyed periods of glory as fighting arenas, sports complexes, meeting places or places of political representation. On the other hand, the intention is to determine those specific features by which current stadium buildings and their uses are different from their historical predecessors. In this context, the stadium will always be viewed not only as a built, but also as a social space, connected to specific social norms and practices, where not only characteristics of national and local cultures but also global economic developments, as well as media and design trends congregate and are expressed.

In this Introduction, we first outline the development, social position and particular fascination of football as a social practice. We then provide a brief summary of the past and present of the stadium as a building type. In order to understand the interaction between football and the stadium, we propose a spatio-theoretical framework which enables us to comprehend the football stadium within a complex interdependency of social practice, spatial representation and built environment. In the final section we briefly outline the content of the chapters and integrate them with the key theme of the volume.

FOOTBALL AS A COLLECTIVE WORK OF ART

Football is currently the most popular sport in the world. It brings together masses of people onto playing fields, into stadia, in front of television screens at home and to Public Viewing events in pubs or city squares. As an integral part of the everyday life of modern society, it has the capacity not only to move people, but also to establish communities that transcend spatial and social boundaries. How can the worldwide fascination with the game of football be explained?

Based on his theory of civilization (1978, 1982), sociologist Norbert Elias has provided the most comprehensive theoretical approach so far to this question. According to Elias (1983), collective recreational events such as football are particularly promising subjects for an analysis of societies since they represent exceptional but also highly regulated areas of human interaction. In this view, leisure activities can act as a mirror to society, the characteristics of which enable us to draw conclusions about the everyday standards and rules of the respective society in which these activities take place. To paraphrase Elias, every society has the pastimes it deserves. In that respect, we can rephrase the question posed above: What does the popularity of football tell us about modern society?

Elias' reply is that football is both a highly chaotic and also a strictly regulated and controlled contact sport, the complexity of which corresponds to the complexity of modern, highly civilized societies in general. In the ancient world, football would have been inconceivable: At this time the arenas of antiquity hosted gladiator fights or public executions and bloodbaths, with the warrior peoples of Greece and Rome taking great pleasure in the violence they observed from the stands. In those days there was no such thing as a sense of fair play, or a fixed set of rules for such spectacles. The fact that 'sport' emerged as a social form during modern times, in which the once excessive battles in the arena were controlled and violence in general was regulated, is proof for Elias of a great degree of civilizing sensitivity in modern societies.

The question of how this form of regulation and control of violent excesses came about, and what function sport as a whole has adopted in modern societies, has been examined by Elias and his colleague Eric Dunning. Their theory is that '[i]n complex industrial societies with a high differentiation of social functions, the correspondingly high interdependence of all activities, public as well as private, occupational as well as non-occupational demands and produces a cover of restraints all round' (Elias and Dunning 1986: 70). In order to be socially acceptable, adults are 'expected to check the rising upsurge of their excitement in good time' (Elias and Dunning 1986: 65). However, the self-control necessary to force people to regulate their impulses has its price: According to Elias and Dunning, sport – which takes place in leisure time, separate from regulated, everyday working life – develops in modernity as 'an enclave for the socially approved arousal of moderate excitement behaviour in public' (Elias and Dunning 1986: 65). For Elias and Dunning, therefore, sport is an exceptional pastime, but also one that guarantees order and fulfils a compensatory function. It allows players and spectators a mimetic 'loosening of social and personal restraints' – always within the framework of certain rules – and thus enables the much more regulated civilized everyday social order beyond the sporting event to remain intact (Elias and Dunning 1986: 66).

For Elias, football is the sport that best represents the highest level of civilization in modern society. He considers it to be a 'collective work of art', the highest civilizing achievement and simply the most mimetic of all pleasures: 'like real events, the played events cause excitement and tension. But it is an uplifting excitement. To put it in my words, a relaxing tension' (Elias 1983: 13, 20).[1] The balance of tension that characterizes football is that between disorder and order: football is never boring, because it allows, theoretically, an endless number of configurations of the 22 players on the field – and thus disorder and chaos. During a football match, the arrangement of players on the pitch always creates new spaces: spaces are 'shifted', either 'narrowed down' in defence or 'opened up' in attack, in order to either score goals or prevent them. In addition, emotional spaces are created by the interaction between the players on the pitch and the fans in the stands. Yet all of these spatial configurations move within a certain order: Events on the pitch are regulated by means of playing rules which are implemented by a referee and which, throughout the history of football, have always been adapted in order to make the game more exciting, an example being the offside rule. Teams or players who are cunning enough to know when and how to break the rules are often particularly admired.

It is the rules of the game, therefore, designed to allow maximum variation on the pitch, that create and reproduce the balance between order and disorder, between excitement and boredom, between emotional and physical excesses and self-control, between the individual and the team, between competition and cooperation on the playing field. According to Elias, these rules are carried over as unwritten rules to the public, since the mimetic physical excesses that are also experienced by the spectators at the edge of the pitch do not, for the most part, cross a certain line. Thus, the highly civilized ordered disorder and relaxing tension of the football match leads to a collective catharsis among the public.

In order to experience this collective catharsis publicly, spaces are needed that enable a large crowd of people to follow and experience the football match and the emotional reactions it provokes. Although football is played in many places – on the street, in back yards, on rough patches of ground, or on the more or less level pitches of lower division clubs – these places form a 'football space' only as long as it is played there, and allow spectators only limited possibilities to follow the game, due to football's speed, complexity and the large space it covers. The growing excitement of the crowd is thus condensed. In contrast, the stadium is not only a building that embodies football beyond its immediate performance (cf. Schroer 2008), but also a building constructed with the specific intention of making the events taking place inside ideally visible and audible to spectators.

THE DEVELOPMENT OF THE STADIUM AS A BUILDING TYPE

The stadium as a building type is certainly much older than the game of football. As already mentioned, stadia have been built since antiquity and their functions were and still are extremely varied. Stadia were always built and used as sporting venues, regardless of whether constructed primarily of earthen walls, wood or stone, as in antiquity; of concrete, as in the nineteenth and twentieth centuries; or, like the newest arenas, of steel and glass. But throughout history they also served as battlegrounds, as gathering places for cults (cf. van Winkel 2000), as prisons (cf. Hachleitner 2005) and, not least, as places of political representation (cf. Kratzmüller 2005). Following the heyday of stadium construction in the ancient world, these buildings thereafter sank into oblivion for centuries, and it was only in the late eighteenth century that stadium construction once again began: the multifunctional arena that was built on the Champ de Mars in Paris in 1790 is regarded as the first permanent modern stadium and is estimated to have held between 400,000 and 600,000 spectators (Verspohl 1976: 39, 42, Figure 16.2).

Stadium construction has seen spectacular advances since the nineteenth century. At present, there are more than 10,000 stadia around the world with a capacity of between 30,000 and 250,000 spectators, though the largest stadia are actually used for motor racing events.[2] The largest arena in which football competitions take place is a multifunctional stadium in North Korea. Eight storeys and more than 60 metres in height, a roof comprising 16 round arches, a building complex that resembles a gigantic landed parachute, the Rungrado May Day Stadium in Pyongyang was opened on 1 May 1989, after a construction period of two-and-a-half years. It contains 150,000 seats. In addition to football matches, other sporting contests are held there, such as athletics, wrestling or gymnastics. The stadium also regularly hosts parades and festivities.

The largest football-only stadium currently in existence was built in India in 1984. The Yuba Bharati Krirangan (Salt Lake Stadium) in Kolkata is an all-seater stadium that can hold up to 120,000 people. The next largest is the Estadio Azteca in Mexico City, which was built as early as 1966 and can hold somewhat more than 105,000 fans, seated and standing. The largest number of people ever to have attended a football match was recorded at the 1950 World Cup final in the Estádio Jornalista Mário Filho (Maracanã Stadium) in Rio. Its capacity of 150,000 set new standards at the time and, in the end, 200,000 spectators squeezed inside to watch the final (Eisenberg *et al.* 2004: 115). As a result of its conversion to an all-seater stadium – due to security restrictions and also the fact that profits in football no longer come primarily from ticket sales, but rather from television rights and advertising – the Maracanã Stadium now contains a mere 96,000 seats. With a slightly smaller seating capacity of 94,700 seats the Soccer City Stadium in Johannesburg, situated 1,750 metres above sea level, has been restructured to host the opening and final matches of the 2010 World Cup. Europe has 4,062 stadia and thus boasts the majority of all existing arenas worldwide. Most of these are football arenas only, and are most prevalent in Germany (510), followed by Spain (428) and the United Kingdom (365).

These figures demonstrate not only the worldwide distribution but also the huge popularity of stadia. Yet the stadia of today not only differ radically from their ancient ancestors, but also from their modern predecessors: Since the late twentieth century, against a background of worldwide interurban competition, stadia increasingly serve as location-supporting, urban representative buildings and as driving forces for urban development (cf. Bale 1993). In that respect, the status of the football stadium of today is comparable to that of museums in the 1980s: 'it has become an absolute must for every self-respecting town or city' (Feireiss 2000: 7). Celebrity architects such as Jacques Herzog and Pierre de Meuron, or Norman Foster, also regard stadium projects as increasingly prestigious projects. Having long been discovered by sponsors as advertising vehicles, stadia have transformed themselves into mediatized market architectures and high-technology multifunctional arenas for different events. But how did this happen?

In his stadia generations theory, the British architect Rod Sheard (2005) presented a periodization of the development of modern stadia. According to this theory, the first generation established itself at the end of the nineteenth century. At this time, stadia were large and uncomfortable and thus little more than large receptacles for as many spectators as possible. An example of this generation named by Sheard is the Maracanã Stadium in Brazil, mentioned above. The second generation emerged with the spread of television in the 1950s, and the opportunity it offered to follow matches from the comfortable atmosphere of the home. Now the familiar receptacles were fitted with proper toilets, beer stalls and food outlets. According to Sheard, the most extravagant example of the second stadium generation is Munich's *Olympiastadion*. The third stadium generation is an American invention. With the rise of Disneyland, stadia were transformed into theme parks, in which sport made way for family-friendly mass entertainment as the main centre of focus. The necessary requirements for a successful family outing included better security, comfortable seating, roofed stands, lighting, shops and restaurants.

Munich's Allianz Arena could be considered a prototype of the fourth generation (Figure 1.7). It represents a highly engineered and mediatized type of stadium, in which the live event, 'football', merely acts as a hook upon which to hang everything else that is happening inside, to be broadcast instantaneously via satellite television all over the world. Sheard sees this represented symbolically in an architectural manner by the luminescent body shell of the arena: The stadium is like a lens, an oversized media and television studio that concentrates the big business of sport and passion in its innards, thus producing enormous profits. The stadium has become a highly segregated space, where private boxes, lounges, corporate and VIP areas are separated from the fan areas. The fifth stadium generation, according to Sheard, will draw the arena back into the cities. People should be able to reach the stadium, the city's landmark, quickly on foot.

As a result, 'live' will once again mean 'on-site'. Before this can happen, however, the stadium must overcome competition from television. Sheard, therefore, predicts the advent of high-tech TV screens on every stadium seat, just as in an aeroplane.

As this overview of the architectural development of stadia shows, each stadium generation has yielded different *spatial* relations, whether between inside and outside, between the spectators' area and the playing field, between fans and players or between the stadium as a built structure and the area surrounding this structure. How, then, can we analyse the complex relationship between the built and the social space of the football stadium more precisely? To do this, some theoretical reflections are needed.

THEORETICAL PERSPECTIVES: SPACE, PLACE AND ARCHITECTURE

Henri Lefèbvre contended that '(social) space is a (social) product' (Lefèbvre 1991: 30). In other words, space is not a neutral (or passive) background *upon* which or *in* which social practices take place and a social order manifests itself. Rather, space can be understood as a built, symbolic and social order, which is always simultaneously a prerequisite *and* a product of human action (cf. Löw 2001, 2008). In this manner, stadium and football, the built and the social, can be seen as constituting each other.

In terms of social theory, this idea is based on Anthony Giddens' concept of 'structuration' (Giddens 1984). In order to get around the dualistic construction of action and structure in social theory, Giddens suggests that social structures are ongoing routines of action that are validated by rules and resources, which on the one hand place an ordering structure on action, but which on the other hand are formed through the reproduction of social action. Applied to space, this simply means that individuals, as social actors, act, and in doing so – because they have a body – create spaces, while at the same time their action is dependent upon social, i.e. economic, legal, cultural, and not least spatial and physical, structures (cf. Löw 2001, 2008). This can be illustrated by an example: The fan sings, shouts, rants and rejoices in the stands and thus contributes to the production of a collective space (she/he acts). Her/his singing, shouting, ranting and rejoicing, however, cannot exist independently of the particular social rules of the fan block, the economic and legal frameworks of the society in which she/he lives, or the architectural and physical structures of the football stadium. Spaces are therefore always the product of action, while at the same time structuring action, in other words, spaces can both constrain and enable action. In examining spaces, one always examines relations: between the built and the social, between action and structure (cf. Reckwitz 2008). This is just as true for the micro level of society as it is for the macro level.

At the macro level, the advantage of such a *relational* concept of space lies in the possibility to examine constellations of space and place. What role does the stadium as a place (of the footballing event) play against the background of an advancing global mediatization of sport? What spaces are created by the medial transmission between the stadium and the world? What impact does the ubiquitous media presence of football have on the architecture of the stadium? Against this background, is the stadium as a place and as a built structure becoming less important? In his groundbreaking analysis *Sport, Space and the City* (1993), John Bale highlighted the location-constituting potential of the stadium. He describes in great detail how stadia

> can not only generate a love of place, a sense of place-loyality, place-bonding and other kinds of localism, but also how some stadia have become what amount to sacred places, worthy, perhaps, of future protection and preservation like other revered monuments and buildings of yesteryear.
>
> (Bale 1993: 6f.)

That which Bale emphasizes in relation to the stadium – the significance of places – is formulated more generally by Helmuth Berking (1998). Berking underlines the fact that, despite the radical shifts in social-spatial criteria, which have greatly altered our perception of proximity and distance in the last few decades (cf. Harvey 1989), places maintain a lasting lifeworldly relevance:

> In countering the by now conventional wisdom that places and spaces are losing significance due to globalisation, it suffices to agree with Clifford Geertz's simple view that 'nobody lives in the world in general' [...]. A sense of orientation and of belonging to a place, the perception and production of places, in short: 'senses of place' [...] belong to the conditio humana. We cannot imagine a world without places.
>
> (Berking 1998: 390)

Equally, we cannot imagine places separate from their physical and material reality. But how can places in a globalized world, and therefore beyond essentialistic modes, be considered?

Doreen Massey has suggested that we consider places against the background of a relational concept of space: as a specific way in which the world is present in them. Such thinking 'enables places to be imagined as the location of particular sets and interactions of such places and relations' (Massey 1995: 63). Places are therefore not simply spatial units that have grown historically and culturally, nor are they mere products of the global, but rather the global and the local constitute each other (Massey 2006: 29). With regard to the football stadium, this means that global flows *and* local cultures always meet in a specific spatial ordering of physical-material objects, symbols and people.

Emile Durkheim (1961) has referred to the social meaning of the material, of the thing, and with it, one of the central aspects of the constitution of space. For Durkheim, physical objects such as buildings, tools, technical artefacts and lines of communication – similar to institutional behaviour and the ruling law of a society – are 'social facts' (Durkheim 1951). Durkheim also sees the built environment as something produced socially: it is the expression of a societal consensus and – like institutional behaviour and the rule of law – exists alongside the acting individual, externally and (apparently) independently. Durkheim's student Maurice Halbwachs developed this idea further. He considers the material factors of society to be a kind of stabilizer. According to Halbwachs, places, buildings, squares, houses and streets give the collective life of society a feeling of regularity and consistency in the midst of permanent change (Halbwachs 1938). He ascribes this to a *symbolic* and a *lifeworldly* aspect of the material milieu: Society, through its buildings, gives itself a form, and thus recognizes, identifies and reassures itself of its self. At the same time, society preserves in its buildings collective practices and memories. Therefore, we pose the question: What form has society given itself in different historical periods through its stadia? Which practices and memories outlive the immediate football match in the materialized form of the stadium?

STADIUM WORLDS: FOOTBALL, SPACE AND THE BUILT ENVIRONMENT

In order to do justice to the complex phenomenon of the football stadium, this book adopts two lines of approach: Following on from our previous consideration of the relationship between space, place, architecture and football, the football stadium can, on the one hand, be approached as a social and material space in which general economic, social and cultural developments are intensified. By this, we are treating the stadium as a lens: Looking at what happens in, with and through football stadia can help us to identify and understand recent social changes.

On the other hand, the football stadium has always been the place of the game, of violence, of community, of mass cheering, and of grief of predominantly male but increasingly also female football fanatics. According to Elias and Dunning (1986), the stadium can be seen as a refuge of social rules of community formation, gender construction and identification that would be unacceptable at almost any other place outside the stadium. In a nutshell, the stadium is at one and the same time a prototypical and an extraordinary place for modern societies. We suppose that the reason for this is to be found in the specific spatiality and materiality of the stadium through which gazes are focused, actions are placed in the spotlight and crowds are celebrated and controlled.

To test and further explore this double perspective, the book is divided into five thematic sections. The first part, 'The Politics of Representation and Design', provides an overview of the past, the present and the future of the stadium. This section approaches the subject of the book from an historical, macrosociological perspective. The stadium is described as a lens which focuses on general social development trends and makes them recognizable.

Parts II and III of the book provide a deeper discussion of the central characteristics of the present-day football arena as identified in the first part of the volume: the trend towards a comprehensive mediatization, an advancing commercialization and a growing professionalization of stadium architecture and stadium events. The second part of the book, entitled 'Architecture and Media', first illuminates the complex interrelation between the built space and the medial space of the stadium. The third part of the book, 'When Global Flows Meet Local Cultures', then delves deeper into the subject of commercialization. By accessing different spatial scales, encounters between global flows of finance and people on the one hand with persistent national and local cultures on the other hand are examined.

The fourth and fifth parts of the book are devoted to the stadium as an extraordinary place, in which certain behaviour is displayed that would be unacceptable outside the stadium. Part IV, 'Gender and Space' first casts an eye on the specific social rules of community formation, gender construction and identification in the stadium. Part V of the volume concerns itself with the intimate and precarious relationship of 'Emotions and the Body' and provides a further starting point with which to examine the stadium as a special place in society, as a refuge.

With essays from the fields of architecture, archaeology, history, sport, film, cultural studies, sociology, social anthropology, philosophy and geography, and illustrative examples from Europe, North America, Africa and the Arab World, the book offers an international and multi-disciplinary range of perspectives on football's built environment. For those interested in architecture and stadium design, it offers many insights into the stadium's atmosphere, its relationship to the local communities, and the broader socio-spatial, cultural and political contexts in which it operates. The themes and main theses of the respective chapters are outlined below.

The politics of representation and design

In the programmatic opening chapter of the volume 'The New European Stadium' sociologist Anthony King analyses the type of football arena that emerged in Europe with the shift from modernity to post-modernity. The author draws parallels between the newly created seating areas, the apparently weightless roofs and the glass façades of contemporary stadia and the social and political-economic hierarchies of postmodern societies: Where the modern stadium with its terraced stands was a massive, clearly defined, inward-looking, functional building, the postmodern stadium presents a lucid space that is characterized by the power of global and geographically unidentifiable capital flows. Referring to Foucault, King interprets the introduction of seating as a concentrated attempt by governments and football associations to ensure security by means of the isolation and control of spectators. This opens up the new arenas to those sections of the public that have deep pockets and a desire for comfort, thus supplanting the original fan milieus. At the same time, the sweeping roofs and glass façades have enhanced the stadia to unmistakable brand architecture. According to King, the power of a growing global alliance of clubs, sponsors, media, consumers and capital can be seen in this new stadium type, which by now can be found all over the world.

In Chapter 2, ' "Show Yourself to the People!": Ancient Stadia, Politics and Society', archeologist Bettina Kratzmüller demonstrates numerous parallels between the design and function of ancient and modern stadia. The Greek *stadion* and *hippodromus*, as well as the Roman *circus* and *amphitheatrum*, were specifically built to stage sporting contests in front of a large crowd. The actual spatial use of the buildings also illustrates the social order of the ancient city-states: The spectators' stands were segregated according to provenance, social status, sex and fan allegiance, while marginalized groups were excluded. In addition, the stadia of antiquity were, to a great extent, spaces of political representation: Since the public was never so concentrated as in the stadium, the rulers used the arena to publicly display themselves and their power. But those rulers exposed on the stands often met not only with the jubilation of the crowd, now also in a position to observe itself, but with its displeasure too. And so, even ancient stadia show the ambivalence of an architectural form that both organizes the confrontation between the individual and the crowd, as well as the confrontation of the crowd with itself and its own power.

While Bettina Kratzmüller traces the history of the stadium up to its temporary disappearance in the Middle Ages, sport and event management expert Hans-Jürgen Schulke asks in his chapter 'Challenging the Stadium: Watching Sport Events in Public' why football in particular played such a large role in rediscovering the forgotten, ancient architectural type of the stadium in modern times. His theory is that popular street football, irrepressible in its vitality and disorder, was transformed into a competitive sport in the context of standardization, which then required a building which would maintain the consistency of the rules of play and allow large numbers of people to watch and place bets on the action. In contrast, current arenas are attractive to spectators only to a limited extent: high admission prices, numbered seats and segmented tiers prevent the development of the kind of marketplace atmosphere traditionally connected to football. The recent triumph of Public Viewing, which poses a serious functional challenge to the building type that is the stadium, can be explained by the fact that Public Viewing combines the advantages of television (close-ups) and those of the stadium (shared emotions), thus bringing football back to its origins: the public space in the middle of the city.

Architecture and media

In his contribution 'The Stadium as Cash Machine', the artist, curator and architectural theorist Michael Zinganel analyses by means of three multifunctional arenas the progression of what Rem Koolhaas has called 'junk space', very flexible and with an affinity for capital. Taking as his examples the Veltins Arena in Gelsenkirchen, the St. Jakob Park Arena in Basel and the Amsterdam Arena in the Netherlands, Zinganel shows that events other than football are starting to play a considerable role in determining the use and architecture of stadia: In Gelsenkirchen, the removable pitch makes way for rock concerts; in Basel, offices, shopping centres and a retirement home have been integrated into the stadium; while entire entertainment areas have been installed in Amsterdam.

Zinganel's theory is that the stadium as a building is ultimately too immobile, despite all attempts by clubs to transform it into a space that is flexible and conforms to the market. This is demonstrated by the many temporary stadia that can be quickly erected and taken down in any place at all. The most minimal version consists of a flagpole, a sportsman or -woman, a DJ, a VIP, and enough room for a few spectators. Stadium architecture, therefore, is a model for a mediatized, commercialized and ubiquitous event architecture in which the public voluntarily poses for the camera.

In contrast, architectural theorist and historian Angelika Schnell analyses in Chapter 5, 'The Mirror Stage in the Stadium: Medial Spaces of Television and Architecture', a moment in which the seemingly (according to Zinganel in this volume) hermetically fused-together spaces of the built stadium and of the medial event were critically separated, so that the distance between them became reflexible. When Diego Maradona lamented his defeat in the 1990 World Cup final and the media showed close-ups of his face not only on the television screens at home, but also on the video cubes in the stadium, it led to an unplanned interaction between the spectators in the stadium and the television viewers: As the spectators in the stadium, confronted with the television cameras, simultaneously experienced the situation before them and the voyeuristic medial staging of this situation on television, the actual television viewers found themselves exposed to an immediate chorus of whistles from the stadium crowd. Based on this, and referring to Lacan and Le Corbusier, Schnell interprets the stadium architecturally/psychologically as a gigantic eye: Its architecture represents on the one hand the dominance of the camera that constantly observes, controls and drills the stadium and its environment. On the other hand, the stadium acts as a permeable medium, as a window on the world, which pulls together the images that have been fragmented by television.

While the merging of media and stadium architecture is observed critically by Michael Zinganel and positively by Angelika Schnell, media and literary theorist Bruno Arich-Gerz deals with the opposite case in his chapter 'Killing Sports Fields: The Amahoro Stadium Complex in Kigali, Rwanda'. In his example, the barbaric events that took place during the Rwandan civil war in 1994, in which the Amahoro Stadium in Kigali was one of the main settings, were precisely *not* reflected in the media. As thousands of Tutsis fled from the attacking Hutus to the shelter of the stadium, many were killed in front of its closed gates. For others it did actually provide the desired refuge, but it soon became a besieged concentration camp, with many wounded, and precarious hygienic conditions. Although the stadium had suitable media equipment, this was not used at any stage to transmit images or sounds of the terrible events to the wider world. The stadium also hardly appeared *ex post* in the many cinematic treatments of the conflict. It only takes on a collective meaning as an open-air theatre for the screening of such movies, becoming, for many Rwandan viewers, a cinema-induced site of memory. Arich-Gerz concludes that the Amahoro stadium is notably untypical for stadia at the turn of the twentieth century.

When global flows meet local cultures

In the chapter 'Global Players and the Stadium: Migration and Borders in Professional Football', sociologist Christian Banse analyses the influence of the global transfer market on events in the stadium. According to Banse, professional football has always been characterized by migration: Until the twentieth century, footballers of different nationalities played in teams together. In the course of the nationalization and regulation of professional football and the setting of quotas for foreign players, former colonial connections began to take hold between the centre and the periphery, and with their help, talented 'foreign' players were nationalized. However, since the deregulation of markets in the 1990s, the migration of professional footballers is no longer a migration of the elite: With the help of football agents, an increasing number of mediocre players come as cheap labour to Europe. Only a few ever reach their desired destination which is, according to Banse, no longer a particular European country, but rather the football stadium in general: Only those who play in the stadium can escape the financial dependency on agents, the precarious contracts and everyday racism of the lower divisions. Professional football is therefore a marketplace that produces distinctions along the line of ethnic dissociation, and the transnational space of the football stadium is a space that – by crossing the border – reproduces the national border and distinctions as an institution.

The following two chapters deal with the case of Manchester in England, where the fans of not one but two clubs were forced, in the last few years, to bid farewell to their original and emotion-filled stadia – albeit in very different ways.

In their piece 'Going to the Match: The Transformation of the Match-day Routine at Manchester City FC', geographers Tim Edensor and Steve Millington break down the global economic changes in football to the level of the everyday match. The experience of 'going to the match' is at the centre of their chapter. The stadium, according to their central argument, only takes effect as a place through the spatial practices and rituals of football fans, by the way in which they approach the stadium on match day, where and how they meet friends and opponents, drink beer, eat fish and chips and together get in the mood for the game. Through a complex mix of heterogeneous social interactions, materialities and mobilities, imaginaries and social effects, a specific and definitely irreplaceable atmosphere of dense geography is created, which leads to a strong bond between the fans and their stadium, and which can clearly be seen, especially in defeat. The case study refers to Manchester City FC, a club that moved out of the old Maine Road stadium in the south of the city in 2003, to the City of Manchester Stadium (COMS), a modern arena in Manchester's East End.

Sports scientist and cultural theorist Adam Brown is also interested in the role of places in the formation of fan communities. In ' "Come Home": The Stadium, Locality and Community at FC United of Manchester', the second local study on Manchester, Brown argues from the perspective of a political economy of football. In protest against the progressive commercialization of Manchester

United, which culminated in the sale of the majority share to the American family of entrepreneurs, the Glazers, a considerable number of fans founded an alternative football club in 2005: FC United of Manchester. The renunciation of their favourite club also meant the loss of an emotion-filled place, the Old Trafford stadium. Brown traces in great detail the politicization of the fans and their actions in and around Old Trafford, the painful dislocation of a community, plagued by conflict but consciously political, and the desire for a place of their own, which seemingly could only be realized with the construction of their own stadium. Brown's analysis ends with a confrontation between the different purposes that today's stadium must fulfil: While the modern arena is, in many places, financed by investors and seen as an income property, the majority of fans simply want a place that they themselves can define and use, without any commercial background.

Gender and space

Anthropologist Christian Bromberger shows in the chapter 'Sport, Football and Masculine Identity: The Stadium as a Window onto Gender Construction' that every sport has a gender-specific image that mirrors the construction of gender and the power relationships between the sexes in a society. Football is a sport that in Western Europe is associated like no other with masculinity. According to Bromberger, the football stadium is a profoundly sexualized place, in which men continuously affirm their identity in relatively homogenous groups, and where 'masculine' attributes such as strength, expert knowledge, camaraderie and solidarity can be put to the test. In spatial terms, the masculine biography is really illustrated by the age-based segregation of tiers. The youth battles in the matey community of the terraces for acceptance as a man, while the enamoured young man, accompanied by his partner, sits in a remote corner of the arena and middle-aged men test new forms of male sociability in the stands. Stadia are also places of chauvinism and machismo, for example when fans shout slogans that question the masculinity of the opponent, attitudes that would be unacceptable *outside* the stadium. The masculine rituals carried out in the football arena therefore also provide an indication of the fragility of Western masculine identity constructions.

Along similar lines to Bromberger, urban geographer and feminist Tiffany Muller Myrdahl traces, in her historically grounded analysis 'Producing Gender-normative Spaces in U.S. Women's Professional Soccer', the formation of a social field influenced by strong heteronormative values. Her examples are the American women's professional football leagues WUSA (2000–3) and WPS (since March 2009). Muller Myrdahl argues that through the verbal and visual framing of women's football in the USA, and by means of the specific decoration and use of the stadia, a realm of experience is created in which women are (and must be) displayed as (good) women. In contrast to the clearly male connotated American sports such as American Football or baseball, in which men are self-evidently men, sportswomen are continuously forced to prove their (heterosexual) femininity.

One reason for this is the fact that tackling, physicality and athleticism, i.e. constitutive parts of football, are seen as genuinely masculine. Muller Myrdahl's article shows clearly how the stadium, as a place for staging heterosexual femininity, unleashes its strong normalizing power.

In contrast, the article by filmmaker Corinna Assmann and political scientist Silke Gülker is about emancipation from normative gender roles. At the core of their analysis, entitled 'Football Under Cover in Tehran's Ararat Stadium', is the first match played by a female Iranian national football team on Iranian turf since the Islamic Revolution in 1979. The Ararat Stadium in Tehran was the location for this extraordinary event and the socio-political context in which it took place is significant: It is against the law for women to enter football stadia in Iran. In addition, they are not allowed to play football in public places where there is a risk that they might be seen by men. Cautious liberalization led to the foundation, in 2005, of an Iranian national women's team, which, however, had not yet appeared in public in Iran. The particular role of the stadium in questioning and challenging normative gender systems becomes clear in the description of the match, which was attended only by women: In the stadium, cut off from the outside world and thus a protected yet public space, around 2,000 Iranian women sang, shouted, celebrated and applauded. In doing so, they carried out actions that in Iran are actually the preserve of men alone.

Emotions and the body

Sociologists Mike S. Schäfer and Jochen Roose devote themselves in their chapter 'Emotions in Sports Stadia' to one of the most important features of the stadium: The emotional intensity that exists there. They take a look at the spectators' stands and investigate how sports stadia provide a physical, architectural and social framework for the emotions of the fans. Referring to and developing the civilization–sociological works of Norbert Elias and Eric Dunning, they argue that stadia constitute emotional niches in a modern, rationalized society and that these niches fulfil a specific function in that society. They are socially legitimate places of exceptional emotions and therefore both act as a relief and stabilize order. Their architectural form underlines this function: stadia are spaces that are marked off from the outside world; by steering the attention of the spectator to a common focus (the playing field) and by enabling the visual and bodily experience of community through the arrangement of the tiers, they become ideal catalysts for spectators' emotions. According to Schäfer and Roose, stadia are segregated not only socially, but also emotionally: The ultrafan standing on the terraces may, indeed must, sing, shout and insult the opposition. The spectator sitting comfortably in a seat in the grandstand is critical, well informed, and follows the game with balanced applause.

In 'Heroes, Myths and Magic Moments: Religious Elements on the Sacred Ground', philosopher Gunter Gebauer examines the role of the stadium for football as a religious-ritualistic and thus socially cohesive practice. At the centre of his observations are the forms of homage and worship of the heroes and 'saints' of football by the community of fans. Gebauer compares the stadium, as a modern site of worship and a predestined place of quasi-religious experience, with the cathedral. Both building types are, in their size and architecture, spectacular elements of the cityscape, they also mark the separation between the weekday and Sunday (or Saturday), and in both places, collective rituals take place that are based on common experiences and memories. Within the stadium, Gebauer differentiates between two ritual spaces: the pitch, which is influenced by rules and the disciplining of emotions, and the spectators' stands, where both positive and negative emotions are effusively expressed. According to Gebauer, these spaces can only be understood in the context of each other. A double transmission of power takes place: the strictly regulated emotions of the players find expression during the match in the stands; conversely, footballers become heroes or 'saints' only when a 'community of believers' is formed around them.

The German language and literature scholar Johannes John goes a step further than Gebauer in his contribution 'Beckhamania: Promoting Post-modern Celebrities beyond the Stadium'. According to John, footballers nowadays can be characterized more as pop stars than as heroes. The immense media hype surrounding David Beckham is paradigmatic for this development. Using different approaches, John investigates the causes of the global popularity of the English midfielder – and finds his answer above all *outside* the stadium. John sees the reason for this in a radical transformation in the world of football: Once associated with inhospitable terraces, violence and yobs, football was reinvented *culturally*, starting in England in the 1980s. The advent of both excessive references to football outside the stadium in film, art and literature, and the assertion of a new model of manliness, iconically condensed in Paul Gascoigne's tears after the World Cup semi-final defeat in 1990, are indicative of this development. Football stars, concludes John, are therefore not created primarily in stadia (as Gebauer in this volume would have it), but rather in the media and by professional producers of images. Only the market value of the brand thus created is validated on the pitch, i.e. *in* the stadium.

The concluding chapter, 'The Stadium – Lens and Refuge', authored by the editors, draws together the findings of the articles and theorizes on the central idea of the book to analyse the stadium both as a window to and a special place in society. It concludes with a reflection about the stadium as a built structure.

NOTES

1 All translations from German by Carolyn Kelly.
2 All figures are taken from the website www.worldstadiums.com. Accessed 17 November 2009.

REFERENCES

Bale, J. (1993) *Sport, Space, and the City*, London/New York: Routledge.

Berking, H. (1998) ' "Global flows and local cultures". Über die Rekonfiguration sozialer Räume im Globalisierungsprozeß', *Berliner Journal für Soziologie*, 8: 381–92.

Durkheim, E. (1951) *Suicide, a Study in Sociology*, Glencoe: Free Press.

Durkheim, E. (1961) *Die Regeln der soziologischen Methode*, Darmstadt: Luchterhand.

Elias, N. (1978) *The Civilizing Process: The history of manners*, vol. 1, Oxford: Blackwell.

Elias, N. (1982) *The Civilizing Process: State formation and civilization*, vol. 2, Oxford: Blackwell.

Elias, N. (1983) 'Der Fußballsport im Prozeß der Zivilisation', in Modellversuch Journalisten-Weiterbildung der Freien Universität Berlin (ed.) *Der Satz 'Der Ball ist rund' hat eine gewisse philosophische Tiefe. Sport, Kultur, Zivilisation*, Berlin: Transit.

Elias, N. and Dunning, E. (1986) *Quest for Excitement: Sport and leisure in the civilizing process*, Oxford: Basil Blackwell.

Eisenberg, C., Lanfranchi, P., Mason, T. and Wahl, A. (2004) *FIFA 1904–2004. 100 Jahre Weltfußball*, Göttingen: Die Werkstatt.

Feireiss, K. (2000) 'Foreword', in M. Provoost and Nederlands Architectuurinstituut (eds) *The Stadium: The architecture of mass sport*, Rotterdam: NAi Publishers.

Giddens, A. (1984) *The Constitution of Society: Outline of the theory of structuration*, Cambridge: Polity Press.

Hachleitner, B. (2005) 'Das Stadion als Gefängnis', in M. Marschik, R. Müllner, G. Spitaler and M. Zinganel (eds) *Das Stadion. Geschichte, Architektur, Politik, Ökonomie*, Vienna: Turia + Kant.

Halbwachs, M. (1938) *Morphologie Sociale*, Paris: A. Colin.

Harvey, D. (1989) *The Condition of Postmodernity*, Oxford: Blackwell.

Kratzmüller, B. (2005) ' "Quae beneficia e medio stadio Isthmiorum die sua ipse voce pronuntiavit" – Stadion und Politik in der Antike', in M. Marschik, R. Müllner, G. Spitaler and M. Zinganel (eds) *Das Stadion. Geschichte, Architektur, Politik, Ökonomie*, Vienna: Turia + Kant.

Lefèbvre, H. (1991) *The Production of Space*, Oxford/Cambridge: Blackwell.

Löw, M. (2001) *Raumsoziologie*, Frankfurt a. M.: Suhrkamp.

Löw, M. (2008) 'The constitution of space. The structuration of spaces through the simultaneity of effect and perception', *European Journal of Social Theory*, 11: 25–49.

Massey, D. (1995) 'The conceptualization of place', in D. Massey and P. Jess (eds) *A Place in the World? Places, cultures and globalization*, Oxford: Oxford University Press.

Massey, D. (2006) 'Keine Entlastung für das Lokale', in H. Berking (ed.) *Die Macht des Lokalen in einer Welt ohne Grenzen*, Frankfurt a. M./New York: Campus.

Reckwitz, A. (2008) *Unscharfe Grenzen. Perspektiven der Kultursoziologie*, Bielefeld: Transcript.

Schroer, M. (2008) 'Vom Bolzplatz zum "Fußballtempel". Was sagt die Architektur der neuen Fußballstadien über die Gesellschaft der Gegenwart aus?', in G. Klein and M. Meuser (eds) *Ernste Spiele. Zur politischen Soziologie des Fußballs*, Bielefeld: Transcript.

Sheard, R. (2005) *The Stadium. Architecture for the new global culture*, Berkeley: Periplus Editions.

van Winkel, C. (2000) 'Dance, discipline, density and death', in M. Provoost and Nederlands Architectuurinstituut (eds) *The Stadium: The architecture of mass sport*, Rotterdam: NAi Publishers.

Verspohl, F.-J. (1976) *Stadionbauten von der Antike bis zur Gegenwart: Regie und Selbsterfahrung der Massen*, Gießen: Anabas.

Part I

The Politics of Representation and Design

Chapter 1: The New European Stadium

Anthony King

INTRODUCTION

Consider two images of Manchester United's ground, Old Trafford, the first taken in 1984 (Figure 1.1) and the second in 2006 (Figure 1.2).

A radical transformation has manifestly taken place. With the exception of the South Stand (furthest away in Figure 1.1 and on the left in Figure 1.2),[1] the ground has been entirely rebuilt. A low, dull structure has been replaced by a bold edifice of bright steel and glass. Old Trafford's renaissance may be striking but it is far from unique. On the contrary, since the 1990s, new stadia have proliferated across Europe. One of the first examples of this renovation was the San Siro Stadium in Milan reconstructed in 1990 for the World Cup. Visitors, at the time, were awed by the monumental new ground with its concrete bastions and latticed roofing.

In Germany, Schalke has recently moved from the Parkstadion to the bright dome of the Veltins Arena (Figure 1.5), while Bayern Munich relocated to the radical new Allianz Arena in 2004 (Figure 1.7). In France, the Stade de France in

Figure 1.1
Old Trafford, from the north-east, looking towards the South Stand, 1984.

Figure 1.2
Old Trafford, from the
east, looking towards the
West Stand, 2006.

Paris represented the pinnacle of stadium redesign which occurred for the 1998 World Cup. In Portugal, Benfica's new Stadium of Light, Porto's Dragão Stadium (Figure 1.4) and the extraordinary Braga Stadium, abutting an open quarry, all appeared for the 2004 European Championship. In Holland, Ajax now plays in the innovative Amsterdam Arena, built in 1996, while PSV Eindhoven's Philips Stadium features a bold new stand. Central and eastern Europe has not been excluded from these developments. Although many grounds remain unchanged, FC Moscow Lokomotiv now plays in a new all-seater stadium which demonstrates the new design features.

However, especially in Western Europe where capitalist investment has been highest and international football tournaments, the European Championship, World Cup and the Champions League, have consequently been played most frequently (cf. Banse, Chapter 7 in this volume), the transformation has been particularly dramatic and widespread. In themselves, each of these structures is impressive but together they represent an architectural paradigm shift in Europe. The football ground of the twentieth century has been replaced by the stadium of the twenty-first century.

Although local conditions have produced unique structures at each location, there is a strong family resemblance between the new stadia. In particular, three distinctive features distinguish them from the old European grounds of the twentieth century: seats, roofs and glass. The new European stadium is all- or nearly all-seater (sometimes with the capacity to turn standing areas into seating for major matches), its stands are covered by roofs and it has a glass façade.

As an important cultural artefact, architecture has always embodied and been a reflection of wider social reality, as European history demonstrates. From the first century BCE until the fall of the Roman Empire in 476, the European political landscape was similarly studded with arenas. In each city, the arena was a decisive landmark and even today, the city of Rome is dominated by the Collosseum. The spectacles which occurred in these arenas illuminated Roman culture in all its stark brutality. Although the crowd might plead for the life of a gladiator, the decision of life and death – as in the rest of Roman life – rested with the emperor alone. The Roman spectacle was a central ritual in later Roman civilization whereby the social hierarchy from Emperor, to citizens, slaves and criminals was re-affirmed. The arenas which appeared in Europe from the first century BCE were a manifestation of the *pax romana* then. Today's new stadia might be seen in a similar light. Although Europeans live under a quite different political regime, the new European stadium may similarly illustrate contemporary social and political hierarchies as the Roman arena once invoked the authority of the Emperor (cf. Kratzmüller's Chapter 2 in this volume).

The new stadium may be seen as a manifestation of globalizing economic flows which have coalesced around professional football, pointing to the wider transformation of social and political hierarchies. They represent the appearance of a new social and political settlement in Europe. Indeed, the new European football stadium is, perhaps, emblematic of much wider developments. This stadium has itself proliferated globally as a result of international football tournaments and above all the World Cup. The new European football stadium can now be found in Brazil, Korea and, for the 2010 World Cup, in South Africa. Indeed, the stadium has become a generic model for all sporting arenas today, with Olympic stadia in Sydney, Athens, Beijing and (now) London demonstrating the same features as the new European football stadium. As the physical embodiment of wider social and political processes, the new European stadium may provide a perspicuous focus for understanding fundamental changes which are being precipitated by globalization not only within football but within society much more widely.

SEATS: COMMERCIALIZATION AND CONTROL

The introduction of seats into European stadia occurred most radically in Britain following the Hillsborough stadium disaster in 1989, when 96 died. There had been a number of disasters in Britain in the post-war era, notably at Burnden Park in 1946 (33 dead) and Ibrox in 1971 (66 dead), where spectators were crushed as a result of collapsing stands or poor stadium design. At Bradford in 1985 (56 dead), victims were burned to death as a result of a dropped cigarette igniting rubbish, which had accumulated for decades under the main stand. Hillsborough proved to be the catalyst, however, not only because it was the most lethal, but also because it convinced Margaret Thatcher that radical change was required. After Hillsborough, a fundamental renovation of British football grounds was demanded by the Conservative Government and dominant sections of British society. To that end, Lord Chief Justice Taylor, commissioned to write an inquiry into the disaster, outlined a fundamental reformation of British football. His report (1990) into the Hillsborough Stadium disaster surprised most commentators and interested parties with its breadth and insight. It sought to create a 'new ethos' in British football in which stadia would be more welcoming, fans would be treated better and the catastrophes of Bradford and Hillsborough would be impossible.

Having weighed up various proposals, including identity cards which were favoured by Margaret Thatcher, Taylor argued that the single most likely measure to be effective was the installation of all-seater stands and the destruction of standing terraces: 'I therefore conclude and recommend that designated grounds under the 1975 Act should be required in due course to be converted to all-seating. I do so for the compelling reasons of safety and control already set out' (Taylor 1990: 16). Consequently, by the mid-1990s, all grounds in the top divisions of English and Scottish football were required to be all-seater.

The radicalism of Taylor's report was a product of the depth of the crisis in British football in the late 1980s, but his report was consonant with a wider trend in European football at the time. Following the Heysel disaster in 1985, in which poor facilities played a role, UEFA (Union of European Football Associations) was forced to consider the issue of stadium design. Today, UEFA has established its own specialist Stadium and Security Committee, chaired by Vice-President of UEFA Senes Erzik, which has developed a system of stadium rating and a series of inspection trips. As Erzik has emphasized, UEFA explicitly saw the Heysel disaster as the origins of their current approach: UEFA

> was at the forefront of moves to improve safety and security at football matches in the wake of the Heysel Stadium disaster in Belgium in 1985, with stringent security requirements and provisions for all-seated spectators put into place at UEFA matches. By doing this, UEFA made a key contribution in the development of modern, multi-purpose venues in which fans can watch football matches in total comfort and safety.[2]

In 1985, FIFA (International Federation of Association Football) similarly began to recognize the importance of stadium design and both international federations began to impose stricter stipulations on national federations and clubs. Consequently, starting with Italia 1990, successive World Cups and European Championships have propelled a cycle of ground reconstructions in Europe. Thus, France 1998, Netherlands and Belgium 2000, Portugal 2004, Germany 2006 and Austria and Switzerland 2008 have all redefined the concept of the stadium in Europe.[3] The all-seater stadium had become the norm in European football.

The introduction of all-seater stadia represented a profound transformation of football grounds in Europe which has required enormous levels of investment. However, despite this obstacle, there were clear advantages to the new all-seater paradigm for clubs and federations. These advantages were particularly obvious in England, where the grounds which they replaced were among the worst in Europe for violence and poor facilities. Above all, seats encouraged a more restrained consumption of the sport, in place of the sometimes aggressive masculine displays typical of the 1980s (cf. Chapter 10 in this volume). In his famous analysis of the penal system, Foucault (1995) utilized Bentham's idea of the panopticon to describe the distinctive features of the modern prison. In contrast to the corporal tortures of the medieval and early modern periods, Foucault sought to highlight the distinctive features of the modern prison of the nineteenth century. The modern prison did not focus on the body of the prisoner, as did medieval torture, but specifically on the mind of the inmate. By isolating prisoners into single cells and submitting them to total surveillance, the modern prison sought to inscribe legal codes of conduct onto the consciousness of criminals who had irrationally committed themselves to crime. For Foucault, isolation and surveillance were the two central mechanisms of state control. In comparison with Foucault's panopticon, the plastic-bucket seat seems an innocuous innovation. It does not suggest itself as an obvious method of social control. Yet, in fact, the installation of seats in European stadia has profoundly altered the social space within grounds and has had a potent disciplinary effect. Certainly, football clubs, UEFA and FIFA all recognized the pacifying function which the seat could serve (cf. Conclusion).

As with the prison cell, the plastic seat disciplines through two basic functions. First, in contrast to the terrace, the seat isolates. It, therefore, obstructs close physical interaction between fans. The atomization of the spectator hinders the group dynamics which lead to crowd activity and potentially to violence. It is particularly noticeable in English grounds where, unlike Ultra groups in the rest of Europe, fan cultures are unorganized that the institution of seats has dissipated atmosphere in the grounds. The isolation of fans from one another into single seats individualizes spectators impeding the initiation of chants or choreographies. Second, by isolating spectators and assigning them a particular seat in the ground, supporters are now subject to highly effective surveillance from the club and police within the ground. Most clubs have surveillance systems

Figure 1.3
Plastic-bucket seats.

which can quickly identify spectators and seat numbers in any part of the ground. As Lord Chief Justice Taylor himself noted:

> It is possible to have disturbances in seated areas and they have occurred, but with the assistance of CCTV [Close-Circuit Television], the police can immediately zoom in with a camera and pinpoint the seats occupied by the troublemakers as well as the troublemakers themselves.
>
> (Taylor 1990: 12)

Seats are not simply about control, however. Football's audience was severely restricted in the 1970s and 1980s substantially due to the intimidating atmosphere and the threat of crowd violence in the grounds, especially in Germany and England. Seats, therefore, represent a second reform programme which was intimately related to the disciplinary element: commercialization. Seats have been a means of widening the market for football by appealing to new consumers and increasing revenue by raising ticket prices (cf. Conclusion).

In terms of both re-marketing the game and increasing revenue, this commercialization was most evident in Britain. Taylor's report on Hillsborough was not intended as a manifesto for the introduction of market forces but, although clubs initially complained about the cost of the Taylor reforms, many quickly embraced the proposed transformation as an opportunity to re-market themselves and to increase their revenue. In England, Manchester United was at the forefront of this entrepreneurial drive (cf. Chapter 9) and it had transformed Old Trafford into an all-seater stadium by 1993. Other clubs, notably Arsenal, followed United's lead in exploiting the Taylor Report as an opportunity to overhaul their ageing stadia into a facility compatible with other leisure activities. As clubs rebuilt their grounds, they increased ticket prices, partly to fund the renovation but also because the facilities on offer were now improved. Between 1993 and 1995, the most intense period of stadium renovation, the ticket prices for English clubs increased by an average of 102 per cent, though prices at Manchester United rose by 240 per cent (King 2002: 135). Inflation continues to the present. The cheapest season tickets for the 2008–9 season at the four dominant clubs (Arsenal, Chelsea, Liverpool and Manchester United) averaged £680, although, of course, the actual average season ticket price was almost £200 more than this figure.[4] All-seater stadia became a way of increasing the revenue of the club.

The commercial opportunities offered by all-seater stadia have been well-recognized across Europe. Indeed, the successful exploitation by English clubs of their new all-seater stadia has exerted considerable pressure on rival clubs, especially in Germany, Italy and Spain. In 2000, Italian clubs were exploring the financial potential of the all seater-stadia. In response to this pressure, for instance, Juventus aimed to develop the unpopular Stade delle Alpi or build a new stadium elsewhere in Turin. It is notable that Milan took over the running of the San Siro in July 2000. Nevertheless, as yet, no fundamental revision of ground ownership or design has occurred in Italy. In the face of financial pressures, clubs have not transformed their business models. On the contrary, in the 2005–6 season,

Juventus, with other major Italian clubs, AC Milan, Florentino and Lazio, pursued a strategy of systematic corruption, manipulating the selection of referees in critical matches. Partly as a result of this scandal, Italian football has now declared itself to be in crisis and is actively looking to implement 'the English model' of radical commercialization and all-seater stadia. It is possible that Italy may be going through its own equivalent of the Taylor reform, some 20 years after England. In Germany, the move to all-seater grounds is also observable. Many clubs, such as Schalke and Bayern Munich, have retained small convertible areas of terracing for league matches but the all-seater stadium has become accepted as the standard form. The German fan movements, such as BAFF and 15:30, have mobilized themselves out of fear that the development of all-seater stadia will involve the kind of ticket price inflation which has occurred in Britain. In the event, although ticket prices have increased with the move to their new arenas, the inflation is less than feared. Britain – and England, in particular – remain at the forefront of marketization but, in Europe, as a whole the installation of seats represents the commercialization of football, through the introduction of higher ticket prices.

Although the increase in ticket prices has been the object of critique by English fans and commentators, the introduction of seats has also had a liberating effect on spectators. It has been designed specifically to enfranchize social groups, especially women, ethnic groups and children, who were once intimidated by the football ground. UEFA have sought to emphasize this familial dimension very strongly with their Fair Play Campaign in which the style of play on the pitch represents standards which are appropriate for the family audiences in the stands (cf. Chapter 4). Of course, the commercial significance of attracting new consumers to the ground in the form of women and ethnic minorities has not been lost on some club directors and administrators in Europe. They recognize that the improvement in the ground has increased the market for football. Consequently, the introduction of seats has altered the social constitution of the crowd, in many cases attracting a more affluent group of supporters than in the 1970s and 1980s. The result is that the football ground is no longer the domain of the male members of the urban working class. It is becoming the arena of the new post-Fordist family. The apparently benign plastic seat represents a profound social transformation.

ROOFS: THE CONGREGATION OF TRANSNATIONAL CAPITAL

Since the erection of San Siro's extraordinary roof in 1990, one of the most impressive aspects of contemporary stadium design has been the new roofing structures which have appeared. Initially, the appearance of new roofs can be explained in purely functional terms. The installation of seats necessitated an expansion of the grounds because seating takes up far more space than terracing. The stands which began to house seats from the 1990s had to be much larger than the old terraces, if ground capacity was not to be reduced radically.

Moreover, especially in northern and central Europe, once seats were installed, it became essential to provide them with cover from the weather. While standing in the rain or snow may be an unpleasant experience, sitting through inclement weather is intolerable. The installation of seats demanded the erection of roofs to protect spectators against weather and because the stands were much bigger than the old terraces, the roofs had to be very large.

Yet, the expansion of the roof is not merely a matter of size. With its bold carapaces, the contemporary stadium roof is qualitatively different from its predecessor. In place of grey roofs, brightly coloured steel or translucent perspex superstructures have appeared. Moreover, they are no longer supported by heavy, often rusting iron girders, but light, almost delicate steel or titanium latticing. These titanium strops do not buttress the roof from below, obscuring the

Figure 1.4
Estádio do Dragão,
Oporto, 2003. Estádio do
Dragão was designed by
RISCO (Manuel Salgado,
Jorge Estriga and Carlos
Cruz), Photography: Luis
Ferreira Alves.

pitch and emphasizing their ponderous load. They rise into the sky above the new roofs, holding them from above. As these elegant strops lift upwards, the roofs assume an airy lightness. Roofs are no longer monolithic but float above the stands to frame the pitch in majestic sweeps. In many cases, such as the Stade de Paris or Porto's Dragão Stadium, the design explicitly emphasizes the buoyancy of the roof by leaving a gap between the back of the stand and the roof. The roof floats. The stand is no longer a squat bunker of steel and concrete but a transparent observatory.

Although fraught with difficulties, the execution of architect Norman Foster's Wembley Stadium project evinces precisely this new concept. Foster himself has emphasized the centrality of the prodigious roof in the design:

> At almost four times the height of the original, covering twice the area, and with 90,000 seats, the new Wembley Stadium will be the largest covered football stadium in the world. The key feature of the new stadium is its partly retractable roof, supported structurally by a spectacular 133-metre-high arch. Dramatically illuminated at night, the arch will be visible from across London.[5]

It is clearly visible from the air as planes approach Heathrow. To spectators, approaching along the Wembley way, the roof seems to be suspended in the sky by the arch; the entire structure floats airily above the ground. At Gelsenkirchen in Germany, the terraced depression of the Parkstadion with a single small roof sheltering the main stand has been dwarfed by the dramatic white dome of Schalke's new Veltins Arena. The new stadium appears like an inflated zeppelin. Similarly Munich's new Allianz Arena represents a radicalization of the concept (Figure 1.7). The roof does not simply enclose the stands from above but actually

Figure 1.5
Schalke's Veltins Arena,
Gelsenkirchen, 2007.

envelops the entire structure. The stadium has become a single encompassing carapace.

The new roofs are not simply functional; they are evocative symbols of a new social order. In his work on architecture, Anthony D. King[6] has examined the way in which structures are both the product and constitutive of global political and social forces; 'the built environment, the material, physical and spatial forms of the city, is itself a representation of specific ideologies, of social, political, economic and cultural relations and practices, of hierarchies and structures' (King 1996: 4). For King, the inescapable dynamic underpinning contemporary design is globalization. To Arjun Appadurai's five dimensions of cultural flows, King adds '*towns* and *landscape* which are produced by the global diffusion of information, images, professional cultures and sub-cultures and supported by international capital flows' (King 1997: 11).

The appearance of the new roofs has been facilitated by new patterns of global investment in football since the 1990s. Following the deregulation of broadcasting in the 1980s, a range of new satellite networks in Europe employed football as a 'battering ram', as Rupert Murdoch had described it, by which they could create markets for themselves (Harveson 1996, cf. John's Chapter 15 in this volume). From the late 1980s, television networks, such as SAT 1 in Germany, Mediaset I Italy, BSkyB in Britain, Canal Plus in France and Spain, made a series of strategic alliances with European football clubs. The inflation in the value of television rights for football has enriched clubs very significantly. Thus, in Britain, ITV and the BBC paid £1.5 million for the second half of the 1986 season. For 2010–13, the rights of the Premier League were worth £1,782 billion.

Similarly, the German *Bundesliga* rights were sold for 12 million DM in 1985–6 but, between 2000 and 2004, the rights were worth 300 million DM (approximately 150 million euros) a season (King 2003: 109–10). Real Madrid, for instance, had a five year contract, ending in 2008, with Canal Satellite Digital worth £259 million. In Italy and France, a comparable inflation is evident. At the same time, these clubs have also benefited from related increases in sponsorship deals. Of course, the new alliances with global media companies and corporate sponsors have not been equally beneficial to all clubs. On the contrary, these global alliances have accelerated the economic inequalities in European football to such an extent that the major European clubs, engorged with their new resources, have begun not merely to dominate their national leagues but to establish themselves as transnational actors, interacting with each other across borders and often operating at the global level (cf. Chapter 7). It is at this precise moment, when the currents of global capital have coalesced at the favoured football clubs in Europe that the most impressive new roofs have appeared over the new stadia.

The new European stadium appears at those meeting points where new media and sponsoring finance congregate. The physical construction of the new stadium was itself the product of new alliances between football clubs and global capital. In Britain in the early 1990s, clubs developed a distinctive, if short-lived strategy for sponsoring building work. Manchester United was undoubtedly the most successful club to follow this strategy, recapitalizing itself through the new influx of stock market money (cf. Chapter 9). Significantly, the primary rationale for the launch was to pay for the rebuilding of the famous Stretford End into the new all-seater West Stand. Soon after the initial completion of Old Trafford into a double-tiered, all-seater ground with a single cantilevered roof in 1994, the club quickly realized that at a capacity of 44,000, the ground was far too small for their potential audience. Consequently, throughout the 1990s, the club rebuilt, first, the old United Road (North) Stand into a triple tier tribune, then the old K (East) Stand before returning to expand the two-tier West Stand. The club's increased revenue from television, flotation, merchandizing and sponsorship facilitated renovation in each case.

It is significant that in the photograph of Old Trafford in 2006 (Figure 1.2), the Nike 'swoosh' is plainly visible on the seats of the new West Stand, physically denoting this alliance of football and capital. With new sponsorship deals in place, the West Stand now displays the word 'Vodaphone' while the Nike 'swoosh' is emblazoned on the seats of the East Stand. The new stadium at Old Trafford is the manifestation of an alliance between the club, its investors and current owners (the Glazers), Rupert Murdoch's BSkyB (and ultimately News International), Umbro (a British sportswear and equipment supplier), Nike, Sharp (a Japanese electronics manufacturer) and later Vodaphone (a British mobile network operator) and AIG (an American insurance corporation). The new roof is the structural embodiment of this global patronage. Arsenal's new ground, the Emirates Stadium, was similarly underwritten by financial support from Emirates Airlines.

In Germany, similar processes have been at work. Schalke's new Arena is also manifestation of private capital (Figure 1.5). Schalke formed a strategic alliance with Veltins Brewery which sponsored the development of the new ground and after whom the stadium is now named (for a detailed discussion of Schalke's Veltins Arena cf. Zinganel's Chapter 4 in this volume). Like Schalke, the hugely expensive construction work on the Munich Arena has been sponsored by Allianz (a German finance and insurance service supplier) which has bought the name of the stadium for 30 years. Elsewhere in Europe, in Holland, Belgium, Scotland and Portugal, at clubs like Ajax, Anderlecht, Celtic and Porto, the equivalent transformation is evident where stadium reconstruction, facilitated by private capital, has produced dramatic new structures. The towering structures represent the new geography of football today as flows of transnational capital crystallize at particular points.

The roofs, then, are not consistent with twentieth-century industrial regimes. They do not signify the heavy metal of mass production or state hegemony. Instead, they are light and flowing. The new roofs signify the concentration of power at decisive nodes in the European order. As such, the new roof of the European stadium might be seen as the economic and symbolic manifestation of the flows of global capital which have congregated at particular locales;

the new stadia may be the structural manifestation of liquid modernity (Bauman 2000). Although much larger than the old structures, they do not signify traditional hierarchy and power. They do not impose vertically upon mass spectators, implying domination. They signify a new political and economic regime. They have arisen in an era when football has been colonized by global capital as a vehicle of market mobilization and the clubs have been inflated through massive increases in financial investment. The new stadium dominates the new urban landscape, as a commanding height, but this new order is not repressive or ossifying. It is highly mobile, shifting and malleable. The roofs of the new stadium reflect the fact that while private companies have become increasingly powerful their potency rests on their ability to liberate, inspire and attract new consumers, not dominate them. The roofs ideally shelter individuated family units who together enjoy the spectacle of sport in a restrained and safe environment. The roofs preside over a changed social order in which hierarchies of gender, class, ethnicity and race have all undergone a profound revision.

GLASS: THE NEW CONSUMPTION OF FOOTBALL

While the roofs have been a necessary change, the appearance of glass façades is one of the most innovative aspects of the new European stadium. The new East Stand at Old Trafford was an early example of this, but most new stadia, including Schalke's Veltins Arena, FC Chelsea's Stamford Bridge and Eindhoven's Philips Stadium, feature large glass façades.

It is possible to identify a symbolic meaning to these glass façades which speaks to changing social hierarchies. In their now famous article on organizations, Paul J. DiMaggio and Walter W. Powell (1983) describe how institutional change is often the product of what they call 'mimetic isomorphism'. Subordinate institutions will deliberately imitate the dominant institutions in any period as a means of attaining legitimacy and status. Consequently, in any era, diverse institutions will assume very similar forms. The glass façades may be an example of 'mimetic isomorphism'. As clubs have become more powerful, through alliances with global capital and media organizations, they want to assert their status publicly. Saskia Sassen has noted the emergence of this new architectural paradigm:

> The particular kind of form that dominates our image of today's advanced urban economy is the agglomeration of high-rise corporate offices we see in New York, London, Frankfurt or Tokyo. It has emerged as a kind of representation of the advanced city form, from the image of the post-industrial city.
>
> (Sassen 1996: 23)

The structures have become 'global command centres' (Sassen 1996: 33). Affirming Sassen's point, architects Norman Foster and Jaques Herzog and Pierre de Meuron, who designed Wembley and the Munich Allianz Arena respectively, are also famous for their contributions to urban and corporate architecture.

The stadium façade signifies the isomorphism of football clubs and global capital but they also represent the new contours of this social order symbolically. This symbolic function can be seen most clearly by comparing the architecture of the new stadium with twentieth-century modernism. From the early twentieth century, functional modernist architecture prioritizing reason and order became dominant. State ministries, international headquarters and corporate headquarters were housed in clean symmetrical edifices, represented in the architecture of Le Corbusier and the Bauhaus. Modernist architecture symbolically signified the hegemony of the state and monopoly capital.

Since the 1970s, there has been an architectural revolution against modernist rationalism. Postmodern architects like Norman Foster, Frank Gehry and Daniel Libeskind have employed new building materials, wood, titanium and glass, to defy the principles of modernism. They have designed structures which reject symmetry, order and function. Glass, communicating a new global geography, has been very important in this postmodern revolution (Jones 2006: 563) as Fredric Jameson has shown. For Jameson, the era of multinational capital and postmodern culture is embodied architecturally in new structures like the Bonaventure Hotel in Los Angeles. He describes how the Bonaventure Hotel subverts the codes of rational modernist architecture, defying mappable space and disorienting the individual (Jameson 1991: 44). The reflective surfaces of the Bonaventure subvert notions of externality and internality. Mirroring its surroundings and mutating as light conditions change, the borders of the building are not definitive. Moreover, the building is functionally confusing. The entrance is obscured and once in the foyer, the reception area is disorienting. Glass lifts are bizarrely externalized, running up and down the walls of the foyer. They are not secreted away in their private shafts. For Jameson, the Bonaventure Hotel marks a decisive divide from the modernist enterprise of Le Corbusier and the Bauhaus. Function no longer dictates form. On the contrary, postmodern architecture deliberately manipulates the rational certainties of modern architecture to confuse, to surprise and to excite.

Norman Foster has exploited the potential of glass to create a series of structures which challenge conventional notions of in- and outside. His Reichstag dome in Berlin actively sought to invert old categories of political order and hierarchy; 'the dome aimed to place the public above the politicians answerable to them' (Wise 1998: 130; Delanty and Jones 2002). Forster's structures typically consist of transparent shells which deny the spatial integrity of the building. His designs enclose exterior space while, at the same time, publicizing once-private interiors. His buildings are inside out; established classifications and hierarchies are subverted and rejected.

The façades of the new stadium play precisely on this confusion of in- and outside which has become typical of postmodern architecture. The stadium's interior is exteriorized while the outside has been incorporated into the structure. The new stadium transgresses conventional notions of boundaries and space. At Old Trafford, for instance, supporters outside the East Stand can see fans within

Figure 1.6
View through the glass
roof of the lobby of the
Bonaventure Hotel, Los
Angeles, 2009.

the building, while they are simultaneously mirrored in the tinted panes. There is an overlap and confusion of space; it is not clear where the stadium ends and the surrounding streets begin. In contrast with the fortress-like K-Stand, the new façade transforms Old Trafford into a paradoxically publicized, private space. It opens the stadium out to its new consumers.

Herzog and de Meuron's Allianz Arena in Munich is, perhaps, the most striking example of this transgression of boundaries. This structure consists of titanium lattice which supports inflated, transparent plastic covering. A lighting system has been installed beneath the covering so that the stadium can change colour, becoming red, blue or white depending on whether Bayern Munich, TSV 1860 Munich or the German national team are playing. The ground is not a

Figure 1.7
Allianz Arena, Munich,
2005.

unitary but a multiple structure assuming different forms in the light of the circumstances. Its mutability contrasts markedly with the functionality of the modern terraced ground.

The Allianz Arena represents this dislocation of expectation. Among supporters, the stadium has been nicknamed *Das Schlauchboot* (the dinghy) because it has the appearance of an inflated life-raft. Such a parallel was certainly not the architect's intention. However, the Arena is intended to question conventional understandings of what a stadium is. It does not look like a stadium. The Allianz Arena is undoubtedly the most innovative stadium to have appeared in Europe but it stresses only a fundamental feature of the new stadium more generally. These structures reject modernist categories of space and function. They embody a new social order which supersedes old boundaries and borders. Under the grand roofs and inside the glass façades of Europe's new arenas, new modes of masculinity and celebrity have emerged (cf. Chapter 15) to reflect the new familial and in many cases more ethnically diverse audiences and to signify a new form of social solidarity (cf. Chapter 4). The new stadium structurally embodies a new transnational social order in Europe.

CONCLUSION

As the dynamics of globalization accelerate, a strange new social landscape is appearing in Europe today. On this terrain, the new stadium with its seats, roofs and glass stands as a prominent feature on the urban horizon. Together, the new stadia constitute an architectural network. The stadia have become nodes in an emergent transnational order, representing the alliance of global capital, football clubs and consumers. They denote profound institutional transformations at the level of state and capital. They signify the emergence of a transnational order in which concentrated nodes of economic power interact across national borders with increasing ease. However, they also represent a transformation of the twentieth-century social order, with the renegotiation of old hierarchies of race, class, gender and ethnicity. In particular, the new European stadium has prioritized the affluent and respectable family as the prime consumer in place of the mass masculine spectatorship of the twentieth century. The new European stadia embody a historical transformation of profound significance.

Of course, the new European stadium is by no means exclusively European. On the contrary, just as the new European stadium is a manifestation of global currents so has this architectural form germinated globally. European architects have had a privileged place in this structural dissemination; Herzog and de Meuron have played a prominent role here. In addition to the Allianz Arena, they also designed the stadium for the Beijing Olympics, the now iconic 'Bird's Nest'. That building represents the same features as the Arena. The roof – a complex lattice of interwoven titanium – swallows the entire structure to produce a new form which appears more as an organic entity than a sports ground. The Bird's Nest links itself to processes of globalization through a series of connotations. While its lattice work suggests global interconnections, it too subverts notions of in- and outside. In this way, although constructed by one of the world's most authoritarian twentieth-century regimes, it points forward to a quite transformed social and political order in which old boundaries and hierarchies are overcome. In his famous essay on the Balinese cockfight, Clifford Geertz claimed that in this strange and violent ritual the Balinese were able to tell themselves a story about themselves (Geertz 1973). The new European stadium similarly tells us a story today about ourselves. It is a narrative of social transformation. If we look very closely at the seats, the roofs and the glass which are these stadia's central features, it may be possible to glimpse the strange new transnational landscape in which we now live – in Europe and beyond.

NOTES

1 The old structure has been retained because it has proved architecturally impossible to develop over the railway track.
2 www.uefa.com/uefa/aboutuefa/newsid=2483.html, accessed 20 November 2009.
3 The 2002 World Cup had a similar impact on Korea and Japan.
4 The figures were taken from the clubs' websites.
5 www.fosterandpartners.com/Projects/1015/Default.aspx, accessed 20 November 2009.
6 Urban and architectural sociologist, Anthony D. King, of Binghamton University SUNY, is unrelated to the author, despite sharing a name with him.

REFERENCES

Bauman, Z. (2000) *Liquid Modernity*, Cambridge: Polity Press.

Delanty, G. and Jones, P. (2002) 'European identity and architecture', *European Journal of Social Theory*, 5(4): 453–66.

DiMaggio, P. and Powell, W. (1983) 'The iron cage revisited: Institutional isomorphism and collective rationality in organisational fields', *American Sociological Review*, 48: 147–60.

Foucault, M. (1995) *Discipline and Punish*, New York: Vintage.

Geertz, C. (1973) 'Deep play: Notes on the Balinese cockfight', in C. Geertz (ed.) *The Interpretation of Cultures*, New York: Basic Books.

Harveson, P. (1996) 'It's a new ball game as takeover talk hits fever pitch', *Financial Times*, 16.

Jameson, F. (1991) *Postmodernism, or the Cultural Logic of Late Capitalism*, London: Verso.

Jones, P. (2006) 'The sociology of architecture and the politics of building', *Sociology*, 40(3): 549–65.

King, A. (2002) *The End of the Terraces*, rev. edn, London: Leicester University Press.

—— (2003) *The European Ritual*, Aldershot: Ashgate.

King, A.D. (1996) 'Introduction: Cities, texts and paradigms', in A.D. King (ed.) *Re-Presenting the City: Ethnicity, capital and culture in the 21st century metropolis*, Basingstoke: Macmillan.

—— (1997) 'Introduction: Space of cultures, spaces of knowledge', in A.D. King (ed.) *Culture, Globalization and the World System*, Minneapolis: University of Minnesota.

Sassen, S. (1996) 'Rebuilding the global city', in A.D. King (ed.) *Re-Presenting the City: Ethnicity, capital and culture in the 21st century metropolis*, Basingstoke: Macmillan.

Taylor, Lord Justice (1990) *The Hillsborough Stadium Disaster, Final Report*, London: HMSO.

Wise, D. (1998) *Capital Dilemma*, New York: Princeton.

Chapter 2: 'Show Yourself to the People!'

Ancient Stadia, Politics and Society

Bettina Kratzmüller

Today, ancient stadia (that is, the Greek *stadion* and the *hippodromos* as well as the Roman *circus* and the *amphitheatrum*, Figures 2.1 and 2.2) are perceived as places of architectural ingenuity which attract a large number of visitors interested in history. Moreover, in modern times ancient stadia have continuously been used for a wide variety of spectacles such as theatrical performances, concerts and athletic competitions. In 1896, for example, the ancient Panathenaic *stadion* in Athens hosted the first modern Olympic Games and the shotput competition was performed in the ancient *stadion* of Olympia when the Games came back to Greece in 2004 (Kratzmüller 2005: 117–20).

In ancient times stadia were not solely constructed to host athletic tournaments, horse and chariot races or gladiator fights. They were widely known

Figure 2.1
Plans of the *stadion-amphitheatrum*-complex of Ephesos and the *hippodromos* of Olympia as reconstructed in the nineteenth century.

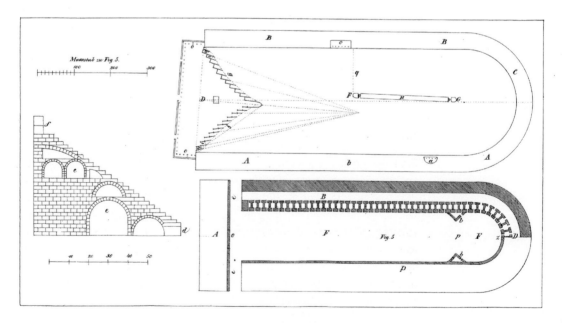

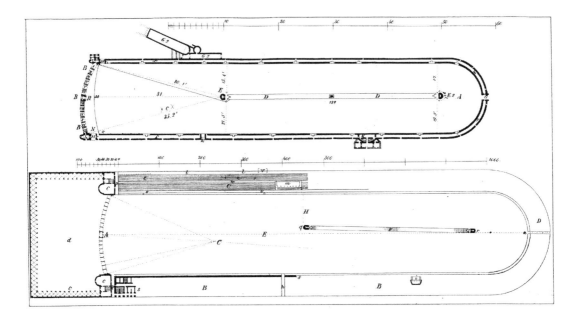

Figure 2.2
Plans of the *circus* of
Caracalla and the Circus
Maximus in Rome as
reconstructed in the
nineteenth century.

locations for the celebrations of – in the widest sense – sports events as spectacles. Moreover, they were places where people convened to attend organized events. While the athletes would have been content with a sports field to carry out their disciplines, the enormous interest of the masses necessitated the construction of large raised floors, making stadia one of the largest building types we know.

Constructed to accommodate vast masses, both the sports fields and the tribunes of ancient stadia also served as public spaces. In this manner, stadia not only provided an architectural frame for the social assembly of athletes, spectators and sports organizers. They were also used by those who intended to present themselves to the crowds. As statesmen and politicians wanted to profit from the concentration of people to impress and to influence them, stadia were also important places for the representation of power. Ancient stadia have to be seen against the background of the interplay of the organizers, active players, audience and built space.[1]

ANCIENT STADIA: GREEK REQUIREMENTS

Even though many ancient sources concern events in the Roman stadia, the ancient *stadion* as a place for the performance of Greek athletic events will be discussed first. In principle the Greek *stadion* offers the required facilities for a fair realization of the athletic *agon*. The term *agon* originally meant a meeting or assembly of men on the occasion of political or cultic events and was later assigned to related competitions. Originally a supporting programme, the sporting events gained in importance, but they have always to be seen in their religious and especially their political framework during the Greek and Roman periods (Herz 1997: 239–40).

The Greek term *stadion* originally meant a distance of 600 feet and was assigned to the footrace of the same distance which was performed on the race track called the *dromos*. This term was later used for the place of the actual sporting activity, even when a certain type of building was developed for the place of athletic competitions which was called a *stadion*. The *stadion* as an architectural structure thus defines that part reserved for the audience (Decker 1995: 158), and the way of naming reflects the importance of the audience, the people within the whole system and environment of athletic competitions.

The terms *stadion* and *hippodromos* are missing from the list of buildings which Pausanias viewed as absolutely necessary for a proper *polis* (city) in the tenth book of his *Description of Greece* (Pausanias, *Description of Greece*, 10.4.1) – such as *archaia* (official building), *theatron*, *agora*, and *gymnasion* (Decker 1995: 174). Nonetheless they existed as venues for athletic and equestrian competitions in many cities. Unlike the buildings named by Pausanias, these venues were not seen as essential for the preservation of political and social life, yet as buildings they always carried a political connotation.

As a sporting competition the *agon* took place in the middle of the *polis*, the Greek city state and amidst the *politai*, the male citizens, who were the decisive element of the society. In particular, early race-tracks which were not part of extramural sanctuaries were situated near the main intra-urban sanctuary. Besides they can frequently be found on the *agora*, the centre of municipal life, as for example at Athens, Corinth, or Argos. Certain equestrian events could even be performed there. In the political centres of the cities, various memorial monuments could also be erected for the outstanding victors of the games.

The integration into political life was omnipresent. In late classical and early Hellenistic times the needs of a huge audience made it necessary for many places to transfer athletic venues to a place outside the actual political or religious centre where more space was available, both for the audience and the necessary buildings. Here, the transition to a more monumental, political architecture was made (Kratzmüller 2005: 113).

This is not the place to treat the typological development of *stadion* buildings in detail (Decker 1995: 158–64; Welch 1998a: 120, 131). In principle hillsides were good places for spectators, while narrow valleys provided a natural advantage in providing the use of both sides. Larger logistic preparation was needed by means of extensive earth walls in order to create monumental artificial slopes. In Greek times the optimal *stadion* consisted of a *dromos* of the required length of 600 feet. This was surrounded by slopes on three sides so that the audience could watch the games, both laterally and from one of the narrow sides. *Stadion* architecture was subject to vast changes when Greece was conquered by the Romans. Especially in Asia Minor new and specifically Roman construction techniques were used. It was only the official Roman method of construction using *opus caementicium*, the ancient type of concrete, that made it possible to build huge multi-storey buildings. Now the tribunes rested on huge sophisticated substructures which could be built quickly (Figure 2.1) and which provided a controllable circulation of the masses when entering and leaving the building. This construction method had been successfully used for the auditoria of Roman circuses and amphitheatres (Kratzmüller 2005: 113–14). By closing off the second narrow side as well, the ground plan of the *stadion* was changed into an all-round quasi-circular building and converged typically towards the Roman amphitheatre; some of the ancient traditional Greek *stadia*, for example those at Olympia or Athens, were eventually converted into such a structure (Welch 1998a, Welch 1998b: 565 n. 68).

Apart from recognizing that the Greek *stadion* was a politically construed building type, political influence was also brought to bear on the organization and performance of the games in the stadia (Kratzmüller 2005: 92–112). Though not always obvious, this can be seen on different levels: reflected intra- and inter-urban, politics influenced all processes of the competitions, the preparation and organization as well as the actual realization. It impacted all persons involved, athletes, judges, as well as onlookers and fans.

The preparation and organization of the local Greek but also the Pan-Hellenic games was not only incumbent upon the particular administration of the nearby sanctuary, the regulation also lay in the hands of that political power that controlled and administered the site. Hosting the games provided different benefits for the actual *polis* (Kratzmüller 2005: 93–5). The games were considered not only as sporting meetings but as occasions of all-Greek assembly. They provided the possibility for an active exchange of views under good conditions because they attracted a broad audience from all Greek settlement areas. They played an important economic role and conferred political influence on the organizer. The organizers had the right to exclude other cities from taking part in the games, for example, because of breaching the sacred peace. On the other hand, the organizers could also be browbeaten through boycotts, or the organization of 'counter-games' by other cities. By offering athletes valuable prizes or by imprisoning or enslaving them, the athletes were kept from taking part in the proper games.

The performance of the games in the stadia was directed by a collegium of judges. Ideally this collegium should have guaranteed a fair, neutral, and objective course of events (Figure 2.3). However, political influence proved to be

Figure 2.3
Attic black-figured *amphora* by the potter Nikosthenes showing two pairs of heavy athletes in action, *c.*530 BCE.

stronger, especially for the Olympic Games, about which we are best informed (Weiler 1997; Sinn 2004; Kratzmüller 2005: 95–6). Amongst other things the *hellanodikai*, the judges who came from the surrounding country, did not always make neutral and objective decisions, but often local or patriotic ones. Occasionally interventions by high ranking rulers allowed more experienced athletes to participate in the contests of lower age groups.

In archaic and classical Greece, athletes were free male Greeks; non-Greeks, women, and slaves were excluded from participation in the competitive events of the sacred games (Crowther 1992). The rule that only male Greeks were allowed to participate was relaxed relatively early on for the equestrian events where politically influential individuals had the possibility of playing to the gallery as owners of the horses (Decker 1995: 122; Sinn 2004: 180, 187–90; Kratzmüller 2005: 96). As early as the fifth century BCE the Macedonian king, Alexander I, was allowed to take part in the Olympic Games because he had proved that his family was of mythical Greek descent. Towards the end of the third century BCE the Romans, whose political and military power was highly visible, were given the right to take part in the Isthmian Games, one of the four ancient Pan-Hellenic sacred games (Decker 1995: 54).

On site the athlete attended not only in a private capacity but also as a representative of his home town (Miller 2004: 216; Kratzmüller 2005: 96–8). Victorious athletes (Figure 2.4) were offered numerous rewards by their home town (complimentary banquets, financial rewards, *proedria* – that is, special seating

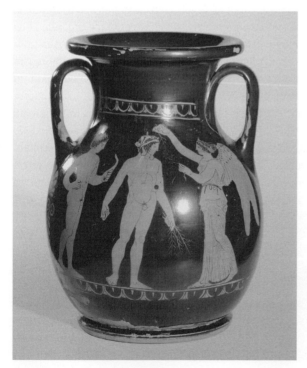

Figure 2.4
Attic red-figured *pelike* showing a victorious athlete crowned by Nike, end of the fifth century BCE.

places during public performances). They were also offered political offices or played an important political role, took part in wars and were given special treatment if taken as a prisoner of war. They were chosen as official ambassadors of their city in political as well as in sporting events. In return the cities used their athletes to display their position of power on the occasion of agonistic games. Victories in the sacred games heightened the prestige of the particular *polis* all around Greece. Sometimes victorious athletes were proclaimed as victors not under the name of their home town, but occasionally under that of another city (Baltrusch 1997: 511; Miller 2004: 216–17), particularly if that city made an attractive offer, not least in monetary form. In the Roman period especially the buying and selling of victors was a current practice which trainers also advised their athletes to accept.

The majority of the spectators were local, although fans also travelled vast distances (Decker 1995: 128) to cheer for their idols at a foreign location during the Pan-Hellenic games. All participants – the athletes, their company, and the spectators – were protected by the institution of the so-called *ekecheiria*: the sacred peace proclaimed on the occasion of the games. The *ekecheiria* referred solely to the site of the event and the arrival and departure of athletes and spectators and was by no means a general truce imposed all over Greece (Decker 1995: 117; Crowther 2001; Kratzmüller 2005: 102–3).

During great games the particular city was represented on site by the so-called *theoroi*, official political cultic ambassadors (Decker 1995: 54, 116; Kratzmüller 2005: 103). The public office of a *theoros* was often taken up by wealthy men as a form of public duty, a certain kind of tax payment which enhanced their prestige and added authority. These official ambassadors had to attend to their athletes' affairs and had, for example, to pay a penalty in case of an athlete's inability to pay. This system meant that honourable people, religious and political notables, and magnates of different city states attended the games in the stadia. It was, however, not only official representatives who, recognizing that the games attracted many spectators, exploited them as a platform on which to expound their own political as well as private aims (Miller 2004: 77, 123; Sinn 2004: 172–3, 185–6). Politicians such as Themistocles or Alcibiades are just two examples of men who understood that an appearance at the Olympic Games was useful to promote themselves. Furthermore, authors such as Herodotus chose the gathering during the Olympic Games to recite his history of Greece in public.

In their political capacity as ambassadors of other *poleis*, the *theoroi* were entitled to the right of *proedria* (special seats) in the stadia, a right also awarded to others as a special distinction. These separate places of honour had to be clearly defined (Kratzmüller 2005: 103–4). The way the seats were distributed, not only the reserved honorary ones but also those of ordinary spectators, can be based on what is known about various details in some stadia, and reflects sometimes social, sometimes also ethnic-political circumstances. An interesting possibility to accommodate the political affiliation of the spectators can be found in the early Hellenistic *stadion* of Nemea which was used for Pan-Hellenic games. On the basis of coins which were lost by the spectators, it was revealed that most of the onlookers originated from the immediate vicinity and that given political-ethnic groups favoured particular areas within the *stadion* (Knapp 2001). The Argive people moved into the place near the reserved seats for the judges who also came from Argos. On the basis of the concentration of Cretan coins found also near the judges' seats, a group of ambassadors from far away can be recorded. Further details regarding reserved spaces for spectators from other specific cities argue for the theory that the seating arrangements were decided officially, at least along general lines.

Since a large auditorium was present in the Greek stadia – scholars assume that there were c.40,000 seats for the Olympian *stadion* of the fourth century BCE (Petermandl 2005: 130) – events were organized from the public political side that, in principle, had nothing to do with sports. These might include vast processions which processed nearby or even directly through stadia using the available auditorium (van Nijf 1997: 133; Welch 1998b: 558; Kratzmüller 2005: 105). These processions were hierarchically organized and mirrored the social structure of an urban society. Here a particular person did not take part as an individual but as a holder of titles or as a representative of a social group. As such the person was immediately recognizable for the spectators, as well as the social hierarchy which they symbolized.

Various announcements and pronouncements were made in the stadia in front of the assembled people (Roueché 1993: 144; Kratzmüller 2005: 106), for example the release of slaves or similar acts of mercy. Thus Alexander the Great, in an act of political calculation, proclaimed an amnesty at the Olympic Games for more than 20,000 Greeks who had been banned from their home cities and who had come to the Games (Petermandl 2005: 148). On the occasion of games it had also been common since the Hellenistic period to pronounce public tributes to benefactors. The ancient *stadion* of Isthmia in particular was used for important political rallies. Here the assembled Greeks deliberated on their military tactics against the Persian army in 490 BCE, here the Roman T. Quinctus Flamininus pronounced the freedom of all Greeks in 196 BCE, a pronouncement that was renewed by the Roman emperor Nero in AD 67 (Decker 1995: 52; Sinn 2004: 196–202).

POLITICS: THE RISE OF ROME

The Romans, however, also pronounced important news on the occasion of competitive events in their home towns; the final military victory against the Macedonians, for example, was proclaimed to the masses in the Circus Maximus in Rome in 186 BCE precisely at the time when the chariot races should have begun. Because of the Roman politics of expansion towards the east, two worlds faced each other in a political and military conflict, one that at least militarily went better for the Romans.

Two traditions faced each other also in the sporting area (Miller 2004: 196–206; Kratzmüller 2009). The Romans had their own traditional sporting culture (Heucke 1994; Thuillier 1999; Horsmann 1998; Kratzmüller 2009: 210–11, 213–15), even though it did not play such a large role in the social and political life of the individual citizen compared to the situation in Greece, but instead was rather meant to satisfy the desires of the spectator. The equestrian events in particular could look back on a long tradition, but also boxing and wrestling, as well as foot-racing, were performed competitively. Here the athletes did not compete totally nude as their Greek counterparts did, but wore the *subligaculum*, a kind of loin-cloth. Alongside these, a new medium for entertainment developed with the world of gladiatorial spectacles. Two special types of architecture emerged for the Roman events, the *circus* (Figures 2.2 and 2.5) where the equestrian events (especially different chariot races), and also athletic competitions, were performed, and the *amphitheatrum* (Figure 2.6) for the various types of gladiatorial shows.

From 186 BCE onwards Greek athletes were brought to Italy and competed in the so-called *certamina athletarum*, that is, sporting events which took place

Figure 2.5
Roman *sesterce* showing the Roman imperator Caracalla and the Circus Maximus in Rome, AD 213.

Figure 2.6
Roman *sesterce* showing the Collosseum in Rome, AD 81.

occasionally and where competitions were performed based on Greek models (Mann 2002; Kratzmüller 2009: 207–8, 213–14). These *certamina athletarum* were only one element within other, typically Roman spectacles. Moreover, they were viewed as curiosities by the Roman spectators mainly due to the public display of nudity by the Greek athletes, which was uncommon for the Roman people.

Within conquered Greece, the Roman potentates were well aware from the outset of the possibility of exploiting the Greek games and the stadia in particular – as a manageable space where the populace was assembled – to demonstrate their own political power (Kratzmüller 2005: 107–8). The old Greek festivals and games were further celebrated and assumed an important place within competitive affairs in the Roman Empire; nevertheless the Roman authority interfered with the administration of the games. The Roman representatives were also honoured with the *proedria* like all other dignitaries. Even the Roman emperor was symbolically present, although not in person. Portraits of the respective ruler were carried in the processions and were set up at the place of competition or performance (Herz 1997: 249–50).

In the period of the Roman takeover of power, other important sportive-social developments also occurred (Kratzmüller 2005: 108–12). From the first century BCE onwards associations of athletes can be found (Pleket 1973; Caldelli 1992; Roueché 1993: 53–60). They united to become an empire-wide association throughout the whole Roman Empire with its head office in Rome at the end of the first century AD and the respective Roman emperor acted as patron. The existing local associations were still concerned with local sporting matters. They were integrated into the life of the city, and their members often enjoyed a variety of public privileges or treatment such as, for example, tax exemption.

Contemporaneously a special system emerged within the area of Roman equestrian sport when circus factions (Cameron 1976; Roueché 1993: 143–56) were established which were named after particular colours (originally the 'Greens', 'Blues', 'Reds', and 'Whites'). These were professional racing associations who, at the beginning, managed their own chariots but who later took over the entire organization of chariot-races in the circuses, at first in Rome and then, from the fourth century AD onwards, also in the Greek East. From the fifth century AD onwards the circus factions of the Greens and the Blues exerted influence on other events and organized the theatre business as well as the sporting affairs in the *stadion*. At the same time the former associations of athletes were also integrated into the factions of the Greens and the Blues.

The development from the unification of athletes in associations which eventually merged into the two circus factions of the Greens and Blues can also be archaeologically documented in ancient stadia (Kratzmüller 2005: 110). As in other auditoria of theatres, *odeia*, and amphitheatres, the stone seats of some *stadia* – for instance those in Didyma, Saittai, and Aphrodisias – bear inscriptions which show who or which social groups were entitled to take certain seats (Kolendo 1981; Small 1987; Roueché 1993: 83–4; van Nijf 1997: 209–40; Kolb

1999). In this way, the authorities wanted to avoid potential conflicts. The stadia of Aphrodisias (Roueché 1993: 83–128; van Nijf 1997: 229–32; Welch 1998b) in particular preserve not only many private graffiti but also official inscriptions, among them those of members of the circus factions of the Greens and the Blues. Moreover, several different public associations, groups of cultic functionaries, foreign traders, or Roman colonists as well as Jews are represented. The fact is that the spectators wanted to represent themselves intentionally as members of certain groups when sitting together in fixed parts of the auditorium (Kratzmüller 2005: 111–12). At the beginning the political hierarchy of the city was reflected in this system. When in the fifth century AD the circus factions took over the organization of the games, the old structures were overlaid. Former opposing groups gained admission into the factions of the Greens and Blues, resulting in the transfer of rivalry from small associations to larger and well organized structures, and the absorption of these former groups into the larger factions. The political authorities therefore sought to place the fans of the Greens and Blues in separate opposing spaces within the auditoria of the various stadia – like theatres, circuses, *hippodromoi*, and *stadia*. The competitiveness of the two fan-groups can, for example, clearly be seen in the graffiti. Fans of the Blues, for example, wrote the words 'bad years for the Greens' on the seats within the space of their opponents in the theatre of Aphrodisias who in return tried to erase these words (Roueché 1993: 102). In AD 561 under the reign of Justinian a revolt broke out which originated in the *hippodromos*; the situation escalated when the Blues entered the seating space of the Greens. Ancient authors comment that the citizens of the cities had been fans of the Greens or the Blues for a long period but that the violence only exploded after they were divided and forced to sit in certain opposing areas within the auditoria (Roueché 1993: 129). Previously, citizens had been members of certain groups but these groups had not exercised any real power; the two circus factions offered the possibility to identify with certain, and indeed powerful groups (Roueché 1993: 154, 156).

Independently from these internal conflicts between groups and factions, the mass of spectators, the crowd itself, formed a sort of 'political institution' worth taking into account (Roueché 1993: 99–102, 128–32, 154–6; Kratzmüller 2005: 110–12); the Circus Maximus in Rome (Figures 2.2 and 2.5), for example, could hold as many as 150,000 people during the Roman Imperial period (Petermandl 2005: 130). The sporting events were politicized (Baltrusch 1997: 512), and the sporting arenas constituted the only spaces where the people assembled at one place at that time. Here individuals could distinguish themselves in front of the populace and gain their support (Petermandl 2005: 148). Political authorities could be boosted by public applause – the assembly of people acquired a political function again (Roueché 1993: 133, 154).

The political reality was that an attempt was made to influence the masses by organizing different events during the Roman period, and to keep the masses quiet by satisfying their principal needs, a fact which is well known under the keywords *panem et circenses* – 'bread and circuses' (Juvenal, *Satires*, 10.77–81).

It is interesting to note that the circuses – that is, the various entertainments – were seen as the more important part. They were called for more urgently by the crowd, and the authorities knew that not only the hungry plebs but also the entire populace could be won over through the games. While, during the Republican era, an attempt was made to canvass potential voters and to manipulate the people by organizing such events, during periods of autocracy such endeavours increased in importance even more. During the Imperial period, when it was no longer necessary to influence the voters but the people had to be kept in good humour, the emperors organized massive events in the different stadia.

Moreover, the Roman politicians and rulers were aware that it was of great benefit to appear personally in the stadia (Petermandl 2005: 148). Information recorded by Cassius Dio, Suetonius, and the *Scriptores Historiae Augustae* (Karl-Franzens-Universität 2007) describing the lives of the Roman emperors, reveals the participation of politicians, potentates, and emperors as spectators in the stadia. These appearances were intentionally calculated to please the masses and to win their sympathy or even just to guarantee their good behaviour. Not only emperors such as Nero, Commodus, Caligula, or Elagabalus, generally infamous for their extreme behaviour and brutality, appeared before the people – Caligula, for example, forced people to remain in the amphitheatre with the sun beating down on the *velia* (awning) during the height of the midday heat, while Elagabalus let snakes loose on the spectators, resulting in the death of many from snake bites. In addition, emperors such as Hadrian, Titus, or Domitian were aware of the importance of their appearing in person. Some emperors such as Marcus Aurelius appeared in the stadia although they took no pleasure in the performances and even hated this form of bloodshed.

Following the political motto *da te popule, committe ludis* – 'Show yourself to the people, emerge at the Games!' (Cicero, *Against Lucius Calpurnius Piso*, 65) – was not always easy for politicians, since the crowd tried to proclaim their wishes or to carry their point when important policymakers were present. The games and the gladiator shows provided some of the rare occasions when the assembled people had the opportunity to voice their political opinions and ideas (Petermandl 2005: 148). Here the individual could disappear in the crowd and feel secure without being held personally accountable for the person's own opinion or loudly voiced criticism (cf. Conclusion). Some politicians were accused by their opponents of not having the courage to appear in the stadia, so as not to be at the mercy of the masses. Sometimes they were told to tell the crowd what it wanted to hear because *ubique igitur populus dominatur et praepollet* – 'everywhere the crowd dominates and is very powerful' (Fronto, *To Marcus Aurelius*, 1.8.1–2). Unpopularity was shown by booing, popularity by clapping and shouts of joy (Petermandl 2005: 135). Sometimes these acclamations were so loud that the sporting competitions which had already begun were forgotten.

SOCIETY: SEX, ETHNICITY, AND FAN-CULT

The audience of Greek and Roman times included enthusiastic onlookers (Peter-mandl 2005) of different origin – residents as well as foreigners – social classes, ages, and sex. Criticism of various events in the stadia and the behaviour of the spectators by ancient authors reveal how great the interest in such events was. Not only is the enthusiasm of the anonymous masses or interested individuals documented, but also that of such population groups who were sometimes banned from active participation, for example, the members of different ethnicities or women.

For the Greek regions, we have some information that athletic competitions existed for (unmarried) girls (Dillon 2000; Kratzmüller 2002; Miller 2004: 150–9) which were not only of local importance. An example is the so-called *Heraia*, which were held in the Olympian *stadion*; nothing is known, however, regarding the involvement of spectators in these footraces. Women were strictly excluded from active participation within the male-dominated athletic competitions; to compete against a man within an organized athletic event was unimaginable. On the other hand, women could emerge as victors in equestrian events, because in these cases neither the charioteer nor the horses, but the owner of the stable was acclaimed the victor after the race was won. It is only in the Roman period that women can sporadically be found in different events that served as additional interludes, such as competitions between abnormally small people or as charioteers. Sometimes they can be found as professional gladiators or athletes, but even these women were viewed and treated as curiosities.

Women, however, were principally allowed to follow the events as spectators (Dillon 2000; Herrmann 1992; Petermandl 2005: 144–6). Only seldom did prohibitions exist which forbade them from attending. These bans, however, only applied for certain places and then often only for special age groups, periods, or occasions. The most famous ban concerned married women (excepting the priestess of Demeter) who were forbidden to enter the sanctuary of Zeus during the Olympic Games; Pausanias, however, explicitly tells us in the sixth book of his *Description of Greece* that *parthenoi* (unmarried women) were allowed to watch these games (Pausanias, *Description of Greece*, 6.20.8–9). Another prohibition concerned women in Rome during the Augustan period and had to do with the fact that women should be forbidden from watching nude competing Greek athletes, because this did not conform to Roman tradition and Roman standards of decency. Apart from that the events were open to spectators of both sexes. Occasionally seating was separated, but in general, and especially in Roman times, the circuses were famous for the opportunity they provided for members of both sexes to sit side by side without attracting a great deal of attention.

In a certain way the stadia also mirrored the social position of sportsmen of different ethnic origin; this can be shown, for example, by analyzing the participation of Africans and blacks (Coates and Kratzmueller 2006). During all periods blacks could be found as helpers, servants, or grooms within the field of sports activities; in Greece these attendants were viewed as a type of 'luxury good' and were symbolically used to heighten the owner's prestige. Fundamentally the *aithiopes*, blacks, were foreigners and like all other non-Greeks on principle excluded from playing a role which might result in victory: as athletes, or as owners in the equestrian events. The situation changed when the *aithiopes*, as direct neighbours of the now Hellenized Egypt, could also acquire a Greek education which included taking part in physical athletics. Pictorial sources provide sporadic evidence for the participation of blacks in different Greek sport events after this period, as wrestlers or horse-jockeys.

In Roman times blacks can be found in the world of the theatre and as active gladiators, charioteers, and competitors in Roman boxing events, as well as in Greek track and field sports and heavy athletics. Moreover, some blacks even became 'heroes of the arena' such as the gladiator Olympius, the boxer Nicaeus, or the wrestler Pannychus, as well as the charioteers Fuscus, Crescens, and Trimalchio. Nothing suggests that they were treated as 'others' in a negative fashion by the spectators or the sporting opponents.

Even long before sunrise the first spectators (Karl-Franzens-Universität 2007) of different social classes arrived at the stadia in order to secure the best seats. Programmes were set up, bets were made. Important announcements were noted on large tablets and carried around so that the audience was always kept informed. The stadia were protected against intervention or rioting by fanatical spectators during the competitions by fixed boundaries (Scobie 1988). In spite of these measures, however, it occasionally was the case – in particular during chariot races – that fans entered the race-track and were run down by the horses or chariots.

Those competing were cheered on by the crowd, but the crowd could also be cruel when an accident occurred (Crowther 1994; Petermandl 2000; Petermandl 2005: 135–6, Figure 2.7). During footraces those in the lead were generally urged on, whereas during heavy athletic contests it was often the weaker opponent who was cheered on by the crowd. To heat up the atmosphere, during animal-baiting or chariot races it became the practice for paid claqueurs to mingle in the crowds; these began their work when the applause was too weak. Also outside the actual competitions people were interested in the active competitors. During the Roman period, the masses tried to influence the authorities by shouting to demand the release of certain captive protagonists such as charioteers, or they surrounded them to keep them from being imprisoned. Furthermore, fans urged and persuaded charioteers not to retire.

Often support for an individual was not based on the person's sporting achievement on offer, the ability of the individual charioteer or gladiator, or personal feelings for a particular protagonist. Other reasons played important roles in cases of partiality (Petermandl 2005: 141–4); even banal motives, such as the beloved being a fan of a certain protagonist, or the role of patriotism, might affect the behaviour of the spectators. Partiality was enhanced by the existing fan-communities within the gladiator-system, where the fans followed not only

Figure 2.7
Campana relief of the
Early Roman Empire
showing an accident
during a chariot race in
the Circus Maximus in
Rome, circa middle of the
first century AD.

individual gladiators but often also entire gladiatorial types, and by these means supported the system of circus factions. Neither the crowd, nor the persons who were otherwise deemed responsible, based their judgements upon objective criteria, but followed solely the participant of their own faction or party. Even some of the Roman emperors were supporters of certain participants and more often of one of the circus factions (Petermandl 2005: 144). Lucius Verus and Caligula supported the Greens. Commodus and Elagabalus were avowed fans of the same faction, too, and acted as charioteers wearing their costume at private meetings, an action that was performed by Nero in public. The emperor Justinian was a follower of the Blues, providing one reason that his political opponent, the Persian king Chosroes I, began to support the Greens as a matter of principle.

The fans wore clothes in the colour of their faction (Petermandl 2005: 143), and the potential achievement of the competitors of the different factions was a topic not only at school, but also during feasts and symposia. Once the fan cult went to such extremes that a follower of a particular faction threw himself on to the funeral pyre of his favourite charioteer, Felix. In the case of outstanding achievement on the part of a particular competitor, partiality was sometimes abandoned and the different factions united to applaud the same victor. Occasionally it was the case that Greens and Blues together called for the erection of a monument.

Women also shared an interest in the lives of the competitors. Pindar writes in his ninth Pythian Ode as early as the fifth century BCE that victors in sporting games had a great appeal to members of the opposite sex (Pindar, *Pythian Odes*, 9.79–103). The fanaticism of some women went so far that they not only did everything possible to watch the competitions, but also presented all their property to youthful athletes. In the area of the theatre in particular, women were mocked by Roman authors such as Juvenal for their enthusiastic, even ardent worship.

'SHOW YOURSELF TO THE PEOPLE...': A KIND OF CONCLUSION

Sporting, political, and social events in ancient stadia, both in the Greek and the Roman world, were designed to include or exclude certain (groups of) people. Keywords such as confraternity and the construction of identities (as apparent in the exclusion of non-Greeks from the Olympic Games), fan-cult (to be demonstrated through the carrying or wearing of certain colours), socialization and sex, mass phenomena (leading to a violence-prone atmosphere on the tribunes), or political representation (such as the manipulation of the masses by Roman emperors, known as *panem et circenses*), testify to the highly important and complex social dimension of ancient mass sporting events.

Ancient stadia provided for a mass gathering of people with basically similar interests. The world inside these stadia and that outside were two completely different atmospheres. The stadia enabled people to withdraw from daily life and all the problems waiting 'outside' its walls. The confined space of the stadia gave to those within its walls a sense of commonality. This allowed the individuals within the stadia to feel a special sense of belonging, as well as self-esteem, and power. Therefore, by virtue of their built space and the social practices that came along with this space, the social dimension of ancient stadia reveals intriguing parallels to behaviours apparent in modern football stadia – the only exception being that football was unknown in Greek and Roman antiquity.

'...EMERGE AT THE GAMES': AN OVERVIEW OF POST-CLASSICAL PERIODS

With the end of the Western part of the Roman Empire an important period of European monumental sporting architecture came to an end in the sixth century AD. In Byzantium, the Eastern part of the former Roman Empire, sporting games and chariot races in particular continued to be held until the beginning of the thirteenth century (Thuillier 1999: 56–8). Nevertheless, we know that jousts and other equestrian events were performed at the Coliseum in Rome in 1332 and the amphitheatre of Verona as late as the sixteenth century. These events, however, were exceptional. Several of the large Roman sporting structures could still be seen in the landscape, however the people did not remember what they had been used for in prior times (Verspohl 1976: 24–6, 92–6; McClelland 2007: 35–6, 152 n. 3; McClelland 2009: 218–21).

During the so-called Dark Ages of Western Europe, and from the seventh to the eleventh century in particular, sporting or 'non-violent, physical activities' have very rarely been documented. Only a few idioms about athletic activities and knowledge concerning former ancient sports can be found in the literal and pictorial sources from the ninth century onwards (McClelland 2007: 36–8). 'When a recognizable athletic ethos does emerge in the eleventh century, it owes nothing to the Roman past and it arises within the context of a new policy' (McClelland 2007: 73; McClelland 2009: 222–3). New sporting activities came to the fore and some of them – such as different ball games and tennis in particular, as well as fencing and archery – needed special architectural surroundings. Particularly large grounds were needed for tournaments and jousts. However, no permanent sports structures were built for most of these activities (McClelland 2007: 22, 48, 56, 123–4, 136; McClelland 2009: 223–8).

The early tournaments of the twelfth and thirteenth century needed and destroyed huge parcels of the land so that the areas for the performances had to be limited by the authorities (Barber and Barker 1989: 25, 190). The individual jousts which replaced the mass tournaments from the late fourteenth century onwards, were performed in limited manageable areas (Barber and Barker 1989: 163). Indoor jousts, which were only seldom performed, were held in closed wooden halls (Barber and Barker 1989: 36, 43). Usually wooden barriers, stands, scaffolds, and lodges surrounded the required sporting venues to permit an unhindered performance of the sporting activities. This helped to separate the performers from the audience which consisted of people of both sexes and different social classes. These 'arenas' were often built on open fields near towns but also around open public squares, for example, marketplaces including the windows, galleries, and balconies of the surrounding houses as additional spectator perches (Barber and Barker 1989: 7–8, 32, 44, 58, 97–8, 193–6, 206–7; McClelland 2007: 22, 80–1, 119–20; McClelland 2009: 223–8, Figure 2.8).

Figure 2.8
Engraving by H.S.
Lautensack documenting
a tournament in Vienna,
June 1560.

Besides these occasionally built sporting structures, some further details like hooliganism – for example, at Pavia in 1453 where the celebration of a victory in a joust ended in a 'medieval equivalent of a football riot' (Barber and Barker 1989: 88) – the preference of ruling authorities for holding, watching, and sometimes taking part in risky and bloody spectacles, and the existence of tourneying societies (Barber and Barker 1989: 188–90) show that certain processes or patterns of behaviours can still be found throughout the Middle Ages and the Renaissance. One major difference still remains – no comparable large permanent architectural structures like those of ancient and modern times can be found in this intermediate period.

During the following centuries wood remained the preferred material for building square arenas or galleries and was sometimes also used to build oval, amphitheatrical, and *circus*-shaped structures. Such ephemeral 'buildings' were erected, for example, in eighteenth century England for different tournaments, fight shows, or animal fights. A contemporary wooden amphitheatrical construction in Vienna can be taken as an additional example. Here about 4,000 female and male spectators used to watch the so-called *Wiener Hatz*, a meagre copy of ancient animal fights (Verspohl 1976: 49–51, 113–14).

According to Verspohl (1976: 7) the arena which was built on the Field of Mars in Paris in 1790 deserves to be called the 'first permanent stadium of modern times'. The artificial earth walls of this oval arena held about 600,000 spectators (Figure 16.2). Whereas it had primarily been built for political reasons, it also served for different spectacles, but also hosted horse and footraces as early as 1796 (Verspohl 1976: 39–43, 46). The starting stages towards building arenas for the masses had begun again (cf. Chapter 3, cf. Conclusion).

In the aftermath, arenas became a part of European representative architecture of the early nineteenth century. Moreover, a series of commercially used amphitheatrical buildings spread from the nineteenth century onwards. Their concept, however, was based on the ancient sporting architecture. This fact responded to a growing interest in these ancient structures in numerous essentially academic studies of the eighteenth and early nineteenth centuries (Verspohl 1976: 61, 144–62).

The fact that permanent large sporting structures are lacking in several historical periods seems peculiar to us only when judging history from a Helleno-Romano-centric Western perspective. This view often prevents us from seeing that we are the exception to the rule when today so much energy and money is being invested in erecting monumental sporting buildings because, on a worldwide scale, they are still negligible, particularly those for sports and football. As sport scientists are we sometimes really asking the right questions? We ask questions like: 'Why didn't some people build huge permanent sporting structures?' But should the question not be: 'Why did the ancient Greeks and Romans need them and why do *we* need them again today?'

NOTE

1 These considerations are based predominantly on the studies done for Kratzmüller (2005), as well as on Karl-Franzens-Universität (2007), which also contains a comprehensive bibliography concerning ancient spectatorship (www-gewi.uni-graz.at/ spectatores/bib?action=pdf&ch). Many of the themes discussed here have also been treated elsewhere, compare especially Verspohl (1976). On research into Greek sports, see Decker (1995), Sinn (2004), and Miller (2004). Thuillier (1999) treats Roman sports, McClelland (2007) sports during the Roman Empire, whereas Weeber (1994) approaches the areas of mass-entertainment and *panem et circenses*. Müller (1995) analyzes the status of the athletes; Horsmann (1998) does the same with the world of Roman charioteers. Petermandl (2005) provides a useful overview of the behaviour of spectators in the ancient stadia, while Bollinger (1969) treats the circumstances in the early Imperial period. Heucke (1994), Baltrusch (1997), Golden (1998), and Morgan (2007) address such themes as society and politics. Finally, McClelland's (2009) analysis of the interrelation of organizers, sports spectators, and (the lack of) sports arenas from the Middle Ages to the end of the eighteenth century is highly relevant. Explicit reference is not always made, however, to these publications. I thank Alfred Bernhard-Walcher for helping to get the permission for publishing the objects of the Kunsthistorisches Museum Vienna and Edith Hütter for helping to prepare the photos for publication. Special thanks go to Sarah Cormack as well as James R. Coates, Jr. for help with the English translation; any errors remain my own.

REFERENCES

Baltrusch, E. (1997) 'Politik, Kommerz, Doping: Zum Sport in der Antike', *Gymnasium*, 104: 509–21.
Barber, R. and Barker, J. (1989) *Tournaments: Jousts, chivalry and pageants in the Middle Ages*, New York: Weidenfeld & Nicolson.
Bollinger, T. (1969) *Theatralis Licentia*, Winterthur: Hans Schellenberg.
Caldelli, M.L. (1992) 'Curia athletarum, iera xystike synodos e organizzatione delle terme a Roma', *Zeitschrift für Papyrologie und Epigraphik*, 93: 75–87.
Cameron, A. (1976) *Circus Factions*, Oxford: Calderon Press.
Coates, J.R. Jr. and Kratzmueller, B. (2006) 'Being the "others"? – Blacks in blood games', in J. Aquesolo (ed.) *Sport and Violence*, Seville: Universidad Pablo de Olavide.
Crowther, N.B. (1992) 'Slaves and Greek athletics', *Quaderni Urbinati di Cultura Classica*, 40: 35–42.
—— (1994) 'Reflections of Greek equestrian events. Violence and spectator attitudes', *Nikephoros*, 7: 121–33.
—— (2001) 'Visiting the Olympic Games in ancient Greece: Travel and conditions for athletes and spectators', *International Journal of the History of Sport*, 18: 37–52.
Decker, W. (1995) *Sport in der griechischen Antike*, Munich: C.H. Beck.
Dillon, M.P.J. (2000) 'Did parthenoi attend the Olympic Games? Girls and women competing, spectating, and carrying out cult roles at Greek religious festivals', *Hermes*, 128: 457–80.
Golden, M. (1998) *Sport and Society in Ancient Greece*, Cambridge: Cambridge University Press.
Herrmann, M. (1992) 'Zur Frau als Zuschauerin bei Wettkämpfen in römischer Zeit', *Nikephoros*, 5: 85–102.
Herz, P. (1997) 'Herrscherverehrung und lokale Festkultur im Osten des römischen Reiches (Kaiser/Agone)', in H. Cancik and J. Rüpke (eds) *Römische Reichsreligion und Provinzialreligion*, Tübingen: Mohr.

Heucke, C. (1994) *Circus und Hippodrom als politischer Raum*, Hildesheim/Zurich/New York: Olms-Weidmann.

Horsmann, G. (1998) *Die Wagenlenker der römischen Kaiserzeit*, Stuttgart: Franz Steiner.

Karl-Franzens-Universität (2007) *Spectatores: Sources of spectators in antiquity*. Online. Available www-gewi.uni-graz.at/spectatores/ (accessed 15 March 2009).

Knapp, R.C. (2001) 'The pre-Christian coins from the stadium', in S.G. Miller (ed.) *The Early Hellenistic Stadium, Excavations at Nemea*, vol. II, Berkeley/Los Angeles/London: University of California Press.

Kolb, F. (1999) 'Die Sitzordnung von Volksversammlung und Theaterpublikum im kaiserzeitlichen Ephesos', in H. Friesinger and F. Krinzinger (eds) *100 Jahre Österreichische Forschungen in Ephesos*, Vienna: Österreichische Akademie der Wissenschaften.

Kolendo, J. (1981) 'La répartition des places aux spectacles et la stratification sociale dans l'Empire Romain', *Ktema*, 6: 301–15.

Kratzmüller, B. (2002) '"Frauensport" im antiken Athen?', in A. Krüger and W. Buss (eds) *Transformations: Continuity and change in sport history*, vol. I, Hoya: NISH.

—— (2005) '"Quae beneficia e medio stadio Isthmiorum die sua ipse voce pronuntiavit" – Stadion und Politik in der Antike', in M. Marschik, R. Müllner, G. Spitaler and M. Zinganel (eds) *Das Stadion. Geschichte, Architektur, Politik, Ökonomie*, Vienna: Turia + Kant.

—— (2009) 'Metallbewehrte *caestus* – römerzeitliche Boxsportrealität oder "scholarly fiction"?', in S. Scharenberg and B. Wedemeyer-Kolwe (eds) *Grenzüberschreitung: Sport neu denken*, Hoya: NISH.

Mann, C. (2002) 'Griechischer Sport und römische Identität: Die *certamina athletarum* in Rom', *Nikephoros*, 15: 125–58.

McClelland, J. (2007) *Body and Mind: Sport in Europe from the Roman Empire to the Renaissance*, London/New York: Routledge.

—— (2009) 'Sports spectators and (the lack of) sports arenas: From the Middle Ages to the end of the eighteenth century', in S. Scharenberg and B. Wedemeyer-Kolwe (eds) *Grenzüberschreitung: Sport neu denken*, Hoya: NISH.

Miller, S.G. (2004) *Ancient Greek Athletics*, New Haven/London: Yale University Press.

Morgan, C. (2007) 'Sport and the construction of socio-political identity in archaic and classical Greece', in B. Kratzmüller, M. Marschik, R. Müllner, H.D. Szemethy and E. Trinkl (eds) *Sport and the Construction of Identities*, Vienna: Turia + Kant.

Müller, S. (1995) *Das Volk der Athleten*, Trier: Wissenschaftlicher Verlag.

Petermandl, W. (2000) 'Der verlachte Athlet. Überlegungen zum Sport und Humor im Altertum', in C. Ulf (ed.) *Ideologie – Sport – Außenseiter*, Innsbruck: Institut für Sprachwissenschaft.

—— (2005) 'Geht ihr aber ins Stadion...', in M. Marschik, R. Müllner, G. Spitaler and M. Zinganel (eds) *Das Stadion. Geschichte, Architektur, Politik, Ökonomie*, Vienna: Turia + Kant.

Pleket, H.W. (1973) 'Some aspects of the history of the athletic guilds', *Zeitschrift für Papyrologie und Epigraphik*, 10: 197–227.

Roueché, C. (1993) *Performers and Partisans at Aphrodisias in the Roman and Late Roman Periods*, London: Society for the Promotion of Roman Studies.

Scobie, A. (1988) 'Spectator security and comfort at gladiatorial games', *Nikephoros*, 1: 191–243.

Sinn, U. (2004) *Das antike Olympia*, Munich: C.H. Beck.

Small, D.B. (1987) 'Social correlations to the Greek cavea in the Roman period', in S. Macready and F.H. Thompson (eds) *Roman Architecture in the Greek World*, London: Thames and Hudson.

Thuillier, J.-P. (1999) *Sport im antiken Rom*, Darmstadt: Wissenschaftliche Buchgesellschaft.

van Nijf, O.M. (1997) *The Civic World of Professional Associations in the Roman East*, Amsterdam: J.C. Gieben.

Verspohl, F.-J. (1976) *Stadionbauten von der Antike bis zur Gegenwart: Regie und Selbsterfahrung der Massen*, Gießen: Anabas.

Weeber, K.-W. (1994) *Panem et Circenses*, Mainz: Philipp von Zabern.

Weiler, I. (1997) 'Olympia – jenseits der Agonistik. Kultur und Spektakel', *Nikephoros*, 10: 191–213.

Welch, K. (1998a) 'Greek stadia and Roman spectacles: Asia, Athens, and the tomb of Herodes Atticus', *Journal of Roman Archaeology*, 11: 117–45.

—— (1998b) 'The stadium at Aphrodisias', *American Journal of Archaeology*, 102: 547–69.

Chapter 3: Challenging the Stadium

Watching Sport Events in Public

Hans-Jürgen Schulke

PRELUDE

Spectacles, songs, circuses, contests between athletes, horses or gladiators – these have all won audiences since ancient times. From a very early stage, theatrical storytelling, announcements of news and tests of strength have had platforms and grandstands and thus an architecture of their own. These can be seen in all their varied and large-scale glory in the arenas, stadia and amphitheatres of the Mediterranean region. The Circus Maximus in Rome still fascinates visitors with its functionality, monumentality and enclosed atmosphere. It gives us a clue to the thrilling spell that existed between players and spectators, by means of which spatial, acoustic and visual arrangements were intensified. Spectators became immediate witnesses to events that had never been seen or heard of before (cf. Chapter 2).

It is possible to identify two anthropological points of focus that evoke the unique atmosphere in these spaces, even in those days. On the one hand there is the human quest to experience the unknown, here and now – humans are characterized by a life-long, life-saving and unquenchable curiosity. They wish to experience what is happening with their own eyes and ears, a meaning reinforced by terms such as 'eyewitness'. On the other hand there is the endless yearning for an all-embracing commonality, for concordance with as many other people as possible, which crowd psychologists refer to as infectious emotion (in German, Canetti's *Gefühlsansteckung*, 1960). Both instances – which can be seen from both an emotional and a cognitive point of view – are phylogenetically important for the cohesion and development of the human species.

It would be almost 2,000 years before such profane monumental buildings for spectators were once again erected in Europe. In England, the first football stadia were built at the end of the nineteenth century, following the construction of stands at some larger racecourses. The period between was dominated by cathedrals as places of ritual assembly, in which information and emotions were channelled under sacred auspices (cf. Chapter 14). In many places they formed an immobile inwardness with the character of a lighthouse, visibly defining the profile of the city.

Just in front of the cathedral and after work, the fair was unleashed, an informal gathering of believers, traders, innkeepers, jugglers and fools – the space for which was provided by the marketplace. What was, a short time before, a strictly organized parish of hymns and prayer was now a place for sauntering and laughing, for curiosity and small talk, bargaining and music, and sometimes even fist fights. Status and position were put into perspective in the mobile crowd, social barriers disappeared – a hint of freedom and equality enchanted the market square.

Showgrounds, theatres, ballrooms and dancehalls – none ever quite achieved these dimensions, not even the stationary circus buildings of the late nineteenth century. The closest events ever came to the magnitude of the cathedral was on level ground, in public spaces where aristocratic weddings, parades, markets and burnings took place. Particularly in Italian regions, physical activities such as football-like games and horse races were staged. Then, at the dawn of modernity, numerous public exercise grounds emerged in Germany, in which – unusually for a class-based society – all young men could train strength, coordination and collective acts in an egalitarian manner. All of this took place under the watchful gaze of parents or officials, who were curious about form and function, but also keen to limit the risks inherent in such strange activities – spectators who watched at ground level.

Sporting exercises were a further product of modern physical activity, and were first introduced in the schools of middle-class English youths, intent on advancement. Faithful to the capitalist ethic of free competition and its political mentality of being the conqueror, these young men competed in athletics, boxing, cricket, hockey, golf, badminton, baseball, soccer, rugby, rowing and swimming, attempting to achieve the highest placing on the internal ranking scale. Orientating itself toward measured 'records', peak performance became ubiquitous and overcame the boundaries of its local anchor. Sport, with its combination of adolescence, selection and asceticism, was to become the most important social entity of the aspiring middle class; physical fitness became a modern lifestyle. The sportsman took to the stage of everyday self-promotion and remains there to this day, while his alter ego, the gentleman, fades into memory.

In essence, sport does not need special spaces. Rivers, meadows and marked-out park areas were sufficient to allow creativity, organization and passion to unfold. This was especially true when the educational authorities were worried about the risks of injury, and the puritanical clergy viewed the uninhibited appetite of youth for games with scepticism. The sportsmen were themselves enough, no spectators were expected and not even referees were needed – conflicts between the teams could be settled by the captains (cf. Chapter 7). Amateurs by conviction – amateurs in the sense that they distanced themselves socially from the physical activities connected to occupational and everyday positions such as running footmen, horsemen and boatmen – they wanted no entry fee to their sporting battles.

Today it is surprising to learn that sport initially had no spectators and therefore neither grandstands nor stadia (Pfister 2006). At the first modern Olympic Games in Athens in 1896, the participants in some disciplines outnumbered the viewers. And even in St. Louis in 2004 there were tug-of-war and long jump contests, organized spontaneously for seamen of different nations who happened to be present at the time. Their philanthropic ancestors of the late eighteenth century, who, with their knowledge of the ancient architecture of stadia and coliseums were keen to revive the Olympic Games, were also satisfied to run a few rounds of a sunken circular course.

Nevertheless, sport nowadays enthrals people and draws them into arenas, stadia and to their television screens like no other activity, and is, economically speaking, by far the most important part of the entertainment industry. As a matter of course, it claims the space it requires and designs this space according to its needs and rules.

SPECTATOR MOTIVES IN SPORT

Different impulses are needed for the formation and distribution of spectators in sport. First, this unknown, often still incomprehensible form of physical activity must become a habit for a large group of people. The growing number of experts among those who take part themselves will successively and chronologically create potential spectators.

A further, and probably the most decisive, impulse comes from betting on sporting competitions. Betting gives carefree, youthful tests of strength a serious economic aspect, leads to the development of rules and encourages the philosophy of fairness. The English landed gentry, with more or less nothing to do after Cromwell's Revolution, sought distraction (Latin: *disportare*) and thrills in the boredom of everyday life. Physical comparisons, on whose outcome bets were placed, provided this. Later, we see the advent of the industrial worker, who had (too little) cash and desperately hoped for sudden wealth, to be gained by placing bets. The gentry and the proletariat converged as gamblers in race-course totalizator betting, then in the realms of boxing and football. Without the modern possibilities of electronic data transfer, they wanted to be eyewitnesses to their own triumphs. They were no longer smug observers of sweat-inducing physical activity or uncomprehending commentators on the luxurious waste of energy, but were rather following, with increasing curiosity and nervousness, the whereabouts of their money. Thanks to competitive sport, the thirst for information and passion entered into a new kind of symbiosis.

This inevitably led to a new type of sports architecture, for not only must ever growing crowds of spectators be accommodated, but they all wanted to know the complete and immediate results of their bets – sudden wealth or financial loss, the greatest triumph or the deepest depression. Stands were erected at the finishing line and along the home stretch, then stadia with higher and higher tiers, and finally weatherproof arenas. At the same time, conditions that ensured the formal principle of equal opportunities for the athletes could be put in place. Procedures unknown to antiquity, such as precisely measured tracks, standardized competitive surfaces, standardized goals and sports equipment, uniform penalty areas, a change of ends to cancel the effect of poor weather conditions, and different weight classes became a matter of course.

The construction of stadia is also connected to the increase in the importance of ball games, particularly football. The first types of sport were not the now worldwide popular game of football, but rather horse-riding, rowing, running and boxing. Ball games followed later, first baseball and cricket with their hard, stuffed projectiles, then rugby with an irregular, egg-shaped ball. Tennis and football required technical innovation before they could triumph.

While countless young people at the end of the Middle Ages kicked an unpredictably bouncing swine's bladder on the streets between the city gates, and attempted, amid collective laughter, to shove it through the opposing goal, the invention of vulcanization and the valve presented the possibility of a uniform ball size with stable flight characteristics. Ball-handling techniques could now be practised systematically and tactics could no longer fall victim to coincidence. It helped to have cultivated, well-drained grass surfaces – the arbitrariness of nature became a part of sports architecture. A level and dry playing field, as well as grandstands that can protect the flight of the ball from the vagaries of the wind should also be considered.

Multifunctional athletics grounds can still be found in many places, incorporating a running track around the football pitch; a few decades ago, not only football but also field handball was played, cycle races were held, gymnastic festivals were celebrated and band music was performed. Mono-functional football

Figure 3.1
Kampfbahn Rote Erde,
Dortmund, 1935.

arenas with high technological equipment have only emerged in the past ten years (for a discussion of a new multi-functionality of football stadia cf. Chapter 4).

A further impulse was provided by the identification of the spectators with the sporting participants, the projection of the self onto the great sporting performances of talented contemporaries. School children in English boarding schools overcame certain fears and educational opposition to cheer on their 'own' team. Sports clubs, created during the course of rapidly growing urbanization, came to represent their locality or district, their social class (middle-class clubs against working-class clubs) or their religion. Eventually, during the course of the development of nation-states (more or less), an entire population identified itself with the national team, and its colours, flags and hymns. This process of identification takes on a political meaning with the medals table at the Olympic Games. Along these lines, demonstrative and monumental examples of sports architecture were created that far exceeded the functional uses of a sports ground for athletes and spectators. Here, sport sometimes even becomes the backdrop to political self-projection.

The great sport has irrevocably distanced itself from the level market square of chance and familiarity. The stadium has become a high security area, voluntarily entered, that channels and at the same time localizes the emotions that are intensified by its architecture. The open and anarchic market can still be found among the beer stalls and the chat outside the heavily protected stadium gates.

THE DYNAMICS AND LIMITATIONS OF THE STADIUM

Today, stadia are the most popular, often the most distinctive and frequently the most expensive edifices in a particular region. Here, many aspirations come together: to facilitate the highest possible sporting performances, to measure the results of these performances in an exact and incontrovertible manner, to make the event visible to all participants as well as to television viewers, to place the focus on passionate solidarity in victory and defeat, to offer spectators the highest possible comfort and the best possible protection, to demonstrate political prestige on behalf of the clubs or the national powers-that-be, and to secure the highest possible profit for the organizers. Not exactly a small number of requirements, and ones that constantly change the character of the stadium and lead architects to probe new dimensions. Current examples include large video cubes, installed above the centre of the pitch, and LED walls that allow spectators a twofold view of events (cf. Chapter 5), as well as ever more comprehensive VIP areas, which illustrate a clearly tiered system of spectator groups (cf. Chapter 4).

Stadia are primarily property that has been constructed to facilitate spectating. Comfort is of importance to spectators, who are in no sense passive consumers. Their ticket purchases, their acoustic support of the team, and their identification with the club make them a constitutive part of a complex system of interaction. Nevertheless, their role, structure and influence are changing. The new generation of stadia, originating with the World Cups of the 1990s, determines more than ever before the routes to and within the stadium, organizes electronically controlled entry, assigns fixed sectors and seats, and stipulates behavioural rituals by means of loudspeakers and fans' representatives. Police attention outside and inside the stadium, video surveillance and security in the

Figure 3.2
VIP lounge, Frankfurt,
2006.

Figure 3.3
The stadium as a high
security area.

spectator areas leave nothing unnoticed – the spectator in the stadium is himself an object of observation, temporary inhabitant of a high security area (cf. Chapter 1).

This development in stadium architecture presents us with a contradiction, which can only be partially, and perhaps to an ever decreasing extent, balanced out: In essence, the spectator is provided with a publicly approved space, found nowhere else, in which, on the one hand, excessive emotions are facilitated and can be intensified (cf. Chapter 13) while, on the other hand, the emotional dynamics are prevented from getting out of hand, in other words, emotions are regulated and channelled in this space. Raucous bawling, alcoholic excesses and threats of violence are seen by many spectators as abhorrent, by club officials as damaging to their product's image, and by security personnel as a reason to intervene in order to protect peaceful spectators. And yet they form a constitutive part of the whole production.

Since the 1950s, decades during which the electronic entertainment community has grown ever faster, a new type of spectator outside the stadium has emerged – the television viewer. Despite initial fears that it would compete with stadium attendance, television has greatly contributed to the popularity of sport, and of football in particular. This medium has led to a worldwide popularity and expertise, which in return encourages stadium attendance.

Television viewers are also real-time witnesses, albeit no longer directly. Their perception is mediated and has no direct retroactive influence on the participants on and around the pitch (for a counterexample see Chapter 5). When they follow a football match on their television at home, either alone or among friends, their infectious emotion remains separate from that of the crowd. On the other hand, their curiosity is better served than in the stadium: Close-ups of match scenes, replays, different camera positions, speed and distance measurements and expert commentary provide extra information which the spectator in the stadium doesn't have. And indeed shouldn't have since, for example, the display of a clear refereeing mistake on a video wall could well cause thousands of spectators in the stadium to lose their practised and spatially controlled emotional composure.

Looking more closely, however, one can see that the television broadcast, which both creates and sates curiosity, is already making inroads into the stadium itself. Those spectators in the stadium with mobile television have the choice of following the entire match or specific players, as well as important situations and constellations. On the video screens, goals that have been scored can be relived, and in the increasingly expansive corporate boxes, the game is shown parallel on pay-per-view television. To an extent, at least, the television viewer with his or her thirst for knowledge already has an influence on the events in the stadium (cf. Conclusion).

Today the link between curiosity and shared experience in the bowl-like arena is crumbling. On the one hand, the stadium is numerically limited to perhaps 60,000 seats (the demand for tickets for big matches is much higher, interest in football is growing and is further boosted by the football authorities), on the other hand, the shared experience is becoming increasingly segmented and classified, and the thirst for information about the actual events on the pitch can no longer be satisfied by the current methods of electronic transmission. The growing social attraction of large-scale football, the somewhat curious yet distanced interest of many people in this strange and fascinating game, can no longer be completely satisfied in a convincing or affordable manner in the stadium.

PUBLIC VIEWING AS A NEW QUALITY OF SPECTATING IN SPORT

One can observe a number of different impulses, very often of a technical nature, throughout the history of sport, and in particular that of football and its spectators. Vulcanized balls, drained pitches, roofed stands, television broadcasts with multifaceted additional information, electronic betting, referees' headsets, artificial grass and many more features influence playing style and spectator behaviour.

A further technical innovation at the beginning of the new millennium triggered an entirely unexpected enhancement of spectator behaviour, football being the first instance: The emergence of LED walls, often still referred to – incorrectly – as big screens. These can be interconnected to form a viewing surface of up to 200 square metres. Around 300,000 people gathered in public spaces to watch important matches during the 2002 World Cup in Japan and Korea, albeit on considerably smaller video walls. It was the birth of Public Viewing (PV), which is unconnected to big-screen presentations (Schulke 2007).

What is technologically innovative about these large-scale presentations of images is the fact that they no longer reflect images from a surface – as a cinema screen does – but rather are composed of thousands of tiny, gas-filled diodes that can create different full-colour pixels electronically. Just as with domestic televisions, they produce a complete picture with such vibrancy that pin sharp images can be seen at great distances and in every weather – simultaneously, more comprehensively, more exactly and in a different manner to that which can be seen in the stadium.

The new technology is mobile. Within a few hours it can be erected and taken down again in any place, it can be set up on the level ground of an urban square or in the semicircle of an outdoor theatre, on a mountainside or upon pontoons on a river. The football match is staged in an ephemeral architecture (cf. Chapter 4) – on the following day, nothing remains to remind one of the passionate spectator behaviour during the match that was shown there.

This new LED technology offers a new means of linking the two fundamental moments of spectator sport: The satisfaction of curiosity and the experience of shared emotion. The as yet short history of Public Viewing has shown that its spatial form is not only anticipatory, from the viewpoint of football functionaries or event managers, but is also driven quite considerably by the spectators

– thanks to their spontaneity, joy and celebratory attitude. It is no coincidence that the first Public Viewing concept published in 2003, in advance of the 2006 World Cup, was entitled *The World Cup on the Market Square* (Schulke 2007).

THE BREAKTHROUGH OF PUBLIC VIEWING AT THE 2006 FIFA WORLD CUP

Prior to the 2006 World Cup in Germany, the organizers were confronted with the problem of providing suitable spectator areas and gathering places to accommodate the more than three million ticket requests, as well as the expected one million foreign visitors (in the end, there were over two million). Building on the experience of hosting international gymnastics events and religious congresses, the concept *The World Cup on the Market Square* was developed, according to which central contact points for all fans would be created for the four-week duration, to act as places to meet, board, get information and partake in cultural events. The highlight was the broadcast of all 64 games on large-scale video walls to at least 50,000 visitors. In a complicated process lasting a number of years, details on costs, logistics and safety issues, as well as marketing, broadcast and events rights, were hammered out. It remained unclear right up until the opening of the World Cup whether what was being offered would be accepted by the fans, and thus be an organizationally controllable festival.

As is now well known, the field study was a complete success (Bundesregierung/BMI 2006). Over 27 million people gathered at Public Viewings in Germany, as well as innumerable spectators in large cities around the world. It is widely accepted that Public Viewing was the decisive factor in creating the joyous mood during the 2006 World Cup (it was termed *Sommermärchen*, or the Fairy

Figure 3.4
Public Viewing during
the 2006 FIFA World Cup
in Berlin.

Tale Summer). FIFA has since decided to make 'Fan Fests' a fixed part of events at future World Cup championships.

From a sociological point of view, two approaches toward an explanation present themselves: Organizational sociology to determine the success factors of this unique event, and cultural sociology to interpret the 'collective rapture' of hundreds of thousands of people in public places.

The large number of visitors to the Fan Fests, which were much more uncomfortable than watching television at home would have been (lots of standing, remote sanitary facilities, expensive drinks) can be attributed to six organizational factors (FIFA 2006; Schulke 2007):

- The central location and easy accessibility of the architecturally attractive city squares (including the national rail company's World Cup Ticket, which made transportation between cities easier; many vagabond 'World Cup nomads' travelled from city to city).
- Free and flexible entry, as well as the possibility to change position within the area (in contrast to the strictly segmented 'high security area' of the stadium). Where higher entrance fees were charged, PV failed.
- A versatile and attractive choice of information and sales stands (market character).
- Good weather, or locations not dependent upon weather conditions (roofed stadia, large factory halls).
- The early success of the home team at the beginning of the tournament – after the good start, the party mood propagated itself.
- The permanently changing and varied life on the 'fan miles', particularly due to the large number of foreign guests, for whom these were ideal gathering places, all day long.

Pragmatic organizational reasons alone do not suffice, since pubs and cinemas would have proved (and in many cases did prove) more comfortable places for Public Viewing. They cannot explain the 'collective rapture' of the Fan Fests. For this we require a cultural-sociological interpretation (cf. Schulke 2006 and 2007):

- Professional sport, and football in particular, fascinates because of its authentic excitement, being easy to understand yet also involving complex coordination. Prior to the game, its course and result are unknown. The consequence is a passionate following of, and identification with, the sporting event. Coping with the huge suspense is easier in larger groups of people (infectious emotion and catharsis, cf. Chapter 13).
- The growing curiosity of the people about the exciting event is more cheaply and comprehensively satisfied on the video walls than in the stadium; here one can see close-ups, slow motion replays and visual aids for spatial constellations such as the offside rule.
- The architecture of the stadium concentrates the tension, but also regulates it almost to the point of punishment. The 'mobile anarchy' of the Fan Fest, the

ability to wander freely to another position, leads to an intermingling of people from different places and with different interests. This relaxes the atmosphere, which in the stadium can often be martial, and makes it easier for women, in particular, to linger. It isn't rare to see Fan Fests develop with a wink into Flirt Miles.

- New stadia are usually built on the periphery. Public Viewing takes place in the heart of the city – a return to the place where football began: On the street, inside the city gates.
- Regulated encounters between two equal competitors at top-class sporting events produces great tension, which releases jolly equanimity among fans of all nations on the market square. Colourful make-up, the happy waving of flags and the singing of playful songs demonstrate an identity with their team, without being chauvinistic gestures of superiority. Schiller's theme 'All human beings become brothers' hovered tangibly above the mediatized events in public spaces during the 2006 World Cup.

Public Viewing provides a new technical, organizational and cultural quality of watching football. Until now, it has been a quality influenced by fans of all persuasions (from skilled experts to violent hooligans in search of a public stage). What all have in common is their identification with their own team and its stars, the passionate, often irrational partisanship in victory and defeat, the high value placed on the matches as well as the everyday communication that they engender.

THE FLÂN AS A NEW KIND OF SPECTATOR: FAN AND FLÂNEUR

The new quality becomes apparent when one compares the traditional sports fan with the figure of the flâneur, a figure first discussed in German sociology some 100 years ago – and indeed almost 100 years earlier in France and England. The flâneur was the successor of the nature-loving roamer of the romantic age, and a product of the rapidly growing city. Here, it is necessary to keep pace in a world where traffic is faster, factories and living quarters are being built at an astonishing rate, and where new technical sensations and strange new consumer products hold sway.

Benjamin (1983) talks of gawking and idleness as a balance between greed for the new and how this is specifically treated. It is bound up with the habitual pattern of prosperity, in which time and money are abundant: Bonvivants stroll along the majestic Champs Elysées with a tortoise on a leash, while in the new cathedrals of labour, the Ford and Siemens factories, human automatons toil away in minute intervals.

Today, innumerable people are immobile flâneurs or flâneuses, who stroll through the internet, linger among items of interest and seek contact with unknown others in blogs or on Second Life. Investigations of the subject from around the world are exchanged in the online magazine *Der Flaneur*.

Public Viewing spectating is a cultural self-image of citizens of the world, who are open to all kinds of sports and everything new that the information society has to offer, and who feel like partying. They deliberately search out stimulating events, in which they take a passionate part while also maintaining an informed distance by strolling through the location and the event and feeling free to leave their chosen standpoint whenever they choose.

This cultural type of spectator, the flân, is an engaged sportsman or sportswoman *and* a critical, luxury-seeking consumer of entertainment, alternating between each option. Even more: at Public Viewing events he or she is a passionate fan and a cosmopolitan flâneur or flâneuse *at one and the same time.* In this symbiosis, the passion of the stadium's sports fan loses its grimness, the idleness of the flâneur or flâneuse its individualistic smugness (for preliminary thoughts cf. Giulianotti 2002).

THE SUCCESS STORY OF PUBLIC VIEWING IN SPORT, POLITICS AND CULTURE

The Fairy Tale Summer of 2006 was not a one-off. During the World Equestrian Games in Aachen in 2006, Public Viewing was set up on the city's market square. While it brought the event right into the city centre, its resonance was modest. Naturally, it could never have enjoyed anything like the success experienced at the football Fan Fests a few weeks before.

Handball is the most likely sport to inspire Fan Fests. This is a sport with hundreds of thousands of fans and rising in many countries, which also enjoyed intensive reporting and great public interest during the 2007 World Championship in Germany, reminiscent of the World Cup fever of the previous year. After the preliminary rounds at the latest, all of the venues were sold out. There was sufficient free space in the roofed arenas that were no longer in use, and also in those of the ice hockey clubs. However, apart from a few local initiatives, there were no nationally organized Fan Fests along the lines of the Fairy Tale Summer. The possibility of showing the latter stages of national cup championships, either in home venues or outside the actual event, is being investigated. Similar results can be expected at the World Ice Hockey Championships in 2011.

The cultural tradition of certain types of sport also plays an important role. In many countries, rugby is the number one sport, and indeed the Rugby World Cup was transmitted via Public Viewing in many countries and was very well received.

Numerous PV festivals were staged all over Europe, particularly in Austria and Switzerland, during the 2008 European Football Championships. They generally proved that this form of spectating could also be held successfully outside of the host nation. It was, too, confirmation that the weather, the progress of the home team and an accessible location are definitive success factors. In Germany in particular, the locations of the 2006 events proved to be successful places to transmit the 2008 European Championship. It is noteworthy that the

2008 European final, played in Vienna, was broadcast live to a packed Frankfurt football stadium.

Until now, international club football has seen only a few attempts to show important away games in the team's home stadium. Aside from a lack of clarity where licensing rights (broadcasting and marketing) are concerned, there is also the strain on the grass and the small economic yield to consider. All the same, the signs are that these options may be used in the future, either by setting up a video wall outside the stadium or, with the introduction of artificial pitches, even inside.

With its growing acceptance and popularity – in 2006, Public Viewing was declared to be the Word of the Year in Germany – this form of spectating is also being offered in non-sporting areas. Public Viewing has long been integrated in religious events (papal visits, national church congresses), as many members of the large congregations would otherwise miss announcements or prayers, for example. Sunday Mass from St. Peter's Basilica is shown on a video wall. Recent papal visits have also been broadcast to remote churches or public spaces abroad. It is to be expected that the continued spectacularization of these events will lead to (even) larger audience numbers, who will seek space and form for their religious celebrations.

Musical performances, in particular, enjoy such popularity, that they even suffer a shortage of space in stadia and other large spaces. Therefore the Wagner festival in Bayreuth and current opera productions in Berlin for example are broadcast near the playhouses – apparently with great success. Public Viewing also developed quite spontaneously during the election and inauguration of President Obama. Election night was followed on video walls in New York, Chicago, Kenya, Hawaii, Asia and Europe by hundreds of thousands of people.

This brief overview (see also Praum 2008) clearly shows that Public Viewing has become an important issue in sporting and other large events, and will continue to develop creatively, though the solutions, to be found locally and according to topic, certainly remain open. The cultural context of the event and its technical, organizational implementation must be taken into consideration, while productive and economic aspects play no small role.

At the 2002 World Cup, the relatively small video walls were rare commodities with somewhat unstable technical functionality. At the 2006 World Cup, six-figure sums had to be found by the event organizers to fund the hire and operation of complicated electronic equipment for the five-week Fan Fests. Now it is possible to hire a truck – and personnel – for 15,000 euros for a weekend, from which a screen measuring 60 square metres can be unveiled and set up practically anywhere, thus providing more than 50,000 people in a public space the enjoyment of an exciting Public Viewing event. Further technical developments will make PV cheaper, more flexible, more spontaneous and more intense (for example, by means of concave projection surfaces, which will increase the 'stadium feeling').

CONCEPTUAL CLASSIFICATIONS: EVENT ENHANCEMENT, CORPORATE AND PUBLIC VIEWING

These days, the electronic presentation of images can be found at many sporting events, they are natural and indispensable sources of information for the spectator (triathlon, biathlon, ski jumping, gymnastics, athletics etc.). They clarify on television screens, simultaneously and repeatedly, the events that are occurring authentically and perceived individually. It is – in a sense similar to that in the football stadia – an electronic, informative event enhancement. The same is true for political rallies or large-scale economic and scientific congresses.

Another form is Public Viewing in public institutions, but with limited attendance (cinemas, pubs, clubhouses, community centres). What we have here is a common experience – after all, the intimacy of the television at home has been left behind – but not a mass psychological phenomenon. By now, many companies use such an event as a carefully staged marketing activity, for example when a large number of customers is invited to watch an important football match in an elaborate room with a video wall, where they receive entertainment and refreshment. These forms are often known as Corporate Viewing.

Electronic event enhancements such as Corporate Viewing are grey areas that cannot be equated with Public Viewing in public spaces. The tracking of important events in a multitudinous crowd of people in front of an oversized television screen, the central and spacious location, free entry and mobility and the freedom of decision in a collective interest are all criteria that make a new quality of spectating possible. The visitors themselves have already made Public Viewing into their own cultural experience, independent of sporting, cultural, religious or political content. It is, at any rate, an entirely different setting to the architecturally structured stadium (cf. Chapter 1).

SOUTH AFRICA 2010: THE TWO-FOLD WORLD CUP CHAMPIONSHIPS

There will be fewer and smaller stadia available at the World Cup in South Africa than there were in Germany in 2006, and therefore considerably fewer tickets for those who wish to see the games in person. In addition, the infrastructure (transportation) serving the stadia will not be of a European standard, thus making it difficult for many people to get to the venues; the security situation will also be more difficult to control. The costs, as well as the time and effort involved, will be prohibitive to many South Africans and other football enthusiasts when considering a stadium visit (Schmidt 2010).

On the other hand, this will be the first World Cup to be held in Africa, which is intended to encourage a broader popularity for football on that continent and in other less developed countries. As a result, the interest of the poorer (i.e. mostly black) population in the competition will be immense, while the white population is more likely to maintain its preference for rugby and cricket. For the former, staging the World Cup in their own country is an honour, provides hope and presents an opportunity to prove themselves as good hosts.

The South African government, in particular, associates the World Cup with sustainable tourism interests and wants the country to profit from many guests from around the world. Many of these will not have any opportunity to visit a stadium; however, memories of the Fan Fests in 2006 will encourage many football fans to set out for South Africa. In this respect, there are many arguments in favour of a comprehensive Public Viewing solution, either in individual World Cup stadia on days where no match is taking place there, or in other places without a stadium, the most likely situation being temporary stands in public squares.

As things appear at present, it is certainly realistic to expect that Fan Fests, and therefore Public Viewing, will be as important a part of the 2010 World Cup as the actual matches in the stadia. Not least the fact that PV is free of charge will draw people to celebrate the World Cup together, and the fact that private television ownership is much lower than in European countries will also play a role. In addition, the public Fan Fests present South Africa and its multifaceted population with a much-desired opportunity to use the celebratory transformation of their public spaces to bring their own history and cultural roots to life.

The 2010 World Cup could be the first which the (mainly television) spectators learn more about events from the public Fan Fests than by watching them live in the stadium. The media will continuously report on the festival atmosphere in the public places, groups of supporters will create their own choreographies, players and managers will appear on the stages of the Fan Fests after matches. There will be two World Cups – one in the stadium and one at the Fan Fests – and it remains unclear which one will excite the greatest enthusiasm among the spectators.

SCENARIO OF THE FUTURE, 2020: THE DISAPPEARANCE OF THE STADIUM

Let us dare to jump ahead in time to the year 2020. Professional football matches are now held in a new generation of stadia, first seen in the European Championships that have just been staged in Germany (there is only one national stadium for the opening ceremony and the final, with a capacity of 10,000 seats). In general, they provide room for 25,000 seated spectators along the length of the stadium, while the stands at each end are equipped with permanently installed video walls, upon which each spectator can observe, in a large-scale close-up, the reactions of the Public Viewing spectators who are out in the public squares, as well as image sequences from the match itself and, more importantly, advertisements. The stands along the length of the stadium contain mainly VIP areas, where matches can be watched from the balconies either on the pitch below or on the flatscreens installed on the seat back in front. There are no referees and consequently no occasions for abuse, offside and sideline infringements are determined in real time by means of sensors and are made known to the public and the players simultaneously. The same goes for fouls. A lawyer monitors the decisions.

The spectators in the normal seats remain immobile during the match and in the breaks. Drinks and 'wakamin' energy drugs are served directly to the seat by means of an ingenious transport system, the quick, frenzied images on the LED screens remain unnoticed, every now and then a signal is transmitted to headphones, urging the crowd to press buttons which will illuminate the seats in a particular colour constellation for the purpose of wide-scale choreography. Hooligan riots are unheard of.

Football remains the most attractive form of entertainment there is. Matches are broadcast daily on TV, the online media informs instantaneously and interactive chatrooms are heavily frequented. The FIFA Football Game is the most popular product on the electronic game market, the World Robot League, founded in 2001, reaches seven-digit viewing figures and even higher bets, the fourth season of the TV format 'Adidas Soccer-Idol' for 4–6-year-olds enjoys its highest ever audience rating, particularly among those with the most purchasing power, the over-70s.

The demand for stadium tickets is modest. While the VIP areas continue to be full, many of the remaining seats must be filled by soldiers, school classes, student assistants and idle security personnel. Cheers of elation and encouragement, as well as booing and whistling and fan chants are all inserted by means of a mixing desk. Alternatively, they are simply transmitted to the stadium from the public squares hosting PV events. No imaginative choreography, no original fan songs, no banners are present in this arrangement; they are shown on the video walls every now and then as relics.

Those responsible for the top professional clubs express great satisfaction with this solution. Construction costs and the accompanying interest payments are considerably lower than those incurred by the stadia of 2006, parking and transportation are easily managed and entertainment and security at match venues are much cheaper. The lower income generated is of little concern, particularly since the area of cheap standing room has been reduced. Besides, the clubs' budgets are primarily earned through income from television and sponsors.

The same level of acceptance can be found at FIFA, the International Football Federation and by now the largest concern in the international entertainment industry, along with its continental confederations. The reduced size and costs of the stadia enable emerging nations to host international championships. In addition, these stadia can continue to be used in a number of ways after the end of tournaments, thus avoiding future white elephants such as those left after the World Cup championships in Japan and Korea in 2002.

The impressively large crowd of football spectators can be found in the open spaces of the city centres; some of the places are in the immediate vicinity of the stadia and allow interaction with the stadium audience before and after the game. They have become the marketplaces of the entertainment industry, with sporting events, concerts and films being shown on mobile video walls many times a week. During the day, markets and gaming booths are set up, which can, depending on the evening event, remain in place, thus offering refreshments, information, competitions, cultural attractions and shopping. Barriers and entry points can be erected hydraulically to suit the various numbers of visitors, and electronic surveillance oversees the many entrances, through which fans and flâneurs can enter and exit at any time. The fans merely need to register once a year for a small fee, and to activate admission online per mobile phone before each visit, to prevent congestion at the event.

The video walls are transported on big trucks and installed a few hours before the match, as are the portable roofed stands for up to 10,000 spectators. There is a charge to sit in the stands, as opposed to the more than 100,000 free standing places. The video walls are convex, so the spectators feel as if they were in the middle of a stadium bowl, or even like players on the pitch. Peripheral video walls provide ongoing additional information about specific match situations, ball speeds, bodily contact and refereeing decisions.

The colourfully painted spectators in the open space of the interior cheer on their teams, sing newly composed songs, determine substitutions by means of mobile phone voting and interact with those in the stadium thanks to reciprocal television transmissions. The centre of all communications focuses on the stages in front of the LED walls, from which hosts speak to the public, fans present new songs or electronic designs, experts opine and betting is coordinated.

The PV is a colourful folk festival at and around the match, a constantly self-regenerating event. It begins long before the game and ends long after the final whistle, after the players and managers have arrived, the most original costume or the funniest song has been chosen, all the important match incidents have been replayed and expertly analysed. Many have already moved on, with new-found friends, to the next entertainment.

These five or so hours form an inexhaustible networking opportunity, since the large number of people in the unregulated area, and the interest in the game, create an effortless sense of community, which makes it much easier to establish eye contact, get closer spatially and physically, address others, exchange telephone numbers and photos or arrange to meet at one of the many stands.

While the spectators certainly cheer for 'their' team, they are also always aware that these teams are inaccessible and unresponsive to them – passion with a nod and a wink, toothless aggression. Between the gates of the marketplace of great entertainment, football has revived some of its origins.

This future scenario is one option. Another one is the consistent marketing of Fan Fests by FIFA, along the lines of the 2006 World Cup (Hamacher and Efing 2006). PV becomes 'stadium lite', without allowing the cultural potential of the open marketplace to unfold. It is questionable whether this has a sustainable future.

In such a case PV may face a similar fate to that of the stadia. As the largest properties in the cities they are safe, well thought-out, provide unimpeded views

– and remain immobile. There are limits as to how far they can react to the ever-changing needs of a spatially and electronically mobile society. For most of the year they remain unused (for a discussion of strategies to diversify the revenue of stadia cf. Chapter 4). Visitors' spontaneity and confidence are hampered by the architecture. Sport architects of the future must give the visitor more spatial flexibility.

The privilege they possess, of bringing crowds of people together in a collective infection of emotion is qualified by electronic Public Viewing. This does not only affect sport. Other cultural and political events can arouse collective feeling. Within sport, the same is true for contests that are not organized by sporting organizations such as FIFA. Whether in singing, modelling, cooking or climbing, multi-episode television series such as 'Pop Idol' provide dilettantes with a receptive stage for exciting competitions. Now, even newly invented sports are being presented. The remarkable viewing quotas and visitor numbers in these competitions are portents for the sporting entertainment industry.

REFERENCES

Benjamin, W. (1983) *Das Passagenwerk*, Frankfurt: Suhrkamp.

Bundesregierung/BMI (2006) 'Die Welt war zu Gast bei Freunden', *Bilanz der Bundesregierung zur FIFA-Fußball-Weltmeisterschaft*. Online. Available http://wm2006.deutschland.de (accessed 14 December 2006).

Canetti, E. (1960) *Masse und Macht*, Hamburg: Claasen.

FIFA (ed.) (2006) *Fan Fest: Dokumentation*, Zürich: FIFA.

Giulianotti, R. (2002) 'Supporters, followers, fans and flaneurs', *Journal of Sport and Social Issues*, 26(1): 25–46.

Hamacher, K. and Efing, A. (2006) 'Das WM-Erlebnis auf der Großbildleinwand – Zur Frage der rechtlichen Zulässigkeit von Public-Viewing-Events bei der Beteiligung von Sponsoren', *Sport und Recht*, 1: 15–19.

Pfister, G. (2006) 'Sportzuschauer: Eine historische Perspektive', in M.-P. Büch, W. Maennig and H.-J. Schulke (eds) *Der Sportzuschauer als Konsument: Gast, Mitspieler, Manipulierter?*, Köln: Sportverlag Strauß.

Praum, K. (2008) *Eine kleine Geschichte des 'Public Viewing'*. Online. Available www.folks-uni.org/index.php?id=165 (accessed 27 August 2009).

Schmidt, H.R. (2010) *Fußballgroßveranstaltungen: Sportpolitische Herausforderungen*, paper presented to the 9th International Hamburg Symposion 'Sport und Ökonomie' 31 July/1 August 2009, in print, Handelskammer Hamburg.

Schulke, H.-J. (2006) 'Perspektiven und Werthaltigkeit des Public Viewing', in M.-P. Büch, W. Maennig and H.-J. Schulke (eds) *Zur Ökonomik der Rechte bei Sportveranstaltungen*, Köln: Sportverlag Strauß.

—— (2007) 'Fan und Flaneur: Public Viewing bei der FIFA-Weltmeisterschaft 2006 – Organisatorische Erfahrungen, soziologische Begründungen und politische Steuerung bei einem neuen Kulturgut', in D. Jütting (ed.) *Die Welt ist wieder heimgekehrt: Studien zur Evaluation der FIFA-WM 2006*, Münster/New York/München/Berlin: Waxmann.

Part II

Architecture and Media

Chapter 4: The Stadium as Cash Machine[1]

Michael Zinganel

The realm of stadium planning is rife with experts and consultants with mathematical minds, who quickly grasp not only the direct but also the indirect, in fact even the 'immaterial', profits that may be generated by competitive sports in a public arena. The economic development potential of sport is no different from that of the cultural sector: to build a stadium (or museum) boosts the local economy and allegedly constitutes a sustainable investment in a location's profile, at the local and perhaps also the international level. The ensuing opportunities for diversification of revenue streams generally compensate the publicly funded maintenance of a stadium (or museum).

Revenue is generated by ticket sales, parking fees and the wages of people employed by the stadium management and teams, who partly reinvest their income as consumers. Employees' income tax is another revenue stream, as are the taxes levied on tickets and parking fees, the sale of refreshments and souvenirs, transport and accommodation, and entertainment before and after the game. This value-added chain reaches as far as the wage earned by cooks and bartenders for serving the fan his or her last meal and beer before they set off to the grounds; not to mention the many service sector industries, without whose care and attention most competitive sporting events would never see the light of day. The most important (strictly speaking) immaterial (yet oddly calculable) profit ensues from mass media advertising campaigns. Experts and consultants assure us that simply to mention a town repeatedly in league table announcements boosts economic growth throughout its entire region. According to this type of potent formula, even a second-class team would in absolute terms generate direct, indirect and immaterial profits for a community well in excess of what it would cost a public authority to build and maintain a stadium. And the rationale behind such formulas is, doubtless, to get more stadia built, for this in turn drives demand for experts and consultants (Spirou 2005: 426–30).

What the stadium owner or manager may reasonably regard as identifiable or, at the least, probable revenue – namely ticket sales from a few dozen

$$\$25{,}000 * \frac{1}{1-MPC} = \$25{,}000 * \frac{1}{1-0.9} = \$25{,}000 * 10 = \$250{,}000$$

Figure 4.1a
Formula to figure out the diversified revenue streams of a newly built stadium.

$$y_{it} = \sum b_{it} X_{it} + b_T T_{it} + b_S S_{it}$$

Figure 4.1b
Formula to calculate the overall economic impact of stadia on cities' budgets.

matches a year – could evidently never finance the construction and maintenance of a stadium. However, compared to the potential revenue from sponsorship, the sale of naming rights of teams and stadia, the lease of VIP boxes, TV rights and merchandizing, the sum of gate receipts is negligible.

This shift in value creation transforms not only marketing strategies but also stadium cultures. A conscious effort has been made to break down proletarian, masculine fan culture. This has made stadia more attractive to women and families and acceptable to VIPs (cf. Chapter 1). In addition, the branding strategies of potential sponsors (as well as individuals' desire to pose) has put traditional stadia under pressure to compete with new trend-sport hybrid events. Stadia are increasingly 'enhanced' for the latter by ephemeral event architecture, generally comprising only a few standard, mobile and easily assembled elements that TV teams use as an instant set on which to record 'extensive live coverage' – and not only of the players: fans are equally happy to thrust themselves, logos and merchandize in front of the cameras (cf. Conclusion).

Not everyone can afford the luxury of a mono-functional (i.e. football only) stadium, however, and a stadium boss is thus constrained to rent his or her premises to a broad medley of event promoters, whose fragile, temporary experiential worlds often seem wildly at odds with the stadium's solid structures.

However, given the huge expense, enormous size and complex transport logistics of any new stadium venture, the primary and usually indispensable source of support is public funding. Major sporting events (such as the Olympic Games and World or European Championships) are cited to legitimize extensive investment, as also the specific cultural or economic benefits that a new stadium (or modernization of an older one) is expected to bring to its vicinity. The architecture of a stadium may prove beneficial in and of itself, especially if it flaunts the primary sponsor's logo. Many stadia have become potent landmarks that heighten their city's regional or even international profile and, at the local level, spur gentrification and new investment.

The newly created, VIP 'premium' or 'corporate' boxes in stadia are booked up years in advance while below-tier areas and concourses are packed with cinema screens, exhibition spaces, retail outlets and restaurants. The stadium has evolved as part of a mixed-use development, a stage for celebrities from popular culture, the economy and the media (cf. Chapter 15), and a top leisure destination for the urban tourist or local resident.

MULTIPURPOSE ARENAS

The pitch leaves the stadium

When the new Arena Auf Schalke opened in 2001 in the former mining town of Gelsenkirchen in Germany, it was one of the most modern stadia in Europe (Figure 1.5). It had the best sound system ever and a huge video cube hanging from the ceiling above the centre of the ground, each of the four screens 36 square metres in size. The complex retractable roof, 560 tons in weight, provided 61,000 spectators[2] with permanent protection from the elements and could be extended to cover the entire stadium. This wasn't good news for the pitch. Grass deprived of sun, rain and fresh air soon threatens to wither (Theweleit 2004). In consequence, not only do fans leave the stadium after a game now but the pitch, too, is rolled up and taken outside. It takes over three hours for hydraulic motors to shunt it along tracks under the suspended tribune south of the stadium, then unroll it in a specially built, sunny recovery area, secured against would-be trespassers.

Yet rolling up the pitch is first and foremost part of an effort to maximize year-round operations. The Arena Auf Schalke in Gelsenkirchen prides itself on being able to pull off three different mega-events within 96 hours (Schmidt 2004: 24). For a beer-swilling *Oktoberfest*, pop concert, opera, biathlon or super-cross rally, a grass pitch is more than superfluous.

Pressure to keep Auf Schalke in permanent use is due to the fact – proudly proclaimed by its management – that it was the first stadium in Germany ever to be built solely with private finance. There is a certain historical irony to this, for the Schalke 04 club long epitomized the traditional mining community culture of Germany's industrial heartland, the Ruhr District, a culture also evident in former club president Rudi Assauer's earthy manner and rough profile. While, in the US, business-minded teams seek public funding for stadium developments (cf. Chapter 11), at the heart of a region where primary industries have surrendered to public schemes for post-Fordist solutions, the role of neo-liberal pioneer was taken up by of all things a traditional workers' club.

This alleged 'workers' association' treated itself to a new stadium worth 191 million euros. In the absence of property development and below-tier poten-tial, Rudi Assauer found himself increasingly constrained to play the role not just of the moody club manager but also the event impresario. The Arena Auf Schalke ultimately became not only the most modern stadium in Germany with the biggest video cube to date, but also the largest stage for operas and the biggest beer tent outside Bavaria (Guratzsch 2001).

To finance this vision, Rudi Assauer 'sold the future of the club to a London stockbroker for 75 million euros, with an option on a further 25'. The deal was thought to cost Schalke 'nine million a year or about 30 per cent of revenue from matches played' (Schmidt 2004: 24). This was a sum that subsequently would have to be raised by other means. In 2005, due to pressing liabilities, naming rights for the stadium were sold for a ten-year period to the brewery

C. and A. Veltins – in direct contradiction of Assauer's earlier assurance that the workers' club Schalke 04 would never countenance such a break with tradition.

In the meantime individual stands in the stadium have been named for various sponsors. The medium-term lease of 81 boxes in Auf Schalke or, of late, the Veltins Arena, has naturally become a vital source of income. Each box comprises 32 square metres and accommodates up to ten guests. Despite such exclusive accommodation, the stadium management promises genuine stadium atmosphere: the sliding glass doors that separate VIP areas from the stadium can be opened to allow guests to follow the game from their comfortable business-class seats. A further eight 'event boxes' accommodating up to twenty guests each and three variously sized VIP clubs are also available for hire. All have a view of the pitch (for a Frankfurt example cf. Figure 3.2).

Multipurpose developments

The St. Jakob Park Arena in Basle, Switzerland, was also built in 2001 but its pitch is a permanent fixture. There is simply no space for it to be rolled out in the densely built neighbourhood. Nor does it have a retractable roof. And, with initial seating for only about 32,000 spectators, the site was considerably smaller than the Veltins Arena and still is, in fact, despite the addition of a further 6,000 seats installed in time for the European Cup 2008.

The St Jakob Park Arena was built by a public private partnership[3] that manages all of Basle's major sports venues. The proposed inner-city location, served on one side by the city overland railway and on the other by trams and buses, seemed to those in charge too valuable a site for mono-functional development. Architects were therefore commissioned not only to design a football stadium incorporating an extensive commercial development, but also to come up with a sensible concept for the area beneath the pitch. Accordingly the whole arena now virtually rests on a dual-storey underground car park, this is a space below tiers that begins by the pitch and accommodates, on its outward-facing periphery, a shopping mall that benefits from the stadium's privileged transport provision and underground car park. The mall's protruding flat roof serves in turn as a generously sized, raked concourse, where celebrity guests can mingle. Here, too, one finds press and hospitality areas of equally impressive dimensions. They can be hired, together with the dual-storey VIP areas above them, as a luxurious conference centre. Conceived at least in part as a roof for the street-side of the concourse on the first tier, a transom-shaped structure hovers above the plinth-like mall. This is an old people's home where the inhabitants are kept awake by noisy football matches, at least once a week. Even on the last tiny plot of vacant land beside the arena – the only one not marshalled into service as an emergency escape or loading bay – an office block towers over the arena's roof, a vertical landmark on the skyline.

Extreme spatial and economic rationalization was the trademark of this arena. Its demonstration of how below-tier spaces in inner-city arenas may be put to practical use made it a much-debated model for subsequent stadium

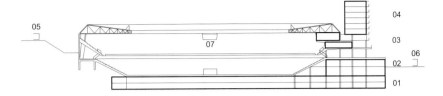

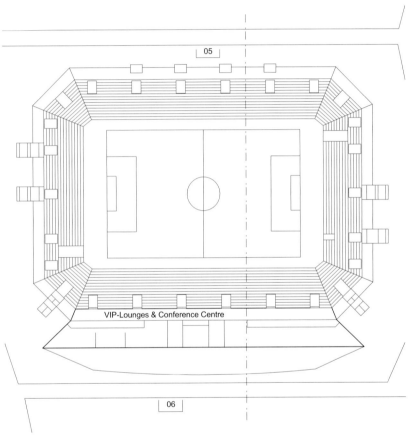

Figure 4.2
St. Jakob Park Soccer
Stadium, Basle (site plan
and vertical section).

01. Underground Parking Garage
02. Shopping Mall
03. VIP-Lounges & Conference Centre
04. Old People's Home
05. City Overland Railway Station
06. Tram and Bus Terminal
07. Videoscreen

developments. Admittedly, any overly 'organic' multifunctional mix within a single structure appears to counter the real estate market's penchant for 'prime cuts'. These require that investment areas and their structural cladding be carefully filleted.

Another unusual architectural feature of the St. Jakob Park Arena is its structured façade. Galleries giving onto public space are clad in prefabricated, convex acrylic glass elements. While these appear cold in the daytime, at night they reflect the ambience of events inside by bathing the street in different colours: in the club colours red and blue during home games of FC Basel, for example; or, when the Swiss national team is playing, almost exclusively in red, except for a white Swiss cross. And the fans moving to or from their seats behind the translucent façade look like characters in a shadow theatre.

The façade is a clear sign of the trend towards state-of-the-art stadia with a cultural agenda. St. Jakob Park Arena was the first stadium built by star architects (and natives of Basle, incidentally) Herzog and de Meuron who were later to build the Allianz Arena in Munich (Figure 1.7) and the Olympic 'Bird's Nest' stadium in Peking. Commissioning architects such as Herzog and de Meuron guarantees optimal media coverage. Sketches and models of their stadium designs can be viewed at international architecture exhibitions and real estate trade fairs, years before anything is actually built. Specialist journals and lifestyle magazines run full-colour spreads, featuring photos and renderings of a quality that underlines their importance as precious cultural artefacts at the cutting edge of progressive design.

From the start of their professional partnership, Herzog and de Meuron sought to position their work in the realms of art and culture, or succeeded at least in suggesting to their clientele that this was where it belonged. They did of course design important cultural edifices such as the Tate Modern in London or the Schaulager in Basle. Yet they honed their profile with equal success by upgrading shopping malls (the Sieben Höfe in Munich) or fashion emporiums (the Prada flagship store in Tokyo), and as such are proven experts at using architecture to imbue brands with cultural cachet (cf. Chapter 1).

It is a fact that the shift from an industrial to a post-industrial economy has long since turned sport into a major cultural industry. The new 'economy of signs' (Lash and Urry 2004) makes profit from symbols, images and desires. Stadia are not only signifiers and veritable desire-machines but also public arenas in which cultural symbols can be exhibited, observed, marketed and acquired (Spirou 2005: 421).

Entertainment city

The Amsterdam Arena in the Netherlands, one among several precursors of Arena Auf Schalke's design, was built as early as 1996, with a similar ground capacity and a retractable steel and glass roof that can be opened and closed within 20 minutes. The pitch was meant to stay inside from the start, however – and consequently withered several times during the first season. It has since either been fed artificial sunlight or simply thrown away and replaced by a new one.

The Amsterdam Arena's location and transport facilities have proved more enduringly spectacular. The stadium was built directly above a stretch of motorway in the southeast of the city and appears impressively monumental to traffic approaching from either direction. The exit slip roads lead almost immediately to a gigantic underground car park, above which the actual stadium is perched. These elaborate access solutions benefit both the stadium and the leisure complex that was subsequently developed around it.

This particular location was selected in 1992. The decision was based largely on the site's potential to become a high-capacity traffic hub as well as the immediate neighbourhood's dire need of regeneration (cf. Chapter 8).

> The adjacent Bijmermeer housing estate was synonymous with just about
> everything that could go wrong on the edge of a city. Amsterdam therefore
> consciously placed its Arena next to a problem neighbourhood and [...] started
> to build an entire new sub-centre around it, the Arena Boulevard.
>
> (Metz 2002: 144)

Some 200,000 square metres of office space and 20,000 square metres of megastores are clustered around the 600-metre-long, 70-metre-wide boulevard. The main attraction is the Villa Arena at its end: a huge closed mall that accommodates 75,000 square metres of different furniture shops.

> The 'entertainment triangle' on the Arena Boulevard is formed by the Pathé
> Multiplex with 14 auditoria, by the Heineken Music Hall and by the GETZ, the
> name of which is an acronym for the four Dutch words for Health,
> Entertainment, Theatre and Business. Two blocks accommodate 150,000
> square metres of fitness and beauty centres, a climbing wall, disco, casino,
> theatre, theatre bar, shops and culture [...]. The whole complex will be
> crowned by two tower apartment blocks [...]. The cultural part is new in every
> respect. It is to be a merger of two new institutions, the Cosmic Paradiso
> Centre for the Arts and Imagine, the 'museum' for immigrant culture. They
> want to offer a joint podium for music, theatre, dance and film and a meeting
> point for the representation of migrant cultures in southeast Amsterdam.
>
> (Metz 2002: 146)

The critical mass of fans with spending power that might be expected to attend a match fostered hopes that many of them would hang out with their families and friends before and after the game – or even return to the centre when no game was scheduled. Moreover, as at Auf Schalke, football was not the only sport foreseen: 'a crowd of 50,000 meritorious citizens paid to come together in the Amsterdam Arena in February 2002, on the eve of the royal wedding between Willem-Alexander and Máxima, to celebrate on behalf of the nation' (Metz 2002: 143). It was further expected that the proposed high-density retail space would draw new consumer groups, who might subsequently book guided tours or other stadium events. The synergetic spheres of leisure and consumerism ideally generate both financial and symbolic surplus value, which in turn benefits city residents, particularly those in the immediate neighbourhood. Furthermore, costs incurred in developing and maintaining the stadium can be offset against the sale or lease of commercial outlets.

As has often been the case with large-scale development schemes, much of the above proved to be wishful thinking. Frequent adjustments were necessary because the anticipated effects had unexpected side effects. And certain great hopes were bitterly dashed. Yet, in the real estate market, the pressure to invest at times produces its own stubborn logic. And, at a pinch, teams of consultants are always ready to peddle their magic formulas regarding the diversification of revenue streams, which maintain that a new stadium stimulates sufficient growth for profits ultimately to exceed investment.

Junkspace

The aforementioned strategies are considered highly viable means to diversify revenue streams. Naturally, their implementation also hybridizes the form and function of a stadium and its locality.

In one of his typically affirmative critiques, Rem Koolhaas (2001) introduced the term 'junkspace' to describe those highly versatile structural agglomerations capable of adjusting themselves constantly to new demands of the market. The prototypical junkspace, argues Koolhaas, is the contemporary airport. Far from being simply a place where one can take off or land, the airport is today a channel for a critical mass of goods and services and for a public with a compara- tively high level of purchasing power; a potent economic mix comprised of shop- ping malls, gastronomic outlets, entertainment centres, hotels, car parks, freight halls and so forth. And leasing real estate – the salvation of the stadia discussed thus far – has long since proved more profitable for airports than air travel.

Like airports, stadia consist of optimized economic mega-structures, ideally with a regional catchment area. Like airports, Koolhaas asserts, they are no longer immutable architecture, no longer a spirited monument to modernist functionalism but rather multifunctional hybrids, obliged to undergo continuous conversion or extension in order to accommodate the constantly shifting palette of attractions, sign value systems or perhaps, new management concepts that is part and parcel of transnational competition.

Critics of such hybridization posit the loss of 'authenticity', which they allege can be found only in the mono-functional stadium, where only football is played. It is almost as if, in the tradition of Fordist planning mythology, a segre- gated stronghold of authenticity might be established amid estrangement and alienation – and maintained: preferably (if *aficionados* of architecture could have their say) in a stadium of *beton brut*.

However, if identity and community are today constituted solely by con- sumerist practice, a space 'beyond the economic sphere' does not exist, not even for a stadium. How on earth might a football team composed of expensive professional sportsmen (cf. Chapter 7) and integrated in an even more expensive infrastructure be able to develop unconstrained by the laws of a post-industrial economy? In a panel discussion that took place in Vienna on 22 November 2007, Stefan Ziffzer, the manager charged with upgrading the club 1860 München in the years 2006–8 gave a prosaic response to frequent criticism regarding dictates of the economy: 'Of course it would be possible for a club to evade economic pressure', he argued, 'namely by playing exclusively with bargain basement home-trained players and third leaguers somewhere at the back of beyond' (Ziffzer 2007). As for the fans, their escape route is apparently the catharsis and sheer delight of an afternoon in the pounding excitement of a stadium, plus the ecstatic realization of their own corporeality and the mass corporeality of sub-cultural bonding in the stands (cf. Chapter 13). Yet, even radical kenosis or rebellious misbehaviour ultimately play into the hands of the attention economy.

TV RIGHTS, FEMINIZATION AND CULTURALIZATION

The enormous sums paid for broadcasting rights to major sporting events ultimately assured the latter prime-time TV slots and improved viewer ratings, which finally put an end to the intimacy of male bonding rituals in the stands. As TV channels demanded ever-higher prices for advertising, companies demanded viewers that were willing to buy more than just beer, hot dogs and badly cut clothing. They wanted expert consumers with a particular feel for the cultural cachet of commodities: women and children, in other words (even if the latter's spending power is largely in the hands of the former, cf. Chapter 1).

TV turned women and children into football spectators. Even if they did not yet personally go to the stadium, they could see what men got up to there – and how they looked. The advertising industry thus got what it wanted and was able to offer its clients totally new market segments. Companies consequently raised their marketing budgets. Viewing from a safe distance also accustomed women to the signs of male culture in the stadium, signs that gradually became socially acceptable. George Best's long hair triggered male angst, for men realised how popular he was with their women. During the 2002 World Cup in Japan and Korea, British superstar David Beckham's hair seemed to have been styled primarily for the young women in the audience – and triggered hysteria like that generally reserved for boy bands in the Pop world (cf. Chapter 15). And despite its connotations of badly dressed young men in souped-up Opel Mantras, the 1980s Viking hairstyle is now acceptable on the pitch. Fan memorabilia and badly cut Adidas bomber jackets are now coveted accessories also among girls.

From an economic viewpoint, the once disdained symbols of working-class subculture thus now take centre-stage. The clubs accordingly see matches increasingly as theatre, dramatically staged to raise the stakes for broadcasting rights. The broadcasts serve, for their part, to advertise memorabilia and the stadium as a locus of family entertainment. But since from that point of view players are entertainers, many team managers started to cast their stars to fit to the needs of their newly diversified audience: aside the essential proletarian pit-bull type of player there now is a demand for types that suit as sex symbols, Latin lovers, but also as the caring family father, who appears to interview with his son or daughter in his arm and, finally, the nice smart young boy mothers would wish to get their daughters married to. Yet broadcasts also report which celebrity football fans are sitting in the VIP boxes or behind the mirrored glass façade of the specially built VIP-lounges, high above the common crowd and engaged in the small talk so vital to business success. But the key to economic success for the clubs is still 'bums on seats', claimed *The Economist* in an article about Manchester United (2002). To assure its success, a club must lure the greatest possible number of fans to the stadium – and preferably sell them season tickets, not for direct profit only but for filling the stands and producing an authentic stadium atmosphere. To this end it must demonstrate that the stadium is a safe place, where people have a good time. Stadium visitors therefore become part of the staged (advertising) scenario. As in TV ads, the joyful discovery of their own image on the huge video monitors prompts them to show their pleasure in clear view of all the other fans, at home or in the stands (cf. Chapter 5, cf. Conclusion).

TV also constrained stadium managers to put a brake on boisterous aggression in the stands: however, spectators also experienced the new medium as a fantastic means to stage violent spectacles which created precisely the thrill of authenticity that young men are desperate to experience. But TV coverage of fighting fans frightened away most female fans as well as the more cultivated citizens seeking distinction in the VIP areas. The security machine for stadium spectacles must therefore be refined constantly. It must present a credible image of the stadium as a place for family entertainment, as well as for spills and thrills.

THE OTHER STADIA

Ephemeral staged scenarios from the adventurous worlds of urban and alpine subcultures gained a competitive edge on the classical stadia because new sport-event promoters – Hannes Jagerhofer and his ACTS agency, the minds behind beach-volleyball tournaments in Klagenfurt; or Andrew Hourmont and his Blue Wings agency, the promoters of Air & Style snowboard events – are not bound by sentimental memories of grassroots club culture. Unlike Rudi Assauer in his threatened workers' stronghold, Gelsenkirchen, they have no need to bolster a sense of local identity. The new promoters gained their stripes in an urban club scene synonymous with mobility, improvisation and flux, a scene geared to punters in search of thrills and innovation, with no interest in yesteryear identities. Nobody in clubland seeks 'authenticity' by passively following a game played by other people. This audience wants to take the stage personally. It wants excess and corporeality. It wants to see it on TV – and to be seen.

Years of experience in event culture, from the early days of subculture parties through to the mega-events of today, gave these newcomer impresarios the dramaturgical and audio-visual tools with which to whip up an audience and hype an event. Pop-stars, scene celebrities, VIPs, 'also rans' and a dose of the community appeal so beloved of clubs all play at least as important a role at their events as do sportspeople.

Air & Style 2004, for example, advertised only 30 snowboard stars but lined up six live bands on two evenings as well as further sideshows at eight 'locations' in Seefeld, Austria: a snowboard event with more musicians than 'riders'.[4] The A1 Grand Slam presented by Nokia in Klagenfurt, Austria, provided far more than 30 sportswomen and sportsmen but also promoted club events scheduled to run on all four nights of the sport event, in and around the main venue. Hopes generally run high that VIPs will step into the limelight without being pushed, for they thus become significant multipliers of media coverage, which is valuable capital in the attention economy. A private jetty is provided for VIPs in Klagenfurt, so that any who choose to arrive by fancy yacht, motorboat or even seaplane may be received in the style to which they are accustomed.[5]

Even though it may appear to be the case and – at least in Klagenfurt – to function admirably, keeping people happy is not all that is at stake at these sporting events. Social events serve above all to convey to viewers at home the ambience and delight of 'being there' (and, hence, of 'belonging'). The size or monumentality of a football stadium is no longer a decisive factor. What now counts is cleverly composed architecture and a well-lit set. Temporary stadia consist of tubular steel and planks, originally designed as basic scaffolding. Most essential now are their immaterial elements: sophisticated camerawork and lighting, and canned sound as a mood-enhancer. Thus all that remains of the classic stadium is the ephemeral scaffolding that used to be removed when an arena was completed: scaffolding that is a last reminder of traditional stadium architecture.

Of course, even this new form of stadium requires a site. But it need not be an expensive building lot or close enough to major metropolises to easily draw a crowd. A site in any town will do for a temporary stadium, as will even the roof of a mall, or a vacant lot on the outskirts of a tiny town, which the mayor, delighted at the prospect of some media attention, will happily make available for free.

A small community that welcomes an Air & Style type snowboard event has a unique opportunity to be in the public eye and improve its international ranking, though it possibly also risks altercations with its traditional visitors and residents. Seefeld hosted Air & Style in 2004 and suffered the hordes of young tourists badly, for they turned the quiet little town into a non-stop party zone for 48 hours; so successfully, in fact, that Seefeld considered its aspiration to be perceived as a chic yet cultivated destination for culture vulture tourists to be seriously at risk. Not that the residents had to worry for very long: Air & Style quickly shifted to Munich and in 2005 signed a six-year contract (Snowborden.de 2004). Frei Otto's Olympic Stadium, largely abandoned since the clubs Bayern and 1860 München moved to the Allianz Arena, was to prove a perfect venue.

Air & Style demonstrates a further important aspect of the new stadium: sponsors' advertising media. Unlike the classic stadium with its horrendous construction and running costs, the new stadium creates a new revenue stream. Instead of persuading sponsors to place its advertising in what may be unfavourable spots, the new stadium simply packs itself up and goes wherever the sponsor wants it. As a listed historical site, the Frei Otto Stadium in Munich is unable to be decked out with banners, for example. So sponsors now look elsewhere, and the opportunities certainly seem to be endless: airships, cranes, hot-air balloons, inflatable objects can all be emblazoned with sponsors' colours and logos to create the vibrant 'skyline' of the very latest in arenas.

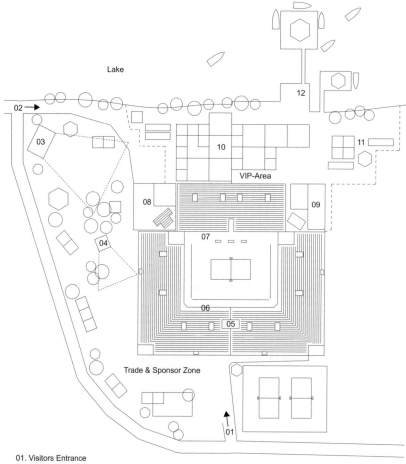

01. Visitors Entrance
02. VIPs Access
03. Open Air Concert Stage
04. DJ Stage
05. Sponsor Car
06. Stands
07. Roofed Terrace
08. VIP Terrace
09. Organisation Office
10. VIP Tents & Catering
11. Press Area
12. Landing Stage & VIP Water Taxi

Figure 4.3
A1 Grand Slam Beach
Volleyball Tournament,
Klagenfurt (site plan).

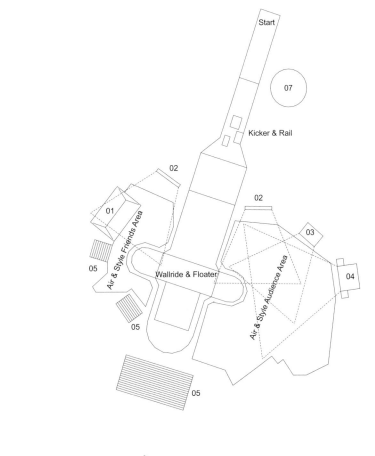

Figure 4.4
Red Bull Air & Style
Snowboard Contest,
Bergisel Stadium
Innsbruck (site plan and
vertical section).

01. Catering Tent
02. Videowall
03. DJ Stage
04. Concert Stage
05. Stands
06. Lighting Cranes
07. Sponsor Balloon

   Ephemeral event architecture consists of a few standardized elements such as scaffolding, tents, containers, barriers, floodlight systems and cameras on cranes, temporary stage sets and long rows of Portaloos®, all of which can be installed at short notice at just about any site, then equally quickly dismantled and taken away. The classic stadium directs the spectator's gaze at the pitch.

The architecture of the new stadium corresponds to whatever a film director or camera operator momentarily requires.

Whilst a nostalgic arena like Munich's Allianz Arena has a duty to its main sponsor and relegates all others to the perimeter strip or expensive TV clips, the ephemeral event stadium has room enough for endless main sponsors: each can have a personal arena. In no time at all, ad media can be inflated, kiosks built or tents erected for further events in the programme. If one's own VIP guest list happens to include the favourite stars of a TV channel's target audience, one need barely concern oneself with media coverage. Cameras will pop up of their own accord.

The planners of ephemeral event stadia play with social barriers as a matter of course. The club scene with its countless subcultures and obligatory bouncers taught them how. Unlike in the classic stadium, they here forego ostentatiously merging as 'a whole' (however illusory) the various groups of a fractured society and thereby symbolically abrogating social divisions. For social barriers necessarily evoke a desire in people to transgress them. They provoke covetousness – the gratification of which is, admittedly, most often limited to voyeuristic aspects. Yet an illusion of 'the whole' is in fact conjured also in ephemeral event stadia, even if only in front of television cameras. One therefore requires (almost) no spatial equivalent. Event experts plan their arenas in a way that will satisfy the TV audience's wish to 'be part of the action' and allow for easy control of different visitor groups. They offer individual guests opportunities to pose for the cameras and to experience ecstatic kenosis with a group of like-minded people. An event stadium therefore always consists of several arenas (cf. Chapter 5).

The first arena is the realm of the car. Huge parking areas are intended to facilitate rapid arrival and departure, yet they also allow visitors to showcase their cars and engage in initial greeting and bonding rituals. The first arena also serves TV cameras that, installed ideally in a helicopter, capture and broadcast images of amassed metal and traffic jams. The TV audience at home associates such images with vacations and action. Slowly snaking traffic and packed parking areas are simply indispensable if an event is to be a success. In fact, their absence signals a flop.

The reception area of a sports stadium with its various sponsored party tents constitutes the second arena. At the Snowboard World Championship at Kreischberg in Austria, this encompassed among other things the Trade Village, a medley of containers and tents for company presentations, a VIP tent, a tent for the rank and file, a sportspeople's tent, a press centre, an area for TV broadcasts and a beach-party tent. The latter comprised a double-walled circus tent dotted with artificial palms and pools, heated to a temperature of 30°C in an effort to entice visitors to take off their winter wraps and 'get in the mood'. Each tent was a world unto itself with its own events and local and media marketing strategies. A defining characteristic of this second arena and its many sub-arenas is access control. As the audience is simultaneously a protagonist in the version of events relayed to the viewer at home, security staff take on a role similar to that of the referee: they control the flow of the game and decide which players are to be excluded from it – or included. The best-case scenario for the second arena foresees an endless mass of surging spectators, or at least enough of them to fill a TV-screen. Cameras are hand-held or installed on cranes or in helicopters. Selected camera angles and timing should suggest to the public (rather than actually show) that a huge crowd has gathered: optical tricks here include a party crush filmed in a limited space or a mass of people on the move, picked out of the darkness by a floodlight.

Finally, the third arena is the competition showcase. This comprises a natural or, more usually, an artificial landscape that is not only essential to the practice of a particular sport but optimizes the latter's dramatic aspects for the benefit of a live or TV audience. Sportspeople take centre-stage in the third arena – although their sponsors' logos enjoy an equally prominent role. These are emblazoned on sportspeople's clothes, on the playing fields, on the obstacles in a race; in a word, on whatever is likely to be caught in a zoom focus. A range of hosts is a further element in the third arena. DJs replace traditional commentators and provide an almost uninterrupted stream of incredibly loud noise. Also on hand are VJs (video jockeys) or, if the sponsors so wish, go-go dancers, whose job is to whip the crowd into a frenzy. There are many ways to do so. At the last Beach Volleyball Grand Slam in Kärnten, Austria, for example, 'Eskimo' go-go dancers on hydraulic platforms turned fire hoses on the crowd (Figure 4.5d). Besides cooling down guests in the stands, this provided the cameras with handy eye candy, namely a 'wet t-shirt look' on fans not yet stripped to the waist. The 'Eskimo girls' of course also consciously played to the cameras, and their exalted position ensured that the sponsor's advertising was not drowned out in the crowd.

Figure 4.5a
Beach maniacs: A1
Grandslam presented by
Nokia in Klagenfurt
(Courtesy of ACTS,
Photograph: Norbert
Jalitsch).

Figure 4.5b
Annual beach volleyball
tournament (Courtesy of
ACTS, Photograph:
Daniel Raunig).

Figure 4.5c
Temporary party zone
(Courtesy of ACTS,
Photograph: Norbert
Jalitsch).

Figure 4.5d
Stage for the self-
representation of people
and brands (Courtesy of
ACTS, Photograph:
Bernhard Horst).

Despite their complex nature, ephemeral stadia provide promoters with a number of advantages such as precise budget costing and timeframes. They are viable in sparsely populated regions and their technical parameters can be easily adapted to a broad range of conditions and demands. The ephemeral stadium thus represents a route back into the attention economy for those who for a while looked like losers alongside the major promoters: the minor sporting associations, young event promoters on a tight budget, subcultural agencies and small communities. The ephemeral stadium marks the comeback of 'small is beautiful'.

An annual event such as Air & Style demonstrates how even a subculture from a Tyrolean ski region can become a major brand within only a few years, one that an international player like Munich was quick to snap up for its home market.[6] The original snowboard station may have been a makeshift structure but at least it stood in a snow-filled Tyrolean landscape; whereas all that remains of it now is a logo that can be applied at will to any structure, anywhere – in Munich today, and perhaps in Abu Dhabi tomorrow. But no matter how it looks or where it is, fans will always find 'their' stadium.

Sponsors such as Red Bull® have invested heavily in their brand image for years and are therefore now in a position to stage an ephemeral stadium wherever they plant their logo (Penz 2004: 12). A fan without a clue as to what's in store relies simply on the Red Bull® logo, which – as confirmed by Eurosport and DSF live coverage of these events – has become synonymous with a fat slice of sporting entertainment.

Taken to its extreme, the smallest type of an ephemeral 'stadium' consists of a flagpole (more specifically: an inflatable/inflated arc) with a logo, a TV crane, at least one sportsman or sportswoman, a DJ, a VIP and a small crowd of spectators. This signalizes that an event is taking place. Be there, no matter what it's about. Your chances of seeing yourself on TV are good.

People used to visit a stadium to see a certain event but today, anyone with a viable media concept could set up an event stadium outside their own front door. Snowboard freaks used to take to the mountains; today the snowboard slopes come to town: to Vienna, Berlin, Hamburg or Munich, for example. Austria's contribution to the EXPO 2005 in Japan was a sledging hall. Vienna is considering setting up indoor ski slopes, which are already familiar to people in Japan, Holland and Germany's Ruhr District.[7] Mediatization has robbed sport of its original locus. It can now take place anywhere.

THE FUSION OF SOLID AND EPHEMERAL STADIA

Traditional solid stadia are not being replaced but, rather, complemented by ephemeral stadia. Whenever a stadium must prove it is multifunctional, not only the space in front of a stadium and the below-tier areas but also the functional and emotional core of the stadium – the pitch itself – become an adaptable hybrid, the 'junkspace' identified by Koolhaas.

The story thus returns to where it began, to the Arena Auf Schalke or, of late, the Veltins Arena. Born of a football fan's nostalgic dream, the Veltins Arena suffered in a flash the entire demise of football, as we knew it: just as the pitch was carried out through the door, the event marched in. The Veltins Arena obeys the laws of event tourism and therefore now epitomizes the consumer's dream of 'two for one', an ephemeral stadium in a cladding of concrete and steel.

Instead of the sacred ground with its strictly configured football match oriented to two delimiting goal areas (cf. Chapter 14), organic gaming configurations are moved in as required, the origins of which lie in more complex and more extensive natural or, at least, cultural landscapes. It is no secret that motor racing, once banned for security reasons from hilly rural highways to specially secured racing arenas, has now returned to public highways in urban agglomerations. Manoeuvrable vehicles such as go-carts or motorbikes have long since made their way into sports arenas. Indoor-motocross is now one of the major highlights at the Veltins Arena, and takes place in a specially built artificial course incorporating grandiose, three-dimensional, sculpturally compact adventure landscapes. Even solitary winter sports that previously took place in rural obscurity are now served to mass audiences in the stadium and on screen. The most significant example of this transfer at the Veltins Arena is the Veltins Biathlon World Team Challenge.

Sensibly enough, the competition modus was modified. It is no longer members of only one sex who brave an artificial cross-country ski run set up in an equally artificial forest of fir trees: each team now comprises two competitors of different gender – yet still of the same nation, at least. The masked, lonely, male alpine runners of yore, trappers of the north who were previously paid a

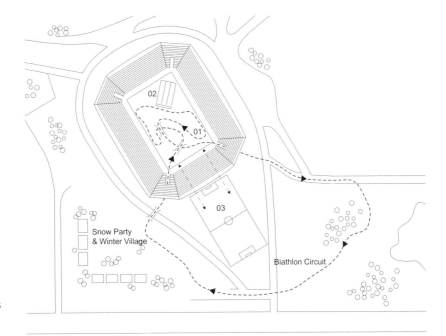

Figure 4.6
Veltins Biathlon World
Team Challenge, Veltins
Arena, Gelsenkirchen,
(site plan).

01. Start & Finish
02. Shooting Stand
03. Mobile Pitch

Figure 4.7
Veltins Arena
Gelsenkirchen,
multifunctional football
stadium, transformed
into a roofed artificial
forest landscape hosting
the annual Veltins
Biathlon World Team
Challenge (Courtesy of FC
Schalke 04).

modicum of attention only during the Nordic World Championships or Olympic Games (and spent the rest of their lives working as border guards) have been joined by attractive female competitors in figure-hugging sportswear (cf. Chapter 11). The man and woman in each team take turns to run laps in the sold-out, air-conditioned arena, and each runs a single outdoor lap around the stadium.

The women appeal not only to female spectators in the stadium or at home but also to men. Like cheerleaders or skimpily dressed female beach-volleyball players, they are part of the re-sexualization of stadium sports, above all, when prostrate and aiming a gun at a target. Gigantic, full-screen shots of the women and the small targets are visible on the video cube – and every hit draws a yell from the crowd.

Enthusiastic fans without money for a ticket flock instead to the Winter Village erected on a stadium car park: a cluster of log-cabins covered in artificial snow and pumped full of après-ski muzak, where stadium events are broadcast live, on huge screens. From the promoters' viewpoint, this is a handy means to swell stadium capacity and, for the fans, a chance to drink more of the main sponsor's beer than if they'd had to buy a ticket; and with such high-resolution coverage, it's almost like being in the Public Viewing zone at a World Cup final.

The Veltins Arena therefore perfectly illustrates the current transfer of stadia into junkspaces and cash machines that can be adopted to any demands of the contemporary cultural industry. If the stadium structure becomes too small for specific events, it even transgresses the solid borders of its terraces – not only by being broadcast in real time on TV sets at millions of homes (cf. Chapter 5) or video screens in public spheres (cf. Chapter 3) but also by physically spreading and sprawling into its neighbourhood, into the urban and suburban fabric – into real space.

NOTES

1 Many thanks to Christian Zillner for his support and advice. Translation: Jill Denton.
2 The stadium was designed with seats and standing areas. But for the FIFA World Championship in 2006 only seats were allowed. Therefore the capacity then was only 50,000. Afterwards the seats were dismantled and the capacity increased again.
3 The GFS (St. Jakob Park Arena Cooperative) commissioned a Bern-based contractor to build the stadium. He immediately provided his own personal investors (two insurance companies, the Suva and Winterthur, and the City of Basle's staff pension fund) and also the main tenant.
4 It is to be noted that Air & Style has to date acknowledged only male riders as the genuine article. The question thus arises as to whether a new male subculture is emerging or whether sportsmen's better performance is simply being exploited in a clever marketing ploy that is meant to appeal also to women.
5 VIPs' significance in Klagenfurt can be measured not least by the number of personnel per head put at their service, which greatly exceeds that made available to the 'normal public'.
6 ACTS, the Vienna-based event agency behind Klagenfurts's beach-volleyball event was also invited to organize a competition along similar lines in Montreal.
7 Salzburg's regional authority secured branding rights to the year-round indoor ski-hall in Neuß, an investment of about four million euros. Austrian tourism experts in other cities use snowboard or ski-jumping events, or marathons in German city centres and such like, with their attendant side-shows and gastronomy stands, to increase their tourist appeal. In this context, snow itself can serve as an advertising medium: 100 tons of snow was transported 800 kilometres from the Söldner Glacier to Ski and Snowboard Festivals that took place in Berlin and Hamburg.

REFERENCES

ACTS (2004) *That's the Way! Beachvolleyball. The story of a hype*, Vienna: ACTS Communications.

Guratzsch, D. (2001) 'Der Rasen kommt durch die Hintertür', *Die Welt*, 28 July. Online. Available www.welt.de/print-welt/article472513/Der_Rasen_kommt_durch_die_Hintertuer.html (accessed 26 October 2004).

Koolhaas, R. (2001) 'Junkspace', in C.J. Chung, J. Inaba, R. Koolhaas and S.T. Leong (eds) *Harvard Design School Guide to Shopping*, Cologne: Taschen.

Lash, S. and Urry, J. (1994) *Economies of Signs and Space*. London: Sage.

Metz, T. (2002) *Fun! Leisure and landscape*, Rotterdam: NAI Publishers.

Penz, O. (2004) 'Praxis und Symbolik. Zur Ökonomisierung des Sports', *Kurswechsel*, 2: 7–14.

Schmidt, C. (2004) 'Kicken auf Kredit. Zur Finanzierung seines Fünfsternstadions verpfändet Schalke 04 seine künftigen Siege', *du*, 748(6): 24–5.

Snowboarden.de (2004) 'Air & Style verlässt nach 12 Jahren Österreich', *Das Snowboard Online Magazin*. Online. Available www.snowboarden.de/home/show.php?id=MS2004-10-12-4720 (accessed 12 October 2004).

Spirou, C. (2005) 'Die Expansion von Stadien als kulturelle Strategie der Stadtplanung und Stadterneuerung in den USA', in M. Marschik, R. Müllner, G. Spitaler and M. Zinganel (eds) *Das Stadion. Geschichte, Architektur, Politik, Ökonomie*, Vienna: Turia + Kant.

The Economist (2002) *For Love or Money*. Online. Available www.economist.com/surveys/displaystory.cfm?story_id=E1_TTQNRJV (accessed 30 May 2002).

Theweleit, D. (2004) 'Feldforschung. Moderne Fußballstadien sind schlechte Gewächshäuser, das Gras verdörrt dort. Wird in der Bundesliga demnächst Kunstrasen ausgerollt?', *Die Zeit*, 5 August. Online. Available www.zeit.de/2004/33/Sport_2fRasen_33 (accessed 26 October 2004).

Ziffzer, S. (2007) *Hightech-Arena oder Gstettn? Welche Orte des Fußballs wünschen sich die Fans?* Public debate held in the framework of the Club 2x11 in the bookshop 'Hauptbücherei am Gürtel', 22 November, Vienna.

Chapter 5: The Mirror Stage in the Stadium

Medial Spaces of Television and Architecture

Angelika Schnell

When considering medial spaces in architecture, one immediately thinks of spaces that have been created by means of highly developed technology and that therefore have highest cultural meaning. The medium of television, being popular and devoid of a recognisably artistic or scientific pretension, is seldom given any attention in this context. Nevertheless, there are some medial spaces, created by and shown on television, that are remarkable enough to be examined further. They are, in fact, medial spaces in many senses, created by technical media on the one hand, but indeed only made present in the first place through 'mediation', or through communication, on the other.

Medial spaces in television are not so much the result of an ingenious idea, mathematical acumen or imaginative simulation, but rather emerge from different spatial and temporal overlaps and interactions, when pictures and sound are sent here and there – in effect a kind of TV cyberspace that is created indirectly, as a space or as spaces that find themselves between various places, times and persons. Indeed, the complexity of such processes usually only becomes noticeable when unplanned discrepancies occur between the different senders and receivers of the actual product, i.e. directors, presenters, audiences, etc. Live broadcasts, in particular, sometimes present an opportunity to look behind the scenes of a mass medium that often appears to be hermetically sealed, and that anxiously clings to the highest standards of technical and content-related congruence. For this reason, one must wait for an 'accident' to allow, for a brief moment, a view through the gap between the pictures, placing the viewer in the position of being able to observe television making its own images.

One such remarkable medial space that was created by television was the image transmitted live and worldwide immediately after the final whistle of the World Cup Final in Italy on 8 July 1990.[1] The screens showed a close-up shot of Argentina's most famous footballer, Diego Armando Maradona, who was obviously struggling to come to terms with defeat. The medial space that we are about to examine was not itself visible in the image, but was created by it. It came about because of the simultaneity of space and affect, transported back and forth, thus briefly allowing the public to influence both events in the stadium and on television. As a result, the spatial and temporal construction of this televisual moment is complex and must be explained.

THE CATASTROPHE OF SIMULTANEITY

Let's start with the easiest definition, the spatial-geographic definition of the content of the image: At the moment his image was being transmitted, the legendary 'Number 10' was at the edge of the pitch in the sold-out Stadio Olimpico in Rome. This had once been intended to form part of the Foro Mussolini, but was then only opened for the 1960 Olympic Games and had now been extensively rebuilt for the *Mondiale*. The architecture of the stadia received more attention than for any other previous World Cup. Renowned architects such as Renzo Piano and Vittorio Gregotti Associati, among others, were charged with constructing new or rebuilding existing stadia. Never before had such an architectural upgrade of all venues been carried out for a World Cup, even if not all results were of equal quality. But the important point was that architecture was used as a sort of corporate identity for the *Mondiale*. A total of approximately 750,000 million euros was spent on the conversion and, in some cases, new construction of the stadia, which at that point was the highest sum spent since the beginning of World Cup competition (see the special 1990 edition of *Stadtbauwelt* on stadia). It was also fitting that the Italian organizers of the World Cup chose as the official emblem an image of the Roman Collosseum, the architectural prototype of the arena, with the spatial structure of the pitch being imposed upon its perfect oval.

Today, however, this pitch is surrounded by dozens of television cameras, and since their spatial arrangement is constrained by the requirements of the pitch and the stadium but while also producing images that are perceived spatio-temporally the pitch is also overlaid and saturated by this much more complex structure. Between 20 and 30 cameras are required for so-called multilateral broadcasts, in which the signal is sent to numerous broadcasting institutions in various countries, as during larger tournaments or at a Champions League fixture. Aside from the main cameras positioned on the two opposite stands, the majority of cameras are 'atmosphere cameras'. These capture the action on the sidelines and goal lines by means of either hand-held cameras or camera track systems which are placed particularly close to the penalty and goal areas; there are even miniature cameras in each of the goal nets. In addition, there are cameras for the substitutes' bench in order to provide images of disappointed reserves and hysterical managers. There are cameras in the so-called Mixed Zone, where television reporters fish for players' first impressions of the game just ended, and naturally there are also cameras for the public and the stadium itself, such as the Beauty Camera, mounted on the edge of the roof

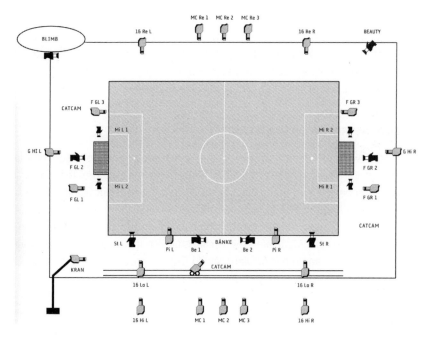

Figure 5.1
Diagram of camera positions during a multilateral football broadcast. MC = Main cameras, GHIL and GHIR = cameras behind the goal post, 16 LoL and 16 LoR = slow motion cameras, PiL, PiR, StL, StR, FGL 1–3, FGR 1–3 = Handy cams along the side of the field and behind the goal post, Be 1, Be 2 = Bench cameras, MCRe 1–3 = fixed cameras for the reverse angle, CATCAM-cameras, BEAUTY = cameras positioned at the roof or at a crane, BLIMP = camera with bird's air view (airship or helicopter).

(FIFA-Fußballweltmeisterschaft 2006/Organisationskomitee Deutschland 2002, cf. Chapter 4 in this volume).

This proliferation of cameras has two known effects. First, the fragmentation of the unity of place, time and activity by means of a completely independent choreography. Phenomena such as slow-motion replays, for example, or constant interruptions for interviews and expert analysis, together produce a similar effect to that of a cubist painting. While watching, we must forego a sense of coherence but, in return, the medium of television implies that it has captured everything *in toto*. Second, there is the expansion of spatial and temporal parameters. A football match may well last only 90 minutes, but the potentially worldwide television broadcast of the event can go on for hours.

In accordance with these conventions, therefore, the cameras of the host broadcaster – the television company that was awarded the FIFA contract to produce television pictures and to send them to other broadcasters – were present on 8 July 1990, incessant in their quest, with the help of a zoom lens, to capture the close-up image of Diego Maradona's face, an image broadcast on screens around the world, so that those who wished to do so could either celebrate or lament the defeat of 'El Diego'. At the same moment, however, something happened which nobody had anticipated. A shrill chorus of whistles started up, which was, of course, perfectly audible to television viewers at home. It was in fact the reaction of the mainly Italian fans in the stadium to the very same television image, simultaneously projected onto two large video screens within the stadium – at the time, quite an unknown phenomenon. And because Maradona – despite playing for SSC Napoli and considered to be a god in Italy – had been responsible, along with his Argentinian team mates, for throwing Italy out of the World Cup in the semi-finals, the *tifosi* did not think highly of 'El Diego' during this final. Not even the victory of the new World Cup champions could dampen their anger.

The simple possibility of sending television images anywhere at all leads to the astonishing fact that they can also be shown at the scene of the action. Television is present in Rome's Olympic Stadium and is sending images of the defeat of the Argentinian team in this stadium all around the world, including back into the stadium itself where it generates a vehement reaction and which is itself seen and heard worldwide. We witness, therefore, first a visual, then an acoustic reflection. Although the moment didn't last long – the camera director of the television company responsible took immediate steps to correct this gaffe by panning to less provocative images such as that of Rudi Völler, at that time very popular among Italians – such behaviour simply proves how explosive and dramatic the moment is[2] because it is suddenly possible *to watch television*, to actually observe the process of television itself, so that we spectators are in the position of both watching and being watched. We are being watched because we, as a supposedly private television audience, are made to feel caught out in our voyeuristic behaviour when the audience in the stadium can suddenly see what we see on our screens at home. Their immediate aggressive reaction must suggest to us that these supposed representatives in the field are not so much our accomplices but rather our denouncers, publicly pointing a finger at our uninhibited curiosity, seeking only to see Maradona in tears.

At the same time, the whistles reveal our passive role as couch potatoes, and thus we perceive ourselves as watchers. One could almost say that an additional contest arises, between the 'real' and 'fake' audience, which has almost emancipatory potential, but in which there is also the short-term threat that things could get out of control. However, because the anarchistic behaviour of the crowd is equally threatening to organizations, associations, institutions and even broadcasting entities, the possibilities provided by this medial space that has emerged remain, naturally, unexploited.

EMOTIVE THEATRE: THE PUBLIC IN THE STADIUM

In such a reflection, which leads to contention and even competition, one can certainly also observe competition-by-substitution between a medial structure (the television viewer) and a spatial structure, normally referred to as architectural (the stadium audience). Both the media and architecture continue to nourish a jealous relationship, which is why it is always a matter of debate as to which of the two is more suitable for the presentation of the event that is a football match. There is, indeed, much to be said for television. It allows more people to participate and shows them details – for example, close-ups of players in 'moving' moments – that they would normally be unable to see in the stadium if a large screen were not provided (cf. Chapter 3). Television corresponds better to the event structure of the game, since it is also organized spatiotemporally. This also means that it is spatially indeterminate as a result of its 'cubist' structure: whether the television viewer considers himself to be sharing an inner space with the rest of the television viewing community, or instead quite literally as a terminal, at the edge or on the outside, depends entirely on the viewpoint of the observer, and does not need to be defined geometrically. Therefore, television as a spatial product is flexible.

The architecture of the stadium, on the other hand, is quite clear in this respect. It provides the spatial parameters of the receptacle as a clearly defined inner space, which can be so architecturally perfect that it can symbolically reinforce the specific function, such as in the previously mentioned Collosseum in Rome. And this symbolic reinforcement has itself a purpose of its own: it has the result that, as Johann Wolfgang Goethe put it in his *Italian Journey*, 'the people' become 'ornaments' (effectively an early thesis on the topic of the 'mass ornament', cf. Kracauer 1928) and are 'astonished at themselves' when seen converged together (Goethe 1976: 55f.).[3]

According to Peter Sloterdijk, it remains the case that it is the stadium itself that, through its formal perfection, coerces the 'many-headed beast' of the multitude, as Goethe put it. Nevertheless, visual power alone is not sufficient. In the third volume of his *Spheres* trilogy, Sloterdijk emphasizes, in an expression similar to that of Goethe, that what happens in the 'large receptacles' is the 'formation of the many-headed [...] crowd into a present "mass" ' (Sloterdijk 2004: 619). Yet he sees an organisational and ritual difference to large events of modern times. According to Sloterdijk, the celebration of the confederation on 14 July 1790 on the Champs de Mars in Paris (Figure 16.2), in which the revolutionary mood of euphoria was channelled by means of a calculatedly staged ritual of the fraternization of the National Guard units, and which hundreds of thousands attended, marks the de facto and *de jure* origin of 'modern "mass" culture as event staging' (Sloterdijk 2004: 620).

Although the architectural template of the Collosseum remains a spatial organizational model, the astonishment of the people at itself, as described by Goethe, can no longer be simply ascribed to that. Rather, the people – the new sovereign, in spite of everything restricted to its place in the auditorium – steers the 'emotional stage direction', the task being to transform the astonishment into a 'collective enthusiasm' that should obviously create a (democratic) 'consensus'. In order to be convinced, or even overwhelmed by this consensus, a 'pervasive, penetrating rule of ritual' is needed, rehearsed exercises in commonality, visible and above all audible to all (Sloterdijk 2004: 620). Thus, Sloterdijk refers to large modern events in the architectural 'collector' of the stadium or arena as a 'plebiscite of screams' (Sloterdijk 2004: 626). In the 'mass containers', surrounded on all sides by ascending stands it is, in his view, the acoustic bell over all heads that conveys the 'phantom of unanimity' through 'sonospheric consolidation', the 'fusion of the audience in the face of a narcissistic-narcotic spectacle' (Sloterdijk 2004: 622, 626, 620, 627).

It is therefore not the architecture of the stadium alone that coerces a large crowd of people as a 'many-headed beast' to a unit. A key role in this process is played by the media in general and television in particular. These contribute significantly to the renaissance of stadium attendance and with it an improvement in the value of the place, because they make a football match into an 'event', in a manner so complete that previously determined functions can simply be abandoned and defined anew.

By the 1970s television was already becoming ubiquitous; like all new media which are simpler and more user-friendly than their predecessors, it was expected that it would out-compete and replace them. Yet the horror scenario of empty stadia failed to materialize. The fact that television broadcast football matches, sometimes even live, did not have a negative effect on stadium attendance, in fact, the opposite is the case: it actually motivated attendance. People flowed into stadia not *despite* the fact that the match was being shown on television (due to e.g. fan loyalty), but rather *because* the cameras were in the stadium. The explanation is, at first, simple: as well as images of the game, the television cameras are increasingly showing images of the spectators in the stands, even in close-up. And what could be more attractive to the public than the notion of one day appearing on television? Thus, television can fulfil the function of being mirrored even more effectively than the perfect architectural form referred to by Goethe – 'the simplicity of the oval': the public sees itself, or rather, is aware that it is being seen by the cameras and therefore by the 'other' spectators on their television screens (cf. Chapter 4).

The fact that it is indeed a mirroring mechanism can be seen from the multitude of voluntary choreographic formations that have been practised by spectators in the stadium over the last ten or 20 years. These go beyond normal fan behaviour, since they are usually extensive and large-scale activities that are connected to the spectators themselves and are independent of specific club affiliation. The most prominent of these is the Mexican Wave, which washes over the stadium, where thousands stand up, one after the other like trained monkeys, raise their arms in the air and then sit down again.[4]

But there are also the enormous banners, many square metres in size, covering the heads of hundreds and probably not very comfortable for claustrophobics, and the increasingly shrill costumes, with the quite obvious goal of attracting the attention of the television cameras and leaving Granny's scarf knitted in the club colours a thing of distant memory. More dangerous activities also fall into this category, such as flares or fireworks, not to mention large crowds of hooligans, who were perhaps the first to realize that a football match broadcast on television is a stage (cf. Chapter 13). And this, precisely, is the switch in dimension, from a public that, according to Goethe, is astonished at itself, to a public that itself becomes a protagonist. Here also, the camera is more potent than architecture; it makes an actor out of everyone, which is why we no longer see spectators in stadia where commercial football is played and broadcast, but rather unpaid actors, taking on the role of spectators (cf. Conclusion).[5]

Figure 5.2
La Ola wave in German
football stadium during
World Cup 2006.

Figure 5.3
Grandstand camera.

THE MIRROR STAGE

Nevertheless, one could argue that the probability of getting on television, as one individual among so many people gathered in a full stadium, is pretty low. The behaviour is also too bizarre, or at least far removed from Goethe's idea of the public as a 'noble body', to figure it out. The desire of the spectator to become a protagonist cannot be explained by simple vanity, since the same people don't pursue self-portrayal in other situations. The hypnotic power exercised by the specific stadium atmosphere, by competition in a collective receptacle, requires other explanations.

Jacques Lacan's essay on the 'mirror stage as formative of the function of the I as revealed in psychoanalytic experience' (1986) is not actually about football fans but about the child that sees itself in the mirror for the first time, yet it is also an examination of the kind of behaviour outlined above. According to Lacan, that moment of jubilation, when one discovers something about oneself, is the moment when 'nature and society meet', because, for the first time, one confronts oneself as a biological phenomenon and at the same time, as one who is able to far outgrow this mere biological existence:

> This act [the first look in the mirror], far from exhausting itself [...] once the image has been mastered and found empty, immediately rebounds in the case of the child in a series of gestures, in which he experiences in play the relation between the movements assumed in the image and the reflected environment, and between this virtual complex and the reality it reduplicates.
>
> (Lacan 1986: 63)

Thus, the first view of the mirror image leads to certain 'gimmicks' of movement, which Lacan interprets as feelings of potency, as the childish attempt to forestall 'the maturation of power' through the mirrored 'imago'. Lacan assumes that, at the earliest infant stage, we perceive our own bodies as merely composed of individual limbs, arms, legs, hands, mouth, etc., that operate of their own accord. For this reason, the first sight of one's own coherent 'gestalt', which one had previously imagined in fragmented form, causes jubilation. But this narcissistic identification by means of an imago is an illusion, Lacan calls it a 'mirage', which from that point on accompanies every person as a 'delusional identity'. And that moment, when we understand not only the power but also the deception of the virtual image of ourselves, which is as we would like to be, is a dramatic moment:

> The *mirror stage* is a drama whose internal thrust is precipitated from insufficiency to anticipation – and which manufactures for the subject, caught up in the lure of spatial identification, the succession of fantasies that extends from a fragmented body-image to a form of its totality that could be called orthopaedic.
>
> (Lacan 1986: 67)

In the mirror stage, we concoct phantasms about ourselves, but at the same time these 'mirages', these 'alluring deceptions', can only virtually assuage our fears of fragmentation that are, according to Lacan, firm components of our unconscious repertoire.[6] The 'stage', a temporal structure, transforms in this dramatic moment into a 'stage', a spatial structure. We enter an 'inner arena', in which we must engage in a lifelong battle with ourselves (Lacan deliberately utilizes the double meaning of the French word *le stade*, which means both 'stage' and 'stadium'). This moment brings us back to the example of Maradona's close-up, mentioned at the beginning, which caused the spectators in the stadium to whistle: the – from the spectator's perspective – simultaneous sighting of body and imago also means the awareness of their spatial separation.

If we therefore allow ourselves to use Lacan's psychoanalysis to interpret the narcissistic behaviour, generated by television, of spectators in the stadium, we must also recognize that this primary identification, as Lacan termed the mirror stage, is, quite in contrast to what one would expect from television and its shows, a process with highly symbolic power; it concerns nothing less than a creation myth. Nevertheless, if we take Lacan's pessimistic evaluation to its logical conclusion, the mirror stage leads to an alienation from the self – where one is obliged to defend the delusional identity – and this feeling of instability releases aggression in 'every relationship to others'.

This, however, explains yet another unanswered question connected to football and its self-aggrandizing fans, and that is the question of violence. In football, the childish fear of the fragmentation of the body is encouraged precisely by the manner in which television and all other image media present the game, with a particular image rhetoric that displays individual parts of the body and glories in each injury and every strain (cf. Chapter 15). The fear must now be defeated by means of a virtual image that promises unity, for example, a collective formation and, on the other hand, the fragmentation fantasies must be projected onto others, must be expressed in a sadistic manner: the showing of the images, the violence in the stands, the aggressive chorus of whistles, while close-ups of the individual body parts of players, managers and referees are simultaneously shown on screens in the stadium.

INTERNAL AND EXTERNAL BATTLES

Fragmentation fantasies are well served by the media in words and in pictures. The multiperspectivity of the camera and the presentation of the occurrence in real time, in slow-motion replays and in post-match analyses are the tools of the media makers. Every scene can be shown at will, from any angle, as often and as close-up as required. In particular, the number of close-up images has increased immeasurably since the early days of professional football on state television. More zoom lenses are constantly on the look out for that most precious of goods, 'pure emotion' – the heated faces of players, hysterical managers, yelling fans – which, parallel to actual attendance in the stadium, is naturally intended to communicate the same feeling of a very close participation in the event, if not more ('In the thick of things, rather than simply being there' – *Mittendrin statt nur dabei* – was, for a long time, the motto of a German sports channel).

In addition, these images are integrated into an understandable and easily recognized dramaturgy. It is common for contemporary football shows to model themselves on movies, particularly on the popular genre of the action film, influencing even the presenter's choice of words ('Roy Makaay thrilled once again as the ice-cold, attacking Torminator', a pun on *Tor*, the German word for 'goal'[7]). This is probably the reason why the self-made formats of various football shows barely differ from one to the other: hectic image direction, made possible by the proliferation of cameras, contrasted with generally banal content which, in addition, is repeated like a mantra and amazingly corresponds to that which is said on competing channels or printed in the media. The effect of this monotony resembles the uniform practices of the stadium entertainers, charged with the task of harmonising the spectators in 'commonality'.

That which is accepted with equanimity by the majority in the stadium, namely 'emotive stage direction' (as long as ostensibly non-political sporting events are involved), is increasingly becoming a process that is attracting criticism, particularly in television ('Once upon a time there was the mass media, it was evil', Eco 1987: 162). This is where the controversial process begins, a process known as mediatization, which includes the allegation that the media does not present reality, but rather – in anticipation – forms reality according to its own (dramaturgical) principles, so that the game's, the players', the spectators' and the venue's rights to exist are dictated by their media suitability: 'Many participants don't yet seem to have realized that it is not they, the performers, who make the "product" football, but rather those who transmit, comment upon and classify their performance', in other words, media representatives of the popular sports channels (Schindelbeck 2004).

As early as 1967, Guy Debord wrote 'The spectacle that falsifies reality is nevertheless a real product of that reality' (Debord 1996)[8] and, indeed, one cannot submit the process of mediatization to a cultural critique alone. The fact that violence plays a role gives the combination of stadium and event – both communicated via the media – a deeper social and political meaning. Tellingly, television still does not know how it should deal with racism and violence in the stands: broadcast it, as part of the duty to provide information, or completely ignore it, in order to remove the opportunity for troublemakers to draw attention to themselves?

The modern mass media has yet to provide an answer to Jean Baudrillard's controversial theory that the very presence of the media is responsible for provoking the violence lurking secretly within many (in contrast to the self-assessment, that one is merely reporting on an event, Baudrillard 1998: 2)[9] – despite the fact that the occasion for Baudrillard's essay came directly from the world of football and was written more than 20 years ago. On 29 May 1985, on live television, just before the start of the European Cup Final between Juventus and Liverpool in the Heysel Stadium in Brussels, rioting English hooligans caused a decrepit wall to collapse, which led to the deaths of 39 people (over 400 people were injured, some seriously).

In contrast to other reporters and commentators of this tragedy, Baudrillard was not outraged at the UEFA, which was not prepared to abandon the game, but rather analysed the behaviour of the broadcasting company present, as well as television companies throughout Europe. None of them saw fit to cease broadcasting, so that the images of people fleeing in panic, and others crushed and suffocating against the fence of section Z, were transmitted live into the living rooms of Europe. And they continued to broadcast – naturally, in the service of providing information – even when, after the game kicked off (with a delay of one-and-a-half hours), the rescue workers and security personnel were trying to carry away corpses and treat the injured. A year later, Baudrillard wrote in the French journal *Autrement* of a 'worldwide derangement', which '[concerns] not so much the violence as the global dissemination of the events by means of the television, the simultaneity of event and globalisation'. He called this worldwide derangement the 'Heysel Syndrome' (Baudrillard 1998, cf. Arich-Gerz's Chapter 6 in this volume).

But, as long as the balls roll and the money flows, no derangement can be detected, as can be seen, for example, in the recently reignited debate about so-called video evidence in cases of controversial refereeing decisions, which would be 'clarified' in retrospect by the television pictures. Although the innumerable cameras all around the pitch have time and again demonstrated that different camera angles, settings and focal widths can make the same scene look entirely different and result in contrary interpretations (from one viewpoint it looks as if Player X has fouled Player Y, while from a different angle it is clear that she or he didn't even touch her or him), the television people are clamouring for the introduction of the 'incorruptable' camera, ignoring the fact that the neutrality of the machine does not automatically mean the neutrality of the image produced, and is therefore no replacement for making anything approaching an objective judgement.

Once again, it is the screen in the stadium that increases the (medial) pressure on the actual event. In the 41st minute of a *Bundesliga* match between Bayer Leverkusen and VfB Stuttgart on 27 February 2005, the referee Franz-Xaver Wack, a dentist from Biberach, appeared to have corrected his decision of a goal kick as a result of the slow-motion replay on the stadium's screen, and instead awarded a corner kick to Leverkusen. This assumption was vehemently denied by the head referee, pointing to the fact that it is forbidden to show disputed scenes in club football. Nevertheless: the associations are under pressure, because they have failed to prepare themselves for the question regarding the criteria that determine how correct or truthful the images shown on television are.[10]

Of course, the question of the veracity of media images is not easy to answer and it is a question with which we are constantly confronted. Whether, for example, the public death of Pope John Paul II gave the modern media society an 'aesthetic shock' (Maslowska 2005: 39), because he didn't hide his ailing body, or whether, in fact, Karol Wojtyla, the media pope, sold his death to the

Figure 5.4
Video cube with close-up
of an Argentinean
football player, World
Cup match Netherlands
vs. Argentina, Frankfurt,
2006.

mass media so well, that 'the bad poet, the mediocre theologian, the conventional philosopher, the narrow-minded Bishop Wojtyla, the impresario of sainthood' would very soon be forgotten (Sloterdijk 2005), has not been decided. The only thing common to both positions is the (culturally critical) assumption that an ephemeral, and therefore 'false', medial reality disengages itself more or less completely from the physical and material, and consequently from the 'real' reality, only to superimpose itself on it and then enter into unfair competition with it. The fact that this competition sometimes favours 'reality', however, can be seen in the example of the football stadium. Not only was the original mass arena not replaced by the mass media of television, it is indeed questionable whether a similar regeneration of the place and its atmosphere could have happened in the absence of television. A modern stadium could hardly exist without the media.

MEDIAL ARCHITECTURE

Le Corbusier certainly anticipated this development, or rather, saw at an early stage that the media is an inherent part of modern architecture. In a particularly radical sketch from *La ville radieuse*, he envisages an exclusively medial architecture, consisting solely of the technical provision of gas, water, electricity, air, telephone, as well as the undisturbed view from one of the higher apartments. However, the blatant affront to 'Architecture with a capital A' does not lead to the abandonment of creative and artistic design. Rather, it is, once again, the media, according to Le Corbusier, which influences and guides the design process. In the same sketch, one can see a giant eye in the square box that

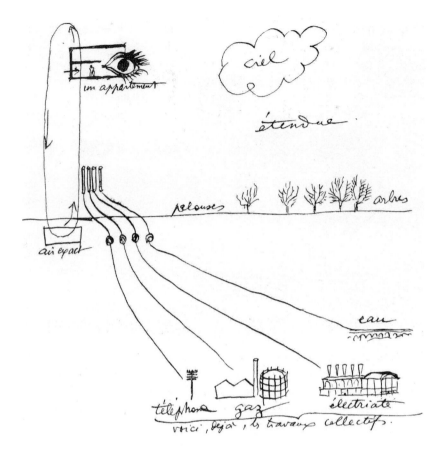

Figure 5.5
Le Corbusier, sketch from
La ville radieuse, 1933
(FLC/VG Bild-Kunst, Bonn
2009).

represents an apartment on the top floor, which is obviously not identical to the user of the apartment, since s/he is portrayed much smaller in the background, without any reference to the eye.

Beatriz Colomina has suggested that it represents the symbol of a camera (1992: 121ff.), but the eye can obviously do much more: it is a kind of artistic element that represents 'seeing' in general, and is therefore not restricted to one particular viewing device. It is eye, camera, computer, monitor, terminal and cyberspace all at once. In this respect, it could represent Corbusier's ribbon window, through which one can look at other Corbusiers in the area; it could be a digital screen, upon which continuous images are projected; it could be an organic prosthetic that vastly improves 'normal' sight, or it could be a virtual space with unlimited possibilities of presentation.

What Corbusier emblematically sketches here is not only a cognitive model, but also a simulation machine, which, just as in the earlier discovery of perspective, can create architectural images and image architecture (we see ourselves as watching and being watched). The sketch as a concept therefore greatly exceeds the designs of digital worlds, because it included them long ago, i.e. as an historical event. Corbusier's model is so comprehensive and radical that it even calls

Vitruvius' primitive hut into question. What we are seeing here is not only *the* paradigm for modern architecture, but the model for every kind of architecture, at least that which has emerged since Corbusier: in other words, the entire architecture of the twentieth century, which from now on is dependent upon and reflected through the media, and is thus constantly simulated. With this sketch Corbusier makes it clear how seriously he takes this historic break, effectively this new beginning of modernity. 'Nothing remains for us any more of the architecture of earlier epochs', as he said in his famous *Five Points of Modern Architecture* (quoted in Joedicke 1990: 50).

The creation myth is, of course, the agenda: through architecture, which permanently renews (simulates) itself, humanity should also be placed in the position to create itself anew, at least potentially. And on Corbusier's terms, an architecture structured entirely by media would succeed simply thanks to mastery over nature and rational control: the last emancipatory action of the free individual from his or her self-inflicted immaturity, which not only allows him or her to tame natural phenomena such as water and electricity, but also, naturally – if only implicitly – to control his or her impulses, since these do not arise in this model. Since Le Corbusier obviously didn't incorporate the dramatic process of the mirror stage, one can only speculate that the eye, the medial machine, also produces relieving images that make the phantasms of a 'gestalt' more tolerable.

The most interesting thing of all about Le Corbusier's model is the fact that it suspends the conventional difference between architecture and media. Each is continuously engaged in producing the other. Medial images produce architecture and architecture produces medial images. The historic order in which the 'solid' buildings are followed by the 'ephemeral' media no longer exists. To exaggerate only slightly: Peter Weir's Truman Show exists. We are our own reality show, not only in the football stadium, but also in our 'ideal home', which is itself a result of medial images. Le Corbusier's medial architecture has long since become reality.

NOTES

1 The 1990 World Cup Final in Italy between Germany and Argentina ended in a 1:0 victory for the German team, thanks to a penalty from Andreas Brehme.

2 In contrast to the 2006 World Cup, FIFA decided at the time to forbid the simultaneous broadcast of television images in the stadium during the match (although in 2006 a FIFA representative sat in the director's studio and filtered the images before they were shown on the stadium's screens). In particular, contentious scenes which might focus on the referee were not shown. In 1990, FIFA had no problem in allowing the transmission of images before and after the game. In Germany, for example, the German Football League DFL asserted in paragraph five of their guidelines on media rights (*Richtlinien über individuelle Verwertung und Vermarktung medialer Rechte*) that only replays of goals, with a maximum duration of ten seconds, could be shown on the by now omnipresent stadium screens and video cubes. It is clear that the association directors are skeptical of methods of visual synchronicity.

3 All translations from German by Carolyn Kelly.

4 The Mexican Wave really was invented with this intention. Tellingly, it emerged in the USA, where sport was exposed much earlier and more obviously to commercial involvement. A professional cheerleader, George Henderson, decided in October 1981 to practice something new with the spectators in Oakland's baseball stadium. Five years later, this choreographed wave caused a sensation at the World Cup in Mexico (Lissmann 2006).

5 The 2006 World Cup in Germany proved this in an impressive manner. Even the spectators who were in the so-called Public Viewing areas demonstrated their acting abilities (cf. Chapter 3).

6 On the one hand, Lacan explains this from his practice of psychoanalysis. His patients told him about continuing dreams, in which they fantasize about the fragmentation of their bodies. On the other hand, he uses the paintings by Hieronymus Bosch as proof of the widespread existence of such visions.

7 This was, for example, the first sentence of a press report by the German Press Agency dpa from 29 September 2004 about the Champions League match between Bayern Münich and Ajax Amsterdam, during which the Dutch striker, Roy Makaay, scored three of Bayern's four goals.

8 First published in French as *La Société du Spectacle*, Paris: Editions Buchet-Chastel (1967).

9 First published in French in the journal *Autrement*, May 1986, pp. 159–63.

10 It is even the case that the German Football Association DFB and others still allow themselves to be drawn into the defensive against the argument that the 'cold gaze of the camera' is superior to the 'fallible view of the referee'. Opponents of video evidence therefore have no other option than to praise 'human failings', a position that can hardly prevail (Soboczynski 2005: 72).

REFERENCES

Baudrillard, J. (1998) 'The Heysel syndrome', *Le Monde Diplomatique*, 5554: 2.

Colomina, B. (1992) 'The split wall: Domestic voyeurism', in B. Colomina and J. Bloomer (eds) *Sexuality and Space*, New York: Princeton Architectural Press.

Debord, G. (1996) *Die Gesellschaft des Spektakels*, Berlin: Bittermann.

Eco, U. (1987) 'Die Multiplizierung der Medien', in U. Eco (ed.) *Über Gott und die Welt. Essays und Glossen*, München: dtv.

FIFA-Fußballweltmeisterschaft 2006/Organisationskomitee Deutschland (eds) (2002) *Stadion 2006. Profile und Anforderungen für Städte und Stadien zur FIFA-Fußballweltmeisterschaft 2006™*; also Online. Available www.fifa.com/documents/static/regulations/media-guidelines-D.pdf (accessed 6 November 2002).

Goethe, J.W. (1976) *Italienische Reise*, Berlin: Rütten und Loening.

Joedicke, J. (1990) *Weißenhofsiedlung Stuttgart*, Stuttgart: Karl Krämer.

Kracauer, S. (1928) 'Das Ornament der Masse', *Frankfurter Zeitung*, 9/10 June; also in S. Kracauer (1992) *Der verbotene Blick. Beobachtungen, Analysen, Kritiken*, Leipzig: Reclam.

Lacan, J. (1986) 'Das Spiegelstadium als Bildner der Ichfunktion', in J. Lacan (ed.) *Schriften I*, Weinheim/Berlin: Quadriga.

Lissmann, C. (2006) 'Die Erfindung der Welle', *Zeit Online*, 24 (audio story). Online. Available www.zeit.de/online/2006/24/wm-geschichten-03 (accessed 1 November 2006).

Maslowska, D. (2005) 'Ich weiß erst jetzt, was Geschichte ist', *Frankfurter Allgemeine Zeitung*, 4 April, p. 39.

Schindelbeck, D. (2004) 'Mittendrin statt nur dabei? Zur Entwicklungsdynamik von Fußball, Medien und Kommerz', *Aus Politik und Zeitgeschichte*, B 26.

Sloterdijk, P. (2004) 'Indoors: Architekturen des Schaums', in P. Sloterdijk (ed.) *Sphären III: Schäume*, Frankfurt am Main: Suhrkamp.

Sloterdijk, P. (2005) 'Zwei Johannes Pauls im Gedächtnis', *Frankfurter Allgemeine Sonntagszeitung*, 3 April.

Soboczynski, A. (2005) 'Der kalte Blick', *Die Zeit*, 17 March, p. 72.

Stadtbauwelt (1990) No. 106, 'Großstadien 1990'; combined issue with *Bauwelt* No. 24.

Chapter 6: Killing Sports Fields

The Amahoro Stadium Complex in Kigali, Rwanda

Bruno Arich-Gerz

At one point in *The Soccer War*, ever since its publication in 1978 a modern classic of football literature next to Norbert Elias and Eric Dunning's *Quest for Excitement* (1986) or Nick Hornby's *Fever Pitch* (1992), Ryszard Kapuściński states about football stadia: 'In peacetime they are sports venues; in war they turn into concentration camps' (Kapuściński 1990: 166). Ariel Dorfman, as a more person-ally concerned eye-witness, ironically speaks of 'an ingenious idea: Turn the National Stadium, our largest sports arena, into a gigantic concentration camp' (Dorfman 2002: 11).

In the first case, Kapuściński writes of the six-day war between Honduras and El Salvador that was actually triggered by a World Cup qualification match between the two countries' national teams in 1969; in the second, Dorfman refers to the internments and killings in the two stadia of Santiago de Chile carried out by Chile's militia under General Augusto Pinochet after the 1973 *coup d'état* against Salvador Allende's democratic government. Both these state-ments blatantly oppose Elias and Dunning's assumption that (stadium) sports events constitute a civilization-stabilizing element for modern societies as they answer to a quest for excitement in leisure which is ultimately both peaceful and vicarious. Taking its cue from the remarks by the Polish journalist and the Chilean-American publicist, the following account focuses on the misappropria-tion of stadium grounds, compared to the function normally attributed to them, and more specifically will examine their deliberate or accidental misuse for com-mitting acts of extreme violence.

The considerations turn to one of the most horrifying non-sports events which have occurred at a sports venue in the recent past: the genocidal occur-rences at Rwanda's national stadium in Kigali, the Stade Amahoro, which in 1994 came to be a United Nations refugee camp that both attracted fleeing victims and marauding killer squads. Conscious of earlier works on this topic by Bernhard Hachleitner or John Bale,[1] the considerations unfolded here will provide an analysis of the role played by audiovisual media in both the actual events at the stadium and their commemoration. It will ultimately argue that today, the Kigali sports venue stands for a material medium of memorialization in its own right precisely because it was neither a TV broadcast scenery at the time when the genocide happened nor figured as its setting in one of the 'docutainment' movies produced in its aftermath. A distinctly non-realtime, non-studio event when mass murder reached its precincts, and not a location for films such as *Shooting Dogs* of 2005, it nonetheless recently figured as an open-air theatre for the screening of these movies. For many Rwandan viewers therefore it was a cinema-induced site of memory, a place notably untypical of stadia at the end of the twentieth and beginning of the twenty-first century.

AT THE TIME OF OCCURRENCE: GENOCIDAL ACTION AT THE KIGALI STADIUM

The Rwandan genocide of 1994 ranks among the most bestial and horrendous ethnically motivated mass murderings of the recent past. The extensive and obviously long-planned killings in Rwanda began on 6 April, when president Habyarimana's airplane was shot down as it flew into Kigali airport. The crash caused the death of Habyarimana and immediately incited tensions between the two major ethnic groups in the country, Tutsi and Hutu. Indisputably, both the world public's initial ignorance of the ethnically motivated mass murders and the insufficient manpower of UN peacekeeping forces at the locale such as the UNAMIR troops (United Nations Assistance Mission in Rwanda) in one way or another contributed to the rapid spread of the killing, which ultimately cost the lives of approximately half a million Tutsis and thousands of moderate Hutus.[2]

While the killings continued with increasing intensity during the first few days, for various reasons news of the events travelled notoriously slowly, impeding urgent counter-measures, such as the reinforcement of the few hundreds of UNAMIR and UN peacekeepers. Instead approximately 1,500 UN soldiers on the ground in Kigali, a major scene of the murderings in the early days of the genocide, were forced to concentrate in a handful of strategically crucial places.[3] Headquarters and outposts were established in the hospital and the Amahoro stadium, a multi-purpose sports complex with a capacity of 10,000 visitors that was right from the beginning surrounded by marauding killer squads.[4] Within no time the stadium complex became a site of crime, suffering and death. The events were recounted in the Canadian UNAMIR Force Commander Roméo Dallaire's prize-winning book *Shake Hands with the Devil* of 2003, and feature films such as *The Last Just Man* (2002, based on Dallaire's memories) as well as the scarce sources provided by non-Rwandan journalists.

Weakly defended and protected from the armed squads outside its gates, the arena was transformed into a huge refugee camp without proper ressources or functioning sanitation. Dallaire remembers that on 8 April, '[w]e had about 15,000 Rwandan civilians taking shelter in our compounds, with the highest numbers at the King Faisal Hospital and the Amahoro Stadium' (Dallaire 2003:

270). Four days later on 12 April, a date Dallaire retrospectively marks 'as the day the world moved from disinterest in Rwanda to the abandonment of Rwandans to their fate', the refugee camp at once turns into a besieged locale of armed conflict: 'A few bombs exploded around my headquarters [...] and a few of the thousands of civilians cowering at the Amahoro and the King Faisal Hospital sites were wounded' (Dallaire 2003: 291).

Three days later on 15 April, BBC world affairs correspondent Mark Doyle, one of the few foreign journalists who had managed to get into the country following the outbreak of hostilities, filed from Kigali:

> The 5,000 displaced in the main Kigali football stadium are being protected by the Bangladeshi [UNAMIR contingent], but have very little food, no running water and no medical supplies. Many of them were wounded in the fighting or are suffering from malaria and other easily preventable diseases. There are several Rwandan doctors in the football stadium, but they have no drugs or bandages. The Bangladeshis have shared some of their combat rations with the refugees. At a makeshift clinic under one of the main spectator stands, a Rwandan volunteer was handing out small sachets of apricot jam to sick people. 'It's all we've got', he said. 'I know it's not medicine but I've got to give them something.'
>
> (Doyle 2007: 151)

Moshed Ali Khan, then a translator with the Bangladeshi units and later a correspondent for the Daily Star's weekly magazine, corroborates the catastrophic circumstances inside the arena:

> On the morning of April 9, 1994 the air smelt foul with corpses rotting everywhere. The night before we had received scores of Tutsis fleeing the massacre. Sanitation problems at the stadium became so acute that we had to look for a site to set up makeshift latrines. Just as I walked within the perimeter fence of the stadium looking for a safe site, I saw a few corpses of children and babies strewn on the ground near the fence.[5]
>
> (Khan 2004)

The death squads outside the stadium gates all the while waited for further Tutsi refugees to arrive at the Amahoro sports venue, which at one point even led to a critical situation between the troops inside and a shelter-seeking UN contingent when the Bangladeshis

> refused [...] to open the gate of the stadium [...] to admit a group of Belgian soldiers who were entrapped just outside by a crowd of Rwandan military and militia. The standoff between the Belgians and the hostile crowd went on for some two hours until the Belgians opened fire, ran to the stadium, and climbed over the fence.
>
> (Des Forges 1999: 598)[6]

The genocide ended in July 1994 and it was only then that the Amahoro stadium complex, too, 'slowly emptied [...] as at first one person and then a family and finally all of our companions left us to find out what had happened to their relatives and their homes' (Dallaire 2003: 478). Resembling 'an overflowing sewer', as Dallaire notes, the locale finally needed urgent refurbishments of various kinds: 'Those [Canadian UN units] who weren't on duty setting up communication and HQ assets carried on scrubbing, building and sandbagging' (Dallaire 2003: 490).

MEDIA COVERAGE: THE AMAHORO SPORTS COMPLEX AS THE OPPOSITE OF A BROADCASTING STUDIO

A disastrous mix of refugee camp, site of siege and slaughtering ground, the stadium complex in Kigali had temporarily lost all the characteristics of a peacetime sports venue. This affected the fast preparation and swift broadcasting of audiovisual material, too, a feature that is otherwise typical of contemporary, highly technified sports arenas. In the case of the Amahoro stadium, broadcasting infrastructure of this kind came to bear (again) in the post-genocide qualification matches for the African Cup of Nations and FIFA World Cup, the first of which took place on 2 June 1996 against Tunisia. Throughout the crucial weeks in the spring of 1994, however, and regardless of existing studio equipments at Amahoro, the national and world public was excluded from what was going on inside and outside the stadium. With the notable exception of Mark Doyle, who was invited by Dallaire to accompany the UNAMIR troops on their reconnaissance trips, and to document what he witnessed to the outside world and transmit his messages to the BBC by using Dallaire's personal media infrastructure,[7] news (re) presentations of the events usually reached the global audience with a delay that is more typical of the print press than of live TV coverage. Arguably, this further contributed to (but was certainly not primarily responsible for) the considerable delay that it took outside Rwanda to realize the dimension of the genocide.

In terms of media coverage, therefore, the Amahoro sports complex figured as the direct opposite of a stadium transformed into an audiovisual realtime studio, i.e. into a broadcasting medium in its own right. As the contributions by Schnell (Chapter 5) and Zinganel (Chapter 4) in this volume show, stadia have increasingly become transmission media; as such they allow the likes of Nick Hornby's financially weak core supporters to come to terms with their forced exclusion from the over-expensive pitch: 'we'll all be at home, watching the box' (Hornby 2000: 189).[8] Visibly closer to the concerns of this chapter, the transformation of stadia into realtime broadcasting media equally play a role in connection with other types of stadium misappropriation that inhere(d) an element of violence. A case in point is the Heysel catastrophe of 1985, which according to Jean Baudrillard was last but not least 'a primitive but devastatingly effective form of "interactive television"' between Liverpool fans and the Thatcher government's previous and provocative handling of the miners' strike via the TV screen: as Andrew Hussey resumes Baudrillard's key message 20 years after the occurrences in the Belgian capital's stadium, Heysel 'did not happen by chance;

it was the inevitable result of the desire of spectators to turn themselves into actors' (Hussey 2005, cf. Baudrillard 1993: 75–81, cf. Schnell's Chapter 5 in this volume). Another such misappropriation of the contemporary stadium-cum-studio phenomenon has been singled out by Tamir Bar-On who, taking his cue from Kapuściński's elaborations on the intricate relationship of football matches and warfare in Latin America, points out that in the 1970s '[i]n El Salvador, the national stadium has even been used to carry out televised, nationwide assassinations against political opponents' (Bar-On 1997: § 3.3, cf. Kapuściński 1990: 185).[9]

Such types of instrumentalization of sports grounds, which obviously ride piggyback on a stadium's quality of being a live broadcasting facility, may be a deplorable corrolary of today's media(tized) culture. Yet neither the stadium-cum-studio misappropriation by Liverpool hooligans for their alleged protest against Thatcherism nor the Latin American variant of notifying the El Salvadorians by realtime transmission that any resistance to the regime will lead to a hanging in public, can be juxtaposed to the circumstances of the Rwanda genocide and the employment of the Amahoro sports facilities. In terms of sheer media presence, therefore, the Kigali national stadium in 1994 instead resembled the many concentration camps established throughout the twentieth century: most of the audiovisual documents of the Nazi concentration camps for instance have been taken and published only after their liberation (cf. Barnouw 1996). If Amahoro was therefore never a local(ity-specific) *Übertragungsmedium* – a medium of instant broadcasting – the question remains whether it subseqently figured as another kind of medium. According to critics such as Aleida Assmann, the former Nazi concentration camp sites today possess the quality of a material *Speichermedium* (storage medium) from which the informed visitor can, in the very act of tuning in to the memorial charge acccumulated there, retrieve the past events as well as the distressful memories that connect her- or himself with the site. In the following pages, this memory-cultural concept will be grafted onto the Amahoro stadium complex.

SITES AS MEDIA: CULTURAL MEMORY AND THE AMAHORO STADIUM

In her theory of cultural memory, Aleida Assmann at one point defines media in very general terms as 'material stabilizers' which 'found and flank cultural memory' while they at the same time allow for 'interaction with human memories' (Assmann 1999: 20).[10] Unusual and unspecific as it at first sight appears, a definition like this allows for a remarkably wide understanding of media in the context of memorial concerns. In this understanding the notion of 'media' includes conventional (or conventionally expected) media such as print publications which, in the case of memoirs, undeniably help to found, flank and interact with individual human memories. Yet the media of memory, in the wider definition that Assmann uses, also comprise other and presumably unconventional types of 'material stabilizers' such as 'locales which due to events of a religious,

historical or biographically significant kind have become sites of memory'
(Assmann 1999: 21).[11] Memory-related material stabilizers, be they monuments
or sites, books or other technical media, or even the human body, figure as
storage media whose memorial content allows for – but cannot per se generate
– retrieval. Instead, restoring these contents requires acts of memorizing – an
agency Assmann subsumes under the notion of *Funktionsgedächtnis* (functional
memory) as opposed to the materio-medial *Speichergedächtnis* (storage
memory). Activities of collective memorization – of the functional memory at
work in groups – include rituals, ceremonies or other social gatherings. Private or
individual acts of memorizing are equally conceivable, though Assmann's model
strongly focuses on the social types.

With regard to memorially charged sites or places, functional and storage
memory thus interact in such a way that 'the site reactivates memories as well as,
vice versa, memories do with the site' (Assmann 1999: 21).[12] One decade and a
half after the genocide in Rwanda, the Amahoro fits well into the memory-
specific theoretical framework propagated by Assmann: the sports ground
figures as a medium of memory in this sense.

At present, though, when sports events and other uses of the arena such
as national celebrations have re-appropriated it, a visit to the stadium alone does
not suffice to unearth its memory-specific underpinnings, and thus to fit the site
into the framework of commemoration on a social or cultural scale proffered by
Assmann. As mentioned, another element apart from the site itself is crucial for
reminding people of – and make them memorize – the stadium's dreadful past
as a site of murder and a refugee camp '[f]or neither biographical nor cultural
memory can be sourced out to these sites; rather these [sites] can trigger and
firm up processes of remembering only in connection with other media of
memory' (Assmann 1999: 21).[13] The 'other media of memory' invoked here can
more specifically be the recollections engraved in the minds of those who had
been at the stadium at the time of the genocidal occurrences that may resurface
in the moment of visiting the stadium site again. Cases of this kind have in fact
been documented in which according to the French memory theorist Pierre Nora
a *lieu de mémoire* comes to (re)gain importance for a person who had lived
through crucial moments in his or her life at precisely this place, and who now
revisits the site.[14] Other visitors than those with a personal, living memory of the
place will require (yet) another material stabilizer or medium of memory, though,
in order to grasp the place's particular quality as not just an ordinary sports
venue, but also a distinctly 'traumatic site'.[15]

For these, books based on the recollections of eye-witnesses of the gruesome murderings such as Dallaire's can figure as one such medium of memory;
other material stabilizers of this kind include the memoir-based, historical or
otherwise non-fictional films produced in the aftermath of the 1994 occurrences.
Among these *Hotel Rwanda*, directed by Terry George and with Nick Nolte star-
ring as Roméo Dallaire, has presumably been the best known production. Apart
from the prize-winning 2004 blockbuster and the previously mentioned filmic

version of Dallaire's memoirs, and at the same time implicitly pointing once more at the worldwide indifference toward the genocide at the time of its occurrence with virtually no preserved documentary audiovisual material as opposed to the time-lagged boom of the topic in the early twenty-first century, these films are *Sometimes in April* of 2005 and *Shooting Dogs* from 2006.

A DECADE LATER: THE AMAHORO STADIUM AS A SITE OF FILM SCREENING

'*Sometimes in April*, a film on the 1994 Rwanda genocide, premieres Saturday in the central African nation at a stadium that was one of the scenes of slaughter over a decade ago', wrote AP correspondent Edward Rwema on 22 January 2005 from Kigali.

> It was filmed mostly in Rwanda, where Hutu extremist militias and army soldiers killed more than 500,000 minority Tutsis and politically moderate Hutus during the genocide that took place between April and July 1994. *Sometimes in April* will be shown at Kigali's Amahoro stadium to an invitation-only audience. Thousands of Tutsis were killed at the stadium during the genocide.
>
> (Rwema 2005)

The announcement points at an, at first sight, unusual, yet on closer inspection familiar appropriation of a football stadium, given the present-day practice of turning the built environment of a sports arena into a large-scale locale for open-air concerts or mass services (cf. Chapter 4). More important for the argument here, the announcement at the same time refers to the fact that the same location had been a killing sports field where a four-digit number of Tutsis had lost their lives, and as such indirectly points to the memorial implications of the stadium site as proposed by Assmann. Presumably not a direct eye-witness of the murderous events that had taken place there, the correspondent well anticipates, and in turn well testifies to, the non-sports-specific role which the stadium plays here as a medium of memory in its own right where yet another material stabilizer of the genocide bears its memorial impact on the visitors: the movie itself in the very act of its transitory screening. Indeed the AP journalist notices that two types of storage memory converge here: the film with the genocidal events re-enacted in them, and the stadium as one of the locales of their original occurrence. Coupled like this, movie and stadium location pave the way for functional memory to have its effects, and trigger commemoration even in those viewers who do not connect any burdensome living memory with the Amahoro 'site as medium'.[16]

While the journalist's announcement well catches the importance of the (site of) screening for the viewers, it must necessarily exclude the reception of *Sometimes in April* by the invited audience he mentions. Reactions of this kind were documented, though, when approximately one year later another movie on the same subject matter was shown in the Amahoro stadium. For some of the viewers, the screening in March 2006 was tantamount to a 'Flashback to Geno-cide', as Cahal Milmo aptly entitles his newspaper report (Milmo 2006). The jour-nalist arranges his feature similarly in a flashback mode by first abruptly introducing what had happened to one of his interviewees in the spring of 1994:

> Joseph Nyamiroko never reached the safety of the Amahoro stadium with his family. On 11 April 1994, he witnessed soldiers hacking his wife and son to death with machetes before shooting his brother in the face as they fled towards the sports complex.
>
> (Milmo 2006)

Then the report (re)turns to the present: 'Sat on the terraces with 2,000 others, he saw a version of the events of that day in the world premiere of *Shooting Dogs*'.

The presence of the surviving witness at the premiere show of the movie adds yet another medium of memory to the memorially charged material stabi-lizer of the built environment itself and the audiovisual material that explicitly re-enacts the genocidal past: Joseph Nyamiroko's own mind, filled as it is with traumatic memories of the site that are now being re-activated.[17] Essentially for the individual witness and those next to him who 'broke the silence in the giant national stadium' with 'muted sobbing' when 'revisiting private nightmares' as expressions of functional memory at work, the Amahoro arena of today has, first, become a memory-infested (and as such highly palimpsested) site only one layer of which points at its original destination as a football ground: a place haunted by the 'ghosts' of the dead and therefore inducing those like Joseph Nyamikoro to better 'avoid[-] the towering arena'.[18]

Second, and presumably of even greater relevance, the movie's storyline actually takes certain liberties with regard to the historical facts it seeks to repre-sent. The Amahoro stadium was one of the places where mass murder occurred in 1994, it clearly is still one for Joseph Nyamiroko – but the arena of screening the film in 2005 is itself somewhat inaccurately not shown as the crime site which it had been 11 years earlier. Then, refugees sought shelter in the stadium, many of them fleeing from a school in a suburb of Kigali, before they were 'spotted by soldiers from the Hutu-controlled army, rounded up and led on a death march to Nyanza-Rebero [...]. After a number of hours, they were slaugh-tered'. *Shooting Dogs* however 'departs from history with its climax – the mas-sacre of the abandoned refugees [abandoned by white teachers and priests, the central characters in the movie] by a baying mob of Interahamwe [Hutu militia] in the ground of the school', reports Milmo in his feature. The storyline leaves out, in other words, that '[i]n reality, the 2,500 victims, including Mr. Nyamiroko and his family, tried to flee their pursuers by heading for the Amahoro stadium' (Milmo 2006). While there may be production-specific reasons for the decision not to make use of the stadium environment as a film setting – as the authentic site of its cruelsome misappropriation as a refugee camp and later as a slaughter-ing place – the instrumentalization of precisely this stadium as an open-air movietheatre actually harbours an interesting aspect of diverting sports venues from their intended use: that of a locale of genocidal action in the past, a site of memory today when event-related movies premiere a decade after the occurrences themselves, and finally and conspicuously, a non-location in these films.

REVISING KAPUŚCIŃSKI THROUGH THE PRISM OF THE AMAHORO STADIUM MEDIUM OF MEMORY: A CONCLUSION

If stadia are sports venues in peacetime, but may instantly turn into concentration or, for that matter and in the present case, refugee camps in times of war, it seems appropriate to modify and expand Ryszard Kapuściński's dictum: as the exemplary case of the Amahoro sports complex has shown, stadia are not automatically – least of all exclusively – re-appropriated by football players and visiting sports enthusiasts once the war is over. Nor are their non-sports re-appropriations restricted to political proclamations or celebrations of national unity. After their temporary misappropriation as concentration or refugee camps, these arenas continue to figure as (mi)lieux de mémoire or sites of memory of a special kind.[19] Unlike the built environments of former concentration camps stadia can, through their capacity of hosting large crowds of people and enhanced by reproductive media infrastructure such as large-scale screens, projectors and sound systems, theoretically carry the audience back to and re-present to them their own wartime past. In practice and in the case of the Amahoro stadium, up to three media of memory actually converge – the site itself, the memories stored in the minds of the survivor-visitors, and the film reeling off on the screen.

Curiously, the interplay of these for the purpose of evoking social acts of commemoration – their flanking and firming of the collective's functional memory – conspicuously refrains, in the documented feature about the *Shooting Dogs* screening, from re-presenting the stadium's own past as a major locale during the genocide. Intentionally or not (but in any case appropriate as far as the imagery resulting from it is concerned), this gap in the filmic representation of the ring-like architecture of the Amahoro stadium at the time of the mass murderings in 1994 is at the same time reminiscent of the 'empty circle' that Dori Laub mentions when discussing the transgenerational late effects of psychotrauma of other, distinctly non-Rwandan survivors of concentration camps.[20] While one may hope for less trauma-ridden scenarios for future generations remembering the 1994 events at Amahoro, the idea of preserving the site's status as a place of past atrocities that has not been visually palimpsested, covered or otherwise blurred by later blockbuster representations may principally be welcome.

NOTES

1 Hachleitner's article focuses on stadia which have in the recent past been misused as sites of detention and secret killings (Santiago de Chile) or even locales of public executions (Kabul) before current political developments turned them into sites where commemorative celebrations take place. Today plaques remind visitors of sports events of the place's past and murderous history (Hachleitner 2005: 278f.) John Bale, on whom also Hachleitner relies, produced a book-length and groundbreaking study on the connection of urbanity, spatiality and stadia, highlighting among other things the issues of mass gatherings, security management and the relatively short way from here to total supervision as known from (Michel Foucault's elaborations on) prison architecture(s).

2 The sum total of victims varies, depending on the sources. The estimate given here refers to Des Forges (1999). Ernest Harsch (1998: 4) estimates the death toll 'between half a million and a million people'.

3 'The mainstay of the force in Kigali was the 440 man Belgian contingent and some 200 Ghanaians recently brought down from the demilitarized zone in the north. The most numerous contingent in the capital [were the] more than 900 soldiers from Bangladesh' (Des Forges 1999: 597f.).

4 In fact, 'the Amahoro (Peace) Stadium and attached athletes' hotel' had been a 'permanent location for UNAMIR headquarters' ever since November 1993. At that time '[t]he complex was in an excellent tactical location, off the major route to the airport in the east of Kigali. The enclosed stadium could accommodate up to a battalion's worth of soldiers, vehicles and equipment' (Dallaire 2003: 109).

5 The startling and somewhat melodramatic climax of Khan's report is the unexpected discovery of a live baby girl amid the small corpses: 'Under the large concrete water reservoir, lay on the ground a tiny newborn baby. She was completely still. Her body was stained with dried out blood with an unusually long umbilical cord torn apart from her dead mother. As I closely examined for signs of life in that lump of flesh, I could not believe my eyes when she slightly moved her hand and feet. I named her Aougny. And Aougny brought joy to the volunteers of the centre. I wondered how a sign of life could bring so much joy to a group of people surviving a massacre of such huge proportions around them' (Khan 2004).

6 Cf. Sénat de Belgique 1997: 28.

7 According to Dallaire, Doyle 'could live with us, be protected by us, be fed and sustained by us, and I would guarantee him a story a day and the means (my satellite phone) to get that story to the world' (Dallaire 2003: 332).

8 According to Hornby, numerous 'young working-class males, the traditional core of support' (Hornby 2000: 212) decided to stay at home and 'watch the box' instead of going to the home pitch stadium. He explains that this was a direct result of the (un)affordability of tickets at a time of extraordinarily increased entrance fees in the wake of the Taylor Report recommendation 'that, post-Hillsborough, football stadia should become all-seater' (Hornby 2000: 67f., cf. King's Chapter 1 in this volume).

9 In a similar way, the Olympic Stadium in Kabul, under the reign of the Taliban, became a location for 'executions and amputations' that were enacted as 'public spectacles [which] took place at regular intervals – much like sports events, yet disproportionately more gruesome' (Hachleitner 2005: 272, trans. Bruno Arich-Gerz). While (secretly shot) moving pictures of these punishment excesses do exist, the regime itself refrained from televising them in any form.

10 Translation from German: Bruno Arich-Gerz.

11 Translation from German: Bruno Arich-Gerz.

12 Translation from German: Bruno Arich-Gerz.

13 Translation from German: Bruno Arich-Gerz.

14 Focusing on the crucial sites of World War I activities for the French cultural memory, Nora relates to a *lieu de mémoire* as a location to which surviving veterans attach their memories: Verdun, the battlefields at the Marne river etc. Observing that with regard to these veterans, their living memory is about to disappear, Nora differentiates between *their* recollections of the places as a *milieu de mémoire* on the one hand, and the commemorative impetus of the afterborn generations who come to visit these sites, but have themselves never come to witness them as places of dreadful events, heroic warfare or otherwise memorable locales on the other. 'We are witnessing a period of transition', he writes with respect to the present and in the light of the decreasing number of (still) living eye-witnesses, 'there are *lieux de mémoire* because the *milieux de mémoire* have gone' (Nora 1997: 23, trans. Bruno Arich-Gerz). Arguably, Nora's generation-specific differentiation can equally well be expanded, and made applicable to the contemporary difference of those who had lived through crucial events, say those at the Amahoro stadium, at the time of their occurrence (for whom the sports fields still contains the characteristics of a *milieu de mémoire*), and those who had not been there in the decisive moments of the past, but who now come to visit it and get confronted with its memorial implications: for these, it will necessarily appear more like a *lieu de mémoire*.

15 The term is again Assmann's. Usually and ordinarily, sites of memory claim pride of place for 'mythical, national or historical memory' because they testify to positively connoted events from the past that often lend an unproblematic kind of identification with the bygone occurrences. Traumatic sites, by contrast, 'differ from [ordinary] sites of memory because they resist any easygoing, affirmative construction of meaning' (Assmann 1999: 328, trans. Bruno Arich-Gerz).

16 Conspicuously and presumably pointing at a culture(s)-specific difference between African sites and sports arenas in other parts of the world, no such appropriation under the sign of commemoration exists in the case of Western stadia that likewise, in one case or another, possess a site-specific traumatic quality. The Heysel stadium in Brussels has never been the locale for a screening of a documentary about the disaster, nor has Hillsborough. Heysel has in the meantime been rebuilt and renamed as King Baudouin Stadium, erasing thus any traces of the tragedy of 1985 except for a 60 square meter sundial in memory of the 39, mostly Italian victims of the Liverpool hooligan riots.

17 Trauma studies in both the fields of clinical psychotrauma and cultural studies have not failed to notice the structural similarities of the sudden and eruptive reappearances of painful memories in the minds of traumatized individuals – a symptom conventionally called Post-Traumatic Stress Disorder – and film. Converging here in Joseph Nyamiroko's identity as former victim on the one hand, and present movie-viewer on the other, the parallels otherwise stretch as far as the vocabulary. Hence 'flashbacks' and 'dramatic re-enactment' are notions oftentimes invoked by experts of psychoanalytic trauma, too, although they have originated from the language of film analysis. By the same token, filmic visualizations of overwhelmingly drastic events such as those in the Nazi concentration camps or, for that matter and more generally, those witnessed by survivors of genocidal occurrences may in the afterborn or uninvolved viewers effect what Geoffrey Hartman terms 'secondary traumatization' (Hartman 1996: 152).

18 This event, memory-infested as it obviously is for many spectator-attendants, resembles the one which according to Ariel Dorfman's description took place in Santiago de Chile's Estadio Nacional. In 1990, survivors of the stadium-cum-concentration camp period in 1973 as well as relatives of people assassinated on the location by the henchmen of the Pinochet regime gathered here after the dictator's ultimate resignation from power. When the new president, Patricio Aylwin, had just delivered a moving speech to the audience, '[s]eventy thousand men and women suddenly hushed as they heard a solitary pianist playing, down on the green field, variations on a song by Victor

Jara, the celebrated protest singer murdered by the military a few days after the coup' of 17 years earlier: 'I had never seen before – and would never want to see again – seventy thousand people crying together as they lay their dead to rest', Dorfman testifies (Dorfman 2002: 12f.).

19 Cf. Morshed Ali Khan, the aforementioned Bangladeshi translator who as a Daily Star correspondent visited the place again a decade after the genocidal actions: 'Amahoro stadium looked exactly the same except that now it houses the Sports and Youth Ministry and some other offices including that of the Genocide Memorial Office'. At the same time, Khan describes a re-appropriation of the stadium by sportsmen and, as himself a former eye-witness, seems much like Joseph Nyamikoro to be puzzled by the incommensurateness of the stadium's present appearance and its disastrous look ten years earlier: 'Male and female athletes practised on the neatly maintained red tracks. Some women carrying their babies on their backs walked leisurely across the green football pitch. Absent were thousands of helpless men, women and children crammed inside the small corridors and rooms. Absent were the gunshots and cries of the wounded and the sick. Absent were the billowing smoke from makeshift cookers lit by some refugees; and the typical smell of African spices that hung in the air. I stood under the concrete overhead water reservoir near the fence and recalled how ten years ago on that spot lay a newborn baby girl, abandoned by her parents' (Khan 2004).

20 Laub refers to the mental afflictions, oftentimes transposed to the next generation, of Nazi concentration camp survivors (1998: 507–29).

REFERENCES

Assmann, A. (1999) *Erinnerungsräume. Formen und Wandlungen des kulturellen Gedächtnisses*, Munich: Beck.

Bale, J. (1993) *Sport, Place and the City*, London: Routledge.

Barnouw, D. (1996) *Germany 1945. Views of War and Violence*, Bloomington/Indianapolis: Indiana UP.

Bar-On, T. (1997) 'The ambiguities of football, politics, culture, and social transformation in Latin America', *Sociological Research Online*, 2(4), § 3.3. Also online. Available www.socresonline.org.uk/2/4/2.html (accessed 12 February 2009).

Baudrillard, J. (1993; 1st edn 1990) *The Transparency of Evil*, London: Verso.

Dallaire, R. (2003) *Shake Hands with the Devil. The failure of humanity in Rwanda*, Toronto: Random House Canada.

Des Forges, A. (1999) *Leave None to Tell the Story: Genocide in Rwanda*, Human Rights Watch. Online. Available www.hrw.org/legacy/reports/1999/rwanda/ (accessed 12 February 2009).

Dorfman, A. (2002) *Exorcising Terror. The incredible unending trial of General Augusto Pinochet*, New York: Seven Stories Press.

Doyle, M. (2007) 'Reporting the genocide', in A. Thompson (ed.) *The Media and the Rwanda Genocide*, London/Ann Arbor: Pluto Press.

Elias, N. and Dunning, E. (1986) *Quest for Excitement: Sport and leisure in the civilizing process*, Oxford: Blackwell.

Hachleitner, B. (2005) 'Das Stadion als Gefängnis', in M. Marschik, R. Müllner, G. Spitaler and M. Zinganel (eds) *Das Stadion. Geschichte, Architektur, Politik, Ökonomie*, Vienna: Turia + Kant.

Harsch, E. (1998) 'OAU sets inquiry into Rwanda genocide, a determination to search for Africa's own truth', *Africa Recovery*, 12(1): 4.

Hartman, G. (1996) *The Longest Shadow. In the aftermath of the Holocaust*, Bloomington/Indianapolis: Indiana UP.

Hornby, N. (2000; 1st edn 1992) *Fever Pitch*, Harmondsworth: Penguin.

Hussey, A. (2005) 'Lost lives that saved a sport', *The Observer*, 3 April.

Kapuściński, R. (1990; 1st edn 1978) *The Soccer War*, London: Granta Books.

Khan, M.A. (2004) 'In search of a daughter in Africa', *The Daily Star*, 1(158). Online. Available www.thedailystar.net/magazine/2004/06/02/index.htm (accessed 24 September 2009).

Laub, D. (1998) 'The empty circle: Children of survivors and the limits of reconstruction', *Journal of the American Psychoanalytic Association*, 46(2): 507–29.

Milmo, C. (2006) 'Flashback to genocide', *The Independent*, 29 March.

Nora, P. (1997; 1st edn 1990) *Les Lieux de Mémoire*, Paris: Gallimard.

Rwema, E. (2005) 'Genocide film premieres at Rwanda stadium, scene of slaughter', *AP Worldstream*, 22 January.

Sénat de Belgique (1997) *Commission d'Enquête Parlementaire Concernant les Evènements du Rwanda, Rapport*, Annexe 5.

Part III

When Global Flows Meet Local Cultures

Chapter 7: Global Players and the Stadium

Migration and Borders in Professional Football[1]

Christian Banse

WHO IS LIVING THE DREAM?[2] THE STADIUM AS AN ASPIRATION

Have you ever heard of Maldini? Anyone interested in professional football will immediately think of the Italian, Paolo Maldini, AC Milan's national player, a man famous worldwide with a record number of World Cup appearances, Champions League winner's medals and Italian League titles (cf. Transfermarkt 2009). However, in this chapter I am not referring to this particular Maldini, but rather to someone as thrilled as I am by his amazing footballing skills.

The Maldini I want to focus on here is a character in the novel, *Le Ventre de l'Atlantique* (*The Belly of the Atlantic*) by Fatou Diome (2003), though that is not his real name. Rather, a young Senegalese boy calls himself Maldini because this famous football star epitomizes for him the chance of exchanging the poverty of Africa for the promise of fame and fortune as a professional footballer in Europe. Because the village television often breaks down during bad weather, Maldini relies on his sister, a student in Strasbourg and the narrator of this book, to give a running commentary on important games over the telephone.

From the narrative of Maldini's sister the reader learns something about the dreams of the boys in Senegal. Their vision of France, as portrayed during the games' commercial breaks, is a paradise, attainable only through the possibilities offered by football. The reader gets to know the ambition and the determination of the youths to fight for their aspirations, becoming acquainted with the failed migrants who return to the village, including those who tell lies in order to hide their failure. There is also the pressure felt by migrants to shower gifts upon their families, and even on the whole village, to prove their wealth. The narrator complains about the horrific sums she must spend on telephone bills, football boots, jerseys and other presents, and about her brother's narrowly focused viewpoint, which sees only the success achievable as a professional footballer, like his Maldini, but not the innumerable failed migrants. It is these who are forced to live illegally in destinations in France, Spain and Italy, because no club will offer them the work that would guarantee them the crucial European residence permit. Many are unable to return to their native country because they have failed, and because this failure will be regarded as a humiliating defeat. As a French talent scout in the novel says to Moussa, another boy from Maldini's village now training illegally in France: Either you succeed in playing in the professional squad or else you'll have to repay me all the money I have spent on flights, bribes, accommodation and training, in order to get you this far. In addition, Moussa must endure the racism of the other players and the impersonal atmosphere in the team. Eventually, his only option is to work on a ship in order to repay the agent.

For gifted African players, those footballers of the periphery, the fight for the few places in the larger European clubs is hard, and the way in which the novel describes the situation is quite accurate. Based on extensive research, Pierre Lanfranchi and Matthew Taylor (2001) conclude for instance that

> with few exceptions, football in Africa is not professionalized and so a move to Europe has traditionally been the only way of becoming a recognized international footballer. [...] Football is Africa's most popular male leisure activity and from an early date African footballers in Europe have become important symbols of international recognition and achievement.
>
> (Lanfranchi and Taylor 2001: 167)

Some recent figures illustrate just how attractive a migrant career as a professional footballer can be, and not only for young Africans: In 2005, Chelsea's Ghanaian-born player Michael Essien earned £55,000 a week when the average annual income in Ghana at the time was £300 (Runciman 2006). In 2005 alone, 878 players migrated from Brazil to Europe and Ronaldinho, at that time the most expensive football player in the world, had a market value of 70 million

Figure 7.1
Have you ever heard of
Maldini?

euros (Goos 2006). In 2006, Jönsson stated that '[i]n the last four years Brazil has exported 3,078 professional footballers throughout the world. Some dominate the Champions League; others play in the second Russian division' (2006: 31).

More figures show just how different the conditions of Western elite league clubs are compared to, for example, those in Africa: In 2006, only one player of the Ivory Coast's national football team played in a club in his home country; in Italy, however, no footballer in the Italian national team played in a club outside his country (WM-Almanach 2006). In 2005, Chelsea employed 16 non-English players (Runciman 2006). Even the USA, an aspiring 'developing football country', is in a position to secure the highly praised talent of Fredua Koranteng Adu from Ghana, whom they have now nationalized, while in Ghana itself, along with other African countries, the continuing work of developing football is made immensely difficult by migration and the lack of resources (Thomé 2003).

While Lanfranchi and Taylor (2001) and other researchers unanimously claim that it is the move to Europe which is the declared dream of many football players from the periphery, I would like to refine their conclusion. I will argue here that it is not just the move to Europe as such, or to a specific European country, that features as an attractive migrant destination. Rather, it is the European stadium (cf. Chapter 1) as a specialized built structure and activity-dedicated public space that is the yearned-for destination for migrant footballers from the periphery – no matter whether this is located in Milan or Madrid. It is the stadium that represents a new 'promised land', a transnational space to which the dreams cling, where heroes are born and where a player can reach an otherwise unattainable summit of prosperity and popularity that will make his family at home more than proud.

Where does this utopian image of the stadium come from? Perhaps from television, films, the sports pages of the press, books produced for fans. What aspects of the stadium draw these migrant players? Is it the size that most appeals, with the prospect of playing before vast crowds in Europe? Do some stadium types have greater attraction than others? While limited space does not permit discussion here, these questions are worthy of further research.

THE STADIUM: TRANSNATIONAL ARENA AND BORDER ZONE

Whoever enters a World Cup or European Cup stadium in which national teams face up to each other, or the stadia of top European clubs in which a selection of the world's best are playing, is confronted with a hybrid space (Bale 2005). On the one hand, the stadium is a transnational arena, a place characterized by different nationalities of players, coaches, managers, referees, media and advertising professionals and sponsors and by their absorption in a global professional football market.

Professional football can be regarded as a global event: World Cups and other contests entertain millions of spectators. The final of the World Cup in

2002 in Japan and South Korea was watched by more than a billion people. Football is a world sport, regulated by a common system of rules set up by the world federation, FIFA. Regular comparisons are made between teams' performances in the framework of tournaments. For example, every four years since 1930 a competition for the World Cup has been organized, with the only break occurring during the Second World War. 'Universal' criteria to judge teams' performances have been established not only by those tournaments and regulations but also by the media that document records and guarantee the comprehensibility and comparability of criteria for spectators and others (cf. Chapter 3).[3]

In this context, the stadium, as a specialized building form, providing for a pitch of internationally agreed dimensions, uniform marking, standard-sized goal posts, accommodation for spectators, officials, media, controlled entrance and exit points, itself plays a central role in transplanting football, as the 'world sport number one', to different countries round the world.

On the other hand, however, the stadium is a space in which national or European borders are maintained, borders that may not be visible initially, but that nonetheless take effect in many different ways. The stadium as a space is crisscrossed by boundaries of political affiliation, by the relative costs of training a player, by his salary and his chances on the football market, his reputation within the team and with the spectators. Moreover, the space of the stadium is influenced by local conditions. Just where the stadium is located accentuates, for example, how global players act and how fans react.

One analytical step further, these observations must take note of sociological theory addressing the experiences and conditions of migration in professional football.[4] In doing this, well known phenomena such as illegality and child trafficking can be found even within the peculiarities of the professional football market, which is permanently in the spotlight.

Most scholars theorizing migration and football use the term 'globalization' (Taylor 2006: 9–12), but football is not really *the* global sport or *the* prime example of a new global order, the almost paradigmatic expression of globalization as the notion 'world sport number one' suggests. In the literature on globalization the increase in cross-border mobility is often regarded as one indicator for more cross-national integration and understanding (cf. Held *et al.* 1999; Werron 2005). This claim has been made along the lines of the sociological assumption that a new, open world has emerged from the once closed model of the national state, but it ignores both border crossings in earlier times and the current creation of borders. The migration of professional football players is not a new phenomenon, but belongs to football's long, cosmopolitan history.

Furthermore, the migration of professional players does not reflect a linear progression from a closed national football market to an open world market, or from local or national to global influences. Rather, it is marked by the conflict that exists between, on the one hand, a high level of interconnectedness – for example through the hierarchic and tightly run world football organization FIFA (Eisenberg 2006a), the developments in telecommunication (including a large television audience), and the many new means of transport without which modern football would not be conceivable (Werron 2005) – and, on the other hand, national immigration policy, political limitations (by the nation-state or international organizations), and the national and local specificities of fans and other spectators visiting their stadium.

Finally, the migration of professional football players is not a phenomenon that can be isolated from the general socio-political situation, even if professional sport does have some legal and political peculiarities. The successful migration of footballers has more to do with the economic differences between regions of origin and those of destination, with the political conditions in the respective states, the policies of national and international organizations, the earlier colonial history of the countries of origin and/or destination, the history of post-colonialism, and of language, religion and other factors.[5]

In the case of professional football we can outline how difficult the current relationship is between transnational conditions of exploitation on the one hand and national (and European) citizenship on the other. The football stadium, in which professional players of different origins meet, is a space that – by transcending the border – reproduces national and European borders as an institution. The brief history of migration in football that follows illustrates how closely migration and nationalization (later Europeanization) have always been intertwined with this sport.

FOOTBALL PLAYERS' MIGRATION AND THE NATIONALIZATION OF FOOTBALL

The origins of football show that the migration of players is not a new phenomenon.[6] Football was originally a middle-class activity carried out mainly by students, and this had a social effect on its proliferation (cf. Chapter 3). As the enjoyment of playing ball with the foot instead of the hand emerged in nineteenth-century England, British students travelling abroad (for example to Switzerland) developed an increasing interest in this form of physical exercise.[7] As far as the cross-border mobility of the game and cross-border sporting activities at the end of the nineteenth century were concerned, the attractiveness lay in the values that were promoted in British sport that can still be found today in the lively (hobby) leagues, where no referees are required to judge whether or not a penalty should be given.

In England (and later in many other countries as well) football quickly developed into a proletarian sport, but the values it conveys are closely related to those of the Victorian middle classes (Lanfranchi and Taylor 2001: 15). The appeal lay in the concept of 'fair play', in the – until then unheard of – written rules, in particular clothing, in the use of English expressions such as 'football', 'sport' and so on, many of which still form part of the names of quite a few European clubs today (for example Football Club Barcelona, Genua F.C., Sporting Lissabon, Societa Sportiva Calcio Napoli). All this led to the creation of an anglophile atmosphere that was to convey, above all, modernity, openness, and cosmopolitanism; one was a 'sportsman', as opposed to just being a member of the local and national sports clubs.

This development, which led at the turn of the century to the founding of dedicated football clubs (i.e. clubs operating independently of rugby, rowing and cricket), is reflected in the similar biographies of the first club chairmen. These 'sportsmen' such as the Swiss Hans Gamper, who founded the Club de Football in the Catalan stronghold Barcelona, the Italian Vittorio Pozzo, who would later become a World Cup manager, or Walther Bensemann, who not only established the Karlsruhe football club but also the much-loved German football magazine *Kicker*, were each initially founder, chairman and player in one (Colomé 1999).

The fixtures from this time also show that the character of the sport could in no way be considered in exclusively national terms. Barcelona and Genoa were then closer to each other than Barcelona and Madrid. Furthermore, the first league games were not necessarily considered to be national championships as, for example, a Swiss or a Belgian team could be found playing in the French league. The teams themselves were also multinational: English was generally spoken, and the first clubs were dominated by Spanish, English, Swiss and other nationalities. Not even the umbrella organisation FIFA, which would later become so powerful, was composed solely of representatives of the national organizations.[8]

One could therefore ask what 'national football' actually is, and whether it can be seen as a style (cf. Wilson 2009; Lanfranchi and Taylor 2001), a particular way of playing, or as a competition taking place on a particular territory. While this question cannot be answered adequately, it does clarify existing inconsistencies.

The cosmopolitan game football was met by a counter-movement, in which newly established, nationally orientated clubs insisted on their right to exclude foreign players. Many of these clubs cultivate to this day remains of their animosity and their contrasting attitudes towards migrants, for example CF. Barcelona and Espanol Barcelona. But the powerful counter-movement of the national sporting organizations – founded out of necessity upon the announcement of a 'contest of the nations' – also changed conditions for the sport, and in particular for the travelling sportsman. Basically, one can speak of a complete 'nationalization of football' from the moment when a national association started organizing championships, cup competitions and international fixtures, as well as setting up a separate professional league.

In addition, the term 'football', both as a notion and a myth, was also nationalized and often linked to the prevailing national history. However, the development occurred at a different rate and with differing intensity. Well into the twentieth century, for example, many national associations, such as in Germany and the Netherlands, admitted only amateur players, while others organized no cup competitions or championships. Even the ideological nationalization proceeded differently, as with the Italian association, for example, for whom the English term 'football' was exchanged for the Italian *calcio*, while other associations maintained the Anglicism.

The biography of Bela Guttmann, born in Hungary and successful in countless countries as player and manager (e.g. as manager of famous teams such as Benfica Lissabon, and of some of the world's best players such as Ferenc Puskás and Eusébio da Silva Ferreira), demonstrates the whole ambivalence of these pioneering times in relation to nationalism and anti-Semitism:

> From the beginning, anti-Semitism played a not inconsiderable role in continental European professional football. The perception that some play only for money, while others play for honour, must have fuelled the prejudiced view that Jews could not be relied upon in football. This affected Jewish players, whether they played for Austria Vienna or for Hakoah. It was insinuated that both 'Jewish clubs' simply bought up all their players to make a team, and could afford to do so because they were swimming in money.
>
> (Claussen 2006: 36)[9]

For football migrants such as Bela Guttmann and for those potentially interested in migrating the situation became equally difficult, since they were more than ever a polarizing force – a precarious position that is, to some extent, still true today.

Another example is provided by Sepp Herberger, legendary World Cup manager in 1954 and former *Reichstrainer* in Nazi Germany, who made it clear to every player that a move abroad would lead to suspension from the national team. Cases of non-consideration such as this occurred in many countries, for example in the Netherlands. The term *legionnaire*, which originated in the middle of the nineteenth century, was often used disparagingly (Lanfranchi and Taylor 2001: 206, 211), and the appreciation of Uwe Seeler, German national striker in the 1960s, had as much to do with his refusal to accept a lucrative move to the Italian league as with his fighting style on the pitch.

In observing the nationalization of football it is particularly interesting to examine the strategies, and the changes to those strategies, employed by individual national associations in composing the national team and in attempting to differentiate between native and 'foreign' players in the first division. In particular, the period from the 1930s to the 1950s sheds light on various possibilities and also points to the arbitrariness in determining the nationality of football players.[10]

> From early on, Italy proved to be a magnet in twentieth century professional football. The country started to catch up internationally from the mid-20s, a run that was crowned with victories in the World Cup competitions of 1934 and 1938. The Italian fascists encouraged the building of stadia and were not, in contrast to the later attitude of the German national socialists, averse to professionalism. The Italian league became an attractive place for foreign managers, particularly those from the Danube Monarchy.
>
> (Claussen 2006: 82)

In the 1930s, when Italy was ruled by the fascist dictator and sports fan, Benito Mussolini, emphasis was placed on allowing only Italian players to play in the league and on the national team. But who was Italian? At this time, special rules applied to Argentinian players with Italian roots: it was not required of them to become Italians in order to play in Italy, but rather – such as in the case of the later World Cup champion Raimundo Orsi – all players from Argentina, Brazil and, partly, Uruguay, who had Italian ancestors, were considered to be Italian. 'Of the 351 foreign players who played professionally in Italy between 1929 and 1965, over half (176) came from Argentina, Brazil or Uruguay, and the majority had Italian origins' (Taylor 2006: 17).

The *reinpatriati*, those who were Italian by 'blood' (descent) and not by birthplace, were numerous and a welcome reinforcement to the World Cup winning teams of 1934 and 1938, despite the fact that some of them could not speak Italian. Other countries with a similar emigrant tradition like Spain and Portugal developed similar migration paths for footballers, by more or less nationalizing the sons of one-time natives of their respective countries. While '70% of foreign stars in Spanish football during the 1970s came from South America, only seven South Americans in total played in the German *Bundesliga* between 1963 and 1983' (Taylor 2006: 17).

Although it cannot be examined in further detail here, the fact that some countries were also dictatorships is of great interest, especially as it turns out that many early idols had been players in pro-fascist clubs. Their biographies would demonstrate the inconsistent complexity of football migration in mid-century. Many were, for example, players in the Hungarian team which, incidentally, would lose the World Cup Final against Germany in Berne in 1954. They fled communist lands as political migrants (which was unusual, as most footballers migrate for economic reasons) and went to countries with better opportunities to earn money that were also anticommunist states, such as Spain (Eisenberg *et al.* 2004).

Many developing migratory paths still exist today and some of these methods are still used to recruit players. The recent case of AS Roma and its Brazilian player Cafu provides an example:

> 'I sent five airplanes to South America to find Cafu's grandfather', boasted the President recently, and everyone imagined dozens of qualified genealogists pouring out of the plane. The experts calmly strode through the darkest primeval forests and the loneliest mountains, no path was too rugged, no water too deep. When, after months of intensive searching, they finally re-emerged, they triumphantly held a yellowing document aloft: 'Presidente Sensi, mission accomplished, Marcos Evangilista de Moraes Cafu is Italian. We can attest that his granddad migrated from Italy to Brazil'.
>
> (Schönau 2000)

The migratory paths described here were used by some countries in order to obtain skilful players for a closed nation and to find them in former colonies or in economically dependent countries. 'Significantly, these migratory routes have by and large remained over time' (Taylor 2006: 17).

Great Britain was open to South Africans, and Belgium to the Africans from its colonies. France could access even more African talents because at that time football, in contrast to cycling, was not seen as a stronghold of national feeling to be defended from outside influence. Moreover, the multicultural integration of people from post-colonial states formed, indeed still forms, an important component in the self-image of France. However, the difficulties that exist in determining French citizens who qualify to play in the national team or in the league, can be seen, for example, in the different types of citizens concerned: dual citizens, e.g. Algerians who play in France; children of migrants who are, like the son of Algerian migrants, Zinedine Zidane, French citizens; children of migrants who, like many Algerians, are allowed to play for the land of their fathers, and migrant footballers, who continue to have another nationality and can use the advantages of migration to improve their own living conditions. While the French World Cup winners 1998 have been called the 'migrant world champions', many of the players were actually 'French' from the beginning of their sporting careers, i.e. most of them were born in France or had held French citizenship all their lives.

I emphasized that the migration of footballers does not represent a linear development towards the free market, but rather that the mobility of professional footballers has always been influenced by the regulating nature of national demarcations. The preceding description of certain migratory conditions, the earlier history of colonization and the migration paths that were established and still exist, should not be described as a new form of globalization, but rather as the utilization of migratory paths in a time of expanding international markets. These markets are defined precisely by the differences in the prices of players between countries of origin and destination. What has changed in the last decades, however, is the – at one time valid – restriction of foreigners as professionals in the squads of European national leagues.

THE BOSMAN CASE

Until the 1960s there were no common regulations as to how many foreign players were allowed to play in the national football leagues in the UEFA, the European umbrella organization (Thomé 2003: 157; Lanfranchi and Taylor 2001). In the 1970s and 1980s only two foreign players were permitted to play in a professional team, the rule being extended by the UEFA to a three-plus-two quota in 1991, allowing three foreigners and two 'assimilated' foreign players on the pitch (Lanfranchi and Taylor 2001). Players counted as assimilated if they had played at least five years in the respective countries, and of these at least three years in a youth team (Thomé 2003: 158f.).

These special UEFA rules were maintained, despite many attempts by the EU to achieve compliance with Article 48 of the Treaty of Rome, which guarantees the free movement of workers and which was restricted by the quota. Then the famous Bosman case came about in 1995 (Flory 1997; Berthold and Neumann 2005). Jean-Marc Bosman, a Belgian professional footballer with RFC Liège, brought an action in which he claimed that his right to choose his place of work within Europe was constricted by the prevailing limitations caused by the transfer system. Until then, it was possible for clubs to prevent a player with an expiring contract from leaving the team, either by utilizing an option to extend the contract for a further year (even for less payment) or by imposing a high transfer fee that was often impossible to pay for the new interested club. The UEFA argued that national teams would come under threat if too many foreign players played in the leagues, that footballers could not be considered to be workers in the normal sense, and, finally, that 'Football Europe' and the Europe of the EU, in which this law was implemented, were not identical (Lanfranchi and Taylor 2001). After the decision of the European Court of Justice, which rendered a judgement in favour of Bosman, the consequences were discussed by the media and by players, in Germany for instance, as follows:

> More and more foreigners are taking the ball off German players. German professional football is facing a definite turning point. It can be assumed that already during the course of the rest of this season, the massive import of foreign players will lead to an overwhelming majority in the first teams of the Bundesliga clubs.

> (Frankfurter Rundschau 1999)[11]

Generally, the Bosman decision – a year later also implemented by the UEFA, who maintained the regulation that restricted the number of non-UEFA players on the pitch to three – is an indication of the borderless expansion of markets or, put another way, an example for an increasing deregulation of markets. Considering the transfers of Eastern European players to leagues such as the German *Bundesliga*, it is plain to see what this means. Particular clubs such as Energie Cottbus, which does not possess the financial power of larger clubs, engaged cheaper players from Eastern Europe, to the extent that Cottbus fielded the very first completely non-German team. At one stage, Cottbus had 17 non-German players in its squad (Thomé 2003: 168).

However, the revolution that everyone expected in the wake of the Bosman ruling failed to materialize. While the number of foreign players since 1995 multiplied almost fivefold up to 2005, the percentage of foreign European players did not jump that significantly (Lanfranchi and Taylor 2001: 222). In the German *Bundesliga*, for example, in the 1994–95 season just before the Bosman judgement, 110 out of 460 players were foreigners (23.9 per cent), the vast majority (81 players) coming from European countries. In 1997–98, shortly after the Bosman case, 188 out of 473 players were foreigners (39 per cent), out of which 143 players immigrated from Europe. In 2002–03, after the restriction on non-UEFA players was lifted from three to five, 281 out of 542 players were foreigners (51.8 per cent). More than half of the players (194) came from Europe while out of the remaining 87 players 45 came from South America (out of which 31 immigrated from Brazil) and 27 from Africa (Thomé 2003).

Before Bosman, in short, migration in professional football was a 'privilege' of elite players; since Bosman, those cost-intensive European players are facing stronger competition from countries such as Brazil, Ghana, Argentina, Nigeria and Cameroon, none of which are EU members. What has changed is that an increasing number of agents search for young, cheap players like Maldini, the character in the novel, in poor countries that offer the raw material 'footballer' for comparatively little money. As a result, players no longer migrate to or between top European leagues to play in their famous mediatized stadia. They are also transferred to lower, semi-professional leagues with low wages and without crowded stadia or TV advertisement contracts where, if they do not fail, they are often forced to stay (Lanfranchi and Taylor 2001; Thomé 2003).

HIERARCHIES IN FOOTBALL PLAYERS' MIGRATION

In order to understand these developments certain aspects of the labour market of football migrants have to be analysed. Most importantly, the migration of professional players is hierarchical. There is a small group of elite emigrants such as Diego Maradona in former times and Ronaldo, Ronaldinho or Michael Ballack today, who change their place of work within the European top leagues. They earn millions, which turns them into superstars (Lanfranchi and Taylor 2001: 226). They play in the famous stadia of clubs such as Real Madrid, Chelsea or AC Milan in front of millions of European television spectators.[12] Enormous advertising contracts for commercials featuring football superstars are transmitted worldwide In good weather, such superstars can even be viewed by Maldini of the novel. They are the true protagonists of globalization. To put it another way: The best players in the world are migrants. They play in stadia which form part of a close transnational network.

On the other side there are many clubs which rely on national players, mostly young, aspiring talents who are supplemented by players from abroad, and for whom these clubs are sometimes a springboard to a greater career. Among these, however, there are many clubs that exist on the periphery. They offer precarious working conditions solely connected to football: no advertising contracts and no stardom. In these clubs players are considerably less mobile and are tied to local conditions.

The migration of Franz Beckenbauer from Bayern Munich to Cosmos New York in 1976, near the end of his career, is a very different kind of migration than that of the young Sammy Kouffour, who moved from Ghana to Bayern Munich at the beginning of his career (Lanfranchi and Taylor 2001: 141–166). Some players, like those from former Yugoslavia or from Denmark, who take on short-term contracts and move between European clubs, are primarily concerned with continually improving their financial situation, whereas players who stick with one club and become settled have another motivation entirely (cf. Geyer 2006 on the Serbian player Marco Pantelic).

At the same time, the migration of professional football players has created a (not always transparent) market for players' agents, some of whom are lawyers, managers, or former professional players. These agents try to secure purchase options on talented players for themselves. They deal with transfer rights and provide, for example, many Brazilian players for the European football market. Brazilians, citizens of the land of the most-often world champion, are the most coveted players in the world (Jönsson 2006). Thanks to state borders, there are many possibilities to increase the profit on transfer deals. One example is provided by the Brazilian player Zé Roberto who, prior to his transfer to Europe, was sold to Uruguay for a short period, and from there to Real Madrid. Sometimes players are loaned to their former clubs and then sold. Because the tax on transfers is lower in Uruguay than elsewhere, both the player and the agent thus benefit more from the transfer fee (Spiegel online 2009).

It is also possible that others want to profit from transfers, such as the parents of Brazilian youngsters who, along with clubs, abandon all future rights to the talented boy in return for a particular sum. The trade in footballing children is increasing, which reflects the difficult situation of many talented boys (Goos 2006). Often the future is unclear and the youths disappear, as we saw at the beginning with Moussa, the player from Maldini's village. Sometimes they must work off their debts and probably remain illegally in the new country. Obtaining new passports with the intention of becoming European – a Brazilian becoming Portuguese, for example – can in those cases usually be ruled out. Wherever national borders determine national membership, border violation is sure to follow.

This overview of migratory phenomena among footballers shows not so much a general alignment with a global market but rather a division into geographic segments and spaces, that are heavily influenced by persisting national or European borders. National and European associations continue to get involved in the regulation of the political integration of players – one need look no further than the search for Italian or Spanish relatives of South American professionals by Bayern Munich (such as Claudio Pizarro from Peru, Martín Demichelis from Argentina and Julio Dos Santos from Paraguay) in order to secure their EU credentials by means of dual nationalities and to reduce the proportion of non-EU players. And whenever the World Cup comes around there is usually an outcry at the players' lack of match practice at their clubs and talk of measures to distribute playing time among national players, thus providing them with an advantage. This is a process that is quite common in other sports such as volleyball, where entire national youth teams can partake in national competitions.

Furthermore, the professional players' market is not only dependent on economic factors. Cultural prejudices and integration problems can quickly become economically relevant, as is the case with the Italian first division club Lazio Rom, a team that has drawn media and legal attention due to its rightwing fans (and a player regularly displaying a fascist salute). The Dutch player Aron Winter, dark-skinned and with a Jewish name, was eventually prevented from joining the club (Europäisches Parlament 1996). The lack of willingness among fans to integrate can certainly act as an important factor in the search for a destination and forms, in itself, a sort of border. In the lower Berlin leagues some 70 matches have been abandoned due to racist conflict. Black players have similar experiences even at FC Barcelona as the Cameroon player Samuel Eto'o can testify.

Here again, it is the distinctive space of the stadium and the peculiar characteristics of its form that concentrates an – occasionally hostile – crowd. Much more than an urban street, it is a space where the migrant player is subjected to the power and scrutiny of the public gaze. In this very focused space the player can become the subject of both cheers of approbation, as well as the object of humiliation and racial abuse. Racist filth shouted from the stands can make the game for many migrant players simply unbearable.

While in this respect the migration of footballers does not differ greatly from that of most migrant groups, in other aspects conditions for them are completely different, as with 'green cards' and migration controls. Even as a migrant, the football star cannot be compared to the mass of other migrants, at least as far as sport regulations and other migratory paths are concerned. In Germany this is covered by the current *German Employment Regulation* for 'specific groups of persons':

> Residence permits can be granted without prior consent to professional athletes or to professional trainers, who intend to participate in German sports clubs or comparable competing sporting institutions, providing they have reached their 16th year, providing the club or institution will pay a gross salary that is at least 50% of the income threshold for statutory pension insurance, and providing the confirmation of the sporting qualifications of the professional athletes and the professional qualifications of the trainers by the relevant German umbrella organisation responsible for the sport in question, in cooperation with the German National Institute of Sport.
>
> (Deutsche Beschäftigungsverordnung für Besondere Personengruppen: §7)

Nor can the flow of migration between different countries be regulated. Although 'peripheral' countries such as Brazil and many African countries are suppliers of footballing resources to the European leagues, not all economically important states are affected in the same manner. There is, for example, a growing market for players in the USA and Japan, but their development is not as affected by migratory flow as it is in Europe. Even in countries such as Brazil, which is fighting high levels of poverty, there are large clubs that can hold on to some players that would normally have gone straight to Europe (Lanfranchi and Taylor 2001; Eisenberg 2006a, 2006b).

All in all, it seems that national borders will always maintain a sort of *Lumpenproletariat*. To put it bluntly, who is seriously interested in removing the conditions that lead to migration? Certain conditions will not change in the foreseeable future. FIFA, the recognized head association as far as the organization of the most important international tournaments and the creation of the framework regulating the international transfer market is concerned, has decreed that a player, regardless of where she or he lives or plays or wishes to play, may be a first team player for only one nation. The World Cup championship is therefore safe, and the teams will continue to consist of mandatory national players. But these, too, are increasingly affected by regulation. Brazilians not only play for the Brazilian national team or for their former colonial masters, the Portuguese, but also for the Japanese and Tunisians.

THE STADIUM AS 'PROMISED LAND'

Have you ever heard of Maldini? By now we have gained an impression of the Maldinis of the football world, of their aspirations and migratory routes which may – or, in recent years, more often, may not – lead them to their yearned-for destination. This is no longer just Europe since a move there or, increasingly, to the US or Japan, can no longer be equated with a successful career as a professional. Their dream remains to play in one of the large mediatized European stadia. They are more than ever synonyms for success, as many other football migrants' destinies in Europe end up as members of a cheap workforce in one of the lower leagues. Only when we see them in the stadium have football migrants from the periphery achieved their aim and reached their migrant destination. The stadium therefore appears as a contradictory location. It is a site where some migrants realize their dreams by obtaining one of the few profit-yielding positions in the global contest for better living conditions but also one where national demarcations and the regulations of national and international associations provide the distinctions for sorting out the sought-for from the unwanted. For those who fail, the stadium remains unattainable.

In sum, professional football has developed working conditions that have turned football players into migrants and different countries into suppliers of an inexpensive workforce. For professional football we can outline how difficult the current relationship between transnational conditions of exploitation like the common European market on the one hand and political affiliation on the other appears to be. The transnational space of the football stadium, where professional players of various descent meet, is also a space that – by crossing the border – reproduces the national border as an institution that makes distinctions. This is personified in the individual player's biography and determines his or her migratory path. Whether you are French, Dutch or German, whether from Africa, Brazil or Eastern Europe, can be crucial for your market value since human resources in the case of football players are dependent on origin, price, mobility and cultural acceptance. The playground is a marketplace that produces distinctions along the line of ethnicity.

At one point in the novel we learn that the village team for which Maldini plays is starting to break up. The players are tired of listening to the trainer's warnings about their aspirations to go to Europe. They have made their decision. Professional football can be a curse or an opportunity.

NOTES

1 I wish to thank Carolyn Kelly for her excellent translation. My thanks also go to Jürgen Ehbrecht for our conversations on the subject.

2 *Goal 2 – Living the Dream* is the second part of the football movie trilogy *Goal!* (first part: *The Dream Begins*). In the first part a fictional player from Mexico succeeds to play football in an English professional club; in the second part his dream of playing for Real Madrid in its famous stadium comes true (Goal! 2008).

3 Cf. in this context Werron (2005) who discusses the criteria for a sport to be classified as a world sport. As opposed to football, the different boxing world federations cannot select a common world champion, and a fringe sport like shooting cannot count on sponsors and the attention of the media, except for an important world event like the Olympics. The documentation of records is especially important for a world sport, whereby results can be made comparable. Record holder with regard to the football World Cup is Brazil with five victories. Cf. Eisenberg (2006a) for the history of the FIFA and Chisari (2006) for the relevance of television for the World Cup in 1966 in England.

4 Fundamental in this area is the book *Moving with the Ball* by Pierre Lanfranchi and Matthew Taylor (2001), which also points to the rudimentary nature of the current state of research. Cf. also Taylor (2006) who discusses different theoretical frameworks and Eisenberg (2006b) who reviews academic and popular books and articles on football history.

5 It is therefore very important to use the migration system approach as adopted by Taylor (2006). This helps to see the relationships between countries. 'At a basic level, a migration system is constituted by a group of countries that exchange relatively large numbers of migrants with each other. Such a system may only include two countries, but normally involves all those linked by unusually large migration flows. The existence of a system would also need to include other linkages between countries, such as historical, cultural and colonial ties, along of course with economic connections. [. . .] Systems evolve over time: the product not of short-term flows, but recurrent patterns of migration. But their relative stability and structure does not mean that these systems are not open to change and adaptation over time, responsive to changing social, demographic, economic and political circumstances' (Taylor 2006: 22).

6 Cf. on this and on the following points Lanfranchi and Taylor (2001), Lanfranchi (1999), Schulze-Marmeling (2000). Cf. specifically on Brazil's path to football Goerdeler (2006), for a history of football tactics Wilson (2009).

7 'The early success of football in continental Europe was directly connected with the mobility of economic elites in the second half of the nineteenth century. British citizens were certainly involved in these initial stages but intra-European migration played a major role … [Private schools like the Ecole de la Chatelaine in Geneva] recruited a large number of their students from Britain, and built football grounds on their premises' (Lanfranchi and Taylor 2001: 19).

8 Notably the history of the Mitropa-cup, a contest between clubs and cities of Middle Europe, can be regarded as an illustration of pre-national competitions. This development arose before the First World War and was institutionalized partly between the World Wars. In the course of the formation of new national states institutions came up that helped generating national competitions (Lanfranchi 1999).

9 Claussen addresses the close relationship between football history and anti-Semitism (cf. Schulze-Marmeling 2003).

10 Cf. for an overview of the different entry and playing requirements that were established by each national association Taylor (2006) and Dietschy (2006).

11 For discussions in England cf. King (2007).

12 As far as merchandising is concerned, Manchester United is the most successful global player in the club football market. The sale of their jerseys is booming all over the world. Whoever watches television reports covering the many natural disasters in India, Africa or Asia will spot numerous Manchester United jerseys among the fleeing people.

REFERENCES

Bale, J. (2005) 'Stadien als Grenzen und Überwachungsräume', in M. Marschik, R. Müllner, G. Spitaler and M. Zinganel (eds) *Das Stadion. Geschichte, Architektur, Politik, Ökonomie*, Wien: Turia + Kant.

Berthold, N. and Neumann, M. (2005) *Der gemeinsame Europäische Fußballmarkt – benötigt Deutschland eine Ausländerklausel?*, Würzburg: Wirtschaftswissenschaftliche Beiträge Nr. 75.

Chisari, F. (2006) 'When football went global', *Historical Social Research*, 1: 42–54.

Claussen, D. (2006) *Bela Guttmann*, Berlin: Berenberg.

Colomé, G. (1999) 'Fußball und nationale Identität in Katalonien. F.C. Barcelona und Espanol', in S. Gehrmann (ed.) *Fußball und Region in Europa*, Münster: LIT.

Deutsche Beschäftigungsverordnung (§7) für 'Besondere Personengruppen' (German Employment Regulation for 'specific groups of persons') (2004) *Beschäftigungsverordnung*, Bundesgesetzblatt I, Heft 62.

Dietschy, P. (2006) 'Football players' migrations: A political stake', *Historical Social Research*, 1: 31–41.

Diome, F. (2003) *Le Ventre de l'Atlantique*, Paris: Anne Carrière.

Eisenberg, C., Lanfranchi, P., Mason, T. and Wahl, A. (2004) *FIFA 1904–2004. 100 Jahre Weltfußball*, Göttingen: Die Werkstatt.

Eisenberg, C. (2006a) 'FIFA 1975–2000: The business of a football development organisation', *Historical Social Research*, 1: 55–68.

—— (2006b) 'International bibliography of football history', *Historical Social Research*, 1: 170–208.

Europäisches Parlament (1996) *Bericht über das Problem des Hooliganismus und die Freizügigkeit der Fußballfans*. Online. Available www.europarl.europa.eu/omk/sipade3?PUBREF=-//EP//TEXT+REPORT+A4-1996-0124+0+DOC+XML+V0//DE&L=EN&LEVEL=0&NAV=S&LSTDOC=Y (accessed 25 April 2006).

Flory, M. (1997) *Der Fall Bosman. Revolution im Fußball?*, Kassel: Agon.

Frankfurter Rundschau (1999) *Multikulti im Strafraum*, Zfg A 101, 18 February.

Geyer, M. (2006) 'Der Söldner', *Spiegel Special 'Planet Fußball'*, 2.

Goal! (2008) Official film website (film). Online. Available www.bvimovies.com/uk/goal2/index.html?hbx.hrf=http://en.wikipedia.org/wiki/Goal! (accessed 1 August 2009).

Goerdeler, C. (2006) 'Futebol! Futebol!', *Die Zeit*, 17.

Goos, H. (2006) 'Der König der Heimlichkeit', *Spiegel Special 'Planet Fußball'*, 2.

Held, D., McGrew, A., Goldblatt, D. and Perration, J. (1999) *Global Transformations*, Cambridge: Polity Press.

Jönsson, H. (2006) 'Die Spielerfabrik', *11 Freunde*, 53: 30–46.

King, Stephen (2007) *Football, Migration and the Blame Game*. Online. Available www.independent.co.uk/news/buiseness/comment/stephen-king-football-migration-and-the-blame-game-400988.html (accessed 1 August 2009).

Lanfranchi, P. (1999) 'Die Anfänge des Fußballs in den Regionen des westlichen Mittelmeeres', in S. Gehrmann (ed.) *Fußball und Region in Europa*, Münster: LIT.

Lanfranchi, P. and Taylor, M. (2001) *Moving with the Ball*, Oxford/New York: Berg.

Runciman, D. (2006) 'They can play, but they never can win', *New Statesman*, 29 May.

Schönau, B. (2000) 'Ahnenforschung auf Italienisch', *Süddeutsche Zeitung*, 13 April.

Schulze-Marmeling, D. (2000) *Fußball: Zur Geschichte eines globalen Sports*, Göttingen: Die Werkstatt.

Schulze-Marmeling, D. (ed.) (2003) *Davidstern und Lederball*, Göttingen: Werkstatt.

Spiegel online (2009) 'Dreieckstransfer', *Spiegel online*. Online. Available www.spiegel.de/sport/fussball/0,1518,druck-645773,00.html (accessed 30 August 2009).

Taylor, M. (2006) 'Global players? Football, migration and globalization, 1930–2000', *Historical Social Research*, 1: 7–30.

Thomé, M. (2003) 'Ausländer in der Fußball-Bundesliga', *Volkskunde in Rheinland-Pfalz*, 18(2). Online. Available www.volkskunde-rheinland-pfalz.de/seiten/zeitschrift/2003_02/berufsfussballer.pdf. (accessed 25 April 2006).

Transfermarkt (2009) 'Paolo Maldini', *www. transfermarkt.co.uk*. Online. Available www.transfermarkt.co.uk (accessed 1 August 2009).

Werron, T. (2005) 'Der Weltsport und sein Publikum', *Zeitschrift für Soziologie*, Sonderheft 'Weltgesellschaft': 260–89.

Wilson, J. (2009) *Inverting the Pyramid*, London: Orion.

WM-Almanach (2006) *Spiegel Special 'Planet Fußball'*, 2.

Chapter 8: Going to the Match

The Transformation of the Match-day Routine at Manchester City FC[1]

Tim Edensor and Steve Millington

In December 1999 the English Professional Footballer's Association (PFA) lavished £1.9 million on L.S. Lowry's (1953) oil painting 'Going to the Match', depicting football fans converging on Bolton Wanderers' Burnden Park stadium (Figure 8.1). PFA Chief Executive Gordon Taylor opined how the painting represented 'the heart and soul of the game and the anticipation of fans on their way to a match' (BBC News 1999). This iconic image provides an alluring, if romantic glimpse back to a football world untainted by the excesses of the contemporary game, a world where traditional values of community and loyalty are upheld, where routines built up over generations would cumulate on the terraces at 3 p.m. each Saturday. Importantly, as Kelsall reminds us:

> The identities of these clubs and their grounds was part of, and often a focus
> for, a stubborn pride, that people had for their community. The roar of the
> crowds assembled inside these grounds would be a collective assertion of this
> identity, community and mutual affinity.
>
> (Kelsall 2000: 88)

Burnden Park, like many early English football stadia, was located in an inner-city working-class neighbourhood where many supporters lived and worked (Giulianotti 1999). The style and design of these grounds was constrained by their location, often found on small sites within rows of densely packed terraced houses. These stadia appeared deceptively small from the outside, but their particular layout, comprising long straight tiered stands within several feet of the playing area, combined with vertiginous standing terraces, enabled huge numbers of people to enter and watch the game. Many were designed by Scottish architect Archibald Leitch, and one of his designs, Manchester City's Maine Road stadium (1923), continues to hold the English club record attendance of 84,569 set in a 1934 FA Cup game between the hosts and Stoke City. These functional stadia, accommodating masses, predated the automobile age and so possessed little parking space. For supporters, the experience of

Figure 8.1
L.S. Lowry: *Going to the Match*, oil painting, 1953.

'going to the match' focused upon surrounding sites and spaces, the pubs, shops, take-aways, bookmakers, food-stands, alleyways and streets (Kelsall 2000). The match-day routines established in such landscapes over decades conjures a particular sensory landscape of affordances, spatial practices, performances and power, through which football supporters, street vendors, the police, city authorities and others produced rhythms of fluctuating intensity and meaning.

In the twenty-first century, following industrial restructuring and suburban flight, fewer English supporters now reside in such localities and typically drive into the city to watch their team (Crabbe *et al.* 2006), and the scene depicted by Lowry is disappearing. Yet myths of 'going to the match' continue to resonate in extended fan culture, particularly in fanzines or on radio phone-in debates about how match day routines have been disrupted and dislocated through stadium relocation and redesign.

Despite this, the exploration of the complex and dynamic relationship between fans and their team rarely extends to uncover how football is embedded in everyday life. Stone, for example, calls for greater attention to the 'everyday and the structuring of football in many people's lives: the regularity of the match, the topophilic affinity of supporters for their team's 'home' ground and the habitual behaviours that make up football culture' (2007: 175). And while numerous studies explore fan culture within stadia, few focus on the everyday spaces and routines of match-day experience. Moreover, there is an overwhelming concentration on the most passionate or dedicated fans, football hooligans, or groups who resist the embourgeoisment of football (Duke 2002).

In this chapter we suggest that the relationships forged between individuals and localities through the rituals and performances that comprise 'going to the match', encompassing the everyday spaces that both surround football stadia and comprise journeys to and from them, is a neglected aspect of fan culture. As the experience of travelling to and from stadia is being transformed through the contemporary restructuring of football, this is of particular significance.

The City of Manchester Stadium (COMS) and Manchester City F.C. provide an excellent case study through which to examine how stadium relocation and the loss of a localised place-based identity has impacted on fan culture. In 2003 the club took up residency at the spectacular, iconic COMS, constructed as the centrepiece of an urban regeneration scheme, Sport City, in a former industrial area in East Manchester. This development serves efforts to re-image Manchester at a national and global scale. Previously, City had played at Maine Road in South Manchester since 1923, and the club and fan base was ingrained in this locale.

We first contextualise our discussion by looking broadly at stadium redevelopment in England and then detail Manchester City's particular move. We then develop an analysis of the topophilic homeliness of Maine Road, using fans' descriptions of their experiences of the old ground to demonstrate how 'going to the match' was embedded in localised, place-based sites, rituals and performances. We focus upon the routines, textures, atmospheres and homeliness of the area surrounding the former site, and subsequent feelings of loss and alienation.

MOVING 'HOME': THE CITY OF MANCHESTER STADIUM

Since the 1990 Taylor Report an increasing number of English football clubs have either deserted or are planning to relocate from their traditional homes within working-class neighbourhoods (cf. Chapter 1). Leitch's functional spaces of mass entertainment are now seen as obsolete, a barrier to fulfilling commercial potential (van Dam 2000), for new stadia are the centrepieces of larger retail leisure zones containing a diverse range of commercial activity and niche markets, thereby reducing reliance on football-generated income (cf. Chapter 4).

The geography of stadia relocation is varied. Wealthier clubs, such as Manchester United and Chelsea, have redeveloped their existing grounds. Other developments have occurred close to old grounds, including Arsenal's Emirates Stadium, whereas others have moved to suburban or out-of-town sites, close to motorways or transport hubs, such as Bolton Wanderers' Reebok Stadium. Yet others have relocated to former industrial or brown-field sites, where stadium developments are integrated within broader urban regeneration and place branding strategies (Giulianotti 1999).

However, proposals to move clubs outside of city boundaries can be fiercely resisted by supporters, as with Everton's planned move from Liverpool to Huyton. Kelsall (2000) refers to 'displacement' anxieties when a club moves from its traditional home. Bale (1999) also suggests that new stadia are often highly controlled spaces of surveillance and crowd management, 'isotopic enclaves', whereby behaviours associated with standing on terraces are no longer tolerated (cf. Chapter 1). Similarly, adjacent large open spaces and access boulevards allow the easy deployment of crowd control tactics and extend what Bale (1993) describes as a 'carceral archipelago'. Giulianotti and Robertson (2004) alert us to the spectre of de-territorialisation, the perceived decoupling of football and local identity (Phelps 2005) with the development of such 'sterile sporting spaces' (Silk 2004).

Since the mid-1980s Manchester has undergone extensive regeneration, with stringent attempts to replace the image of a grey, 'northern', ex-industrial image with a new 'cosmopolitan', European, culturally sophisticated reputation. Sport has played an important role in this transformation, notably two Olympic Games bids followed by a successful hosting of the 2002 Commonwealth Games. These sports-related developments have played a key role in shifting regeneration into 'East Manchester', a depressed, ex-industrial community (Gratton *et al.* 2005; Smith and Fox 2007).

In 1999 an Urban Regeneration Company, New East Manchester Ltd, was established to oversee the renewal of a 1,900 ha area east of the city centre through the 'Sports City' complex, which occupied a former gasworks site. Sports City comprises several inter-related facilities including: two athletics stadia; fitness and health studios; the National Squash Centre; a Regional Tennis Centre; and the National Cycling Centre. Although a Supercasino planned for the site failed to materialise, the area has attracted investment in new gentrified housing and a retail park. In terms of future development, Sports City will be connected to Manchester's Metrolink tram network by 2012.

The centrepiece is the 48,000 capacity COMS, designed by Arup Associates. Initially constructed as an athletics stadium for the 2002 Commonwealth Games, it was expanded to host Manchester City F.C., who became permanent tenants in 2003. City added a superstore, café and social club, museum and stadium tour, hospitality suites, extensive corporate boxes and conference facilities. The relocation radically altered the spatial dynamics between the club and the city of Manchester. Maine Road originally had been City's base for 80 years and for most supporters was regarded as the club's spiritual home. Like many British football stadia it was located in a densely populated working-class and multi-ethnic neighbourhood, from which the club originally drew its main support. The spaces around Maine Road evoke a classically Mancunian working-class landscape of small red-bricked terraced houses and back-alleys, interspersed with cornershops and back-street pubs, and latterly, various ethnic eateries. Maine Road could be accessed via a myriad of different routes from all directions, although the ground itself could remain almost invisible to an encroaching supporter until they turned the last street corner.

When Maine Road set the club attendance record the ground was mainly uncovered terraces.[2] In the post-war period, however, successive redevelopments greatly reduced its capacity, which fell to 52,000 in the 1970s as new seated stands were constructed. Following the Taylor Report the club's famous pitch-length terrace, the Kippax, was demolished and replaced by a three-tier all-seater stand which further reduced capacity to 34,000. By the 1990s, the four radically asymmetrical stands, replete with obstructed views and poor sight lines, mirrored the club's well-documented off-field mismanagement. Nevertheless, the ground's quirkiness was cherished by fans.

However, City's dire financial position prevented any form of mass redevelopment, so the allure of a relatively inexpensive move to a purpose-built 48,000 capacity stadium only a few miles away proved irresistible. Relocation, therefore, became a matter of financial expediency, necessary to secure the long-term future of the club. Following an emotional final game in 2003, the turnstiles closed for the last time and the ground was demolished over the summer months. The site is now the home of the Divine Mercy Primary School, located on Blue Moon Way amongst new housing on streets named after City legends. As we discuss, topophilic associations with Maine Road continue to resonate strongly within Manchester City's support, although at the time the planned relocation was met with relatively little resistance.

TOPOPHILIA

The experiential memories of Maine Road resonate with Bale's (1999) use of the concept of 'topophilia', a strong sense of belonging to place informed by fans' experiences inside the stadium: occupation of the same spot over years, the historical catalogue of dramatic events on the pitch, the varying fortunes of the team, half-time refreshments, the smell of bovril and the waft of cigarette smoke, the jokes and chants, and the whole rich panoply of successive shared events that become sedimented in the inhabitation of the stadium as a home from home (cf. Chapter 9). However, we focus on the broader topophilic sense associated with a diffuse area to which the stadium is connected and of which it is part. Accordingly, we explore how these sensations and routines extend out into a wider space of belonging, a space of paths, fixtures, familiar textures and stopping points to and from the match; a space of conviviality and atmosphere.

For Guano the narratives produced by football fans and their descriptions of their movements to and from stadia are 'practical spatial narratives: meaningful actions that organise space into places and that can become more or less explicit prescriptions for walking and looking, for sensing and thinking' (2003: 360). We stress that places at all scales, whether stadia or the areas which surround them or the city to which they belong, are not self-contained envelopes but always exist in relation to other places as part of infinitely complex spatial networks (Massey 1995). Places thus possess no essence but are always in a process of becoming, seething with emergent properties, though often stabilised by regular patterns of activity. Cities as a whole are ceaselessly (re)constituted out of their connections, the 'twists and fluxes of interrelation' (Amin and Thrift 2002: 30) through which 'multiple networked mobilities of capital, persons, objects, signs and information' (Urry 2006: ix) are brought together to produce a particular, but ever-changing, complex mix of heterogeneous social interactions, materialities and mobilities, imaginaries and social effects.

It is thus impossible to place a boundary around a place other than for administrative purposes, and this especially applies to urban areas that are rarely marked off from the rest of the city. A diffuse realm, the place of the stadium is reproduced by fans at different scales, through the routes by which individuals and groups use to make their way towards the match. Specifically, these net-worked characteristics of the place of the stadium are illustrated by the ways in which City fans used to descend upon Maine Road from all over Manchester and beyond, usually making their way via predictable modes of transport, routes and routine procedures. This place around the ground is and was reproduced in many other ways: by the habits and norms of inhabitants, service providers, officials and businesses. However, a distinct sense of place is reproduced by fans on match-days and lingers through the effects of this variegated mass activity. Accordingly, we exemplify how the stadium is not a disconnected entity into which fans pour in and out but is intimately connected to adjacent spaces at various scales.

Besides existing in a particular locational context, the stadium also has a temporal existence. While its physical existence was secured by endless mainte-nance and use, its symbolic significance emerged from its importance as a venue for home matches: the meaning and use of the stadium and its sur-roundings was re-inscribed every match day. Then, areas close to a stadium and connected to it were revitalised, and although these sites were reproduced differently at other times, fans' presence was marked on space, and these absent presences continue to charge the relatively empty streets and bars with heavy significance for supporters, producing a hauntedness following the stadi-um's demolition. This temporality of place for regular fans is further entrenched by continuities in attendance over years through which memories stack up, become sedimented and intensify a sense of homely belonging. A knowledge of the area is consolidated, a competence at how to get to the match on time and rehearse regular routines of sustenance, friendship, anticipation and leisure. Here we acknowledge both cognitive understandings of the stadium's surrounding area as a familiar, homely, communal place, and the affective, sensual qualities through which place is less reflexively experienced through exploring four interrelated themes: fans pre- and post-match spatial routines; the material fabric that constitutes place and shapes fans' behaviour; the sensual and atmospheric associations to which fans allude; and the meaning and feeling of the 'home' ground.

The quotes in the next sections have mainly been taken from the Blue Moon discussion forum, where we posted questions about the stadium relocation and memories of Maine Road. There are several Manchester City forums, but the Blue Moon site is the most active. Established in 2001, it currently has 15,000 members, a sizeable proportion of the fan base. Since then, there have been over 834,000 messages posted to the site relating to 36,000 different topics.

THE ROUTINES AND ROUTES OF PLACE

I remember when i used to get the number 11 bus from Piccadilly to Maine Road, i remember the reason i knew we were approachin the ground were the massive Kippax stand towering above the shops and houses, i'd nip in2 the Sherwood pub for a quick few b4 enterin the North Stand for a sing song with the lads, i bet that poor pub along with others round there have closed down now!!

(Zaba-daba-doo, November 2008, www.bluemoon-mcfc.co.uk)

A couple of pints in the beehive, then to that chippy behind the Kippax (what was it called?) for pudding chips and gravy. Eat that in the Kippax car park and into the ground 10 mins before kick off. Happy days, i used that routine for about 5 years. I have not got a routine at the new ground....

(BigG, November 2008, www.bluemoon-mcfc.co.uk)

Park up near a pub, then have a couple of pints. Go to the ground and buy some Bovril and maybe a Wagon Wheel. At half time grab a pie and a cup of tea. After the match go to the pub again – usually a different one – or a local curry house and talk about the match. After all, where do you go for a decent pint near Eastlands?... And do Wagon Wheels still exist?

(Dave Bishop sings the Blues but loves the booze, www.manchesterconfidential.com/ index.asp?Sessionx=IpqiNwy6IlxiJ0qiNwF6IHqi)

Walk down to the Beehive and sink a few pints ... Usually bought a badge off the badgeman with my hard earned and then off to the ground taking in the atmosphere.... Always liked the walk to the ground better cos it was through the back streets with just lil glimpses of the Kippax before you saw it in it's glory ... Top days. Can't beat em.

(PJMCC1UK, May 2009, www.bluemoon-mcfc.co.uk)

Pink emphasises that '(W)e are involved in a continuous process of emplaced engagement with the material, sensory, social and cultural contexts in which we dwell' (2007: 62). The relationships we have to places, rather than being experienced solely as representative and cognitive, are embodied, sensual, practical and shaped through how we coordinate our movements and organise routes and nodes around which we orientate ourselves and get things done. A moment's quick reflection identifies the regular patterns of use that characterize the rhythms of a place over days, weeks and months, giving it a temporal and spatial particularity (Lefèbvre 1996: 204). For instance, the passage of commuters, schoolchildren, students, tourists and the homeless through a place at regular times bestows a special character upon it that is further grounded in the situated activities of shop-keepers, clubbers, housewives, the unemployed, drug addicts and alcoholics, and football fans. These patterns are well known to residents and users of place, for whom the familiar sites they pass through and dwell in are the unquestioned backdrop to regular tasks, pleasures and routine habits. Further, individual and shared synchronized activities consolidate a powerful shared sense of place, and what Raymond Williams calls a 'structure of feeling', a sense that emerges out of 'the most delicate and least tangible parts of our activity' (1961: 63). Situated, collective practices such as these generate a communal way of seeing the world in consistent terms, sharing a host of reference points which provide the basis for shared discursive, pleasurable and practical habits.

Familiar places contain familiar routines, regular patterns of walking, driving, shopping, eating and socialising that constitute the familiar spatio-temporal experience of place. This braiding of rhythmic, routine activities in and around place highlights how, as Mels asserts, 'humans have always been rhythm-makers as much as place-makers' (2004: 3). Because routines are habitual, often beyond reflection and critique, their common sense practice is grounded, and furthered through the sense of belonging established through 'people together tackling the world around them with familiar manoeuvres' (Frykman and Löfgren 1996: 10–11). Friends, family and fellow fans tend to share habitual routines and these 'familiar building blocks of body, family and kinship' are the basis for a wider sense of belonging (Herzfeld 1997: 5–6). The environs of Maine Road were saturated with meaning and emotion for Manchester City fans, grounded in the familiar routines centring upon and around the stadium. The pre- and post-match visits to various pubs and restaurants, discussion about the game over a pint, the shared walk to the ground and the conjoined anticipation. All these regular experiences carried out over seasons, over decades, became part of the situated, unreflexive practices of fans on match days, and wove the stadium into the spaces outside of it. As the quotations above demonstrate, fans were particularly attached to these routines.

These banal, regular paths collectively constitute the time-geographies within which fan's trajectories separate and intersect in regular ways, merging together as they approach the stadium. This ongoing mapping of space through repetitive, collective choreographies of congregation, interaction, rest and relaxation produce rhythms through which time and space are stitched together. And the accumulation of repetitive events becomes both deposited in individual bodies and grounded in the shared spatio-temporal constellations where numerous paths and routines coincide to constitute what Seamon (1980) refers to as 'place-ballets'.

Hagerstrand (1975) identifies points of spatial and temporal intersection and alerts us to this routinization of action in space (see Gren 2001) through which individuals 'repeatedly couple and uncouple their paths with other people's paths, institutions, technologies and physical surroundings' (Mels 2004: 16). Shops, pubs, cafes, garages and so forth are points of intersection where individual paths congregate, providing spaces of communality and continuity within which fan activities are coordinated; they leave a residue in the landscape and in the habit-body, providing a geography of communality and continuity. Linked by the roads down which fans drive and the paths which they walk along, particular venues for shopping, eating and leisure are 'activity spaces' (Massey 1995), the small-scale congregational sites, where they meet, chat, sing and shop.

Because these routines become so much part of what fans do on match days over years of following the team, they become part of a common sense, unreflexive apprehension of space and time. With the sudden cessation of these routines, and the realisation that these times have gone and that the site of the stadium has disappeared, a sharp, reflexive awareness of the loss of this home from home with all its mundane routines becomes acute. For many fans, the routines that enfolded Maine Road match days have only been unsatisfactorily replaced, and the activities associated with attending a game are now far more dispersed. The potential for multiple routine and path-making in the environs of the COMS is restricted by its functional and material qualities. In contradistinction to the surrounds of Maine Road, there are limited numbers of pubs and shops, no restaurants, and a limited range of routes through which to wend a path to the stadium.

THE MATERIAL TEXTURES OF PLACE AND SENSATION

> My old man used to work at Cordingleys. It was the garage at the start of maine road. Used to always have car of the week on its roof. Memories of parking up there then walking to the ground. Fond fond memories.
> (mancitymick, November 2008, www.bluemoon-mcfc.co.uk)

> i'll never forget parking down on princess road (i think it was called) then walking/running (i was only lil lad so my dads steps = 2 of mine) down the cobbled back alleys to the ground avoiding horse mess and soggy newspapers on the way;-) … good times … good good times.
> (felixbg, January 2009, www.bluemoon-mcfc.co.uk)

> A lonely half eaten chips and curry and the smell of fags and vomit Ah happy days.
> (dannybcity, May 2009, www.bluemoon-mcfc.co.uk)

> I used to go to Claremont chippy I think it was called? About a 10 minute walk from the ground. They did the nicest chips and gravy ever.
> (Jonathan Barnett, May 2009, www.facebook.com)

The materiality of places, their surfaces, contours and textures offer affordances that constrain some actions and enable others. These physical qualities shape the direction fans take to the stadium but also produce a habitual sense of familiar space, a drawing towards particular sites and the installation of these sensations in memory.

Socio-technical networks bond people, technologies, matter and places together for a while. Thus for a period, places may well be 'tightly coupled with complex, enduring, and predictable connections between peoples, objects, and technologies across multiple and distant spaces and times' (Sheller and Urry 2006: 216). At other times however, such arrangements may be more volatile –

as with the recent moves of clubs out of traditional areas and the dismantling of the networks that secured stadia in place. These stabilities do not mean that places are static for they continuously change in small or large ways, and continuous maintenance secures their use for particular practices and hence consistency of meaning. We should beware therefore, of being bedazzled by the notion that the city is a perpetual space of flows, for enormous endeavour goes into the production of stability, reliability and orderliness. The tendency is 'to have things come together in discernible arrangements' (Sack 2004: 248). While grand projects wipe away and replace the material organisation of whole urban areas, in most parts of the city, change is more incremental wherein new transport infrastructures, electricity networks, housing estates and single buildings are enfolded into existing arrangements over time, to produce an ever-different spatial mixity but one which is insufficiently volatile to disrupt a stable material backdrop.

The area around Maine Road has never been static. Shops change hands, new restaurants open up, buildings are demolished, housing developments emerge and new inhabitants move in. For instance, in the terraced housing surrounding Maine Road, a white working class has become less dominant with a growing population of Pakistani descent and the advent of Somali refugees. The famous 'Curry Mile' in Rusholme emerged in the 1980s (Goswami 2009) and has grown ever since. Yet while change has been constant, the area was also experienced by fans as recognisably part of a 'changing same', containing consistencies and reiterations. In this sense, place (and place-image) cannot be made through image and brand but is reproduced at each moment by the practices, processes and experiences that circulate through and within it – in the case discussed here, by fans going to the match.

Fans' route to the stadium involves a bodily involvement with the materiality of the environs, producing placed experiences of heartbeat and breath, the particular movement of limbs and the sensing of textures underfoot, the press of bodies, the assailing of the nostrils by familiar smells, and the sonic melding of one's own footsteps with those of thousands of others. The repetitive pacing of the same tarmac and paving slabs, cobblestones and patches of grass absorb the surfaces of place into the body, producing 'a primary rivet aligning body with place' (Labelle 2008: 189). As can be seen from the quotes above and those from the preceding section, fans' sensual memories of the area around Maine Road are strong – with allusions to touch, taste, smell, texture, and the looming shadow of the ground.

THE ATMOSPHERES OF PLACE

I was invited to my first city match by a friend of my Dad's.... Despite the relative gloom surrounding football and City at the time, I could sense the tangible excitement drifting on a breeze of fried onions and barely edible burgers from the many independent food vans.

(Andy Brady, http://myfirstcitygame.com/time/1980–1989/)

i miss walking down the alley ways and narrow cobbled roads in moss side, the atmosphere and buzz was amazing ... and driving passed moss side being able to see the top of the kippax down the alley ways.

(chrisi, May 2009, www.bluemoon-mcfc.co.uk)

The COMS is an awesome stadium and fits perfectly for the modern game, but for pre-match build-up it has got a very long way to go to get that same buzz that posters on here fondly remember at the great days of Maine Rd.

(Cheltblue, May 2009, www.bluemoon-mcfc.com)

Besides the solid material characteristics of place, the more immaterial quality of atmosphere is an important ingredient of the match-day experience and fans often mourn its loss after their clubs have moved grounds (Armstrong and Young 1999). Atmosphere is an elusive quality that varies continually and depends upon the importance and significance of games. The atmosphere is no less powerful outside the ground, and was a quality perceived in the area surrounding Maine Road on match days, as exemplified in the quotes above.

Conradson and Latham argue that atmosphere might be understood as the 'energetic outcome of encounters between bodies in particular places' (2007: 232). In thinking about the affective qualities such as atmosphere, we may explore how different configurations of objects, spaces and bodies come together to form different experiences of being with and coming together in place, 'temporary configurations of energy and feeling that arise' (Conradson and Latham 2007: 238). The atmosphere of place is produced by the anticipatory charge before a match, or the sense of relief of triumph or disappointment afterwards, feelings clearly communicated in the sound of the crowd, their movements and bearing, through what Thrift refers to as 'imitative contagion' (2008: 231). Yet it is also connected to the rather less identifiable qualities of place. McCormack describes atmosphere as 'something distributed yet palpable, a quality of environmental immersion that registers in and through sensing bodies whilst also remaining diffuse, in the air, ethereal' (2008: 413) and Böhme suggests that atmospheres 'seem to fill the space with a certain tone of feeling like a haze' (1993: 114). These atmospheres are sensual and embodied, and are not something into which fans are merely passively immersed but are produced by how they interact with space and practice fanship.

Atmosphere at Maine Road was thus transmitted between people in their brisk walk to the stadium, by the shouting of sellers of fan paraphernalia, by the dense chatter of fans, galloping police horses off to sort out trouble between rival fans, the chanting through the streets and a host of other energies ranging from the buzz of radios, the smell of food and tobacco smoke, the shadows of the terraced streets, the channelling of bodies through narrow alleyways and the subsequent sudden emergence into the larger space in front of the stadium.

HOME GROUND AND THE LOSS OF HOME

> *SUPER CITY FROM MAINE RD*
> *Moss Side is not the same place anymore . . . all the pubs that shut. Eastlands*
> *will never beat home. If we could go back there i would be back straight away.*
> *RIP thanks for the memories.*
>
> (scottyboimcfc, Febuary 2008, www.youtube.com)

Bringing together these experiential dimensions of place, we further emphasise the strength of belonging by drawing upon the notion of 'home'. Home is the normative phrase given to stadia in which home fixtures are played, but is also grounded in the habitual travels and routines of City fans in and around the stadium. In this sense, Maine Road became home, and while it was extant, was always in the condition of becoming home. 'Home' can equally refer to 'house, land, village, city, district, country, or, indeed, the world', transmitting the sentimental associations of one scale to others (Sopher 1979: 130) but here the sentiment is wholly attached to the place of football. While home can be oppressive, it is also a place of comfort: 'convenience, efficiency, leisure, ease, pleasure, domesticity, intimacy and privacy' (Rybczynski 1988: 231), where the body is relaxed and unselfconscious. Home is made by the accretion of habitual enactions, by our familiar engagement with the space in which we live with others. And as Lippard comments, reinforcing the sensual associations of place cited above, '(I)f one has been raised in a place, its textures and sensations, its smells and sounds, are recalled as they felt to child's, adolescent's, adult's body' (1997: 34). We can extend this idea to the neighbourhood of Maine Road, which was convivially and emotionally inhabited at a larger scale.

> *I remember walking down as a kid, and as an adult, on my way to the match*
> *only to turn the corner and see a big green fence and no Kippax stand looming*
> *over the top of it. Makes me sad just thinking about it.*
>
> (matty, December 2008, www.bluemoon-mcfc.co.uk)

> *I miss Maine Road. I love COMS, but Maine Road was in the middle of the real*
> *areas of Manchester, the places that make Manchester. I used to love walking*
> *down the curry mile and heading to the Stadium . . . Great times!!;-).*
>
> (leftovcenta, June 2008, www.youtube.com)

> *COMS is nothing compared to maine road. Maine road is and will always be*
> *Manchester City. It should never have been knocked down. I used to love*
> *walking round those terraced streets on a match day. COMS or Maine Road on*
> *a cold intimidating wednesday night, i know what i'd pick any day.*
>
> (Supremeo2, March 2008, www.youtube.com)

Many of the material remnants of City's presence in the area of Maine Road have been gradually effaced, with the current construction of a new housing estate on the stadium's site, yet numerous small traces remain including graffiti (Edensor 2008). At the time of the departure and since, an outpouring of books, articles, videos, websites and other media by fans testifies to the loss of the place of foot-ball homeliness. This sense of loss pervades the quotations cited above, highlight-ing the intrinsic association of the area with Manchester City, a fundamental belonging that the move to East Manchester has not dispelled. The nostalgia articulated here binds place closely with memories and comments on a loss of atmosphere and identity. It also refers to a sense of authenticity associated with the 'real' Manchester club (contra United – see Edensor and Millington 2008), located in an 'authentic' part of the city, steeped in history and 'character'.

PLACELESSNESS AND 'NON-PLACE'

> We should never have moved from Maine Road, the capacity should have been increased. Okay it wasn't the best of areas but that was part of the fun. The new place has no atmosphere and no soul. Ahh memories.
>
> (City78, Failsworth, March 2008, www.manchestereveningnews.co.uk).

> Its not just EASTLANDS thats got no Soul ! Just look at all the other grounds that are Prefab like built. And all look the same !! Great names a thing of the past. Look at the new Wembley … Oh dear…
>
> (arthurdawkins, March 2008, www.manchestereveningnews.co.uk)

The routine habits, sensations, atmospheres and memories discussed above are partly grounded in the consolidation of individual and collective feelings built up over time, a time-honoured familiarity with place that was suddenly arrested with the movement of Manchester City Football Club to Eastlands. However, as we have emphasised, the structures, affordances, textures, fixtures and institutions of place are also contributory factors, agencies which exert their force upon people. The ways in which fans discuss Maine Road and its environs conjure up a variegated, complex and looser space (Frank and Stevens 2007) at variance to the much smoother, more highly regulated surroundings of COMS. Where the sur-roundings of Maine Road featured old, tightly packed, working-class terraced housing, cobbled alleyways, a plethora of outlets for eating and drinking, shops and schools, COMS stands grandly apart from surrounding housing and can be seen from far away, notably at night when blue lighting creates an impressive aura. Beyond the stadium's enclosure, the area is undergoing regeneration. The 1970s' housing is being complemented by more upmarket accommodation, and wide roads bisect the perimeter of the ground on three sides. Apart from a huge supermarket there are few shops and only a handful of pubs. Routes to the ground by foot are fewer – there is no myriad of paths, alleyways and streets here. The much smoother materialities, buildings and verges are well maintained and the more planned and segregated spatialities of the houses and streets lack the varied textures of Rusholme and Moss Side.

COMS and its surroundings seem to epitomise what Augé (1995) calls 'non-place' or Harvey terms 'serial monotony' (1989) – the widespread, predicta-ble reproduction of similar retail outlets, forms of urban planning and regulation.

The area seems rather devoid of history and patina, varied cultural presence, 'atmosphere', and sensual diversity. Rather, it is technically organised as a space of flows, a functional realm in which fans get quickly to and from the stadium, and is regulated to banish that which interferes and contrasts with prescribed designs and functions. Consequently, emergent rituals of 'going to the match' are located more in the city centre, where transport, food and drink are easily obtained.

This is what regeneration inflicts on place. Since the new locale had few associations with Manchester City, a marketing campaign was developed around the slogan 'This is our City' (Edensor and Millington 2008). Moreover, attempts have been made to bestow a new symbolic landscape which attempts to recreate a relationship between Manchester City and place. Stands have been named after favourite players, the name of every season ticket holder imprinted in blue plastic swathes on the stadium's external columns, and sculptures have been erected. Nevertheless, as one fan comments:

> *went to the everton game last week and was saying to a few everton fans on the walk to the ground about how much i missed the prematch build up at city games now … things like brekky in the pub … taxi ride to the sherwood or hardys … and the most sickening thing i miss is the walk through the (over) crowded, bustling back streets and alleyways to the ground for you to turn the last corner and the ground came into view above the houses, sending a shiver down the spine. i am envious of everton just for the fact they have kept all those traditions … i was buzzing walking to goodison last week with all the crowds through the backstreets, i had a tear in my eye reminiscing and thinking back to how it used to be. one everton lad hit the nail on the head, when he said going to CoMs now is like visiting any retail park in the country, you drive on, you drive off .. and that just about summed it up for me.*
>
> *(shadygiz, May 2009, www.bluemoon-mcfc.co.uk)*

This final quote underscores the deep emotional attachments supporters may forge with their chosen football team and the area in which they play. The nature of this relationship defies normative understandings of consumer relations and 'brand' loyalties, famously summed up by Rogan Taylor in his remark that 'no one has their ashes scattered down the aisle of Tesco' (Tapp and Clowes 2002). This special attachment forms an important anchor, therefore, for place-bound loyalties and a sense of community in a world in which such notions are seemingly being eroded through homogenising and commodifying tendencies.

Further, this attachment to place is indicative of the quest for *authenticity*, an important element of contemporary fan culture, forming a basis for the assertion of identity and claims on space, whilst simultaneously allowing self-proclaimed 'loyal' fans to distance themselves from the sport's new 'plastic fans' or 'glory hunters' (see Giulianotti 2002, cf. Brown's Chapter 9 in this volume). It is not surprising, therefore, that the fans who responded to our questions about Manchester City's relocation reproduced a particular nostalgic sense of loss associated with long-established routines and traditions, because these practices formed important attributes of their fan identity. Perhaps other supporters feel rather differently about the relocation. A generation of City supporters, for example, is beginning to emerge who never experienced Maine Road and can only ever share a vicarious nostalgia for the place. Further, the negativities associated with Maine Road, Moss Side and the experience of football fandom in the 1960s and 1970s, are absent from the accounts we uncovered. Although supporters are apt to distance themselves from the commercialisation of the contemporary game, they may forget that football in England has became a relatively safe and inclusive leisure pursuit for a broader social spectrum.

But fans aware of the transformed spatialities within which stadia become entangled draw parallels with wider regulatory and regenerational processes. To produce topophilia and a sense of place under these conditions is unpromising and yet while the thick textures, atmosphere and sensuality associated with Maine Road may be impossible to replicate in this more organised, smoother space, attendance over successive seasons, a growing compendium of season-upon-season dramas, and the slow accretion of rituals and sites inhabited en route to and from the stadium may start to consolidate fans' attachment to East Manchester.

NOTES

1 Thanks to Joshua Millington.
2 An aerial photograph of Maine Road as it looked in the 1920s can be found under: www.images.manchester.gov.uk/web/objects/common/webmedia.php?irn=55753.

REFERENCES

Amin, A. and Thrift, N. (2002) *Cities: Reimagining the Urban*, Cambridge: Polity Press.
Armstrong, G. and Young, M. (1999) 'Fanatical football chants: Creating and controlling the carnival', *Sport in Society*, 2(3): 173–211.
Augé, M. (1995) *Non-Places. Introduction to an Anthropology of Supermodernity*, London: Verso.
Goswami, N. (2009) *The making of 'Curry Mile'*, BBC Manchester. Online. Available www.bbc.co.uk/manchester/content/articles/2009/05/12/curry_mile_history_feature.shtml (accessed 29 May 2009).
BBC News (1999) *Footballers' union nets Lowry*. Online. Available http://news.bbc.co.uk/1/hi/uk/545023.stm (accessed 14 June 2009).
Bale, J. (1993) 'The spatial development of the modern stadium', *International Review for the Sociology of Sport*, 28: 121.
—— (1999) 'Parks and gardens: Metaphors for the modern places of sport', in D. Crouch (ed.) *Leisure/Tourism Geographies*, London: Routledge.
Böhme, G. (1993) 'Atmosphere as the fundamental concept of a new aesthetics', *Thesis Eleven*, 36: 113–26.
Crabbe, T., Brown, A., Mellor, G. and O'Connor, K. (2006) *EA Sports Research: Football – An all consuming passion?*, Manchester: Substance.
Conradson, D. and Latham, A. (2007) 'The experiential economy of London: Antipodean transnationals and the overseas experience', *Mobilities*, 2: 2231–54.

Duke, V. (2002) 'Local tradition versus globalization: Resistance to the McDonaldisation of professional football in England', *Football Studies*, 5(1): 5–23.

Edensor, T. (2008) 'Mundane hauntings: Commuting through the phantasmagoric working class spaces of Manchester, England', *Cultural Geographies*, 15: 313–33.

Edensor, T. and Millington, S. (2008) 'This is our City: Branding football and the myths of locality', *Global Networks*, 8(2): 172–93.

Frank, K. and Stevens, Q. (eds) (2007) *Loose Space: Opportunities for public life*, London: Routledge.

Frykman, J. and Löfgren, O. (eds) (1996) *Forces of Habit: Exploring everyday culture*, Lund: Lund University Press.

Gratton, C., Shibli, S. and Coleman, R. (2005) 'Sport and economic regeneration in cities', *Urban Studies*, 42(5/6): 985–99.

Gren, M. (2001) 'Time-geography matters', in J. May and N. Thrift (eds) *Timespace: Geographies of temporality*, London: Routledge.

Giulianotti, R. (1999) *Football: A sociology of the global game*, Cambridge: Polity Press.

Giulianotti, R. (2002) 'Supporters, followers, fans and flaneurs: A taxonomy of spectator identities in football'. *Journal of Sport and Social Issues* 26(1): 25–46.

Giulianotti, R. and Robertson, R. (2004) 'The globalization of football: A study in the glocalization of the "serious life" ', *The British Journal of Sociology*, 55(4): 545–68.

Guano, E. (2003) 'A stroll through la Boca: The politics and poetics of spatial experience in a Buenos Aires neighborhood', *Space and Culture*, 6: 356–76.

Hagerstrand, T. (1975) 'Space, time and human condition', in A. Karlqvist, L. Lundqvist and F. Snickars (eds) *Dynamic Allocation of Urban Space*, Farnborough: Hants.

Harvey, D. (1989) *The Condition of Postmodernity*, Oxford: Blackwell.

Herzfeld, M. (1997) *Cultural Intimacy: Social Poetics in the Nation-State*, London: Routledge.

Kelsall, G. (2000) 'From the Victoria Ground to Britannia Stadium: Remembering and reinventing the experience and identity of place', in T. Edensor (ed.) *Reclaiming Stoke-on-Trent: Leisure, space and identity in the potteries*, Stoke-on-trent: Staffordshire University Press.

Labelle, B. (2008) 'Pump up the bass: Rhythm, cars and auditory scaffolding', *Senses and Society*, 3(2): 187–204.

Lefèbvre, H. (1996) *Writings on Cities*, Oxford: Blackwell.

Lippard, L. (1997) *The Lure of the Local: Senses of place in a multicentered society*, New York: The New Press.

Massey, D. (1995) 'The conceptualization of place', in D. Massey and P. Jess (eds) *A Place in the World? Places, cultures and globalization*, London: Open University Press.

McCormack, D. (2008) 'Engineering affective atmospheres on the moving geographies of the 1897 Andrée expedition', *Cultural Geographies*, 15: 413–30.

Mels, T. (2004) 'Lineages of a geography of rhythm', in T. Mels (ed.) *Reanimating Places: A geography of rhythms*, Aldershot: Ashgate.

Phelps, N.A. (2005) 'Professional football and local identity in the "golden age": Portsmouth in the mid-twentieth century', *Urban History*, 32(3): 459–80.

Pink, S. (2007) 'Sensing cittàslow: Slow living and the constitution of the sensory city', *Senses and Society*, 2(1): 59–78.

Rybczynski, R. (1988) *Home: A short history of an idea*, London: Heinemann.

Sack, R. (2004) 'Place-making and time', in T. Mels (ed.) *Reanimating Places: A Geography of Rhythms*, Aldershot: Ashgate.

Seamon, D. (1980) 'Body-subject, time-space routines, and place-ballets', in A. Buttimer and D. Seamon (eds) *The Human Experience of Space and Place*, London: Croom Helm.

Sheller, M. and Urry, J. (2006) 'The new mobilities paradigm', *Environment and Planning A*, 38: 207–26.

Silk, M.L. (2004) 'A tale of two cities: The social production of sterile sporting space', *Journal of Sport & Social Issues*, 28: 349–78.

Smith, A. and Fox, T. (2007) 'From "event-led" to "event-themed" regeneration: The 2002 Commonwealth Games Legacy Programme', *Urban Studies*, 44(5/6): 1125–43.

Sopher, D. (1979) 'The landscape of home: Myth, experience, social meaning', in D. Meinig (ed.) *The Interpretation of Ordinary Landscape*, New York: Oxford University Press.

Stone, C. (2007) 'The role of football in everyday life', *Soccer and Society*, 8(2): 169–84.

Tapp, A. and Clowes, J. (2002) 'From "carefree casuals" to "professional wanderers": Segmentation possibilities for football supporters', *European Journal of Marketing*, 36(11/12): 1248–269.

Thrift, N. (2008) *Non-representational Theory: Space, politics, affect*, London: Routledge.

Urry, J. (2006) 'Travelling times', *European Journal of Communication*, 21(3): 357–72.

van Dam, F. (2000) 'Refurbishment, redevelopment or relocation? The changing form and location of football stadia in the Netherlands', *Area*, 32(2): 133–43.

Williams, R. (1961) *The Long Revolution*, London: Chatto and Windus.

Chapter 9: 'Come Home'

The Stadium, Locality and Community at FC United of Manchester[1]

Adam Brown

It's that time again when I lose my friends
Go walkabout, I've got the bends from pressure
This is a testing time when the choice is mine
Am I a fool for love or foolish with desire
And I don't believe you're all I'll ever need
And I need to feel that you're not holding me
but the way I feel just makes me want to scream
Come home, come home, come home

(Lyrics of the Mancunian alternative rock band James' song
'Come Home', Fontana, 1990)

Cultural geographer John Bale has argued that 'it is almost impossible to deal with club-community relations without focusing on the changing geographical and social role of the football stadium' (Bale 2000b: 91). He also states that the stadium is a sports facility that always generates both positive and negative effects on the broader urban community and the local/neighbourhood community as well as on fans.

According to Bale, the psychological benefits to be derived from football have led stadia to be seen by some as a source of 'topophilia' – a place that generates feelings of love or attraction (Tuan 1974) which can evoke strong sentiments and attachments – and as a source of 'topophobia', or alienation and fear (especially when visiting opposition stadia, 'away from home'). In this context, referring to the work of Mackay on the feelings of supporters of the Scottish football club Hibernian for 'their' Easter Road stadium, it is suggested that moving to a new ground would 'be like losing someone in the family' (Mackay 1995: 35), a sentiment which it is suggested typifies 'the strength of feeling that can be attached to a football ground as a place, an emotional tie which can take the stadium beyond a simple functional space for the production of football matches' (Bale 2000b: 92). Indeed stadia are also seen as a source of 'geographical memories' which serve as 'a reference that triggers wider memories of friends, relatives and people' (Hague and Mercer 1998, cf. Edensor and Millington's Chapter 8 in this volume).

As such, the notion of 'home' in football reaches far beyond the well reported advantages for one team playing at their ground – the 'home win' – and the disadvantages of 'playing away'. Bale suggests that the dislocation of clubs from the places that bear their name and their traditional location is anathema to fans. Nevertheless he recognizes that this situation 'remains at odds with the logic of a fully marketized industry in modernity' (Bale 2000b: 96) with its emphasis on the commercial interests of clubs over nostalgic sentiment.

It is in this context, and that of wider investigations into the relationships between football clubs and their 'communities' (e.g. Brown *et al.* 2008), that I will consider the issues associated around the development of FC United of Manchester, and the place of the football stadium – former, temporary and new – within those processes.

Bale refers to the dislocation of football clubs from old traditional grounds to new, modernized and corporate stadia (or 'tradia') within a 'fully marketized industry'. Here I consider the impact of a different element of that free market industry – the corporate takeover – and the actions and reactions of fans as a result, creating its own dislocation. I will then explore the (re)creation of 'home' for these fans in both a temporary and permanent sense and its place within wider policy developments in the contemporary city.

FC United of Manchester was formed by Manchester United fans in the 'wake' of the corporate takeover of the club by the American Glazer family in May 2005. The events around this have been described in detail elsewhere (Brown 2008a, 2008b) but in summary the club sought to empower football fans by taking the legal form of an Industrial and Provident Society in which members each own a nominal share and each have one vote to decide club rules, the club board and, at its inception, the name and badge. It is outside of the Football League and is semi-professional, with players who are mostly locally based and have other occupations. Its fan base is overwhelmingly drawn from the Manchester conurbation.

The events leading to its formation and the experience of the club's fan communities emphasize the centrality of the football ground: at Manchester United's stadium Old Trafford, as a site for protest for some years before, up to and including the Glazers; at Gigg Lane, Bury and a plethora of small 'away' grounds in the lower reaches of English football, as sites for the recreation of fan communities and the invocation of 'tradition' and nostalgia in the face of displacement, division and 'exile'; and in the aspirations of the club, its members and fans in its search for a home of its own, the development of its own, new ground.

A DIVIDED HOME

Stand up, for the champions![2]

I have written elsewhere (Brown 2004) of the expression in the late 1990s and early twenty-first century of a distinctly Mancunian local identity by Manchester United fans, and in particular the reinvigoration and reassertion of a rivalry with Manchester City (cf. Chapter 8). Here it was possible to see

> in an age when football has arguably become detached from its sense of place
> [...] a stark reminder of football's enduring local meanings for some fans [...].
> [raising] questions about the place of sport and football in the 'post-Fordist' city
> and the endurance of local rivalries within an increasingly globalized sport.
>
> (Brown 2004: 175)

These expressions of local identity were also wrapped up in notions of authenticity in football fandom and, following this, opposition to the ongoing 'commercialization' of Manchester United and its Public Limited Company (PLC) status. There was here a mixture of both self-promotion of local identity and attacks on their club's policies, partially articulated through demands to reintroduce standing areas at football to aid access for local young fans (IMUSA 1998) and to prioritize local fans in the supply of tickets.

Although at various times this 'politicized' local identity was expressed away from the stadium – on streets, bridges and in the media – it was also in print fanzines, sold to match-going fans outside the confines of the stadium (fanzine sellers were banned by the club from selling on property owned by Manchester United) and within the stadium itself that it was most frequently seen.

As part of a *rapprochement* between supporter groups and the club following the failed attempt by BSkyB to take over the company in 1999, supporters were allowed to hang banners on the top tier of the newly expanded Stretford End (the traditional 'home' end at Manchester United). These allowed fans to 'mark out' territory and express local identifications: one read 'The Flowers of Manchester' (a reference to the Munich Air Disaster victims) and another 'Republik of Mancunia'. As with any other football club, songs and chants within the stadium also re-enforced fans' identifications, a sense of collectivity and their local attachment within Old Trafford.

This relates to Bauman's (2000: 199–201) point that 'spectacles' such as football matches have become events around which people temporarily unite as communities, only to go back to their individualized lives at the end of the game. People 'perform' all the aspects of community and commonality around football for the time they are together 'as one', but do not necessarily knit themselves into deep reciprocal relationships as a result. However, although this can occur in the fan spaces associated with matches such as local pubs, it is within the stadium that this expression finds its most concentrated form.

Where the situation at Old Trafford differed, perhaps, is that this sense of 'community' became imbued with political aims and a 'cultural contestation' (Jary *et al.* 1991) took place. At one level this was about what makes a 'real' supporter (however problematic that concept) – at another level it fed a politicization of a section of Manchester United fans and a contest to the governance and policies of both the club and football more broadly.

As such, Old Trafford was, for some years before the Glazer takeover, a site of protest. The Independent Manchester United Supporters Association (IMUSA), formed to 'roll back the PLC', was itself formed following a club tannoy announcement in the stadium, during a vital match with Arsenal in February 1995. This announcement urged fans to remain seated, when many felt that it was not only their right, but also their duty as supporters to be on their feet actively supporting their team. The immediate response to this announcement was a mass defiance, with almost the whole stadium standing up; the longer term result was the formation of IMUSA itself.

Standing in the stadium itself became a hotly contested topic, both at Manchester United and nationally – the imposition of all-seater stadia following the Taylor Report (Taylor 1990) being resisted by some fans ever since (cf. Chapter 1). IMUSA became prominent in the national debate about re-introducing standing at football but also organized protests around it within Old Trafford. At one stage in 1998 they attempted to use the development of football as a satellite television spectacle and product to their advantage, by placing fans with banners saying 'Bring back terracing' near corner flags or in the front rows of the stadium so that they would be caught on camera and broadcast globally. This picked up where other fan groups had led, notably the Independent Arsenal Supporters Association in 1991 who deliberately organized protests against the club's 'bond scheme' to coincide with televised games (Brown 1998: 56). Here the stadium and its televising became a vehicle through which fans could express opposition and demand change gaining profile and publicity – a manipulation and attempt at appropriation of the globalized and mediatized era of football.

Of course, the staging of protest – or even merely standing – within the modern stadium rarely goes unchallenged. Bale's description of the development of stadia as a panopticon (Bale 1993: 127) where surveillance and social control predominate and Anthony King's description of the 'the panoptic isolation of the seat' (King 1998: 161) are both hugely relevant here (cf. Chapter 1 and the Conclusion in this volume). Fans behaving in ways that are no longer acceptable to authorities, clubs and football's governance in England were given short shrift.

When members of IMUSA stood for matches at Old Trafford, the club responded by ejecting them. This reached a crisis point in December 1997 at a game against Everton when fans, stewards and police clashed during the match as authorities attempted to remove standing fans. However, it was the ability of the club to use their 'panoptic gaze' to identify on camera specific supporters and their seat numbers, and thus be able to issue bans in the post to those fans, that proved a powerful weapon. Although some fans would attempt to circumvent this by sitting in different seats, the club simply threatened to ban the person responsible for the seat in which any fan was standing.

Figure 9.1a/b
'Not for Sale': Fans
protesting against the
Glazer takeover of
Manchester United.

Old Trafford's role as a site for protest perhaps reached its climax during the 'Not For Sale' campaign to prevent the Glazer takeover (Brown 2008a). The campaign was initially targeted in 2004 at the 'Coolmore mafia', two race-horse owners (John Magnier and J.P. Macmanus) who had bought a large stake in the public limited company that owned the club. During this period, in which Magnier and Macmanus clashed not only with the manager, Alex Ferguson, but also the club's chief executive and board, fans in the stadium again used chants and banners to protest. 'Stand up if you're not for sale' replaced 'Stand up for the champions' in the songs of fans.

When it emerged that it was the Glazers, not Coolmore, that were most likely to take over the club, fans' attention turned on them and, in actions designed to put off potential purchases, tactics changed. Supporters 'flash-mobbed' the club's *Megastore* situated within the stand at the east end of the ground in early 2005, disrupting business and chanting 'no customers, no profit'. On 13 February 2005 between 10,000 and 15,000 supporters marched on the ground in advance of the team's home game against AC Milan in the Champions League (Figure 9.1). This protest saw the first serious clashes between fans and police and was typical of a tendency for the anti-takeover protesters to converge on their 'home', as a kind of magnet for their anger and the focal point of the battle for ownership.

The climax of this came in June 2005 when supporters converged on the ground as news that the Glazers were inside spread via text message, internet and phone. Supporters erected barricades at either end of the South Stand tunnel, as well as blocking car park entrances and exits and for some hours an uneasy stand-off occurred. By late evening large numbers of riot police clashed with fans removing them with violent force from the stadium environs. This was to be the last serious expression of dissent – of any kind – that has been seen at Old Trafford, but exemplified a tendency for fans to focus energies and their physical presence on their 'home' ground. For, whilst Old Trafford remained 'home' for fans, club and company, it was a divided one, and it was one to which many would not return.

FROM 'LEAVING HOME' TO 'HOME FROM HOME'?

This is how it feels to be FC
This is how it feels to be home
This is how it feels when you don't sell your arse to a gnome[3]

Although there was never a sustained implementation of a 'no customers no profit' boycott of the club, a few thousand Manchester United fans withdrew their custom and did not renew their season tickets. Although heart wrenching for many, their refusal to support the Glazer takeover meant that they would not pay for tickets, merchandize nor attend games that ultimately would go toward paying the £660 million debt with which the family had saddled the club. It is interesting in this context to reconsider Bale's assertion that:

> there is a feeling, however, that the dislocation of the club from the place
> bearing its name is anathema to fans and something clubs have tended to
> avoid, reflecting a local sense of sentiment, place pride or topophilia.
>
> (Bale 2000b: 96)

However, the dislocation now experienced by fans of the new club, distanced from their 'home' of Old Trafford, was of a very different character to this: in some senses they had removed themselves (however principled), rather than having the stadium removed from them (cf. Chapter 8). Also, for many fans, feelings of topophilia towards their long-standing home ground became replaced by a topophobia, particularly at the climax of the protests. However, their new club, FC United of Manchester, wore this attachment between football club and place on its sleeve: the name of the club embraced an identification with Manchester and the club badge centres around the city's crest, both voted for by the club's founding members and both celebrated since in song.

The formation of FC United of Manchester was, in part, an attempt to 'keep the community together'[4] in the face of this dislocation and keeping together meant at the stadium, re-emphasizing its centrality to these fans. Most Manchester United fans remained going to Old Trafford, others merely resorted to watching Manchester United on television and in pubs, but for those who threw their weight behind FC United there was a belief in the pre-eminence of match-day consumption of football and the importance to their understanding of football support of physically being at the ground – a philosophy embodied in the fan vernacular, 'if you don't go, you don't know'. This understanding of fandom is regularly re-emphasized in official club statements:

> We should never forget that it is our commitment and support that makes the club's very existence possible [...]. Show your support for YOUR club and cheer the lads on in the run up to the end of the season (you'll miss it come the middle of May!) [...] vocal support is just as valued as their financial help. Time and time again, Karl Marginson and the players have spoken of how our fantastic crowd acts as a 12th man for the team and can often make the difference to the outcome of a game. In short, being there counts. So, get yourself to that football ground and get behind the team in these last five games. Sing your heart out for the lads. Thanks for your support, from all at FC United.
>
> (FCUM 2009)

In many ways FC United attempted to embody the principles which had underpinned the protests of the 1990s around standing, supporter control, anti-commercialism, anti-globalization and anti-corporatism. It has also set out to symbolically and practically mark its distinction from the dominant corporate *modus operandi* of English football.

Established as a not-for-profit, member-owned cooperative, and promoted in each of its first three years of existence, FC United now compete in the Unibond Northern Premier League, seven divisions below the Premier League in 'Step 4' of the English football pyramid.

Since formation in June 2005, FC United have played their 'home' games at Gigg Lane, the ground of League Two's Bury FC. Gigg Lane is a 10,000 capacity stadium six miles to the north of Manchester city centre and FC United have access to it only for their matches. The groundshare has been far from unproblematic and has been extremely costly to the new club, although it has fulfilled the basic requirement of competing in English football (and indeed most sport) of having a 'home' ground.

This situation is not totally unique in English football – a new club, born out of conflict at another, locating itself at another club's home ground. Only one club in England has moved significantly from its origins and that is Wimbledon, renamed MK Dons, who relocated much like an American sports franchise from South London to Milton Keynes in the face of fierce criticism. Wimbledon fans who rejected the 'franchise' formed AFC Wimbledon who themselves had to groundshare with non-league Kingstonian (they later bought the ground). However, in that case it was the club that was removed from the fans and in the FC United case it was the fans who felt forced to leave the club. AFC Wimbledon was, however, not only an inspiration but also active in helping FC United become established.

Faced with playing matches at a League Two club's ground (which itself was too big for the 3,000 FCUM fans) and supporting a team initially playing in the North West Counties Division Two was a huge change for those that had been used to the biggest English club grounds and the rarefied atmosphere of the Premier League. Further, formerly cohesive fan communities that were at Manchester United had been split, between those that left the club for FC United and those that remained going to Old Trafford. This meant not only that old alliances, friendships and 'micro-communities' were tested, if not broken, but that new fan community formations had to be established.

One thing fans did to address this was the attempt to 'make it feel like ours' by decorating their temporary home with flags and banners of a huge variety. With supporters occupying just two of the four stands at Bury, these covered much of the empty blue seats with red, white and black, including a huge 'traditional' bar scarf, some 30 metres long. Reflecting a desire for a more 'authentic' match day experience than had been possible at Old Trafford (as the failed standing protests had shown), supporters resolutely stood up in the all-seater ground and sang songs both old and new throughout matches (Figure 9.2).

Figure 9.2
FC United of Manchester fans celebrating at Gigg Lane (Courtesy of Andy Barker, andy@ fcutdphotos.co.uk).

The voluminous 'atmosphere' was remarked upon by the team's manager, Karl Marginson, early in the first season, dubbing it a 90/90 atmosphere – '90 per cent of the fans singing for 90 minutes'.[5]

This was particularly true of the 'Manchester Road End' ('MRE') where the majority of fans congregated behind one goal in a recreation of the popular ends characteristic of a much earlier epoch in football where the 'large working class audience stood on the terraces' (Giulianotti 1999: 61). The average attendance in the leagues the club has played has ranged from 50 in Northwest Counties League to around 300 in the Unibond Premier League, dwarfed by FC United's own crowd, which averages between 2,250 and 3,000. As such, at 'home' FC United fans have lacked the traditional 'away' opposition fans with whom to conduct the vocal jousts and bating, part of the 'essence of football' worldwide (Giulianotti 1999: 10).

In response to this absence, and as the club's fan communities developed and favoured locations for different groups of friends within the ground emerged, playful rivalries developed, in particular between the 'MRE' and the Main Stand. Thus, over time, a familiarity with Gigg Lane developed and a notion that it was a kind of 'home' to FC United's fan communities – at least temporarily – emerged. Some of this was organic, other aspects instrumental, others performative in attempts to maintain a sense of unity, common purpose and togetherness. In a society and 'sportscape' (Bale 2000a) that is increasingly individualized, it could be argued that here football supporters were attempting to hold on to, or recreate, the *Gemeinschaft* type communities which Tönnies (1974) has described.

However, the creation and consumption of fan culture at FC United matches – the performance of fan identity – represents in part a symbolic re-creation of the fan communities following the Glazer takeover emphasizing what those supporters held dear. This reflects MacAloon's definition of performance as an: 'occasion in which as a culture or society we reflect upon and define ourselves, dramatize our collective myths and history, present ourselves with alternatives, and eventually change in some ways while remaining the same in others (MacAloon 1984 in Carlson 1996: 24).

This seems appropriate in a situation where old and new identities, shared histories and those in formation are played out. However, in this case it is in part with instrumental purposes – one of which is the (re)creation of preferred modes of consumption of football and another is the presentation of an 'alternative', both within FC United fan culture and to the outside world.

However, FC United's tenure at Gigg Lane has been far from unproblematic, eventually undermining senses of topophilia toward the place among fans and by 2007 the 'honyemoon' period was well and truly over. One issue was that it was costing the club huge sums of money – match-day costs were over £5,000 a match, meaning that any advantage of having large crowds (to be reinvested in the club as a not-for-profit enterprise) was largely lost. In 2007 and 2008 the club posted significant losses in its annual accounts and was facing further losses in 2009 at the time of writing. The largest non-staff expense, at around £110,000 a year, was the large sum that Bury charged the club for playing there, and widespread antagonism toward Bury among FC United fans has emerged.

Furthermore, some actions of the host club have exacerbated relations between the two clubs and between sections of FC United's supporters and Bury, based on the use of the ground and making it a site for conflict. One example of this is a sense of unequal treatment, with one supporter calculating that since the ground share had begun, FC United had had 14 games postponed (ostensibly due to poor weather conditions) and Bury had had just four called off.

Another example has been the refusal of Bury to allow FC United to sell its own catering, drink and alcohol at the stadium, thus removing the ability of the club to raise much needed finance from supporters. One exception to this has been the popular pre-match entertainment in one small bar at the ground, an event held at every Saturday match called 'Course You Can Malcolm'. This supporter-organized event not only allowed the club to earn some meagre income, but became a favoured location for one element of FC United's fan communities – with live local and unsigned bands, book readings and poetry all of a resolutely Mancunian flavour (FCUM 2007). At one match in 2009, Bury suddenly restricted numbers to this event, citing local fire department regulations. These proved to be unfounded and this deliberate episode of obstruction – taken as an attack on both that element of the club's support and FC United itself – further antagonized relationships.

The inequitable nature of the relationship further undermined notions of being 'at home', increased topophobic feelings toward it and has prompted two developments for FC United. One is that FC United's board has actively sought an alternative venue for home games, to date without success. Second, the club and its fans have been working to find a permanent home in the shape of a new ground development.

BRINGING IT ALL BACK HOME

Since 2007, the club have been developing plans for their own 'community stadium', closer to the heart of the city of Manchester, that it will own and control itself, and with a target of having this in place for the start of the 2011 season. This is based on a number of factors, the first of which are the cost and lack of control over match-day arrangements associated with playing 'away' when 'at home' in Bury. The distance from most fans' sense of home in Manchester and the lack of sustainability of the situation, has meant that the significant advantages of the large crowds and membership the club attracts, as well as benefits from surpluses being reinvested in the club as a not-for-profit social enterprise (Wheeler and Sillanpaa 1997), are lost.

The club rent their home ground, offices and football facilities for the first team, its youth team and its community programme outreach work. Assessments by the board of the club have cited being in Bury as a deterrent for fans living in

Manchester attending matches and the situation has meant that the club has been unable to fully develop a relationship with, and build a fan base in, local communities. Reversing this would above all enable the maintenance of low, affordable ticket prices, a core belief for the club.

However, the desire, in the words of one fan and author for 'a place finally to call home' (Wood 2007) among fans and club alike is equally strong. Within this is a real longing to realize an identity and sense of place, to be in Manchester itself and to build a stadium that embodies the desires of match-going supporters. The formation of the club had symbolically emphasized its identity as Mancunian – in its name and in the use of the city's crest within its badge. The desire now is to realize that with a permanent 'home' within the city. The anathema of dislocation of name and place that Bale refers to, cited above, is seen here in reverse – the club never has been in Manchester, but it now aims to be.

Discourses about the ground development have embodied many of those problematic notions of authenticity identified earlier. There is a desire to have a very 'traditional' design to the ground, yet this has to be delivered in the context of contemporary stadium design and regulations (Football Licensing Authority 2008). These desires, centred on standing, terraced accommodation, the ability to 'create an atmosphere' and the provision of alcohol reflected the 'freedom' many fans had now experienced when travelling with FC United away from home, often to poorly built, yet 'homely' non-league grounds. In one case there was even a plea to have a chimney to reflect the industrial heritage of Manchester and these associations with more traditional forms of cultural consumption and production, were also reflected in an internet forum discussion, 'Our New Home, What Would You Like?'

> From the grounds we have visited, I would like from:
> Leigh Gen – the terrace behind the goal.
> Glossop – the pies.
> Newcastle BS – the stewards.
> Leigh RMI – the centre spot.
> Accrington – easy access to the pub...
> Only one stand seated, main stand obv[iously]
> big terrace at our end
> smaller terrace at the away side, another terrace opposite main
> pies from my local chippy
> close to a pub as well all i want...
> All stewards to be FC United fans volunteers who understand and respect their fellow fans. (I'm talking about people persons).
> In addition to this I would like to see a permanent home for all FC United fans teams, all weather pitches for 5 & 7 aside games for fans and any other facilities that promote the health & well being of FC United fans. Oh, and a decent bar and a couple of burger vans for the less athletic.
> (FCUM 2009 Forum)

This desire for a 'home' has been the principle motivation for supporters to initiate a Development Fund to raise capital for the ground development.

> We're now into our third year as a football club and with each passing season the realization that we need our own home grows stronger [...] As with the purchase of any home, FC United need to raise a deposit; the Development Fund has been set up to raise that deposit. The Development Fund needs you! Only with your help will the dream of playing in our own ground become a reality. Fundraising will take various forms and will be co-ordinated by the club's Development Fundraising Group, which will meet regularly to plan events, drive fundraising initiatives and review our progress towards the £100,000 target for the season.
>
> (The Punter's Lounge 2008)

Furthermore, despite an expanding community programme – delivering sport, education, health, social inclusion and community cohesion schemes to deprived communities (FCUM 2008) – one of the driving forces behind the ground proposals has also been a feeling that the ambitions in the club's constitution and original *Manifesto* to be 'accessible and of benefit to communities of Manchester' cannot be realized without its own permanent base. This is a markedly different rationale for stadium development than the capitalist, free-market imperatives Bale identifies and emphasizes the origins of the club and its aims to continually challenge the dominant discourses in English football (cf. King's Chapter 1 and Zinganel's Chapter 4 in this volume).

This is all reflected in the plans developed to date, which include a 5,000 capacity stadium, the vast majority of it terraced accommodation in order to recreate conditions for 'ecstatic celebration' (King 1998); a main building with large bar and function area for fans to gather on match day; sports facilities for the local community; and facilities for young people to access on non match days. The rejection of options for a commercially driven stadium development reflect this orientation to both its own fan communities and those of the locale in which it seeks a home. This is in contrast, however, to the historical underpinning of English football's association with 'community' in which teams came from, not to, localities.

The status of the club as a cooperative has also unarguably aided this approach, helping to open doors to the local authorities where a more commercial proposition would not have garnered public or local government support. However, the stadium development must also be seen within the context of studies of stadium building, communitarianism and urban regeneration, such as Smith and Ingham's (2003) study of Cincinnati; as well as the wider shift in city policy in Europe, the UK and Manchester in particular (Brown *et al.* 2004: 11). Whereas the development of the City of Manchester Stadium by Manchester City Council (cf. Chapter 8) was part of a bigger process of city re-imaging and marketing based around major events, the development of a stadium for FC United within these cultural and economic policy processes provides yet another 'new nuance' to this experience.

CONCLUSION: BACK TO THE FUTURE?

The centrality of the stadium as a 'home' site for protest and for the active recreation of fan communities in an oppositional context does not fit easily with Bale's various descriptions of stadia as 'cathedrals', 'theatres' or 'prisons' (Bale 2000b). However, the strength of feelings associated with the stadium in protests at Manchester United and the development of FC United, most notably the fluid notions of 'home' entailed in them, does reflect Bale's emphasis on the importance of the social role of the stadium in football. As Bale argues, that social role is a changing in the face of the marketization of football and the individualization of the 'sportscape'. The example of FC United of Manchester provides an interesting take on these themes, as both an alternative to that free market individualization and in the changing understandings of football's relationship to communities.

Initial survey work undertaken by the club with its supporters has re-emphasized those preferences on internet forums for the construction of the ground to encompass a large, terraced 'end' with acoustics to emphasize the fans' vocal contributions. The desire for emancipation from the 'isolation of the seat' (cf. Chapter 1 and Conclusion) and the preference for 'community' as opposed to 'commercial' spaces stresses the distinction between this (imagined) 'fans'' stadium and the 'cash machine' referred to by Zinganel (in Chapter 4).

The ambitions of the club to develop its own stadium, a new 'home', also provides an interesting contrast to the 'traditional' understandings of football's relationship to its local communities. Formed in the late nineteenth and early twentieth century, most teams came from churches, factories and the new urbanized communities of the industrial revolution.

> The massive expansion in the scale and size of urban communities in the second half of the nineteenth century created new problems of identity for their inhabitants [...] In essence, football clubs provided a new focus for collective urban leisure in industrial towns and cities that were no longer integrated communities gathered around a handful of mines or mills [...] These inhabitants of big cities needed a cultural expression of their urbanism which went beyond the immediate ties of kin and locality. A need for rootedness as well as excitement is what seems most evident in the behaviour of football crowds.
>
> (Holt 1989: 167)

We can see in the FC United story, the persistence of some of these themes and the changing nature of others. The search for rootedness and excitement is certainly evident, though in the case of the former, from a very different perspective. Whereas Holt describes a process that was a result of industrialization, what we can see in FC United is a process that in many ways is the result of *de*-industrialization and the global, mediatized commodification of football. The development of Manchester United as a global leisure brand, the Glazers' takeover, the processes of 'glocalization' that can be seen in the local identity formation and politicization of a section of the fan base, and the resistance to the Glazers that resulted in the formation of the new club, can all in part be seen in this context.

Also, should plans for their own ground come to fruition, it will be a process that is in some ways reversed – a club formed from division and crisis at another, based around *supporter* communities (i.e. ones of consumption, identity and, in this case, opposition) rather than work or residential ones, naming itself after a city which it is yet to locate in but from which most of its fans come, seeking a new home in that city. It will be a paradoxical coming *to* a residential community as well as a coming *from* re-formed fan communities (however diffuse, multiple and fluid both of those are). This fluidity and change will develop as the place of the stadium changes with fans finding their new 'routes and practices by which individuals and groups make their way towards the match' (cf. Chapter 8).

Although these fan-community relationships will develop within a modern urban policy context, with all the added instrumental approaches to community development contained therein, the objective has been to create something that is in sharp contrast to the 'non place' of most modern stadia. The announcement in March 2010 that FC United's stadium will be built in Newton Heath, North Manchester – the location of Manchester United's origins – gives the story a sense of 'back to the future' and a new twist to football's notion of 'coming home'.

Ultimately, the development is being pursued to strengthen the opposition that FC United has represented, to create and sustain, as Noam Chomsky termed it in a very different context, 'the threat of a good example' (Chomsky 1985). In part this must be seen as an *attempt* at *emancipation* from the globalization of football and a fulfilment of the ambitions of FCUM to be a different, more egalitarian and more democratic football club, a challenge, however minor, to the dominant discourse in contemporary football. However, its success will also be heavily dependent on the extent to which the club and its supporter communities can build a sustainable relationship with its new neighbours.

It is in this light that it is useful to re-interpret our understandings of community in the context of football. Rather than relating purely to accepted formulations around tradition, organic development and space and place, it emphasizes the importance of symbolism in such moments for the formation of 'community', the oppositional nature of those symbols in this case and the enduring, but changing, centrality of the stadia as 'home' in football.

NOTES

1 I am indebted to my colleagues, Professor Tim Crabbe and Dr Gavin Mellor, of Substance, with whom some of the ideas and theoretical understandings in this chapter were developed, notably for an unpublished paper (Brown *et al.* 2005) as part of the Football and Its Communities research.
2 This was common song among fans in the late 1990s – one which attempted to both support the team but challenge the all-seater requirements.

3 This has been a persistent song at FC United matches. The 'gnome' referred to is Malcolm Glazer.
4 This was a phrase used by General Manager Andy Walsh at the founding General Meeting of the club in July 2005.
5 Marginson, speaking at FCUM General Meeting, March 2006.

REFERENCES

Bale, J. (1993) 'The spatial development of the modern stadium', *International Review for the Sociology of Sport*, 28(2): 121–34.
—— (2000a) *Sportscapes*, Sheffield: Geographical Association.
—— (2000b) 'The changing face of football: Stadiums and communities', in J. Garland, D. Malcolm and M. Rowe (eds) *The Future of Football: Challenges for the twenty-first century*, London: Frank Cass.
Bauman, Z. (2000) *Liquid Modernity*, Cambridge: Polity Press.
Bianchini, F. (2002) 'Culture and the city', paper presented to Urbis Seminars, 15 July, Urbis, Manchester.
Bianchini, F., Fisher, M., Montgomery, J. and Worpole, K. (1988) *City Centres, City Cultures: The role of the arts in the revitalisation of towns and cities*, Manchester: CLES.
Brown, A. (1998) 'United we stand: Some problems with fan democracy', in A. Brown (ed.) (2008) *Fanatics! Power, identity and fandom in football*, London: Routledge.
—— (2004) ' "Manchester is red"? Manchester United, fan identity and the "Sport City" ', in D. Andrews (ed.) *Manchester United: A thematic study*, London: Routledge.
—— (2008a) ' "Not for Sale"? The destruction and reformation of football communities in the Glazer takeover of Manchester United', in N. Tiesler and J. Coelho, J. (eds) *Globalised Football: Nations and migration, the city and the dream*, London: Routledge.
—— (2008b) ' "Our Club Our Rules": Fan communities at FC United of Manchester', in A. Brown, T. Crabbe and G. Mellor (2008) 'Football and community in the global context', *Soccer and Society*, Special Issue, 39(3).
Brown, A., Cohen, S. and O'Connor, J. (2000) 'Local music policies within a global music industry: Manchester and Sheffield', *Geoforum*, 31.
Brown, A., Crabbe, T. and Mellor, G. (2003) *Football And Its Communities, Interim Report 1: Baseline analysis of case study football and community initiatives*, Manchester: MMU. Online. Available www.substance.coop/files/Football%20and%20Its%20 Communities%20-%20Interim%20Report%201.pdf (accessed 24 March 2009).
—— (2005) *'End of an era': English football, endings and the performativity of fandom and corporate responses*, unpublished paper.
—— (2008) 'Football and community in the global context', *Soccer and Society*, Special Issue, 39(3).
Brown, A., Mellor, G., Blackshaw, T., Crabbe, T. and Stone, C. (2004) *Football and its Communities, Report Three: The impacts of a stadium move on the communities of a football club: The example of Manchester City FC*, Manchester: MMU. Online. Available www.substance.coop/files/Football%20and%20Its%20Communities%20 -%20Interim%20Report%203.pdf (accessed 24 March 2009).
Carslon, M. (1996) *Performance: A critical introduction*, London: Routledge.
Castells, M. and Hall, P. (1994) *Technopoles of the World: The making of 21st century industrial complexes*, Routledge: London.
Chomsky, N. (1985) *Nicaragua: The threat of a good example*, Oxfam America.
Cochrane, A., Peck, J. and Tickell, A. (1996) 'Manchester playing games', *Urban Studies*, 33(8): 1319–36.

Essex, S. and Chalkley, B. (1998) 'Olympic Games: Catalyst of urban change', *Leisure Studies*, 17: 187–206.

FCUM (2007) *A Statement of Beery Intent for Course You Can Malcolm*. Online. Available www.fc-utd.co.uk/story.php?story_id=1183 (accessed 17 October 2009).

—— (2008) *Community and Education Work Report, September 2007–September 2008*, Manchester: FC United of Manchester.

—— (2009) *Only Five Home Games Left*, Club Statement. Online. Available www.fc-utd.co.uk/story.php?story_id=2149 (accessed 24 March 2009).

FCUM Forum (2009) *Our New Home, What Would You Like?*. Online. Available www.fcunited.co.uk/fcumforum_org_uk/OurNewHomeWhat Would You Like.mht (accessed 11 September 2009).

Football Licensing Authority (2008) *The Guide to Safety at Sports Grounds*, London: The Stationery Office.

Giulianotti, R. (1999) *Football: A sociology of the global game*, Oxford: Polity Press.

Hague, E. and Mercer, J. (1998) 'Geographical memory and urban identity in Scotland: Raith Rovers FC and Kirkaldy', *Geography*, 83: 105–16.

Harvey, D. (1989) *The Condition of Postmodernity*, Oxford: Blackwells.

Henry, I. and Salcines, J.L.P. (1998) *Sport and the Analysis of Symbolic Regimes: An illustrative case study of the city of Sheffield*, Loughborough: Loughborough University.

Holt, R. (1989) *Sport and the British: A modern history*, Oxford: Oxford University Press.

Lenskyj, H. (2002) *The Best Olympics ever?: Social impacts of Sydney 2000*, London: Albany.

IMUSA (Independent Manchester United Supporters Association) (1998) *Redprint for Change*, Manchester: IMUSA.

Jary, D., Horne, J. and Bucke, T. (1991) 'Football "fanzines" and football culture: A case of successful "cultural contestation" ', *Sociological Review*, 39(3).

King, A. (1998) *The End of the Terraces: The transformation of English football in the 1990s*, London: Leicester University Press.

MacAloon, J. (1984) *Rite, Drama, Festival, Spectacle: Rehearsals toward a theory of cultural performance*, Philadelphia: Inst. for the Study of Human Issues.

Mackay, D. (1995) *A Sense of Place: The 'meaning' of Easter Road*, unpublished MA dissertation, Department of Geography, University of Edinburgh.

Myerscough, J. (1988) *The Economic Importance of the Arts in Britain*, London: Policy Studies Institute.

O'Connor, J. and Wynne, D. (eds) (1996) *From the Margins to the Centre: Cultural production and consumption in the post-industrial city*, Aldershot: Avebury.

Smith, J. and Ingham, A. (2003) 'On the waterfront: Retrospectives on the relationship between sport and communities', *Sociology of Sport Journal*, 20: 252–74.

Taylor, Lord Justice (1990) *The Hillsborough Stadium Disaster, Final Report*, London: HMSO.

Tönnies, F. (1974) *Community and Association*, London: Routledge.

The Punter's Lounge (2008) *F.C.U.M.* Online. Available www.punterslounge.com/forum/f27/f-c-u-m-66776/ (accessed 17 October 2009).

Tuan, Y. (1974) *Topophilia: A study of environmental perception, attitudes, and values*, London: Englewood Cliffs.

Wheeler, D. and Sillanpaa, M. (1997) *The Stakeholder Corporation: A Blueprint for maximising stakeholder value*, Pitman: London.

Wood, S. (2007) *Trips on Glue*. Online. Available www.tripsonglue.co.uk/index.php?option=com_content&task=view&id=1&Itemid=1 (accessed 17 October 2009).

Wynne, D. (ed.) (1992) *The Culture Industry*, Aldershot: Avebury.

Part IV

Gender and Space

Part IV
Gender and Space

Chapter 10: Sport, Football and Masculine Identity

The Stadium as a Window onto Gender Construction

Christian Bromberger

Whether for practice or play, sport is the perfect observatory for the social construction of gender. We don't have to remind ourselves that competitive sport has long been a bastion of masculinity. Olympic events for women date only to the games of 1928, over 30 years after the founding of the modern Olympics by Pierre de Coubertin. Many women's specialties have only recently been introduced: women's 1,500 metres in 1972, basketball 1976, the marathon 1984, judo 1992, pole vault 2000.

In France, several federations and competitions have accepted women only within the last 40 years: football since 1970, even though a women's team had existed between 1919 and 1932 (a period of emancipation in which sportswomen were characterized as 'tomboys'), weightlifting since 1984, and rugby since 1989. The first female contestant in the Tour de France raced in 1984, although her male counterpart has been competing since 1903. These are contact sports and mechanized disciplines that, despite woman's timid advances (especially in the martial arts), still remain a masculine prerogative. One therefore finds in the gender divisions operating in sport the same contradictions that anthropologists note when studying sexual division in the use of tools: for men tools are percussive, complex and mechanical whereas for women, they are more often a matter of technical gesture, less brutal and usually applied to flexible materials using simpler tools (with regard to the basis for the gender division of technical activities, see Testart 1986 and Tabet 1998).

There is doubtlessly a trend emerging which foresees a less discriminatory future, a trend evident in Seattle, when, on 9 November 1999, in a boxing match, Margaret Macgregor, alias 'the Tiger', won a victory on points over her male rival, Loi Chow. The confrontation was completely dominated by Macgregor who was more aggressive and mobile and enjoyed a distinct advantage in size. Marginal and exceptional as her victory may have been, the event signals release from a double bind: women's access to contact sports and the organization of mixed events. And yet we remain far removed from such ideals.

The French Boxing Federation counts a mere 3 per cent of women among boxing champions, but it is similar in automobile racing, sailing or athletic champions over whom there hovers a suspicion of androgyny.

It is for men then that the contact intensive, percussive sports employing mechanized equipment are reserved. For women, it is practices that recall precision, hygiene and physical grace, as expressed, for example, in synchronized swimming. This is one of only a few Olympic sports that are almost exclusively reserved for females and for which a significant part of the score is given for aesthetics when judging performance. The *Sporting 2000* survey commissioned by the French Ministry of Youth and Sport confirmed this recurring tendency. Sports for which at least two-thirds of practitioners are women include dance, gymnastics and ice skating. More women than men participate in such activities as walking, swimming and even equestrianism.

The large and growing proportion of women who engage in this last discipline is a good example of the differential degree of participation by men and women in the same practice. Since 1973, in France, the number of female riders has increased by 120 per cent, while the number of male riders has increased by only 42 per cent, so that today almost three-quarters of publicly registered riders are women. In riding, men do not particularly care to prepare and groom their mounts, a practice more common among women. Male riders tend to push their horses, whereas female riders are more inclined to persuasion (Digard 1995). One finds then, in male and female practice, the same 'qualities' that are conventionally attributed to men and women: strength and aggression on the one hand, kindness and persuasion on the other. There was a time when the opposition between male and female horse riding was even more marked; between the fifteenth and twentieth century, women generally rode sidesaddle while only men would ride astride. As Puritan pundits might have it, riding astride would warm a woman's lower parts, inciting her to debauchery and lust, while riding sidesaddle would preserve a woman's virginity (Tourre-Malen 2006). The same prejudices could be noted at the beginning of the twentieth century with respect to a woman's use of the bicycle. Feminists reacted against these sexist prejudices: at the Feminist Congress of 1896, President Marie Pognon raised her glass to 'the bicycle, egalitarian leveller'.

Relations between competition and sports institutions also provide insights into sport as a mirror of gender differences as constructed by our societies. If sporting activities broadly defined are, in France, about equally divided between men (52 per cent of the active population) and women (48 per cent), club membership and competitions present quite a different story, from one gender to the other. While approximately one-third of men practice some form of physical activity in a club or association, only one-fifth of women do so; three out of four competitors are men (Louveau 2004). As to responsibility in federal and community associations, these remain a near male monopoly: in France, only four sports federations among 101 have a woman for president, while departmental, regional and federal committees count women as 5 per cent of members.

Let us consider spectator sports. Contrasts are striking here also. In France, women are more likely to attend indoor events which proscribe aggressive physical contact such as basketball and volleyball, and prefer those favoring grace and 'appearance' (as in gymnastics, figure skating, synchronized swimming, various athletic disciplines), practices in which they themselves engage. Their interests are less centered on rankings, records and competition. Such general data, however, are modulated by the scale of the event. A home game, pitting village teams against one another, will attract a mixed gender, family audience and include many women who support their son, husband, a boyfriend or other friend. In the towns and villages of southwest France, rugby, a male sport par excellence, will attract a significant female attendance (32 per cent of spectators, for example, in St. Vincent de Tyrosse, a large village of the Landes region, cf. Darbon 1995). Once removed from this local, family context, rugby quickly becomes overwhelmingly male, consistent with its image as a contact sport (spectators at Bègles-Bordeaux matches, a large urban club among the elite at the time of the survey, are 85 per cent men, Bodin 1998: 119).

Similar findings have been made about football. In surveys conducted in football stadia in the 1990s, it was found that female attendance was significantly higher in local competitions, at the division level and below, than it was for the big national and international competitions (for the principal results of this European study see Lanfranchi 1992). There are also differences in age and social class, where sports, like tennis, attract a larger percentage of older women, with affluent social backgrounds: 41 per cent of Roland Garros spectators are women, even if it is true that racket sports have long been associated with young women of the 'leisured class'.

Differentiation of sporting practices as to whether they are masculine or feminine and differences in the gender composition of the spectating public do not reflect the laws of nature (muscular, hormonal, psychological) universally applied, but vary significantly depending on the sports stories and on the ideological context of each country. A male contact sport, popular in most countries, football (soccer) is mainly practiced by upper-class women in the United States (cf. Chapter 11). We should not interpret this however, as the mark of a radically different treatment of gender categories in the new world, but rather of United States' exceptionalism in the development of their own national sports: baseball, football and basketball (Markovits 1990). Soccer in North America is a minor sport, practiced by immigrants and women, and otherwise deemed slow and boring. 'Real men' however, are passionate about (American) football which is fitful and violent. Hierarchy in sport is, here as elsewhere, homologous to that of gender.

The tendency toward gender segregation and conditions of access to the public arena only harden in regimes obsessed with concealment of the female body. Such is the case in Iran where the only specialities to which women may aspire in the sight of men are shooting, riding, canoeing, mountaineering, skiing and competitions for the handicapped, all practices which, unlike athletics or swimming, accommodate themselves somehow to the Islamic dress code. Such 'victories' are recent, however, and every advance is protested by the fundamentalists.

The practice of women's football – a sport synonymous with international openness and particularly prized by young Iranian women in urban areas (on football and sports in Iran cf. Bromberger 1998, 2003, 2006; Assmann and Gülker's Chapter 12 in this volume) – is also controversial, and it is only recently, in 2002, that a Women's National Team was created. When they practice in Tehran parks or play in official competitions, the players are fully covered, even in the heat of summer. For this reason, the wearing of Islamic dress, Iran's women's football team has been barred by FIFA from participating in the inaugural Youth Olympic Games in August 2010. The principal advocate for women's sports is the spirited daughter of former President Rafsanjani, Faezeh, who in 1993 founded the Islamic Women's Sporting Meet, the fourth of which was held in Tehran in September 2005.

According to 'cultural usages', men may not attend most women's events, which, because of immodest displays of flesh, are also enjoined from public broadcast. Photography is forbidden, of course, and the use of mobile phones, possibly equipped with a camera, closely monitored. The spectacle of national men's football competitions poses a more ambiguous problem in that women are denied access to stadia even though matches are broadcast on television and no *fatwa* (religious decree) exists to sanction this ban.

Challenging the ban has become a leitmotiv for women's rights and every great match is an occasion for women to attempt to enter the stadium. The origin for this series of protests was the hero's welcome given the national team following their qualifying match in Australia for the 1998 World Cup. Several thousand women (especially young women) invaded the Tehran stadium where

Figure 10.1
An exclusively male attendance in Tehran stadium, 2006.

Figure 10.2
Abroad young Iranian
female supporters attend
the matches of their
national team, Lyon,
before the match of Iran
against USA, 1998.

the national team were to be fêted as heroes. The media exhorted the 'dear sisters' to stay home and watch the event on television, avoiding any mention of the mutinous women in their public coverage. 'Are we not part of this nation? We too want to celebrate. We are not ants', proclaimed the upstarts.

The problem of female access to stadia was raised again, in November 2001, during the Iran vs. Ireland qualifying match for the 2002 World Cup when Irish women insisted on attending. Following much equivocation and several reversals the Irish women were finally admitted while Iranian women remained excluded. In January 2003 it was announced that, under pressure from reformers then in power, the ban would be lifted and that sections of the stadium would be reserved for women. The conservative trend prevailed, however, and fans were turned back as they approached the gates. In the fall of 2004, 11 women tried to watch a friendly match between Iran and Germany, but were turned away while German women were admitted. 'How are we different from them?' protested the rebels. The situation seemed to improve in the pre-electoral context of the spring of 2005: on 25 March a small group of women was allowed to attend a crucial World Cup qualifying match between Iran and Japan. On 15 April members of the Women's Federation (footballers, referees and coaches) were admitted to the stadium in Isfahan to attend a match between a local team and the visiting Syrian national team.

But it was only for the qualifying match against North Korea in June 2005 that a threshold seemed to have been crossed. A significant number of female supporters were allowed to attend the match under heavy police surveillance. The fans were placed between sections of Korean fans to avoid any possibility of promiscuity with Iranians. Since then, politicians and candidates have routinely promised – no doubt for electoral purposes – to create special sections for women, proposals which have been systematically rejected by the religious leadership. The 150 women who tried, on 1 March 2006, to attend the friendly match against Costa Rica, waving a banner proclaiming 'We want to support the national team', were strongly rebuffed. The presence of women in stadia has become a major political issue and has even inspired filmmakers. In *Offside*, an Iranian film which won a Silver Bear at the 2006 Berlin Film Festival, but remained banned in Iran, Jafar Panahi depicts the story of a young girl who disguises herself as a boy to go to Azadi Stadium (a large, 100,000 capacity stadium west of Tehran; for an exclusively female attendance at a friendly match of the Iranian women's national team cf. Chapter 12).

The stadium interdiction and the concern for protecting women are driven by an obsession with discipline, moral order and social propriety, but also by the fear of unrestrained public meetings and the excess of free speech. Sports stadia have been the scene of numerous protests and confrontations over the past ten years and are closely monitored. Public exuberance following sporting victories is perceived as a threat to the social order and an affront to public decency, a moral code that prescribes sobriety and seriousness in public demeanour. Loud honking and dancing in the streets are seen as intolerable transgressions of the imposed standards. Daily, conservative authorities are offended by the vulgarity of spectators, who, as elsewhere, consider that the sports arena is one of the only places where you can say bad words (*fohsh*). There is indeed a singular contrast between supporters' slogans (e.g. *shir-e samavar dar kun-e davar*, 'the samovar tap up the referee's ass') and slogans plastered in the cheering sections, indicating that prayer is the key to paradise and that we must build in stages from the example of Ali (the first Shiite Imam) and his family.

In this way and in many others, the sports arena inspires fear among pernickety authorities attached to a puritan ethic. For most conservatives and for those now in power, players must, by their appearance and behaviour, set an example. In October 2005, the Football Federation called on players to respect 'Islamic values', and enjoined them not to wear tight-fitting clothes, earrings, rings or necklaces, to maintain proper grooming of their hirsute selves, avoiding irregular beards, ponytails and long or curly hair. In short, anything that recalls a Western look is prohibited. The stars did not miss an opportunity to repost, noting, for example, that the Prophet himself wore his hair long.

But let us return to our subject, and to Southern Europe where I have conducted a number of surveys, one of the purposes of which was to capture the source of this well-established connection between football and the glorification of manly 'values'. While we are at it, let us also get a measure of the interest each gender may have for its particular practice and the sporting event before scrutinizing the individual meanings.

FOOTBALL, A MAN'S BUSINESS

Except for a fleeting moment in the aftermath of the First World War, women's football did not really take off in Europe until the 1970s, a turning point in defining gender roles, even if this boom remains modest and female participation rates only underscore the contrasts between Northern and Southern Europe. The football associations of the Nordic countries have a high percentage of women in their ranks: 31 per cent in Iceland, 24 per cent in Sweden, 22 per cent in Norway, 18 per cent in Denmark and 14 per cent in Finland. Participation rates are high in Germany (13.5 per cent for a total of 840,000 registered athletes in 2003) and remain significant in the Netherlands (7.5 per cent). They do not however, exceed 4 per cent in the countries of Latin Europe (3.5 per cent in France, 2 per cent in Spain, 1.2 per cent in Italy). In this part of the world, the female footballer is unique and an accident of circumstance. The case of Italian player Carolina Morace is quite extraordinary: scorer of 500 goals during her career, she was, in 1999, the first woman to lead a professional men's team, Viterbese, competing in series C (the third division) of the Italian league. Unfortunately, and perhaps as a testament to the persistence of the old ways, this experience did not last more than 100 days.

Sports practice aside, attendance at principal matches is overwhelmingly male, although a significant trend has emerged over the last 30 years. Surveys in the 1980s and the early 1990s pointed to a modest feminization of spectator attendance (7–14 per cent depending on location, cf. Bromberger 1995: 217; Bromberger and Lestrelin 2008). More recent data from France, Italy, Spain and England show a sharp increase in women's turnout to between 20 and 25 per cent of attendance (for England, see Chester 1994, for France, Spain and Italy statistics are taken from various sources such as theses, study reports, specialized surveys). If we encounter more and more genuine *aficionadas* in the stands, it is rare that they should come on their own. Usually, they accompany a father, a brother, a 'sweetheart' or a husband, and such complicity, or concession, is often ephemeral. It is as a teenager that such outings are most popular. The young and passionate gladly take their place in the end-zones with their friends to particip- ate in the rites of their age group. Adult women on the other hand, especially housewives, rarely attend stadium events, even if it appears that they are more familiar with the event, and in some cases, even encouraged as in England, as a means of imparting a more peaceful ambiance (cf. Chapter 1). Some of these older women, especially the well-to-do, are happy to comply and so to partake of the comfort of a spectator's box in what is essentially a mundane ritual.

Football viewership on television has also been feminized. A survey con- ducted before the 1998 World Cup (a private study performed by SOFRES for the Kronenbourg Breweries in February 1998) revealed the big gap between the football television audiences as they are imagined and as they truly are. For French respondents at the time, assiduous viewers of televised football matches were almost exclusively (97 per cent) male, whereas the reality is that only 62 per cent are men and 38 per cent women, with women watching with a partner in 35 per cent of cases, although one imagines that such shared viewership con- cerns only 20 per cent of households. The intensity of interest varies by gender, and it is common for men to impose or negotiate diplomatically a programme choice. Women will often hold back and view with reserve. They are less fluent in their technical reviews, more distant and less aggressive in substituting their views for those of the coaches and referees. Similarly, the conventional image of the group of friends drinking beer and eating pizza during the game should be revised: only 17 per cent (not 82 per cent as the French think) of men consume beer and only 8 per cent (not 21 per cent) munch pizza when watching a game.

Whatever the nuances and the evolving practices, football remains essentially a masculine activity, a paean to the masculine that crystallizes manly virtues. What boy did not, as he dribbled a ball on the path of adolescence, dream of greatness and impossible feats (cf. Chapter 7)? Modes of attendance over the ages of life, the slogans and metaphors used by fans in stadia are good indicators of how men are constructed and construct themselves.

AROUND THE STADIUM

Whether in the British (that is to say, rectangular) or Latin (which is to say, oval) tradition (with respect to amphitheaters) the stadium is a singular space in which we may observe while being observed, a key function of the 'mass ring' in the words of Elias Canetti (1986). This space is also partitioned into grandstands and ends, sides, curves located behind the goals, often open to wind, sun and rain and summarily furnished. Each of the areas, bounded by grids, forms a sort of territory which comprises a relatively homogeneous population (by age, residential origin and social status). Each step in the life-history of a supporter may be reflected in the differential mode of occupying stadium geography. Early learning takes place in stands or bleachers under the calm guidance of a father, an uncle or some vigilant initiator, with discussion and commentary continuing through family meals (cf. Chapter 14). In adolescence, boys, free of parental tutelage, earn 'their place' among turbulent clusters of friends.

Figure 10.3
Young supporters of
Tehran Esteghlal team,
1998.

Stadium end zones that in France were termed 'popular' (because it brought together an audience with little money), should now be renamed 'juvenile' because they have become emblematic of a class of age rather than a social class. This is where groups of young supporters and demonstrative 'diehards' ('Ultras', as they are called in Italy and France) have established their territory. Participation in one of these self-managed groups is understood as a step in a 'manly career', where one proves oneself and shows that one 'has what it takes' by word and sometimes provocative gesture ('A little bit of violence never hurt anybody' goes the English saying). Within these groups of peers 15 to 25, even 30 years of age (the socialization of youth has increased considerably in recent decades), members test the limits and even break the rules. Such groups of young supporters, however, have ethical standards of their own.

One fundamental principle which operates as a criterion of assessment and as a guide for action is honour. Any aspersion upon a group's name or identity, such as stealing a logo or a banner, for example, are regarded as intolerable offences that must be redressed. Upon such an affront a vindicatory cycle is launched complete with punitive expeditions and retribution. Out of public sight and in the group's most hidden precinct the stolen 'trophies' are admired and serve as reminders of the group's history and great deeds. If the code of honour requires a challenge and an exemplary response to the provocations of others, it prohibits fighting in disproportionate numbers, braggart vainglory: 'We have no right to attack the *Mastres*' says a Marseilles supporter, 'the fight is too uneven' (*Mastre*: a 'wannabe' supporter, wrapped in the signs of membership but of little consequence).

Among such groups of young supporters, self-managed *bachelleries* (in English: 'coterie'; the French word describes what were known in the old days as associations of single males) experimented with marginal forms of socialization such as were formerly supported by large institutions (religious, political, labour) under the guidance of adults. Such coteries perpetuate solidarity and such masculine values as have been corroded over time. These groups have few girls – usually no more than 10 per cent – who are very rarely among the leaders. 'Too many girls soften the guys, it lowers their *gnaque*' (*gnaque*: aggressivity). Young girls who do belong to supporter groups generally accompany their friends, although autonomous girls groups have appeared in recent years.

But such phenomena are rare and often ephemeral, whereas large groups of supporters, numbering several thousand members, with premises and equipment, constitute a major factor in the socialization of young men. Another motivation drives these diehard supporters: it is a need for affirmation, a 'hunger for recognition', in the felicitous expression of Alain Ehrenberg (1986), that drives this youth subculture. 'To be there, to exist, to put up a banner with our name, that was our primary objective', stated the head of a splinter group. Symptomatically, these young fans celebrate as much, or even more, their group as their favorite team. Their banners, scarves and outfits display their name, their initials or their specific colours. The huge sail they unfurl covering the entire end zone of the stadium, minutes before the start of a match is emblazoned with the symbols of their team but also, in a very showy way, symbols of the group. To be seen, recognized and identified, such is the *tour de force* proper endemic to this kind of supporter and that abolishes the conventional boundaries of social representation. Anonymous and invisible subjects contemplating the stars, the Ultras have lifted themselves to the rank of stars commanding spectacular air time and leveraging media as proof of their celebrity status. A former leader of a large Marseilles support group confided, 'I knew we had made it when *L'Equipe* [the national sports daily newspaper in France] ran a front-page article on our group'. This desire for visibility is much like the keen sense of competition unfolding on the field. It is up to each group to affirm that it is first in imposing its presence at the centre of the bleachers behind the goal.

With the passage of effervescent youth, as supporters marry or enter stable relationships, a temporal break is introduced into the cycle of male sociability previously satisfied through the supporter organization: more or less resigned partners, young women may for several months pay sentimental tribute to the passion of a partner who, in a remote corner of the arena, away from the noise and tumult, attempts an unlikely conversion. This gallant interlude is followed in middle age by new forms of male sociability, whether on the sidelines, in forums or among professionals, 'colleagues', drinking buddies, in-laws, former classmates, a time forgotten. To the hale and hearty realm of youth among friends succeeds the wiser, measured reality of adults of a similar class.

In short each new form of occupancy of the stadium space produces a rite of passage on the life-path of a man. These shifts are reflected and set off, symptomatically, at the dawn of each new season.

> It's decided. Next year I'll quit the end-zone and join my brother who has season tickets with his friends on the east side. What do you think? I am 26 years old, and it's just a little too crazy here in the end-zone,

a supporter explained to me in Marseilles. Over time and following successive transformations the supporter may well find he has made his way around the stadium, as if the ring of the arena somehow materialized the circle of life.

FANNING THE FLAMES OF VIRILITY

The virulence of insults against the opponent or the referee varies significantly from one area of the stadium to another, from the ends where young Ultras gather to the sections where upscale spectators have installed themselves. Regardless of whether insults exacerbate or euphemize, taunts are always drawn from one of four registers: discredit of the other (through scathing stereotypes or racial slurs), war (through calls to 'mobilization' and the display of banners by young fans who call their group 'Army', 'Brigade', 'Corps'), life and death (*Devi morire!* parodied the *tifosi* – 'fans' in Italian – at an injured opponent) and finally, sexuality, probably the most employed among the registers of disqualification.

Songs, slogans, gestures of defiance and condemnation (both obscene and suggestive), emblems (oversized bananas squeezed at the base), drawings on banners are most often scathing variations on an opponent's virility. Durkheim and Mauss, had they hung out in stadia, would have been struck by the simplicity of the forms of classification of humanity in the context of a football game: On the one hand, 'we' refers to 'real men' while 'they' or 'them' (opposing players, referees, capital journalists, always hostile to our own), are relegated to the ranks of sub-group, of passive homosexuals, cuckolded husbands, abject wimps, retarded children, sons incapable of defending their mother, which is to say, their honor. 'In Toulon they're all fags/in Bordeaux they've got a stick up...' proclaims one Marseilles Ultra standard, or another, a Marseilles T-shirt that reads 'Paris, stick it up your...', stigmatizing the PSG (Paris Club) by calling PSG supporters 'double-A cups' or even 'Gay-Sado-Fags'. The anthology of these insults suggests the portrait of a dominant male humiliating and subjugating the other: *Ciuccia la, ciuccia la banana, o Veronese, ciuccia la banana* ('Suck it, suck the banana, O Veronese, suck the banana'), scream the Neapolitan supporters at their reviled North Italian adversaries. 'Bordelais, I fucked your mother on the Cane-cane-cane-bière' (after the central boulevard of Marseilles, the Canebière) sung by Marseilles Ultras to the tune of *Chevaliers de la Table Ronde*, following a victory over Bordeaux (see Figure 10.4 in which Marseille challenges AC Milan).

Figure 10.4
Sexual disqualification of
AC Milan's team, 1993.

When a match is dominated by 'the other', the assertion of manly honor is not diminished, but turns the misfortune to its advantage. If all is going well for the adversary, the beaten supporter will taunt the opponent, recalling with more than just a touch of facetious sarcasm that no one can enjoy perfect happiness and that the corollary of such luck – of course, the other's success is mere 'luck' – is male misfortune: 'lucky at bowling, unlucky in love', says the proverb. Or the chant of 'Cuckolds! Cuckolds!' may be heard from the stands, stigmatizing the insolent success of the lucky opponents. But, if one of our own fails, that is, 'concedes without the slightest excuse', 'throws in the towel', abdicates one's masculine duty, retribution is swift and the guilty party denounced as being of incomplete or deficient masculinity: 'Go back to bowling!', 'Pussy, go turn a trick!'

Commentary on the play, on the feelings experienced during the match are often metaphoric, even sexual. 'We get a hard-on watching Papin and Waddle' (star forwards from the 1990s team), maintain supporters of Olympique de Marseille. To speak of a goal is a more or less elliptical variation on the subject of orgasm: 'Did you see how he put it to them? He stuck it right to the hole in the top corner'. As for missed goals, in defeat, these are experienced as frustration, 'impotence' and 'sterility'.

The football game does indeed provide a good 'analogy' for virile sexuality. It is first a competitive tribute to the male body, a sort of 'sexual display' where men look upon one another, glorify themselves, measure their prowess against the competition, behaviour that is often only implied in daily life (cf. Chapter 15). This tribute to the male body takes a startling turn when officials turn out to congratulate the players in the locker room: fully dressed, they become minor characters before the triumphant and eloquent nudity of the protagonists. The match is also an opportunity to display 'our own' capacity for preserving manly honor. Each team defends its cage, just like 'our women', to preserve their virginity, to keep them 'inviolate' – the conventional vocabulary is revealing – seeking to 'penetrate', indeed, to 'drill' the adversary defense and scoring a goal is like 'deflowering' the adversary. Cunning, deception, force and brutality are used to win a man's honor for which 'the other's' submission to 'our own' is the condition. Ultimately, what is the point in exacerbating masculine virility in the stadium, and more specifically, of sexually disqualifying and 'sissifying' the adversary as an incomplete and subordinate male?

Such salacious challenges, 'filthy language whose echo alone would sully a lady's hearing', to quote an English chronicler of the early twentieth century (quoted in Walvin 1986: 3), share the tradition, like calls for violence and bloodshed in the clamour of unbridled partisanship, of shocking and outrageous humiliation to influence the flow of play. Such behaviour also reminds us that a stadium is an arena in which 'values', and more specifically, manly virtues were once boldly displayed. They underscore and highlight in match after match borders now obscured, which reserved to men the right to make war, however stylized as ritual complete with violent contact (symptomatically, it should be noted that the tackle is not allowed in women's football). Machismo, the prestige of a male 'who knows how to fight' and to respond to insults, finds nurture in sporting events all the more as the prevailing ideology advocates the neutralization of sexual differences. The most eloquent poets of manly honor are recruited among popular audiences and inner city youth, refractory and contemptuous of gentrified lifestyles and attached to traditional community values. It is these who especially appreciate the manly challenges thrown out to opponents, the man-to-man settlement of scores, like Zinedine Zidane's headbutt that floored the Italian defender, Marco Materazzi, after he insulted the French player's sister in extra time play in the World Cup final, played in Berlin on 9 July 2006.

The manly displays that accompany each encounter express more than mere aggressive pride to be engaged in the battle being fought on the ground. They are, in fact, a parody of the 'condition' of males in our societies and indicative of surprising fragility. While female destiny is organized as a series of successive and irreversible slices (a mother does not skip except to initiate her daughter and does not get excited about a game of hopscotch), a man's fate is seen as perpetually unfinished, requiring that a man regularly test and prove himself. Support for a team of young males, sexual disqualification of 'the other' are the means by which, through active participation and by proxy, a male will test and reaffirm his manhood. It is at the price of such proclamations that doubt – always latent – is vanquished and that men's gatherings find solidarity, camaraderie and friendship, the very fabric of social life. Only the winning goal and denial of 'the other's' masculinity – conspicuous proof of one's own masculinity – justify intimacy and embraces among peers.

Football shows us how it is we construct our men: from the shelter of the school yards to the field of fortune, are instilled in men from childhood, the core values: strength, cunning, skill, group solidarity ('Don't be so stingy! Pass the ball!'). The sports event dramatizes these virtues and allows the vocal expression of the prerogatives of masculine 'culture': the right to verbal abuse, to expressive gestures, to cursing and whistling – behaviours rigorously excluded from the more decorous female repertoire, and relegated to the marginal areas at the outskirts of cities, where the stadium is usually located. The game and the spectacle thus evoke the uncertainties that mark the virile life, where weaknesses, deceit, shame, dominance and insolent luck harbouring suspicions and solidarity degenerating into ambiguous sentimentality (when a disappointed supporter surreptitiously lets loose a tear): on the field and in the stands there is played out and replayed the fragile identity of men.

As a virility ritual, the football match is being progressively transformed into a sporting spectacle. Increased ticket prices, comfortable stadia and efforts to attract family audiences will probably ultimately rid the major sports arenas of turbulent juveniles (cf. Chapter 1). Already in England masculine support is fading from the main sporting venues to off-premises or to the lower divisions. For the demonstrative and provocative faction chants and choreographies, there is substituted increasingly sophisticated and professionalized programming. Such transformation reflects contemporary developments in sports entertainment and the cracks that now riddle the seawall of masculine companionship.

REFERENCES

Bodin, D. (1998) *Sports et Violence* (Ph.D thesis), Université Victor Segalen Bordeaux II.

Bromberger, C. (1995) *Le Match de Football. Ethnologie d'une passion partisane à Marseille, Naples et Turin*, Paris: Editions de la Maison des sciences de l'homme.

—— (1998) 'Le football en Iran', *Société et Représentations*, 7: 101–15.

—— (2003) 'Iran: Les temps qui s'entrechoquent', *La Pensée*, 333: 79–94.

—— (2006) 'Iran, el balon y el turbante', *Vanguardia*, 20: 112–18.

Bromberger, C. and Lestrelin, L. (2008) 'Le sport et ses publics', in *Le Sport en France*, Paris: La Documentation française.

Canetti, E. (1986) *Masse et Puissance*, Paris: Gallimard.

Chester, N. (1994) *Carling Premiership Fan Surveys (1993–1994)*, Leicester: University of Leicester.

Darbon, S. (1995) *Rugby. Mode de vie*, Paris: Jean-Michel Place.

Digard, J.-P. (1995) 'Cheval, mon amour', *Terrain*, 25: 49–60.

Ehrenberg, A. (1986) 'La rage de paraître', *Autrement. L'amour foot*, 80: 148–58.

Lanfranchi, P. (ed.) (1992) *Il Calcio e il suo Pubblico*, Napoli: ESI.

Louveau, C. (2004) 'Sexuation du travail sportif et construction sociale de la féminité', *Cahiers du Genre*, 36: 163–83.

Markovits, A.S. (1990) 'Pourquoi n'y a-t-il pas de football aux États-Unis? L'autre exceptionnalisme Américain', *Vingtième Siècle*, 26: 19–36.

Testart, A. (1986) *Essai sur les Fondements de la Division Sexuelle du Travail chez les Chasseurs-Cueilleurs*, Paris: Editions de l'EHESS.

Tabet, P. (1998) *La Construction Sociale de l'Inégalité des Sexes. Des outils et des corps*, Paris Montréal: L'Harmattan.

Tourre-Malen, C. (2006) *Femmes à Cheval*, Paris: Belin.

Walvin, J. (1986) *Football and the Decline of Britain*, London: MacMillan.

Chapter 11: Producing Gender-normative Spaces in U.S. Women's Professional Soccer

Tiffany Muller Myrdahl

On 25 February 2009, representatives from the newest incarnation of U.S. women's professional soccer explicitly marked their affiliation with the volatile stock exchange by ringing the closing bell of the NASDAQ stock market. The new league's movement toward an altar of capitalism demonstrates its fundamental reliance upon capital investment. This relationship is notable for two reasons. First, Women's Professional Soccer (WPS), which began play in March 2009, emerged following the 2003 failure of the Women's United Soccer Association (WUSA) league, whose collapse was linked to financial mismanagement, including a reduction in media visibility that ensured a loss of advertising support. According to sports economist Andrew Zimbalist, 'The suspension of the WUSA has nothing to do with the viability of women's sports. Rather, it is the result of a misguided business plan that was poorly implemented, along with an inauspicious macroenvironment' (2006: 108). Thus, the WPS will undoubtedly do everything in its power to avoid the same fate. Arguably, its central strategy must include a heightened responsiveness to its investors and media sponsors.

Second, the link between the WPS and its investors is worth noting because this relationship has very particular implications for the league's game spaces and game-day experience. The league will walk the fine line of creating a game space that is appealing to both funders and fans as it tries to create a sustainable base of support. For instance, the WPS has tapped fewer giant venues for league play, embraced Twitter and other new media (Bell 23 March 2009), and reached out to growing niche markets, like Latino fans, in its attempt to develop a strong following. Yet the most notable – perhaps notorious – tactic that the league has used to attract interest is unveiling the skort, or the PUMA wrap: the WPS uniform kit, designed and supplied by its founding partner PUMA, includes 'tailored jerseys, shorts, and wraps (think a kind of tennis dress),' noted New York Times soccer blogger Jack Bell (26 February 2009). Decried by many followers, the skort component of the uniform, as well as its fashion show unveiling (Figure 11.1), was considered to be an effort to 'girl up/straighten up the look of the

Figure 11.1
Heather O'Reilly and
Christie Rampone
unveiling the skort: the
WPS uniform kit,
designed and supplied by
its founding partner
PUMA, 2009.

WPS' (Doyle 5 March 2009). According to these fans, the skort and the accompanying fashion show hoopla drew exactly the opposite kind of attention to the one the WPS sought: rather than requiring that their athletes be taken seriously *as athletes*, the league and its key sponsor emphasized the beauty of its players and the feminine design of its uniforms; indeed, the unveiling highlighted everything *but* soccer skills. At the same time, the WPS played into a long-standing neurosis about female athletes: that their on-field play translates to off-field masculinity and thus lesbianism.

The 'skort affair' serves as a reminder that the seemingly apolitical business strategies employed by women's professional athletic leagues are important indicators of the balance they must strike to attract fans and satisfy funders within a leisure market that has not been able to rid itself of gender-normative and heteronormative stereotypes (on the 'colonization' of athletes' bodies through marketing strategies, cf. Chapter 15). Indeed, this incident arguably plays into such stereotypes by adopting the sexist philosophy that 'the way to make women's soccer more popular [is] to make the players wear tighter shorts,' a strategy advocated by FIFA president Sepp Blatter (Christenson and Kelso 16 January 2004). Yet, the 'skort affair' is only one element of the league's self-presentation. The 'See Extraordinary'[1] television and internet campaign, a series of eight advertisements that highlight individual WPS athletes in a stylized performance of soccer skills, is the league's primary form of promotion. In contrast to the uniform unveiling, the 'See Extraordinary' campaign emphasizes only skill on the field: the video gives the sense that the audience is watching the actions of one player close up, but under the lights during a night game, so there is very little attention paid to the player's appearance. Taken together, these tactics offer a complex picture about how the WPS will do business: it provides clues into the ways that the league will represent itself and into the game spaces and game-day experience that it will create.

This chapter offers an early reflection on the WPS and its emergence from its predecessor, the WUSA. I argue that league (WUSA and WPS) representations and game spaces create(d) a particular game-day experience and thus a particular vision of professional women's soccer in the U.S. Like the league-deployed discourses they employ, game spaces are material articulations of league self-image; thus, they provide insight into the strategies intended to cultivate enduring support for women's soccer. As such, league game spaces, including discourses and daily practices, are significant for their articulations of, and disruptions to, normative associations of gender and sexuality especially as they relate to long-held cultural anxieties about women's sport and women athletes. Because game spaces, like all social spaces, are produced in and through the context of social life, they are 'integral to the production of social relations' (Massey 1994: 4). In this case, the game spaces of women's professional soccer are especially important for their ability to communicate or reframe relations of power and difference. Analyzing the materialities of professional women's soccer spaces, then, reveals how league efforts to capture fans and create cultural capital has been influenced by, and thus inform, normative gender relations.

U.S. WOMEN'S SOCCER: HISTORICAL CONTEXT

Soccer has been a physical activity for elite women in the U.S. since the early twentieth century when it was a staple of physical education courses in women's colleges (Ladda 2000). The roots of its current success as both a recreational activity and spectator sport are recent: competitive leagues for girls and women blossomed only in the 1970s and thereafter (Knoppers and Anthonissen 2003: 356), and the U.S. women's national team formed in 1985. According to the United States Youth Soccer Association, now the country's largest youth sports organization, there were more than three million registered youth (ages 5–19) soccer players in 2000, 45 per cent of whom were female (USYS 2000). The Sporting Goods Marketing Association, which captures a broader spectrum of participants in terms of age group and recreational status, puts that number even higher: 'In 1999, 7.3 million females aged six and older participated in soccer, a 20 per cent increase over the 6.06 million reported in 1987, the first year the study was conducted' (SGMA 2000).

The evolution of girls' and women's soccer from an activity that occurred primarily in physical education classes and intramural college leagues (Knoppers and Anthonissen 2003: 356) to an activity that is played both recreationally and competitively by millions and is a spectator sport is due to at least two significant factors. First, soccer was long ago eclipsed by other sports, most notably American football, in men's participation. One consequence of low participation rates among men is that U.S. attitudes toward and discourses of masculinity share a much more tenuous link with participation and performance in soccer than they do with American football and other sports that are perceived as more combative (cf. Chapter 10). In the U.S., masculinity has been tied more intimately to sports where play is characterized more in terms of physical aggression and strength than in terms of agility, speed, or finesse. This gendered construction is fundamental to understanding the landscape of sport in the U.S., and especially the normalization of heterosexual masculinity and femininity as read through participation in sport. For boys and men, participation in sports and activities that emphasize the agility and finesse over physical strength and combat (figure skating, for example, as compared to hockey) can come with accusations of aberrant sexuality, a result not only of participating in a 'girls' domain but also for partaking in activities that lack legible 'masculine' qualities (Messner 1988). For girls and women, similar (hetero)sexualized notions of deviant femininity have shaped the growth of women's athletics. As Cahn argues, however, these discourses have shifted such that there is a greater willingness to accept women athletes in the U.S. today:

> Participating [. . .] in sport no longer automatically connote[s] masculinity; an appreciative public generally accepts that a woman can actively pursue athletic excellence with no cost to her 'femininity,' however one defines it. Yet older associations between masculinity and sport linger on, as do cultural fears about physically strong, sexually independent women. This creates a peculiar tension: The growing popularity of women's sport hinges on the athlete's success in reassuring the public that, however exceptional her athletic talents, she is in all respects a 'normal' woman.

> (Cahn 1994: 265)

Thus, in spite of unprecedented participation by girls and women in amateur and professional sports, material and metaphorical landscapes of sport remain important sites of contest over what constitutes 'appropriate' attributes of womanhood and its demonstrative displays: 'legible' femininity and heterosexuality (Messner 1988). Yet, the upshot of this historical, albeit problematic, formulation of sport, gender, and sexuality is that girls' participation in soccer has not been perceived as a challenge to femininity in the same ways that girls' participation in, for example, American football is. Thus, it is possible for girls to play soccer and still be read as 'appropriately' feminine – and therefore heterosexual. Both of these factors have enabled girls and women to participate in soccer more readily than they have in other sports.

The central factor in the rise of U.S. women's soccer was the passage of Title IX in 1972, which institutionalized the demand for equal access to athletic funding, equipment, and opportunities. Title IX, part of the Educational Amendments to the 1964 Civil Rights Act, states that educational institutions receiving federal funds cannot discriminate, or deny equal benefits, on the basis of sex. In other words, the same number of athletic opportunities, for instance, must be available to both male and female students. While athletic programs were not the target of the law, its effects have been most visible in relation to sport.

Although compliance with and enforcement of Title IX continue to be challenged – indeed, the law itself remains contested – and there remain many disparities between boys' and girls' participation in youth sports, Title IX had a dramatic effect on increasing girls' participation in sports. For women's soccer, the numbers have been especially profound. At the collegiate level, women's soccer demonstrated the most consistently strong 'growth pattern within all NCAA [National Collegiate Athletic Association] divisions' (Carpenter and Acosta 2008).[2] The numbers are stark: In 1981, 78 NCAA schools sponsored women's soccer, whereas in 1998, there were 721 NCAA women's soccer teams (Markovits and Hellerman 2001: 281).

As Markovits and Hellerman (2001: 175) note, the surge in collegiate women's soccer is significant in relation to the development and success of both the U.S. women's national team and a professional league. Nonetheless, the audience for collegiate women's soccer has remained small, both for league games and for the championship tournaments. In 2006, only the top two Division I schools had an average game-day attendance of over 3,000 people (NCAA 2006); the vast majority of teams attracted audiences in the range of 100 to several hundred fans. Men's collegiate soccer outperformed the women's side in terms of audience numbers – 24 Division I schools and one Division III college averaged more than 1,000 fans per game in 2006 (NCAA 2006) – but both women's and men's soccer attendance figures are minuscule in comparison to the number of fans at the most popular collegiate sports events. In 2006, 91 Division I schools attracted more than 20,000 fans to (American) football games (four teams topped 100,000 for average fan attendance) (NCAA 2006) and 41 Division I schools attracted more than 10,000 fans to men's basketball games (NCAA 2006). For comparison, consider that 20 Division I schools attracted more than 5,000 fans to women's basketball games (NCAA 2006).

It is easy to understand, given these figures, why there remains a debate over the sudden increase of popularity around the women's national soccer team in the late 1990s. There was no media coverage of their 1991 Women's World Cup victory in China, but support emerged for the team during the U.S.-hosted 1996 Summer Olympics when women's soccer first became a medal event. During the Olympic tournament, the numbers of fans steadily increased from 25,303 during the semi-final game, to 74,489 at the championship between China and the U.S. in Athens, Georgia. These figures were a precursor to the fan frenzy around the 1999 Women's World Cup, which took place in eight venues across the U.S. This team, led by Mia Hamm, gained increasing fame through the course of the tournament, which culminated in the seminal final game between the U.S. and China at the Rose Bowl Stadium in Pasadena, California. It is difficult to overstate the incredible phenomenon that this game was: with 90,185 fans at the game itself and a national television audience of more than 40 million, the record-setting numbers made the game 'the most watched soccer match in the history of [U.S.] network television' (Wahl 1999: 40), men's or women's (Markovits and Hellerman 2004: 21), and equivalent to the number of viewers for the men's professional basketball (NBA) finals (Crowe 2009). As the U.S. Soccer Federation notes, 'The victory vaulted the sport into a rarified air that few sports celebrities ever enjoy, with the covers of [popular magazines] [...] the U.S. Women's National Soccer Team closed out the 1990s with the incredible [achievement] of earning *Sports Illustrated*'s 1999 Sportsmen of the Year Award' (U.S. Soccer Federation 2008). Consider that the *SI* Sportsmen of the Year Award has been given to women six times in its 54 year history, most recently in 1999.

The reasons for the 1999 media explosion remain inconclusive. Scholars Leslie Heywood and Shari Dworkin (2003) claim that the surge of popular attention was a conflux of increasing participation and interest in women's sports at the culmination of a decade during which corporations targeted women as an investment strategy for the first time. Other writers, however, perceive the jolt in popularity to have been a passing fad. *Sports Illustrated* journalist Andrea Canales (15 June 2009) contends that 'women's soccer rode a wave of trendiness.' Despite the ongoing questions, the excitement around the 1999 Women's World Cup demonstrated to many that a market for professional women's soccer exists in the U.S.

THE FAILED PREDECESSOR: THE WUSA (2001–03)

The emergence of the Women's United Soccer Association (WUSA) in 2001 seemed like a logical extension to this excitement. The first women's premier league in the U.S., the WUSA, sought to attract the world's best players and 'was positioned as the premier women's league in the world' (Southall *et al.* 2005: 160). Its founding players were all familiar names from the 1999 women's national team as well as many recognizable international stars. Teams were located in eight cities and eight distinct venues. Several teams, including the Atlanta Beat, the Carolina Tempest, and the San Jose CyberRays, played at college stadia where the seating capacity ranged from 5,700 (Carolina's home field at UNC-Chapel Hill) to 46,000 (Bobby Dodd Football Stadium in Atlanta). Likewise, there was no standard for field cover or size. The Philadelphia Charge, whose home pitch was at Villanova University, played on artificial turf, and both the San Diego Spirit and the Atlanta Beat had home fields that were 3.6 metres narrower than U.S. Soccer Standards. According to Tonya Antonucci, CEO of the new WPS league, such variation in stadium infrastructure and unprofitable leasing arrangements were key obstacles for the failed league. She stated, 'A major part of the challenge that the WUSA faced was that the original five investors were putting a lot of money into capital improvements in stadiums that they didn't own or control' (in Carlisle 2006). In sum, the WUSA was a financial disaster; the league went over-budget, spending approximately US$100 million in three seasons before folding in September 2003.

Two points about the WUSA and league operations require further discussion. First, as Jean Williams stated,

> What we do not have in terms of the 'cultural capital' of women's football [...]
> is a women's professional league with the same prestige, sponsorship or
> support as any of the male domestic leagues around the world, and the
> country-specific reasons for this link women's history, sports and particularly the
> popularity of association football.
>
> (Williams 2007: 10)

Williams speaks of one systemic reason for the WUSA's failure: lack of cultural
capital, or the perceived value or status that popular men's professional leagues
claim and thus endow upon their fans. Although the WUSA's attendance
numbers exceeded projections by the middle of the first season ('Turnstile
Tracker' 17 July 2001), the average audience numbers declined each year. In
2003, its television ratings were one-twentieth of league predictions (Woitalla
2003). The league found neither the viewership nor the corporate sponsorship it
expected, an outcome directly related to the (lack of) cultural capital commanded
and endowed by women's soccer.

This is not to suggest that the WUSA did not try to cultivate more interest
or status for the sport and its players. They did indeed; the second point that
requires attention relates to *how* the league and the athletes approached this
task. The WUSA's attempt to garner cultural capital for women's soccer was
grounded largely in discourses of 'appropriate' femininity and heterosexuality:
the athletes were good role models and the league was 'family friendly' entertainment. As Giardina and Metz contend,

> the WUSA's marketing efforts work explicitly to locate it within a discourse of
> 'All-American' family values [...] the term family values – itself a complex matrix
> of ideals with links between morality, sexuality, politics, and personal
> responsibility – becomes positioned as the always already site from which the
> league defines itself.
>
> (Giardina and Metz 2005a: 113–14)

Examples of this discourse were plentiful in the WUSA. Athletes sang a near-
constant refrain about the league serving the needs of young girls. Player Brandi
Chastain asserted: 'To me, it is so important for young girls to be able to come to
the stadia on a regular basis, not just every four years' (in Wahl 2001: 9). Likewise, coaches touted the power of the WUSA to shape athletes into the model
players and role models the league both created and relied upon. As one
example, former women's national team coach and WUSA executive Tony
DiCicco commented on the league's character-building benefits for the six
Chinese national team players drafted into the WUSA: 'In China [the players]
made practically no personal decisions because the team handled almost everything. Now they have to decide everything for themselves' (in Thomsen 2001:
26). In other words, visiting international athletes with established careers in their
home countries were to be molded into good *individuals*, in contrast to remaining in a system that purportedly produced 'robotic' players (see Wahl 2000,
quoting women's national team coach April Heinrichs).

The strength of this discourse is also evidenced by its use even after the demise of the league. For instance, the 'Keep the Dream Alive' Ticket Fund project, a strategy to generate financial support in exchange for vouchers for future tickets, stated,

> Together [the WUSA and our supporters] are [. . .] Supporting and promoting women's sport, in the U.S. and around the world; embracing core values of determination, good sportsmanship, teamwork, fitness, community spirit, multi-cultural understanding, perseverance and respect; supporting and promoting role models who embody these positive values.
>
> (WUSA Dream)

This stylized emphasis on the ideal female athlete and, by extension, athletic league, offers an illustration of the WUSA's attempt to develop cultural capital.

Efforts to generate cultural salience also had an effect on the game spaces the league created. The material spaces of WUSA games – the sideline and field spaces and the geography of stadia themselves, including the discourses, practices, and identities integral to the production of those spaces – highlight the league's interest in creating game spaces that framed the WUSA and its players in normative terms. For example, the WUSA partnered with, and thus benefited from, corporate sponsors who used the game space to promote products as well as 'shared' values. Gillette For Women Venus (razors), for instance, had a presence in game spaces during 2001 and 2002. Advertised as offering an 'Opportunity to Local Fans to Express Their Inner Soccer Goddess', the Gillette For Women Venus' booth raised brand awareness while rearticulating an expectation of normative femininity – in this case the hairless female body – onto WUSA fans and athletes. The sponsor's press release details their presence and practices in game spaces:

> Located within the Fan Zone outside WUSA stadiums, the Venus Ultimate Soccer Goddess Station is open two hours prior to kickoff and is designed to help fans of all ages bring out the 'inner soccer goddess' within. Fans who visit the station can enter a drawing to be named the game's 'Ultimate Soccer Goddess', have their picture taken at the Goddess Photo Booth and visit an interactive area where hair-decorating and megaphone-making materials are available.
>
> (Philbin 2002)

Those (girls, implicitly) who participated in the Soccer Goddess Station could take part in a time-honored feminine tradition: doing their hair. Fans could also enter a contest to meet a WUSA star: fans selected in the 'Ultimate Soccer Goddess' drawing were honored alongside the 'Player Goddess of the Game' during an on-field half-time ceremony. This game-day practice inscribed a particular type of legible femininity, and therefore heterosexuality, onto both fans and players at WUSA games.

The Fan Zone mentioned in the Gillette press release above provides a second example of the way that social norms inform and are produced within game spaces in ways that contain notions of difference. Housing kid-friendly activities like inflatable games and face painting, WUSA fan zones were located directly outside the stadium ticket booth or immediately inside the entrance to the stadium gates. These zones increased the sense of spectacle occurring in the stadium: fans were encouraged to partake in activities before taking their seats for the game, which in turn created a greater 'playground' environment at the stadium. Fan zones and the fan festival, the larger, end-of-season counterpart, functioned as a branding effort that provided fans with a special game-day experience over and above the game itself. Additionally, they created a game space that emphasized family-friendliness and a connection between league and fans as a way to offset anxiety about gendered athletic performances that are historically read as masculine. Thus, fan zones provided a pre-game site that gave material form to the league's discursive focus on 'good girl' role models and family-friendly entertainment. Jowdy and McDonald connect the game spaces to the WUSA's philosophy this way:

> [T]hrough the fan festival marketers can communicate/reinforce a large number of messages/associations that are tailored to fan consumption motivations, e.g. family values, players as role models, community, and go beyond basic product attributes.
>
> (Jowdy and McDonald 2003: 297)

Fan zones confirmed the focus that the league sought – to build a connection between 'role model' players and young fans. These material practices reframed the game space from an athletic one, notable for its display of non-normative gender through the performance of the athletic female body, to one remarkable for making its athletes accessible, just like 'the girl next door.'

The decision to build a fan base and support for the WUSA through discourses and demonstrations of idealized, normative role models and family values illustrates the endurance of cultural anxieties about female athletes. Yet these game-day practices are also important because they could be read as 'natural' elements of women's professional sport space. Thus, these practices received little critical attention. Likewise, there was little public criticism of the WUSA when it folded in 2003. While attention was paid to the failure of the business plan, the impetus to create a sustainable professional women's league remained. In fact, a reorganization committee was immediately formed with the aim of re-launching the WUSA as quickly as possible. This committee transformed into Women's Soccer Initiative, Inc., which produced the business plan that gave shape to the new manifestation of U.S. women's professional soccer, the WPS. Although the WPS distinguishes itself from the WUSA by featuring integration and shared responsibility with the men's side Major League Soccer (MLS), including sharing soccer-specific stadia, some WUSA tactics linger, as evidenced in the 'skort affair.' Taken together, these strategies paint a complex picture of the new league's attachment to normative values.

THE NEWEST INCARNATION OF U.S. WOMEN'S SOCCER: THE WPS

The Women's Professional Soccer league began play on 29 March 2009 with seven teams: Boston Breakers; Chicago Red Stars; FC Gold Pride; Los Angeles Sol[3]; St. Louis Athletica; Sky Blue FC; and Washington Freedom. Two additional teams, Philadelphia Independence and Atlanta Beat, will begin in 2010. According to FIFA Magazine (2009: 39), attendance at the opening game between the LA Sol and Washington Freedom 'was 14,832 which exceeded the home team's original expectations of around 10,000 fans.'

The WPS touts several key features that set it apart from the WUSA. First, the WPS shunned the WUSA's single-entity structure and instead adopted a strategy that allows individual team ownership. According to Zimbalist (2006: 109), 'teams are better operated by local owners who understand, and have the incentive to cater to, the local market.' Independent ownership enables teams to pursue creative marketing strategies that, if successful, may be picked up by the league. Boston Breakers athletes 'have headed out to city bars to play pool with twenty-somethings and connect with young adult fans,' while the Chicago Stars players 'will hit the bar for viewing parties' of league games (Gregory 29 March 2009). Likewise, Chicago team CEO Peter Wilt relies less on costly marketing techniques and more on inexpensive new media like Facebook and Twitter (Bell 23 March 2009). This tactic has been widely adopted: As of July 2009, all seven teams, 21 players, five coaches, and numerous league executives and staff use Twitter to connect with fans.

Likewise, much attention has been paid to the WPS' shift toward a smaller game venue. League commissioner Tonya Antonucci argues that a 'cozier venue' is cheaper to operate and is better for viewers: 'For fans it's a more intimate, authentic soccer experience when you're closer to the field, instead of in a cavernous environment' (in Gregory 29 March 2009). Although the argument that an 'intimate' soccer experience is more 'authentic' is debatable, the WPS is indeed scaling down in its facilities. Several of the teams in this league, FC Gold Pride, Sky Blue FC, and Boston, play most of their games on smaller campus facilities. Still, small is a relative term: Yurcak Field at Rutgers University, where Sky Blue FC will play all but two of its home games, has a seating capacity of 5,000 in the grandstand, with additional seating on the lawn area opposite the stadium structure, whereas the Boston Breakers play at Harvard Stadium, which has a sizeable maximum capacity of 30,323. Harvard Stadium and The Home Depot Center, the multiuse complex that is the home field of the Los Angeles Sol and seats 27,000, are the largest stadium sites in the league, however. This is in contrast to the WUSA, which housed two teams in stadia that had a seating capacity of approximately 50,000.

Additionally, WPS games will be played primarily in soccer-specific venues. The Washington Freedom play at the Championship Stadium within the Maryland SoccerPlex, a 5,200-seat facility that sits in the midst of 19 full-sized (115 × 75 yards) fields and underwent an upgrade of additional seats and perimeter fencing in order to house the WPS team (Figure 11.2). Championship

Stadium has seating on both sides of the field but has no roof structure; its openness is accentuated by the paved and lighted plaza that connects the stands. Likewise, the home field of FC Gold Pride, Buck Shaw Stadium on the Santa Clara University campus, is an open, 10,300 seat venue that also houses the university's soccer teams and MLS team San Jose Earthquakes.

Two of these sites are soccer-specific facilities within larger complexes: the St. Louis Athletica moved to its new home field in June at the soccer park (seating capacity unspecified) segment of the Anheuser-Busch Conference and Sports Center. The Los Angeles Sol, the team that lured Brazilian star Marta to be the female counterpart to the Los Angeles Galaxy's (MLS) English star David Beckham (cf. Chapter 15), is also housed in a multi-use complex but on a much larger scale. The Home Depot Center is a 125-acre site on the grounds of California State University, Dominguez Hills. Its facilities include the 27,000-seat stadium for soccer and rugby, home fields for the Sol, the Galaxy, Chivas USA (MLS); as well as tennis and track stadia and other sport facilities.

The Chicago Red Stars is the only team other than the LA Sol that plays at a single-use stadium constructed with professional soccer in mind. Its home field, Toyota Park, was opened in 2006 for Major League Soccer and Major League Lacrosse; it has a mix of individual (9,772) and bench (10,228) seats for soccer, with another 8,000 available on the field for concerts. Toyota Park and The Home Depot Center are the only two WPS stadia that boast a roof to cover the seating areas. These sites are also unique among WPS for their premium seating, notable for helping stadium owners turn a profit: both offer 42 Executive/Luxury suites and six Party/Event suites (cf. Chapter 4). The Philadelphia Independence may join the teams who enjoy newly constructed, single-use, professional-centered facilities: the Chester Stadium, scheduled to open in 2010, would house Philadelphia's MLS and WPS teams. Like other stadia designed by Rossetti architects (Home Depot and Toyota Park), Chester Stadium will feature a design with a partial roof, an integrated concert stage, and seating for up to 18,500 fans.

Figure 11.2
Championship Stadium
within the Maryland
SoccerPlex, Germantown,
MD, home of the
Washington Freedom,
2009 (Courtesy of the
Maryland SoccerPlex).

Not everything about the WPS' business model is unique. One prominent holdover is the ticket pricing: tickets and season packages are inexpensive, averaging between US$15–$20, including the option of a cheap seat that is in the US$10–12 range. Inexpensive entertainment options such as these are typically sold as a family friendly value, and the league hopes to tap the family market as well as passionate soccer fans. Commissioner Antonucci has even tried to frame the WPS' emergence during a recession as growth possibility for attracting new fans. She argued, 'We're an attractive and affordable alternative [...] Whereas in a good economy, we might have been perceived as, well, a lower priority among sports fans. We might actually have some sports fans sample us who wouldn't have otherwise' (in Gregory 29 March 2009). Some stadium practices may complement the league's attempt to become a low-cost alternative for entertainment. At Boston and Chicago games, tailgating (gathering in a venue's parking lot to enjoy food, drink, and company prior to a home game) is encouraged. Likewise, many WPS teams have offered special events, like game-day concerts, that are covered by the low-cost ticket.

Another carry-over is the league's apparent attempt to garner cultural capital through associations with normative femininity (see Shugart 2003) and family values. The WPS' choice to feature a silhouette of pony-tailed Mia Hamm on the league's logo highlights such an attachment to a representation of stereotypical femininity. The league announced:

> Mia Hamm retired in 2004 as one of the greatest players in women's soccer. Now she is the image of a new league. Hamm's silhouette is featured in the logo unveiled Thursday by Women's Professional Soccer [...] Hamm is about to strike a ball with her right foot in the navy, red and gold W.P.S. logo.
>
> (Gloster 2008)

One could rightly argue that positioning Hamm prominently in the new league's materials serves to memorialize her role in U.S. women's soccer and draw in fans who remember her name but are unfamiliar with the current roster of athletes. Yet, this logo is a silhouette; it has an extremely tangential likeness to Hamm herself. The function of this logo as an inscription of normative femininity becomes clearer when discussed in relation to FIFA's adoption of the 2007 Women's World Cup logo; as Williams (2007: 8) notes, FIFA's decision to launch a women's soccer logo 'without the image of a woman (particularly without "the ubiquitous ponytail") is a significant departure [...] it implies a move away from a Westernized, white bias and the heteronormative symbolism of long hair as indicative of youthful femininity.' The WPS, on the other hand, returned to and embraced this symbolism in the implementation of their new league logo.

The 'skort affair' is another example of this strategy. Released as an extra piece of the uniform kit for four teams, the 'wrap' was touted by WPS staff as 'designed with the female player in mind': 'They are completely optional and will not be worn in games [...] [they are to] be worn to and from the field, after practice – and if a player really wants to, they can wear it on the field, too, in training or warm-up' (WPS Staff Report 25 February 2009). Whether or not the league intended the wrap to be an attention-grabber, it was met by fans with both disdain and indifference. Blogger Megan Heuter (25 February 2009) wrote, 'Yikes! A skort? Are you kidding me? [...] Seems to me like PUMA/WPS are trying to "rebrand" the female athlete.' Some who responded to Heuter's post appreciated the wrap's feminine and possible money-making qualities; ziba_cranmer wrote,

> As a lacrosse player, I have no problem with 'skorts' because we wear kilts and I kind of like the contrast of apparel item that is so strongly associated with femininity and a sport that is pretty fierce! Maybe this is what is needed for professional women's sports to thrive [...] and finally achieve market viability.
>
> (ziba_cranmer 10 March 2009)

Although these writers differ about the value of the skort, both agree that the skort intensifies the sense of femininity associated with women's soccer. That the WPS would promote this association by including the wrap in its uniform, even as an optional element of its kit, demonstrates that one aspect of the league's marketing strategy is emphasizing that its athletes are feminine, and therefore unthreatening to the hierarchies of either sport or sexuality, both on and off the field.

Marketing strategies that emphasize normativity correspond neatly with game-day practices that highlight family values, narrowly defined. The 19 July FC Sky Blue game, for instance, was dubbed Faith Day and the ticket to the game included a post-game show featuring a Christian rock band (Sky Blue Soccer 2009). The press release for this event spoke to the multiple functions that this event was intended to serve: the post-game concert frames the FC Sky Blue event as family-friendly while it also strives to attract a larger evangelical Christian fan base.

> General Manager Gerry Marrone expressed his optimism for the potential impact the event could have in growing the Sky Blue FC fan base. 'Faith Day is an opportunity to bring family friendly entertainment to an audience that matches up well with what we provide,' Marrone explained. 'With our season-long advertising campaign and partnership with Star 99.1 [contemporary Christian music station] [...] We hope Faith Day and [rock band] can bring a new group of spectators out for the first time to experience our team and product'.
>
> (Sky Blue Soccer 2009)

Here, FC Sky Blue is taking a cue from other professional leagues that have attempted to expand their fan bases by reaching out to a market of evangelical Christians (see Muller 2007). Whether this tactic is successful at attracting fans remains to be seen, but it is clear that Faith Day will have an impact on the game-day environment of Yurcak Field. According to New York Examiner blogger Jeff Kassouf (19 July 2009), the game-day activities will culminate with a post-game show by the Christian rock band, but the Christian radio station and co-sponsor Star 99.1 will also broadcast live from the field prior to the game and the post-game festivities will include a short statement from a local reverend. Under this model, FC Sky Blue will not be the only entity to make attempts at recruiting fans; Star 99.1 and the local reverend will also try to recruit new followers. Thus, in its effort to signal family-friendliness, Faith Day will transform the game space and game-day experience into an exclusive site, potentially unwelcoming for those who do not subscribe to evangelical Christian beliefs or those who are uninterested in mixing religion with sport.

Problematic though these practices are, they represent only a selection of framing and game-day techniques that the WPS and its teams employ to capture audiences and generate cultural capital. The WPS appears to draw on a complex set of marketing strategies that does not begin or end with gender and sexual normativity, or with an exclusive set of family values. For instance, the league promotes a range of personalities to generate attention: tattooed Natasha Kai is one example. An out lesbian and a visible woman of colour in the league, Kai is framed in the media as the exotic exception to the rule of gender and heterosexual normativity. Similarly, the Boston Breakers showcase a range of material on its website as a way to connect its team and players to its fans. Some of this material squarely falls within normative territory: the 'Off the Field' link of feature videos includes 'Battle of the Brides,' in which two players visit a local bridal shop to try on dresses for their upcoming weddings. Clearly, this video reinforces the discursive framing of the WPS as a league full of feminine, heterosexual athletes while also serving to give fans a glance into the lives of soccer stars. Still, the website is also full of content that emphasizes athleticism and the skill of athletes: athletes are shown on the field, in uniform, and performing their jobs. This method of underlining athletic talent without drawing attention to gendered characteristics is unique in U.S. media coverage of women's sport.

CONCLUSION

The materialities of league self-image, including the production of game-day spaces, are central to the success of the WPS. The league has a greater chance to be taken seriously if its venues emphasize sport: soccer-specific stadia rather than cavernous American football stadia offer fans an intimate event experience where the audience is close to the game and to each other. Likewise, the WPS' ability to showcase the sport, the league, and the fan community in its game spaces will go a long way to generate cultural capital. By following this less travelled path to maintain a singular focus on sport and skill, the WPS would undermine the ubiquitous alignment of women's sport leagues with normative associations with gender, sexuality, and 'family values' defined in exclusive terms. If the league pursues the well-worn route of creating a sport niche of 'good girls' and family-friendly fun, however, the WPS will fail to generate a shift in attitudes about women's sport and women athletes *and* the league will find itself at the periphery of professional sport. Further, by positioning itself as a celebratory site of gender- and sexual normativity, the WPS would encourage a particular –

exclusive – set of readings about the league and its intended audience. This tactic would have the effect of exacerbating the troublesome binary between family-friendly spaces and professional sport spaces.

The question of which direction the league will take has already emerged. On the one hand, both athletes and management continue to rearticulate the 'role model' mantra of the idealized female soccer player and league. Abby Wambach, a current star in U.S. women's soccer, offers this case in point: 'I think that this league, the WPS, can really attract all people [...] if you have a young daughter or son who you want to put in front of role models that are good people, that make the right choices, and that are real' (womensprosoccer 25 June 2008). Although Wambach begins with a nod to a wide range of fans, the majority of her comment focuses on the ability of the league to attract fans because it offers good role models. FC Sky Blue General Manager Gerry Marrone provides another example. He believes that middle and upper-class soccer moms and families are the untapped market for the WPS because people want 'female role models for their daughters' (Tomasino 7 June 2009). On the other hand, league management is beginning to acknowledge the limitations of marketing the WPS as a repository of role models. According to Andy Crossley, the Boston Breakers director of business development, 'We need to get out of the ghetto of being a role model for girls' (in Belson 2009).

At the same time, attempts to attract 'regular' male sports fans requires the league to guard against using a similar but distinct set of gendered assumptions: the idealized role model must not be turned into a sex symbol as a way to attract men to follow the WPS. Transforming 'good girls' into sexual objects will also impede perceptions of the league and may hinder lasting financial investment (Lawrence 2008: 22). Andy Crossley's point about moving the league away from an emphasis on role models must be interpreted as a call for the league to capture male fans by moving toward a focus on athleticism and quality of play rather than an endorsement of a 'sex sells' philosophy.

Ian Lawrence (2008: 22) argues that professional women's soccer can succeed if it finds its unique selling point, which he contends is neither the idealized role model nor the sexualized athlete. Yet, pressure to stay on the familiar course remains: recent media coverage memorializing the 1999 U.S. Women's World Cup victory illustrates that role model description of women soccer players continues to shape the discourse about the new league, while league executives seem drawn to the model of objectifying athletes as a way to bring attention to the sport. Both examples reveal that cultural tensions arising from the display and performance of powerful female athletes continue to colour attitudes about women's athletics and may shape the new league's access to long-term cultural capital.

Today, there are two competing narratives about the health of the WPS. While some report that attendance figures are low and that U.S. audience will not follow women's sports (Plaschke 10 July 2009), others argue that the average attendance is good, exceeding 'half the teams in Italy's men's second division this season' (Hersh 14 July 2009). This debate will undoubtedly continue while the WPS struggles to carve out a sustainable niche within an intensely competitive leisure landscape. Given that women's athletics in the U.S. have historically received about 6 to 8 per cent of the mainstream sport media coverage (Messner *et al.* 2003), the league has an uphill battle to make itself known. Neither the constraint of a tight marketing and publicity budget nor the league's penchant for aligning itself with normative family values will make this battle easier. Indeed, the 'skort affair' illustrates that this strategy has great potential to turn away supporters who want to follow women's soccer without attendant gendered hoopla. The key to the league's success, and to its ability to cultivate cultural salience, depends upon its capacity to reject the investment in cultural anxieties and resist a gender-normative self-styling in its material and social articulations, including game-day production.

NOTES

1 Cf. www.seeextraordinary.com.
2 The NCAA comprises more than 1,000 member colleges and universities; these are broken into three distinct divisions, I, II, or III. See: www.ncaa.org/wps/ncaa?key=/ncaa/ncaa/about+the+ncaa/membership/the+divisions/div_criteria.html (accessed 15 September 2009).
3 The Los Angeles Sol existed for the first season of WPS play. Owned by AEG, the behemoth sport and entertainment subsidiary of the Anschutz Company, the team was released to the WPS in November 2009. The league failed to find a new owner for the Sol, and players were drafted to other WPS teams. See: htp://www.womensprosoccer.com/news/pressreleases/100128-sol-discontinues (accessed 13 April 2010).

REFERENCES

Bell, J. (2009) 'Ooh Aah Fashion', *New York Times Goal Blog*, 26 February. Online. Available http://goal.blogs.nytimes.com/2009/02/26/ooh-aah-fashion/?scp=19&sq=WPS%20soccer&st=cse (accessed 26 February 2009).
—— (2009) 'New women's soccer league confident despite economy', *New York Times*, 23 March. Online. Available www.nytimes.com/2009/03/24/sports/soccer/24goal.html?scp=6&sq=WPS%20soccer&st=cse (accessed 23 March 2009).
Belson, K. (2009) 'Women's soccer builds a league from the ground up', *New York Times*, 7 July. Online. Available www.nytimes.com/2009/07/08/sports/soccer/08league.html?_r=1 (accessed 7 July 2009).
Cahn, S.K. (1994) *Coming on Strong*, New York: Free Press.
Canales, A. (2009) 'Can WPS recapture glory of 1999?', *Sports Illustrated*, 15 June. Online. Available http://sportsillustrated.cnn.com/2009/writers/andrea_canales/06/15/wps/index.html (accessed 17 June 2009).
Carlisle, J. (2006) 'WUSA revival looking more like reality', *ESPNsoccernet.com*, 30 December. Online. Available http://soccernet.espn.go.com/columns/story?id=394952&root=us&&cc=5901 (accessed 23 February 2009).
Carpenter, L.J. and Acosta, R.V. (2008) '2005–2006 Sports-sponsorship and participation-rates reports. NCAA, 2007', *Women's Sports Foundation*. Online. Available http://66.40.5.5/~/media/Files/PDFs%20and%20other%20files%20by%20Topic/Issues/General/W/WSF%20FACTS%20MAY%202008.pdf (accessed 10 February 2009).
Christenson, M. and Kelso, P. (2004) 'Soccer's chief plan to boost women's game? Hotpants', *Guardian*, 16 January. Online. Available www.guardian.co.uk/uk/2004/jan/16/football.gender (accessed 24 February 2009).

Crowe, J. (2009) 'Marla Messing's big thinking made the Women's World Cup huge', *Los Angeles Times*, 5 July. Online. Available www.latimes.com/sports/la-sp-crowe6 –2009jul06,0,3167467.column (accessed 15 July 2009).

Doyle, J. (2009) 'I guess PUMA didn't get the skort memo', *From a Left Wing: Meditations on the beautiful game from an unlikely player and fan*, 4 March. Online. Available http://fromaleftwing.blogspot.com/2009_03_01_archive.html (accessed 5 March 2009).

FIFA Magazine (2009) *Women's Professional Soccer (WPS)*, May. Online. Available http://fifaworldmagazine.fifa.com/?vcabid=geeSeaelhSephja (accessed 15 July 2009).

Giardina, M. and Metz, J. (2005a) 'All-American girls? Corporatizing national identity', in M.L. Silk, D.L. Andrews and C.L. Cole (eds) *Sport and Corporate Nationalisms*, London: Berg.

—— (2005b) 'Women's sports in Nike's America: Body politics and the corporo-empowerment of "everyday athletes"', in S. Jackson and D. Andrews (eds) *Sport, Culture & Advertising*, New York: Routledge.

Gloster, R. (2008) 'Mia Hamm's silhouette featured in new women's soccer logo' *Associated Press*, 18 January.

Gregory, S. (2009) 'Is women's pro soccer really coming back now?', *Time*, 29 March. Online. Available www.time.com/time/nation/article/0,8599,1888229,00.html (accessed 20 April 2009).

Hersh, P. (2009) 'Women's soccer 10 years after the U.S. World Cup title: Failure or progress?', *Chicago Tribune*, 14 July. Online. Available www.chicagotribune.com/sports/soccer/fire/chi-14-womens-world-cup-jul14,0,6391801.story (accessed 15 July 2009).

Heuter, M. (2009) 'Women's Professional Soccer unveils PUMA uniforms: A skort?!?', 25 February. Online. Available http://becauseiplayedsports.com/2009/02/25/womens-professional-soccer-unveils-puma-uniforms/ (accessed 27 February 2009).

Heywood, A. and Dworkin, S. (2003) *Built to Win*, Minneapolis: University of Minnesota Press.

Jowdy, E. and McDonald, M. (2003) 'Relationship marketing and interactive fan festivals: The Women's United Soccer Association's "Soccer Sensation"', *International Journal of Sports Marketing & Sponsorship*, 4: 295–311.

Kassouf, J. (2009). 'Sky Blue faces off with Chicago on Faith Day', 19 July, *New York Examiner*. Online. Available www.examiner.com/x-4801-NY-Soccer-Examiner~y2009m7d19-Sky-Blue-faces-off-with-Chicago.

Knoppers, A. and Anthonissen, A. (2003) 'Women's Soccer in the United States and the Netherlands: Differences and similarities in regimes of inequality', *Sociology of Sport Journal*, 20: 351–70.

Ladda, S. (2000) 'The early beginnings of intercollegiate women's soccer in the United States', *Physical Educator*, 57: 106–112.

Lawrence, I. (2008) 'The unique selling point of women's soccer', *Soccer Journal*, September/October: 18–22.

Markovitz, A. and Hellerman, S. (2001) *Offside: Soccer and American exceptionalism*, Princeton, NJ: Princeton University Press.

—— (2004) 'Women's soccer in the United States: Yet another American "exceptionalism"', in F. Hong and J. Mangan (eds) *Soccer, Women, Sexual Liberation*, New York: Routledge.

Massey, D. (1994) *Space, Place and Gender*, Minneapolis: University of Minnesota Press.

Messner, M. (1988) 'Sports and male domination: The female athlete as contested ideological terrain', *Sociology of Sport Journal*, 5: 197–211.

Messner, M., Duncan, M.C. and Cooky, C. (2003) 'Silence, sports bras, and wrestling porn', *Journal of Sport & Social Issues*, 27: 1, 38–51.

Muller, T. (2007) '"Lesbian community" in WNBA spaces', *Social and Cultural Geography*, 8(1): 9–27.

NCAA (2006) *NCAA Attendance Statistics*. Online. Available www.ncaa.org/wps/ncaa?key=/ncaa/ncaa/sports+and+championship/general+information/stats (accessed 19 June 2009).

Philbin, C. (2002) *Gillette For Women Venus Provides Opportunity For Local Fans To Express Their Inner Soccer Goddess*, February. Online. Available www.womensportswire.com/pro_sports/archived_pro_sports/archive_11/body_wusa_gillette.htm (accessed 4 January 2009).

Plaschke, B. (2009) 'The spirit of 1999 Women's World Cup lives on', *Los Angeles Times*, 10 July. Online. Available www.latimes.com/sports/la-sp-plaschke10–2009jul10,0,6134997.column (accessed 15 July 2009).

SGMA (2000) 'Gaining ground: A progress report on women in sports', *Women's Sports & Physical Activity Facts & Statistics, Women's Sports Foundation*. Online. Available http://66.40.5.5/~/media/Files/PDFs%20and%20other%20files%20by%20Topic/Issues/General/W/WSF%20FACTS%20MAY%202008.pdf (accessed 10 February 2009).

Shugart, H. (2003) 'She shoots, she scores: Mediated constructions of contemporary female athletes in coverage of the 1999 US women's soccer team', *Western Journal of Communication*, 67(1): 1–31.

Sky Blue Soccer (2009) *Sky Blue FC to Host Faith Day on July 19*, 10 July. Online. Available: www.womensprosoccer.com/Home/ny/news/press_releases/090710-faith-day (accessed 18 July 2009).

Southall, R.M., Nagel, M.S. and LeGrande, D.J. (2005) 'Build it and they will come? The Women's United Soccer Association: A collision of exchange theory and strategic philanthropy', *Sport Marketing Quarterly*, 14: 158–67.

Thomsen, I. (2001) 'WUSA's Great Haul from China', *Sports Illustrated*, 26.

Tomasino, D. (2009) 'New league targeting soccer moms, families', *New York Post*, 7 June. Online. Available www.nypost.com/seven/06072009/sports/moresports/new_league_targeting_soccer_moms__famili_172907.htm (accessed 15 June 2009).

Turnstile Tracker (2001) *Street and Smith's Sports Business Daily*, 17 July. Online. Available www.sportsbusinessdaily.com/article/57460 (accessed 4 May 2009).

US YOUTH SOCCER (2000) *Membership Statistics*. Online. Available www.usyouthsoccer.org/media_kit/keystatistics.asp (accessed 1 May 2009).

U.S. Soccer Federation (2008) *U.S. Women's National Team History & Information: Rise*. Online. Available http://national.soccerhall.org/US_NationalTeamRec_Intro.htm (accessed 17 June 2009).

Wahl, G. (1999) 'Out of this world', *Sports Illustrated*, 38–43.

—— (2000) 'Heinrichs, 1 v. 1', *Sports Illustrated*, 14 September. Online. Available: http://sportsillustrated.cnn.com/olympics/2000/soccer/news/2000/09/13/wahl_heinrichs/ (accessed 15 July 2009).

—— (2001) 'Strong finishing kick', *Sports Illustrated*, 3 September.

Williams, J. (2007) *A Beautiful Game. International Perspectives on Women's Football*, London: Berg.

Woitalla, M. (2003) 'Women on the verge', *When Saturday Comes*, December. Online. Available www.wsc.co.uk/content/view/2284/29/ (accessed 20 April 2009).

Womensprosoccer (2008) *Abby Wambach Talks About WPS and the Olympics*, 25 June. Online. Available www.youtube.com/watch?v=WqK_BJ4kfiw (accessed 11 July 2009).

WPS-Staff Report (2009) *What's in a Wrap?*, 25 February. Online. Available www.womensprosoccer.com/news/general/090225-Whats-in-a-wrap (accessed 1 March 2009).

Ziba_cranmer (2009) *Comment on 'Women's Professional Soccer unveils PUMA uniform: A skort?!?'*, 10 March. Online. Available http://becauseiplayedsports.com/2009/02/25/womens-professional-soccer-unveils-puma-uniforms/ (accessed 20 March 2009).

Zimbalist, A. (2006) *The Bottom Line*, Philadelphia: Temple University Press.

Chapter 12: Football Under Cover in Tehran's Ararat Stadium

Corinna Assmann and Silke Gülker

On 26 April 2006 a football game took place in Tehran's Ararat Stadium which was later described as a 'historical event': a women's team from Germany, the Berlin Sports Club AL-Dersimspor e.V., played against the Iranian women's national team. This was the first public women's football match to take place since the Islamic Revolution in 1979. It took one and a half years to organize and to arrange this game, as preparations for the match were subject to constant set-backs. After the match, the images of the sportswomen dressed in Islamic cover attracted worldwide attention; these were also captured in the theatrical documentary film *Football Under Cover* (2008). The authors are players of the Berlin team and co-producers of the film. With this chapter they thus reflect on an event in which they were active.

This football match provides much food for thought. In recent research in the sociology of space, the constitution of space is described as a socially repetitive process (Löw 2001). Class and gender are structural principles in this process; spaces are accordingly negotiated in class- and gender-specific battles (Löw 2001: 273). The football stadium has in the past often been described as a site of masculinity: the placement of social goods and people creates an atmosphere which encourages male rapture and female alienation (cf. Chapter 10).

This raises questions about the possible consequences of a female occupation of this 'site of masculinity.' Despite the growing popularity of women's football and the increasing numbers of female spectators in the stadia, and irrespective of the steady rise in female fan clubs, the majority of sports-sociological literature supports the thesis of masculine hegemony in football. Very few surveys focus on women as active participants (e.g. Sobiech 2007). In simple terms, two effective hypotheses can be assumed: 1) by playing and watching football, women change the game, or 2) playing and watching football changes women and also society's expectations of women.

However, this chapter does not attempt to tackle such general questions. Instead, it concentrates on one single, albeit outstanding, event which effectively inverts typical gender roles. That which in other countries is often analysed as a practice of gender-specific segregation is actually law in the Islamic Republic of Iran: women are prohibited from entering the football stadium. For many of the Iranian women involved – not only players, but spectators, referees, reporters, and security staff – this football match offered them the first ever opportunity to visit a football stadium. As the legal framework forbids women playing sport under male observation, men were not allowed to visit the stadium where this game took place. In this way, the traditionally male space of the stadium became, temporarily, a female site of occupation.

By closely examining female behaviour and reactions during the match, this chapter explores to what extent women continued to adhere to prescribed roles under these exceptional circumstances. It should be noted that adherence to roles refers not only to social conventions here. In Iran, numerous behaviour patterns are laid down by law: correspondingly, transgressions entail other risks than in a society which is not organized by religious law. How far can sporting events of this kind be conducive to women transgressing even statutory behavioural expectations?

This chapter first examines the background of the distinctive history of football and gender roles in Iran. We then analyse the effects of this match based on extensive film footage shot inside the stadium during the game. With regard to 'the special quality of the stadium as a whole, that is, not only as the site of a spectacle (the match), but also as a spectacle itself (the behaviour of the crowd)' (Bromberger 1995: 300), it focuses in particular on the spectators' stands. The behaviour of the players will not be analysed here. The concluding section places the results gathered from the analysis of the match into the wider context of research on football and gender.

WOMEN AND FOOTBALL IN IRAN: THE EXCEPTIONALITY OF A PUBLIC WOMEN'S FOOTBALL MATCH IN THE ISLAMIC REPUBLIC OF IRAN

With the exception of the USA,[1] world football today is still largely a male domain. Admittedly, things have changed noticeably in some Western European and South American countries; enthusiasm for women's football has increased and more women regularly attend matches in the stadium. Still, women remain 'the other' (cf. Meuser 2008).[2] Adopting a historical perspective, Dunning and Elias (Elias and Dunning 2003) describe the football match as civilized violence, in direct continuity with martial conflicts between villages; women have no place in this description. The notion of battle and the desire for dominance clings to the game itself.[3] These can be seen as particularly masculine features. The football stadium is a markedly gendered space in that it mirrors the masculinity of the game itself. It is an important place for the creation of a 'hegemonic' masculinity, which isolates and attacks other kinds of 'marginalized' and 'inferior' masculinities (cf. Lehnert 2006: 89). Surveys of the behaviour of spectators and hooligans also demonstrate various rituals of masculinity, often enhanced by excessive drinking. These involve loudly voiced dissociations from everything feminine and disdain for homosexuality (Dunning 2003). This behaviour is essential for the construction of a shared identity and the creation of a collective consciousness among the fans in the stadium (cf. Bromberger 1995: 306). A space-sociological perspective illustrates to what extent the behaviour of male football fans in the stadium complies with the characteristics of male spatial behaviour: large groups, loud, expansive behaviour with sweeping movements (Feltz 2007; Löw 2001: 246–8; Sobiech 2006).

Even if the gender question is left to one side, football has always been a highly political issue in Iran and in other countries of Islamic tradition.[4] The attempts by Reza Shah's government to promote football between 1940 and 1960 instigated the 'religious oppositions to identify official football as one aspect of the moral corruption propagated by the Pahlavi regime' (Chehabi 2006: 243). Accordingly, the Islamic Republic turned against the sport after the revolution, tackling it with an 'official anti-football campaign,' which rejected it 'as a royalist tool of manipulation' (Fozooni 2004: 364). In general, the Republic's policies on sport were affected by a combination of religiously inspired puritanism and revolutionary asceticism (Chehabi 2006: 244). On the one hand, football was condemned as apolitical entertainment which diverted attention from the pressing political concerns of the time. On the other hand, it was suspected of failing to conform to Islamic values and rules. Moreover, the new Republic felt threatened by football's potential for mass mobilization, as it feared all kinds of large gatherings which were not state-controlled. Public gatherings were consequently declared a national security threat and were forbidden in 1980. This served the state as a convenient tool to combat football, as it allowed matches and tournaments to be cancelled arbitrarily (cf. Fozooni 2004: 365).

Despite this, the popularity of football continues to grow in Iran and it is now the number one sport in the country. This, however, only serves to enhance the political explosiveness of the issue. The events of 1997 and 1998 illustrated how football and the football stadium could act 'as powerful catalysts for protest, by awakening rather than anaesthetizing political consciousness' (Bromberger 1995: 295). The qualification of the Iranian national team for the FIFA World Cup in France in a match against Australia on 29 November 1997, followed half a year later by the victory of the Iranian team over the U.S. football team during the World Cup on 22 June 1998, led to exuberant celebrations of a kind not seen before in the Islamic Republic. In 1997, the celebrations which took place at Azadi Stadium to welcome the team home from Australia were crashed by 5,000 women who stormed the gates (Chehabi 2006: 249) and participated in the celebration although they had previously been explicitly excluded from the event. The victory over the U.S. team in 1998 was celebrated even more fervently. After the final whistle, thousands of men and women who had watched the television broadcast poured onto the streets of Tehran, turning the whole city into one giant public party. 'Streets were jammed with revelers at 1:00 a.m, driving around and honking their horns. One symbolism registered in everyone's minds is the sight of young women waving their headscarves out of car windows, daring vigilantes and morality squads' (Gerami 2003: 271). There was nothing which the police or civil guardians could do to stop this breach of the public order. The intermingling of the sexes in both these celebrations represented 'a significant step toward achieving sexual equality' (Fozooni 2004: 367). These events unleashed pent-up emotions and frustrations which are normally repressed in Iranian society.

As football is considered a male sport, female attendance at matches is generally considered exceptional.[5] This is even more the case in Iran where gender roles are more strictly determined and politically charged. The redefinition of gender roles was one of the central concerns of the new government after the Islamic Revolution in 1979; this was an attempt to reconstruct and to purify an Iranian society which had, in the eyes of the traditionalists, become immoral and debauched in the course of the Shah-regime's project of modernization and westernization (Najmabadi 1991: 64). This process can be followed clearly with reference to the 'woman question,' that is, the politics concerning women's place in society and the regulations surrounding dress. Reza Shah's decree which banned women from wearing the *hijab* (Islamic dress) in public places in 1936 was answered by the Islamic Republic in 1983 with the re-introduction of the Islamic veil as a 'mandatory dress and behavior code' (Gerami 1996: 103) in all public areas. The central image in the fight against the 'excesses of modernisation' (Najmabadi 1991: 64) of the Pahlavi regime was that of the *gharbzadeh* ('westoxicated') woman as an embodiment of all social ills (cf. Najmabadi 1991: 65). This image was compared to that of the 'modest' female, represented by the *hijabi* woman. The *hijabi* woman became a political preoccupation of the newly formed Islamic Republic as she 'symbolize[d] the moral and cultural trans-formation of society' (Moghadam 2004: 459). This process of restructuring was not only concerned with how women looked but also with women's role in society, with gender relations and with female sexuality and behaviour. Consequently, the image of the modest woman in *hijab*, a 'fetishized form of female honor' (Moghadam 2004: 102) represents a central aspect of the Republic's identity.

This politics of gender segregation had a direct impact on Iranian social geography; after the revolution, women were increasingly confined to the private space of their homes as their primary role was seen as wife and mother. When tackling the issue of public versus private space in Iran, one 'needs to expand the definition beyond mere spatial dimension and include behavioural segregation' (Gerami 1996: 132), for the 'Islamic hijab is more than a dress code, it is a live and dynamic social ethic that includes a set of values and norms of interaction' (Gerami 1996: 132). Hence, the law of compulsory veiling also implied behavioural rules, e.g. women were told not to laugh in the workplace, or to smoke in public, or even to cross their legs (Gerami 1996: 133). Accordingly, women were not only banned from the public football stadium, but were also prohibited from playing football themselves. In the 1990s, however, when the reform movement slowly caught on, women gained a new presence in public space. With the end of the Iran–Iraq war in 1988, an Iranian civil society developed which encouraged a women's movement to grow, signified by the emergence of a lively women's press. This 'movement for political and cultural reform' (Moghadam 2004: 460) continued during the presidency of Mohammad Khatami (1997–2001). The political and social changes of the time paved the way for the development of women's sport in the 1990s.

If football is part of a ritual of masculinity, then female players are unlikely to be well-received in a country like Iran, where gender segregation and gender roles are of such high importance. The combination of the political threat of football in general, and the sensitivities surrounding gender segregation in particular, combine to fashion women's football as a potential threat to the social and political order in Iran. Hence, it is no surprise that, while all women's sport faces oppression in the Islamic Republic, this is especially true for football, which was established much later for women athletes than other sports. The question of female presence in the football stadium during men's matches is also a highly contested issue. Regarding women and football in Iran, three aspects appear to be of particular interest:

- *The question of dress*. At the beginning of its history in Iran, even men's football was a source of suspicion for traditional religious circles because the players' shorts were in violation of the Islamic dress code for men (Chehabi 2006: 237). In the case of women's football this is an even more sensitive problem: the compulsory *hijab* consists of 'a long and loose robe' usually dark in colour, a pair of wide trousers worn underneath with 'flat shoes, and a head cover that covers all of a woman's hair' (Gerami 1996: 133). The great political significance of this dress code for women is not only evident in Iran.[6] A strict dress code has also been a pivotal point with regard to women's sport in countries of a Christian tradition.[7]
- *The game*. Football is a game about hierarchies which centres on the dominance of one team over another. This can be clearly seen in the language of football, largely comprised of war metaphors: attack, defence, shooting the ball, striker, etc., as well as in the idea of the game, which is for one team to 'occupy as much of the "territory" of the other as it can, culminating in attempts symbolically to "conquer" the other side's stronghold by kicking the ball into the goal' (Chehabi 2006: 233). As a result, football is generally considered to be 'unfeminine' and therefore problematic 'even if [...] practised out of sight of the (male) public' (Pfister 2003: 215). This is not only the case in Iran; it is also a feature in other Islamic countries. In 2004, a national women's football tournament in Bangladesh was harshly criticized by religious authorities who argued that 'women's football is an indecent game. Playing football is not a job of the women' (Rahman 2004).
- *The behaviour of spectators*. As a typical masculine domain, football not only implies loud cheering and shouting amongst the spectators, but it also seems

to encourage a certain degree of aggressive behaviour. The new image of women propagated by the government after the revolution was an exaggeration of positive female features and characteristics which placed much emphasis on women's high social and spiritual status, thereby highlighting the idea of the 'sacredness of women' (Afzali 2008). Consequently, women are expected to act according to this view, keeping their voices down, avoiding laughter or any other kind of behaviour that could attract attention in public. In short, their behaviour should aspire to 'the preservation of "modesty" as a desirable characteristic of a woman' (Najmabadi 1991: 65). This, in turn, makes it difficult for women to legitimize their desire to play sports or to visit the football stadium (Afzali 2008).

These three examples illustrate the difficult situation of women's football in Iran, highlighting why it is subject to the strict regulations and restrictions. Accordingly, lifting the ban imposed on women's football in the course of the Islamic revolution (cf. Ghazi 1999: 20), was an 'extremely controversial issue' that not only depended on 'a lot of hard work on the part of women's sport activists' (Pfister 2003: 215) but also on favourable political and social circumstances.

In the second half of the 1990s there was an enormous upsurge of women's sports due to the victory of the reformist candidate, Mohammad Khatami, in the presidential election in 1997. This victory fostered hope and optimism amongst the Iranian people that change was coming; this was particularly the case for women. In 1998 Faezeh Hashemi, then vice president of the Iranian Olympic Committee, claimed, 'that roughly two million Iranian women participate in some form of sport, compared with 400,000 two years ago' (Longman 1998). This was also a time of an unprecedented enthusiasm for football in Iran which was triggered by the qualification of the men's team for the FIFA World Cup in 1998 and the subsequent victory over the U.S. team. In the wake of these events, women's voices claiming the right to play football became louder and they were eventually heard.[8] A training session was subsequently held at Tehran's Hejab Stadium, in which 40 women of all ages participated. 'The day – 22 August 1998 – is engraved in Iranian history as a victory for women' (Ghazi 1999: 20). However, despite this, women remained confined to the closed space of the inside stadium, playing futsal instead of football. A national team was founded in 2005, despite the fact that there had not been an official women's football match in Iran since the Islamic revolution. The best players of the nationwide futsal-league were chosen for this team. They took up training and, after only two months, they participated in the First West Asian Cup for women hosted by Jordan in September 2005. Surprisingly, they won the runner-up prize. Whereas futsal allowed the women to wear the usual short-sleeved shirt and trousers, football required a different attire. At the tournament in Jordan, played in open fields in front of a mixed audience, the Iranian team wore a special outfit in accordance with the Islamic dress code. This comprised a tight-fitting headscarf, long trousers tucked into the socks and a loose, long-armed jersey that covered the thighs. This has become the usual attire of the women's team and is produced by the sports fashion label owned by former football star Ali Daei, who was, at that time, also the official sponsor of the male national team.

THE FOOTBALL GAME

Roughly 2,000 female football fans attended the match that took place on 28 April 2006, in the Ararat Stadium in Tehran. This was the first women's football match in an open field in the history of the Islamic Republic. In the years preceding the event there had been several attempts to organize a women's football match. The authorities prevented these matches from taking place using a variety of excuses. The match against the Berlin club had originally been planned to take place on a much larger scale. However, all forms of advertisement were prohibited and the match was overshadowed by the threat of cancellation right up until the very moment of kick-off. Given these circumstances, it is remarkable that 2,000 women actually turned up for the match; they had received information about the event through word of mouth.

The game took place in the Ararat Stadium. Situated in the north of Tehran, this stadium is owned by the Armenian community. It is the home ground of the Armenian-Iranian football club Ararat Tehran, which currently plays in the second division of the Iranian national league. The rules of the Islamic Republic are usually suspended in this stadium and (Armenian-Iranian) women are allowed to exercise here together with men, with or without *hijab*. The venue had been selected in a very diplomatic move in order to appease the political opposition to this match. A well known and adequately equipped football stadium in Tehran, Ararat Stadium is a kind of heterotopia. As it is not wholly territory of the Islamic Republic of Iran, somewhat different rules apply here and the Armenian community has its own say. At maximum capacity, the stadium

Figure 12.1
Women cheering and
singing to support their
team, 2008.

can hold up to 10,000 people. On this day, however, only one part of the stands was open to the public: the grandstand to the north.

The match was attended by women of all ages and diverse social background. Although no men were allowed to enter the stadium, the Islamic dress code was still enforced. This was due to the presence of a large number of international and national representatives from the media, who were thus able to take pictures. Consequently all women (except for small girls) wore *hijab*. There were, however, remarkable differences in the style, the colour and the way the headscarf was worn; these differences were not age-specific.[9] Younger and older women appeared dressed in the black *chador* and there were also younger and older women wearing colourful headscarves and fashionable *mantus*. Some women wore their scarf at the very back of their head so that more than half of their hair was visible, while others were completely covered. Some painted the colours of the Iranian national flag on their cheeks; a few even wore the German national colours. Some girls wore baseball caps over their headscarves; in this way, they resembled the usual (male) stadium spectators with football scarves. The women brought along flags in all sizes – many Iranian and some German. Some women were even equipped with instruments for cheering: large plastic horns, drums, whistles, and other noisemakers.

There was a VIP area which was partially covered in the centre of the stands, dividing the northern and the southern part. Officials and a group of moral guardians were seated in this section. In contrast to the public area a more homogenous style of dress was evident here. Most women wore dark colours if not black *chadors* and the few colourful scarves which were in evidence were tightly bound. Before the game commenced, a young girl read a section from the Quran as is customary in Iran.

The first cheer was heard when the teams entered the football pitch for the first time to warm up. There was loud applause, screaming, resounding horns and 'Iran … Iran!'–chants. The following 90 minutes of the match took place amidst continuous loud cheering and singing in support of the home team. We have included some impressions here:

Three young women wearing dark *mantus* and scarves were hopping, clapping and shouting along with the beat: 'That's it! That's it!' Close to them, a woman dressed in a dark *mantu* and a colourful headscarf was blowing her plastic horn in time to the other women's beat, hopping up and down on the steps and holding her clenched fist in the air. An elderly woman sat on the steps, waving an Iranian flag with both hands. She was blowing a whistle to the beat of the clapping women. The trumpets and horns created a shared rhythm, accompanied by the cries of 'I–ran!' Four women stood in front of the others, leading the fan chants. They chant, in singing dialogue with the other spectators: 'What will Iran do?' and 'Kick them goodbye!'

At half-time, the score was 2–0 to Berlin. Initially, during the half-time interval, loud music was played through the speakers while the players were in the changing rooms. This prompted many women to begin dancing. When some

Figure 12.2
Female football fan
swinging the Iranian flag,
2008.

women even began to take off their scarves, the officials realized that turning the music on had been a mistake. To control this problem, the music was imme- diately switched off and a public announcement was piped through the stadium warning the women against inappropriate behaviour: 'I don't want to see any ladies in the grandstand behaving in an improper manner. You are being filmed. I appeal to you! This is beneath your dignity. If you want to dance, go to the disco!' Following this, the moral guardians were admonished to report 'every instance of undue behaviour' (*Football under Cover* 2008: 01,14).

Following this reprimand, the atmosphere began to shift in the stadium. A group of women began to chant a number of slogans for women's rights in Iran. A small group of middle-aged women wearing loosely fitting, colourful head-scarves at the back of their heads shouted: 'Our share of freedom is half the freedom!'[10] and, 'It's our basic right to enter the stadium!' The number of women shouting continued to grow until it appeared as if the majority of the women were joining in the chants. The media representatives in the stadium, whose presence made the situation for the officials even more precarious, incited the female protesters to continue their chants as they were finally being heard. At one point, the camera turned on one woman and she began to complain about the double standards evident in Iranian society: 'Do this, do that.' That only applies to us. 'Don't dance, don't go to the stadium, be polite.' But men can do whatever they want in the stadium. They swear, behave badly, and it doesn't bother anyone. Only women get criticized.' (*Football under Cover* 2008: 01,15) The women in her vicinity applauded this speech. A reporter sitting next to them hurried to write down the words, and then looked up satisfied.

Shortly after this, the players returned to the pitch and the game recommenced. The Iranian team scored two goals in the second half, equalizing the half-time score. Both goals were enthusiastically received by the fans, who waved Iranian flags and continued to cheer, scream, whistle, and sing. Hardly anyone remained seated; time and again individual women adjusted their headscarves which had fallen off.

The game ended in a draw with the final score of 2–2. When the final whistle was blown, this was followed by loud screaming, whistling, and honking. The players all held hands and ran towards the grandstand in a long line. Fans and players threw their arms up together and applauded each other. Hardly anyone left the stadium right away; most people stood around for a long time, talking and laughing together.

CONCLUSION

What happens, when the football stadium, formerly a male domain, turns into a place exclusively for women? This single case study impressively illustrates that the football stadium is a place for women to act against role expectations. We deliberately focused on the spectators and have observed a large number of behavioural patterns and rituals that are usually connoted as male behaviour and can, according to Iranian law, result in prosecution: loud shouting and clapping, the use of certain expressions, negligent violation of the dress code. Furthermore, this example illustrates the affinity of football and politics in Iran in the way that the stadium atmosphere gives way to a political demonstration. It seems a small step from loudly cheering for your team to chanting for your rights.

However, the framework of a single case study does not allow us to tackle general questions. It is difficult to ascertain to what extent the behaviour observed was exceptional or whether this pattern could have been encountered elsewhere at other times. Women have participated in public celebrations in the context of football matches before as well. Moreover, the fact that women played a pivotal role in the recent protests in the wake of the presidential election in June 2009 showed once again that many women in Iran repeatedly test the limits of the law. The law, however, does exist and any breach is severely punished. The question remains: What led to the exceptional dynamic in these 90 minutes?

We can proceed on the assumption that the space of the football stadium greatly influenced the women's behaviour. The stadium is a site of emotional intensity (cf. Chapters 13 and 14 in this volume) which separates the inside and outside world. In this case women are inside while men remain on the outside, an exception in a country where exclusion is mainly a female experience. The site of the stadium, providing inclusion and enclosure, creates unity among the spectators and thus bridges the vast social and generational gap between the women present, uniting them in one large celebration. In this atmosphere of containment a dynamic evolves that induces the women to (almost) discard all rules. This is the more striking because the outside world is present in the form of moral guardians and safety police; it is by no means a lawless area. This suggests that the football stadium in Iran has in recent years established itself as a place of protest, whether it is used as a site to raise attention to women's rights issues, as done by the White Scarves Group (cf. Afzali 2008), or as a place where women transgress gender boundaries, as shown with great subtlety in Jafar Panahi's film *Offside* (2006), where a group of young women tries to enter the stadium dressed as men.

In addition to the special atmosphere inherent in the stadium, the presence of media representatives also plays an important role. The media serves as mouthpiece in carrying news of the events inside the stadium outside and provides international attention for the situation inside Iran. Although the match was not broadcast live, national television featured a short news story. The press covered the match extensively inside as well as outside Iran. Incited by the group dynamics and presented by the media with the rare chance to voice their discontent, the women felt encouraged to test their limits in this way.

The documentary film *Football under Cover* premiered at the Berlin International Film Festival 2008. The film does not have permission to be screened in the Islamic Republic of Iran; but it was successful in countries around the world and has won several awards. At the time, the film inspired a discussion about the possibility of FIFA changing the dress code for international tournaments in favour of Muslim women's teams. Recently however, women's football in Iran has suffered another blow from FIFA's decision to exclude the Iranian team from the Youth Olympic Games in Singapore in August 2010 on the grounds of dress code.

NOTES

1 In the US, what is termed football in Europe and soccer in America, is still inferior to other sports such as American football, basketball, and baseball. Nevertheless, the US was the first country in the world to establish a professional football league for women (the Women's United Soccer Association, founded in 2000 and suspended in 2003).

Markovits (1988) deduces this peculiarity (on the basis of Werner Sombart's thesis of 'American exceptionalism') from the specific history of the US as the first 'new nation', in which sports with an indigenous tradition were firmly rooted before football was imported from Great Britain (cf. Chapter 11).

2 Weblogs such as 'Frauenfußball? Weder sind es Frauen, noch ist es Fußball!' ('Women's Football? It's neither women nor is it football!') show how women's football is still regarded as a threat even in Germany.

3 For an overview cf. Brändle and Koller 2002: 207–9; Kreisky and Spitaler 2006; Meuser 2006, 2008.

4 Loimeier (2000) for example describes the close relation between football and politics in northern Nigeria.

5 This has changed somewhat in top-level football in recent years, but is still largely the case at amateur and recreational level.

6 From a female perspective, the role of the headscarf is extremely complex. It has its theological basis in the Quran, verse 53:33. This verse deals with the relation of public and private space in the house of Mohammad, where the veil (*hijab*) is introduced as a means of separating the guests from Mohammad's wives. Interpretations of this verse are manifold and quite controversial (Mernissi 2002: 113ff.). In Turkey, a women's movement has evolved which advocates women's right to wear the veil. The radical ban by Atatürk is still seen by various groups of women as a serious intrusion on their privacy and a violation of their right to self-determination (Acar 1991, for a historical classification see also Göle 1995).

7 Georg Denzler (Denzler 1988), for example, quotes the congregation of the Catholic Council in 1930: 'Parents are to keep their daughters away from public gymnastic exercises and sporting events. […] If the daughters are under constraint to participate, the parents should aspire to supply them with perfectly decent attire, and should never allow them to wear indecent clothing' (Denzler 1988: 233, trans. C. Assmann and S. Gülker). The Association of Catholic German Women Teachers specified these guidelines from the bishop as follows: 'a pair of trousers that is sufficiently roomy and closed above the knee, and a loose blouse with a high neck-line and arms reaching down to the elbows' (Denzler 1988: 233, trans. C. Assmann and S. Gülker).

8 Before they were finally officially allowed to play football, Iranian women were restricted to futsal, an indoor five-a-side variant of football, which complies more easily with Islamic rules. Since it is played behind closed doors with no male spectators, the players can wear the customary short-sleeved football jerseys and trousers. At the same time it also proved a convenient way of channelling women's football away from public attention.

9 There are many different ways of conforming to the Islamic dress code and the particular dress chosen offers insights into a variety of positions regarding 'individualism, resistance, rejection, commitment, devotion, and fashion, as well as social status' (Gerami 1996: 133). Generally, the Islamic *hijab* consists of a robe (called '*mantu*' from the French *manteau*), which may vary in length, fit, and colour. Despite this, they are mostly either black or dark in colour. However, it is the choice of the headscarf 'that draws the boundaries of segregation, ideology, and social standing' (Gerami 1996: 133). There are three main categories which can be identified (this categorization is based on Gerami 1996: 133ff.): 1) the *hijab* that is mandatory in offices, schools, universities etc., which consists of a long, loose, and dark-coloured *mantu* and a special kind of headscarf ('*maghnae*') which has a small opening for the face and completely covers a woman's hair; 2) the combination of *mantu* with a headscarf which is tied around head and neck called '*rusary*'; this outfit may vary 'from expensive, elegant, and fashionable to, at times, tacky' (Gerami 1996: 134), depending on the colour of the headscarf and on how it is tied; 3) the *Hijab Islami* consists of *mantu* and *maghnae*

as described above. This is supplemented by a *chador*, a long and wide cloak which is tied around the head and covers all of the body. Since the *maghnae* is often obligatory, a woman's social and political standing are generally determined by the rest of the ensemble. Hence, the first category is rather neutral and mostly indicates a college student or woman working outside the home. The second category denotes a non-advocate or may even signify that the woman is in opposition to the system. By opting for the third category, the woman generally shows her commitment to the regime, especially if the *chador* is black. The reasons for this choice of dress may also be informed by the husband's position or it may be determined by the woman's own occupation.

10 This is the main chant of the White Scarf Campaign for women's presence in football stadia; it plays very cleverly with the double meaning of *azadi* as the farsi word for 'freedom' on the one hand and the name of the famous football stadium on the other hand. Thus, besides its meaning with regard to women's rights in general, the chant can also mean: 'Our share of Azadi (stadium) is half of Azadi (stadium)'. For further information on the White Scarf Campaign see Afzali 2008.

REFERENCES

Acar, F. (1991) 'Was die islamische Bewegung für Frauen so anziehend macht. Eine Unter-suchung über Frauenzeitschriften und eine Gruppe von Studentinnen', in N. Ayla, S. Tekeli and M. Akkent (eds) *Aufstand im Haus der Frauen. Frauenforschung aus der Türkei*, Berlin: Orlanda Frauenverlag.

Afzali, N. (2008) *Iranian Women's Campaign to be Football Spectators*. Online. Available www.meydaan.org/English/showarticle.aspx?arid=662; 2008/09/12 (accessed 25 February 2009).

Brändle, F. and Koller, C. (2002) *Goal. Kultur- und Sozialgeschichte des modernen Fußballs*, Zürich: orell füssli.

Bromberger, C. (1995) 'Football as world-view and as ritual', *French Cultural Studies*, 6: 293–311.

Chehabi, H.E. (2006) 'The politics of football in Iran', *Soccer and Society*, 7(2–3): 233–61.

Denzler, G. (1988) *Die verbotene Lust. 2000 Jahre christliche Sexualmoral*, München/Zürich: Piper.

Dunning, E. (2003) 'Sport als Männerdomäne. Anmerkungen zu den sozialen Quellen männlicher Identität und deren Transformation', in N. Elias and E. Dunning (eds) *Sport und Spannung im Prozeß der Zivilisation*, Frankfurt am Main: Suhrkamp.

Elias, N. and Dunning, E. (2003) 'Volkstümliche Fußballspiele im mittelalterlichen und früh-neuzeitlichen England', in N. Elias and E. Dunning (eds) *Sport und Spannung im Prozeß der Zivilisation*, Frankfurt am Main: Suhrkamp.

Feltz, N. (2007) 'Der Umgang mit Bewegungsräumen in biografischen Verläufen', in I. Hartmann-Tews and B. Dahmen (eds) *Sportwissenschaftliche Geschlechterfor-schung im Spannungsfeld von Theorie und Praxis. Jahrestagung der dvs-Kommission Geschlechterforschung vom 9.-11.11.2006 in Köln*, Hamburg: Cwalina.

Fozooni, B. (2004) 'Religion, politics and class: Conflict and contestation in the develop-ment of football in Iran', *Soccer and Society*, 5(3): 356–70.

Football Under Cover (2008) Theatrical documentary film directed by Ayat Najafi and David Assmann. Germany: Assmann/Flying Moon Filmproduktion.

Gerami, S. (1996) *Women and Fundamentalism: Islam and Christianity*, New York/London: Garland.

—— (2003) 'Mullahs, martyrs, and men: Conceptualizing masculinity in the Islamic Repub-lic of Iran', *Men and Masculinities*, 5(3): 257–74.

Ghazi, S. (1999) 'Iranian Women Put on Their Running Shoes', *The UNESCO Courier*, 52(4): 20–1.

Göle, N. (1995) *Republik und Schleier. Die muslimische Frau in der Moderne*, Berlin: Babel.

Kermani, N. (2005) *Iran. Die Revolution der Kinder. Erweiterte und aktualisierte Auflage*, München: Beck.

Kreisky, E. and Spitaler, G. (eds) (2006) *Arena der Männlichkeit. Über das Verhältnis von Fußball und Geschlecht*, Frankfurt am Main/New York: Campus.

Lehnert, E. (2006) 'Auf der Suche nach Männlichkeiten in der sozialpädagogischen Arbeit mit Fans', in E. Kreisky and G. Spitaler (eds) *Arena der Männlichkeit. Über das Verhältnis von Fußball und Geschlecht*, Frankfurt am Main: Campus.

Loimeier, R. (2000) 'Ist Fußball unislamisch? Zur Tiefenstruktur des Banalen', in R. Loimeier (ed.) *Die islamische Welt als Netzwerk*, Würzburg: Ergon.

Longman, J. (1998) 'A quiet revolution in Iran: Beneath coat and scarf, women discover the freedom to play', *New York Times*, 26 May. Online. Available http://query.nytimes.com/gst/fullpage.html?res=9804E7DF1438F935A15756C0A96E958260&sec=&spon=&pagewanted=all (accessed 25 February 2009).

Löw, M. (2001) *Raumsoziologie*, Frankfurt am Main: Suhrkamp.

Markovits, A.S. (1988) 'The other "American exceptionalism" – Why is there no soccer in the United States?', *Praxis International*, 2: 125–50.

Mernissi, F. (2002) *Der politische Harem. Mohammed und die Frauen*, Freiburg im Breisgau: Herder Spektrum.

Meuser, M. (2006) 'Riskante Praktiken. Zur Aneignung von Männlichkeit in den ernsten Spielen des Wettbewerbs', in H. Bilden and B. Dausien (eds) *Sozialisation und Geschlecht. Theoretische und methodologische Aspekte*, Opladen/Farmington Hills: Barbara Budrich.

—— (2008) 'It's a men's world. Ernste Spiele männlicher Vergemeinschaftung', in G. Klein and M. Meuser (eds) *Ernste Spiele. Zur politischen Soziologie des Fußballs*, Bielefeld: transcript.

Moghadam, V.M. (2004) 'A Tale of Two Countries: State, society, and gender politics in Iran and Afghanistan', *The Muslim World*, 94: 449–67.

Najmabadi, A. (1991) 'Hazards of modernity and morality: Women, state and ideology in contemporary Iran', in D. Kandiyoti (ed.) *Women, Islam and the State*, Basingstoke: Macmillan.

Pfister, G. (2003) 'Women and sport in Iran: Keeping goal in the Hijab?', in I. Hartmann-Tews and G. Pfister (eds) *Sport and Women: Social Issues in International Perspective*, London: Routledge.

Rahman, W. (2004) 'Row fails to halt women's soccer', *BBC News*, 4 October. Online. Available http://news.bbc.co.uk/2/hi/south_asia/3714550.stm (accessed 25 February 2009).

Sedghi, H. (2007) *Women and Politics in Iran: Veiling, unveiling, and reveiling*, Cambridge et al.: Cambridge University Press.

Sobiech, G. (2006) 'Im Abseits? Mädchen und Frauen im Fußballsport', in H. Brandes, H. Christa and R. Evers (eds) *Hauptsache Fußball. Sozialwissenschaftliche Einwürfe*, Gießen: Psychosozial.

—— (2007) 'Zur Irritation des geschlechtstypischen Habitus in der Sportspielpraxis: Frauen spielen Fußball', in I. Hartmann-Tews and B. Dahmen (eds) *Sportwissenschaftliche Geschlechterforschung im Spannungsfeld von Theorie und Praxis. Jahrestagung der dvs-Kommission Geschlechterforschung vom 9.–11.11.2006 in Köln*, Hamburg: Cwalina.

Part V

Emotions and the Body

Part IV

Emotions and the Body

Chapter 13: Emotions in Sports Stadia[1]

Mike S. Schäfer and Jochen Roose

> *The ball changed possession, moving fast from one end of the field to the other. The tension mounted; it became almost unbearable. People forgot where they were standing. They were pushed, and pushing back, were again jostled back and forth, up and down the terraces. There was a tussle to the left of the guest team's goal, a quick centre, a header. Suddenly the ball was in the net, and the joy, the delight, of the home supporters went up in a thundering roar that one could hear over half the town, a signal to everyone: 'We've won!'*
>
> (Elias and Dunning 1970: 47)

One of the most striking characteristics of the sports stadium is the emotional intensity found there. On the one hand, stadia play host to an 'adoring audience' (Lewis 1992) of enthusiastic, shouting, celebrating or crying fans, while on the other, they are a place in which deviant and violent behaviour, fuelled by emotions such as anger and hatred, can break out. Thus however it is expressed, sport seems to carry an 'enormous emotional load' (Wohl 1970: 122), something that has repeatedly been described in popular novels such as Nick Hornby's *Fever Pitch*, in countless mass media reports and, also, in academic accounts such as Norbert Elias's case study on football which provided the introductory quote. Although this emotional intensity extends beyond the time and space in which the game is actually played, it is most striking at the site in which professional spectator sports are usually located: the stadium.

However, such emotional intensity is in fact not what social scientific theory would lead us to expect. Several classical sociological authors converge in their diagnosis that modern societies develop in a way that increasingly suppresses, substitutes or regulates emotions. Max Weber, probably the most influential founding father of sociology, sees rationalization as a major and general characteristic of modern societies, a trend that manifests itself not only in bureaucratic institutions but also in cultural leitmotifs which lead to a devaluation of emotions and emotion-based action. In his works on religion, Weber (1993) describes how the specific leitmotif of the Occident, Ascetic Protestantism, not only gave birth to the capitalist regime, but also strongly emphasized a methodical way of living, an inner-worldly asceticism and, connected to that, emotional control and restraint. Similar views, albeit less explicit, can be found in the works of other sociological classics. Emile Durkheim (2001) interprets collective emotions and effervescent phenomena as characteristics of pre-modern societies, characteristics which in modern societies are relegated to the religious sphere and are considered less important overall. Along similar lines, Norbert Elias (2000) assumes that 'civilizing' processes in modern societies involve a more rigid emotional control and an increasing suppression of emotions – although he, as we will see later, also allows for certain exceptions.

This theoretical backdrop can shed interesting light on an analysis of the emotionality associated with stadia. Accordingly, our chapter asks how sports stadia facilitate the emotions of spectators, and pays specific attention both to spatially specific social rules as well as to the built environment. It aims to gather findings, interpretations and ideas scattered in the literature on spectators' emotion in stadia, on its facilitation and containment. In the first section, we will argue that in contrast to Weber's and Durkheim's rationalization hypothesis, sport and sports stadia can be seen as niches in which emotions in modern societies can still be found. Norbert Elias, Eric Dunning and their colleagues have prepared the field for this argument. In the second section, we turn to the built environment stadia constitute for emotions of sport spectators. Emile Durkheim's works on religion and religious rituals, and its subsequent uptake by Randall Collins, provide the material which can be applied to the situation in stadia. In the third section, we turn to the social rules targeting the creation of emotions in stadia. Employing a symbolic-interactionist perspective we can learn how the feeling and expression of emotions is regulated in stadia. As a contrast, we take up Foucaultian arguments pertaining to the containment of emotions. The combination of both approaches illustrates the interplay between the orchestration, control, and performance of emotions in stadia.

SPORT AS AN EMOTIONAL NICHE

Norbert Elias's theory, and its application on sport by himself, Eric Dunning and their numerous collaborators will serve as our starting point, as Elias is one of the few modern classics of sociology who not only explicitly deals with emotions, but also considers sport and sports spectators as a subject worthy of academic interest.

His analyses of sport – and other societal fields – are embedded in a larger framework which Elias uses to interpret the development of societies; a framework that can only be roughly sketched here. As a general trend, Elias describes how modern societies became less emotional over time. In his seminal two volumes on *The Civilizing Process* (2000), Elias views the historical development of several European societies as ever-increasing 'civilization' based on the monopolization of violence in certain regions. He argues that this pacification enabled the emergence of increasingly complex social networks ('figurations', e.g. Elias 1986a: 154) of actors and institutions, and that this societal complexity necessitated increased individual control of affects and emotions. Elias demonstrates this change in norms of violence, sexual behaviour, dealing with bodily functions, table manners and forms of speech and how these were gradually transformed by increasing thresholds of shame and repugnance, respectively, which started with court etiquette and then worked their way outwards to other societal spheres and strata.

Thus, emotional control and restraint pervaded most societal realms in 'civilized' societies and limited emotions to private life and intimate relations. However, Elias, particularly in collaboration with Eric Dunning, also argues that the civilizing of many and most spheres of society creates a 'counter-move' (Elias and Dunning 1970: 31). Although societies are becoming generally less affective, niches continue to exist which serve a basic – almost anthropological – need of human beings for something the authors call 'excitement' (Elias and Dunning 1986d; see also Dunning 1976; Dunning and Rojek 1992). Thus, Elias and Dunning argue that the increasingly controlled and regulated emotions, whose expression was legitimate in many places and in public for long periods of time, do not become entirely extinct but are relegated to certain areas within society (Elias and Dunning 1984: 47ff.). People are on a 'quest for excitement in unexciting societies' (Elias and Dunning 1970); i.e. they search for the 'kick' lacking in most realms of the bureaucratized, rationalized, professional society, the emotional experience they can no longer enact in the wider society with its 'built-in restraints [and] social control' (Elias and Dunning 1970: 35). The authors argue that people seek and find this excitement in their leisure time, and that they do so in a variety of ways: in music and dancing, in movies, in exciting hobbies and also (perhaps even mainly) in sport (Elias and Dunning 1970; 1984).

This standpoint allows Elias and Dunning to interpret sports phenomena and spectators not as isolated 'small group problems', but as connected to a larger societal context (Elias and Dunning 1966: 191), as one of the typical realms of society providing 'pleasurable' (Elias 1986c: 15) forms of 'tension-excitement' (Elias and Dunning 1970: 49). On this theoretical foundation, sport analyses became one of the main applications of this approach. In their works, Elias and Dunning focus on two interconnected facets of the described 'counter-move'. First, they describe changes in sport itself. They demonstrate that, for sportsmen and sportswomen, active participation in sport served as an exciting substitute for violence and battles. Sport is understood as a mimetic alternative to 'real' violence and fights, as 'mock battles' (Elias 1986a), which, according to the authors, explains the increasing 'sportization' of societies, and also that many sports emphasize the element of (often physical) competition (Elias 1986a). Nevertheless, sport itself is also shown to be influenced by the general pacification trend in society: sport in many disciplines has developed from its often (when compared with current beliefs) 'crude' or 'savage' (Elias 1986b: 131), 'wild' (Elias and Dunning 1986a: 197) and 'dead serious' (Elias 1986b: 135ff.) origins in Ancient Greece (cf. Chapter 2) or in Western Europe's Middle Ages, towards a non-violent simulation of battle, an ethos of fairness (Elias and Dunning 1984: 26), the development and elaboration of rules and, eventually, towards a less pronounced expression of emotions. Elements of violence, for example, which are still prevalent in some of today's sports, are no longer expressions of uncontrolled emotions such as anger, hatred or aggression, but serve 'rational' and 'instrumental' ends, like winning according to the rules (Elias 1986c: 16). Such trends can be seen in boxing (e.g. Elias 1986b), football (e.g. Elias and Dunning 1986b), rugby (Dunning and Sheard 2005), wrestling (Stone 1976) and other sports. Moreover, the emotional motivation for doing sport, i.e. inherent 'fun', is, according to Eric Dunning, being supplanted by a 'growing seriousness' and a general orientation towards 'achievement' (Dunning 1986a: 214ff.).

Elias's and Dunning's second focus, which is of particular interest for this chapter, is the behaviour and emotional make-up of sports spectators. The authors claim that not only enacting, but also and even more so watching sport has become one of the most desired exciting leisure time activities. It seems, however, that the authors do not perceive sports spectators as becoming both less violent and less emotional over time. What they do show, on the one hand, is a long-term pacification of sports spectators that parallels a trend in sport itself – they can demonstrate that the violent behaviour of early sports crowds has cooled down significantly (Elias and Dunning 1986b, Dunning 1986b), and they interpret widespread attempts to 'solve' the problem of football hooliganism as another symptom of this trend (Dunning *et al.* 1988). The pacification of violence amongst spectators aside, however, Elias and Dunning argue that watching sport has remained one of the few societal realms in which positive and also some negative emotions – joy, enthusiasm, affection, suspense, but also distress, suffering, and to some extent, even hatred – can be enacted in a way that is widely seen as legitimate and which is usually shared with others (Elias and Dunning 1970: 142). Here, it seems, the authors do not perceive an increasing emotional control, but rather a persisting legitimacy of emotions amongst spectators. Sports spectatorship, they observe, gives people the chance to 'loosen their [emotional] armour' and experience the 'strong emotional excitement' (Elias and Dunning 1986c: 124f.) they are looking for in today's societies.

Accordingly, Elias and Dunning are a useful starting point from which to emphasize the general relevance of an analysis of sport and, specifically, of sports spectators (see also Ferguson 1981). They convincingly argue that even in seemingly rationalized societies, niches continue to exist where the expression of emotions, and even collective emotions, is legitimate, becomes public again and actually takes place (cf. Chapter 12). Sport, in their view and also according to numerous other scholars, is one such (and maybe the primary) niche of this sort, and particularly sports spectators are of interest in this respect (cf. Bromberger 1995; Josuttis 1996; Prosser 2002) – something that is certainly connected to the fundamental openness of sports, where results and outcomes in general are undetermined, and where identification with participants and teams seems relatively easy due to the competitive structure of the game or competition (cf. Riedl 2006: 155). Accordingly, it can be shown that spectators perceive sports settings as legitimate places for emotion-based action in general (e.g. Cachay *et al.* 2005: 17ff., Földesi 1996: 419ff.), and also as places in which they can enact emotions de-legitimized in other fields of society, such as emotions connected with certain notions of masculinity (e.g. Taylor 1976: 359f., cf. Bromberger's Chapter 10 in this volume).

In turn, however, some important aspects seem to be missing in Elias's and Dunning's investigations. For instance, they – like many scholars in this field (cf. Bale 1989: 10ff.) – tend to neglect the spatial dimension of sports, along with an analysis of its concrete and also architectural setting: The stadium as the place in which sport often takes place and, particularly, where it is usually watched in public, is not taken up systematically. An analysis of emotions amongst spectators within the stadium is also absent: Elias and Dunning cannot tell us precisely how emotions amongst sports spectators are orchestrated and performed in the stadium (Taylor 1976). Accordingly, these areas of neglect will be considered in the next sections of this chapter. The chapter will attempt to outline the specifics of the spatial setting of spectator sports first, and then move on to an analysis of the emotional dynamics within the stadium.

THE STADIUM AS AN EMOTIONAL SETTING

Elias and Dunning, while emphasizing the importance of an analysis of emotions in sport, neglect the spatial setting of sport and sports spectators, even though they mention the playing field, the stands or the terraces often in their analyses, and despite the fact that 'spectators' already implies a space in which these spectators actually watch sport. This omission is particularly regrettable, since the stadium can not only be considered as the archetypal locus of sports watching, but also as an ideal environment for emotional behaviour of sports spectators.

Of course, spectators and particularly fans loosen their 'emotional armour' not only in the stadium, but as soon as the social situation becomes defined as a sports setting. On game day, for example, the visit to the local pub or the bus transfer to the stadium will already be charged with a special emotional atmosphere (cf. Chapter 8); and this is even more relevant on longer trips to away games. The stadium, however, is at the very core of this atmosphere, not only because it is a part of an already emotionally charged sports setting, but also because it implies a specific, emotionally relevant code of conduct (Kopiez 2002: 294ff.).[2]

In part, this has to do with the stadium's ability to highlight and aggravate the difference between participants and non-participants. It aims to establish a border between the inside and the outside world (Bale 2005): The carefully monitored gates of modern stadia demonstrate this, as well as the visual borders they

Figure 13.1
The LTU Arena in
Düsseldorf, 2005
(Courtesy of Reinaldo
Coddou H., www.
fussballtempel.com).

erect – modern stadia are closed in the sense that they usually make it impossible to watch games from nearby houses or trees nowadays; the 'closed circle of the bowl breaks the visual connection between the stadium and the town' (Neilson 1986: 42, see also Schroer 2008: 161), 'the sports arena is a bounded universe [and it] is no accident that the best sports stadia are those that do not allow any glimpse of the World outside' (Whannel 1993: 346). The trend for closed (or closable) stadium roofs also aggravates this (Schroer 2008: 164). Moreover, sound is almost hermetically enclosed as well, as recent stadium construction tends to create an intense atmosphere with good acoustics inside the stadium (Alkemeyer 2008: 92). In turn, excluding the outside world also emphasizes the fundamental other-worldliness of the inside, that is, of the stadium (cf. Bromberger 1995).

Furthermore, the architectural make-up of today's stadia provides a particularly advantageous setting for the arousal of emotions. This insight stems from another theoretical tradition which mainly draws from Emile Durkheim's works on religion (2001). In this tradition, it is asked how a social setting should be structured in order to further an intense emotional atmosphere. Durkheim argues that shared rituals arouse individual emotions and (may) result in collective emotions, and that these rituals, especially when coupled with shared emotions, are essential for the stability, cohesiveness and self-affirmation of social collectives – an idea that Randall Collins has taken up and elaborated in recent years (see Collins 2004). For our purposes, it is interesting that both Collins and Durkheim describe a set of 'ingredients' (Collins 2004: 47) which they perceive to constitute a favourable environment to generate collective emotions, and that their descriptions converge in most points (for the following see Collins 2004: 47ff., Durkheim 2001: 221ff.).[3]

First, they argue that participants of rituals should be co-present, i.e. physically present at the place of the ritual. Moreover, they should be visible to each other and, thus, mutually aware of their participation in the ritual (a condition that would usually be fulfilled in smaller rituals, but one which is important to point out when looking at stadia). Second, the participants should share a 'mutual focus' (Collins 2004: 47), for example the proceedings on a stage or certain aspects of nature. A third condition is the physical involvement of the participants in the ritual, preferably in the form of some synthesized motion like shared dances, rhythmical behaviour etc. Fourth, and finally, it is helpful if participants are symbolically unified, e.g. by shared symbols such as totems, signs or banners. These conditions, when present in rituals, not only strengthen the sense of community amongst participants, but are also likely to intensify the individual emotions of the participants and can lead to 'effervescence' (Durkheim 2001: 153ff.), an intensive collective emotional experience.

Durkheim's and Collins's theory was applied quite frequently to sport. Usually, the respective studies focused on one of the above-mentioned 'ingredients' and described its existence and relevance in sports settings and amongst sports spectators. For the purposes of this chapter, it is interesting that they can demonstrate that stadia, particularly modern, tightly packed, monofunctional stadia with steep terraces exhibit, and even emphasize, the characteristics necessary for powerful rituals and, thus, for intensive emotionalization to take place.[4]

First, the spatial organization of the stadium not only excludes outsiders, but also organizes the insiders on steep terraces around a field, pitch or track. Thereby, stadia facilitate the co-presence of a large number of spectators and amplify this by making it visible to all participants at the same time, allowing them to observe each other (Schroer 2008: 167).

Second, the spatial arrangement of the stadium is designed for a main purpose: to enhance the visibility of the game or the competition (Bromberger 1995: 302) – or, when seen through the lens of ritual theory, to further the mutual focusing of a large crowd (Alkemeyer 2008: 90). From early on in stadium history, one of the few constants has been the organization of spectators around or before the respective events (cf. Alkemeyer 2008: 97; Kratzmüller's Chapter 2 in this volume).

A third characteristic of the stadium is that procedures are highly ritualized and often include some kind of physical involvement and synchronized motion. In football stadia, this starts with the extreme density of human bodies occupying limited space (cf. Alkemeyer 2008: 88). The behaviour of spectators follows standardized routines in certain game situations, i.e. when corners or free kicks are awarded and executed, and chants largely remain the same over time and often vary only slightly from stadium to stadium (cf. Klein and Schmidt-Lux 2006). Moreover, many of these situations involve spectators physically; they have to stand up for the 'Mexican Wave', or to jump, sing and shout rhythmically (e.g. Trujillo and Krizek 1994: 311), following the development of the game as well as the rules of the ritual.

Furthermore, these commonalities amongst spectators are amplified by shared symbols (the club logo or colours, for instance), common clothing rules like wearing a club scarf (Kopiez 2002: 289f.), and also by being explicitly addressed by public announcers and others as a 'crowd', i.e. as 'an aggregation of people who do, in fact, have a common focal concern' (Bryan and Horton 1976: 7). With these features, stadia further a sense of community that, in many cases, even exceeds social positions or personal differences. For the time of the

Figure 13.2
Emotions in sport stadia:
Fans of 1. FC Lokomotive
Leipzig, (Courtesy of
Thomas Franke, www.
von-athen-nach-althen.
de).

Figure 13.3
Fans supporting their
team (Courtesy of
Thomas Franke, www.
von-athen-nach-althen.
de).

game, and for some time before and after that, it establishes a 'casual sociability' (Riedl 2006: 169) amongst potentially very different spectators. Moreover, and particularly relevant here, is the fact that intertwined with this sense of community, emotions are aroused.

It is further interesting to note that these features of stadia, which make them ideal catalysts for spectator emotions, seem to have been increasingly emphasized over time. Not only has the place in which the game takes place been increasingly confined in many sports, but the development of stadia has taken quite similar paths in this respect in football, American football, rugby, baseball etc. (cf. Bale 1989: 145ff.). 'If one could watch the history of stadium construction as a fast-forwarded video, a continuing enclosure of the masses would be visible. This movement – like an oyster slowly closing itself – is repeated symbolically by the sliding roofs which can be found in new stadia in the 1990s' (van Winkel 2005: 251).[5] Accordingly, the other-worldliness of the stadium and its seclusion are emphasized more strongly than before. The same is true for the stands, which have moved closer to the pitch and at the same time have become steeper, thus enabling spectators to follow the game(s) from only a few metres away, watching themselves and the other spectators in the stadium more closely, and also allowing for a more intense, noisier, more resonating atmosphere which generates emotions more easily (cf. Bale 1993), something that is not only known to architects but is intentionally created for this purpose (cf. Prosser 2002: 275).

What we can learn from the above is that stadia – and particularly modern sports stadia – can be understood as extremely favourable environments for the facilitation of emotions. They segregate spectators from the wider societal context and from everyday life, show them that they are part of a large collective, try to draw their attention to a shared focus, and involve them mentally and physically in collective rituals (cf. Chapter 14). This is an ideal environment, not only for an individual emotional experience, but also for the perception of other people being emotional and, thus, for the emergence of collective emotional phenomena, an 'enthusiasm about [the others'] enthusiasm' (Bette and Schimank 2000: 315); spectators 'become progressively more excited and outspoken; they become increasingly more agitated and active in venting and displaying their emotions' (Bryan and Horton 1976: 7) – precisely what Durkheim calls 'effervescence' (Durkheim 2001: 153ff.).

Nevertheless, what we have described so far may be more an account of the extraordinary potential of the stadium to induce emotions and to further an intense atmosphere than a description of daily proceedings in stadia. Effervescent phenomena, of course, do not occur every time a game is played or a competition is held (cf. Leistner and Schmidt-Lux 2010). This leads us to the last section of our chapter, in which we will deal with the question of emotional orchestration and control: How are emotions induced in a stadium setting, which social rules apply, and which emotions are targeted?

EMOTIONAL RULES IN THE STADIUM

The stadium is not only an ideal place for emotions, but also characterized by specific emotional rules which aim to impact on the actual experience and performance of emotions. In different ways and from different parties, efforts to steer and control emotions and their expression can be found in stadia: On the one hand, rules can be constituted by peer or reference groups, as symbolic interactionist scholars emphasize; on the other hand, writers in the tradition of Michel Foucault stress the interplay of architectural or spatial configurations and (internalized) social rules of behaviour. Both perspectives are helpful in shedding some light on existing emotional rules for spectators.

Symbolic interactionism has been applied to emotions most prominently in

Arlie Hochschild's *The Managed Heart* (1983), a study of flight attendants and bill collectors describing how both professions imply a certain emotional appearance, how this appearance is regulated by US companies and how individuals try to adapt to these rules. In her book, Hochschild strongly emphasized the sociocultural origins of emotions, and very successfully introduced to the sociology of emotions the terms 'feeling rules' (which apply to felt emotions: what should I feel?), 'display rules' (which apply to the expression of emotions: should I smile now?) and 'emotion work' (individuals labour to synchronize their own emotions and expressions with the emotional rules that seem valid in a given situation).

This view has also been applied to sport. Most of these writers have dealt with sports professionals and their emotion work before and during games, for example in (American) football (Zurcher 1972) or US pro hockey (Gallmeier 1987).[6] Of particular interest to this chapter are several studies which also applied the symbolic interactionist approach to sports spectators, mostly in US college settings (Bryan and Horton 1976; Friedenberg 1967; Zurcher 1972), but also, for example, in German football (Schwenzer 2001).

In line with Elias and Durkheim, these studies demonstrate that the stadium is not only a peculiar place in the sense that there, emotions are legitimate and even furthered by the ritual setting, they also show that stadia are places where the expression and, in fact, the sensation of certain emotions is expected and, at times, demanded by others (cf. Schwenzer 2001). The emotions that are demanded can be both positive and negative. On the one hand, support and enthusiasm for the home team are naturally expected, and spectators are to 'develop a behaviourally overt response to vicarious experiences' (Bryan and Horton 1976: 5). Yet on the other hand, spectators may also be expected to express negative emotions, mainly towards the opponents. '[G]ood fans – like good soldiers – need to be initially hostile toward their opponent' (Bryan and Horton 1976: 6). Such expectations are brought forward from different sides. Before games, for example during 'pep rallies' at US universities, an emotional atmosphere is created in which the spectre of emotions that could be necessary during the game is presented and practiced: Spectators are shown that they should be 'ready to enact, at different times during the game, affection for other fans and hostility or even hatred for the opponents. We might be called upon to show compassion for the injured. If the game went well for the team, we would be expected to show pride, joy, and perhaps ecstasy. If the game went badly, it would be appropriate for us to display anger, disappointment, disgust, and perhaps even shame' (Zurcher 1972: 5).

During games or competitions, a number of 'emotional prompters' or 'orchestrators' can be identified, who try to activate certain emotions amongst spectators. On the one hand, these orchestrators can be spectators themselves, who have acquired a special position in the hierarchy of spectators and work – jumping, shouting, drumming, singing, etc. – as 'informal cheerleaders' (Zurcher 1972: 14) to get other spectators to support the team or to mock the opponent (cf. Bryan and Horton 1976: 4). On the other hand, some orchestration is also provided by the team and its representatives. For them, the emotional atmosphere is 'an important element in this spectacle, and [they] do not risk leaving it to spontaneous self-expression' (Bryan and Horton 1976: 7). Accordingly, cheerleaders, speakers, bands, mascots, stadium announcers, and sometimes even team representatives like managers, coaches or players, will attempt to orchestrate the spectators' emotional performance, for instance by asking spectators simply to 'shout', to 'support the team', 'yell louder' or 'yell like hell' (Bryan and Horton 1976: 6).

Symbolic interactionist writers usually concentrate on social rules and the orchestration of emotions, in most cases strongly focusing on positive emotions such as joy, support, happiness etc. It is interesting to counter this view with the works of Michel Foucault, who also describes rules, but highlights two aspects neglected by symbolic interactionism. First, while rules were mainly understood as trying to evoke emotion, the focus of Foucault's (1977) work on prisons, asylums and similar institutions has been the control and restraint of emotion. Second, he does not limit himself to social rules and human orchestrators, but stresses that rules are also embedded in and emitted by architecture and infrastructures. According to Foucault, built-in devices are crucial to implement and supervise social rules, leading eventually to an internalized control. Foucault emphasizes the interweaving of generalized external supervision and internal control, blurring the border between architectural setting and social rule.

John Bale (e.g. Bale 1989, 1993, 2005) transferred Foucault's view to stadia and emphasized that they inhibit methods of controlling negative emotions and, particularly, limiting violence as their outcome (cf. Chapter 1). For example, Bale shows how the segregation within stadia according to team affiliation – home fans on one side, away supporters on the other – led to fights between 'home' and 'away gangs' who, as they usually watched from fixed locations, could try to 'take' the other side's location, as in combat (Bale 1993: 125). This led to an emphasis on crowd control, which quickly became a major influence on stadium construction. Stadia were soon built in specific ways for safety reasons, not only to ensure fire safety for the initially wooden constructions, but also to decrease fights between spectators. Most notably, subdivisions of the terraces with physical barriers were erected that herded spectators into small pens, and stadium sections were separated from one another. Nowadays, in a 'new phase of spatial control' (Bale 1993: 125), CCTV observation is being used which, according to Bale, shows close parallels to Foucault's idea of panopticism: At any given time, each spectator must assume that he is potentially being watched at that moment, and therefore regulates his behaviour accordingly. Consequently, the containment of negative emotions, especially of aggression and violence, is transferred from physical barriers and specialized control personnel to an internal regulation of each spectator (cf. Conclusion).

In the Foucaultian approach, the effects of controls on emotions are not explicitly spelled out, as the major focus is on the control of violence. But, when considered together with symbolic interactionism, an emphasis on architectural influences on the supervision and internalization of emotional rules results in some interesting questions. For example, it makes clear that while different orchestrators may exist in the stadium, it is important to recognize that some have better chances of reaching the audience and, thereby, of implementing their desired rules because they are advantaged by infrastructural features. Amongst fans, those orchestrators who – like some drummers and 'capos' in football stadia – are allowed to sit in front of other fans are more visible than others and can use this advantage. 'Ultra' fans are another example of this observation, who, due to their established positions within the stadium, are able to use the stands for elaborate choreographies, displays of large banners, etc., and often reflect upon the architectural layout of the respective stadia when planning their choreographies (how steep are the stands?, what will look good from the other side of the stadium?, how big do the banners have to be? etc., see Leistner and Schmidt-Lux 2010). As well as fans, however, team representatives may have even more advantages: By using the stadium's speaker systems, for example, stadium announcers can make their announcements more pervasive, clubs can play certain songs to evoke emotional outbursts (Bryan and Horton 1976: 3) and employ video screens for messages to the spectators, such as 'make some noise', or to show action replays of crucial plays and successful actions of the home team (Bale 1989: 147). Thus, technical equipment establishes a hierarchy among the orchestrating actors, giving the home teams and athletes an advantage.

Furthermore, the room for spectators in stadia is internally differentiated corresponding to emotional rules. According to Bale, the separation, first, mirrors a societal hierarchy, in that social positions are usually displayed in the 'quality' – and price – of the seats; second, it mirrors the hierarchy of the sports world, with managers, ex-players, etc. being privileged; and third, segregation also follows a hierarchy based on the level of emotional support (cf. Bromberger 1995). Die-hard fans are usually positioned in a certain area of the stadium – for instance, behind the goals – while other spectators sit elsewhere. All these sections vary in their emotional rules. Amongst spectator groups such as fan club members or 'ultras', for example, sitting down will already be seen as an illegitimate behaviour and as a lack of identification and support. In other parts of the stadium, in contrast, rules may apply that resemble those of concert halls and drama theatres: Spectators remain on their seats, follow the game as critical connoisseurs and give the appropriate amount of applause whenever necessary.

CONCLUSION

Modern societies have regulated emotions to an astonishing extent. In most social settings we are confronted with extensive rules confining emotional expression. The processes of rationalization, as described by Max Weber and Emile Durkheim, or the 'process of civilization', documented by Norbert Elias, are immediately visible in many areas of everyday life. One of the few ways to escape these rules is to visit sports stadia. During sport events entirely different opportunities and restrictions for emotional expression apply. Thus sports stadia become an interesting setting for the study of emotions. By integrating and contrasting very different theoretical traditions, remarks and observations from a scattered literature, this chapter has painted a multifaceted picture of the social and architectural setting that sports stadia provide.

First, it has shown that sports stadia provide an advantageous environment for the experience and expression of emotions. The architecture of sports stadia is bound to intensify the emotional experience by complying with Durkheim's suggestions for facilitating 'effervescence'. Furthermore, technical equipment and spatial organization in stadia also allow control of spectator behaviour. On the one hand, some social, infrastructural and architectural features help to arouse and intensify team support by enhancing positive emotions; while others are used to control aggression and violence.

Second, the analysis shows that sports stadia in modern societies are by no means places where emotional rules do not apply. Rather, we find an emotionally charged place in which the expression of emotions is regulated in very specific ways, and in which some emotional expressions strictly forbidden in other social arenas are possible, present and even requested. In sports stadia an exceptional emotional experience is not simply left to chance. Architectural and social rules, in close combination, prepare the ground for an emotionally intense event unlikely to be found elsewhere in modern rationalized and civilized societies.

Whether such high emotionality ultimately occurs is another question. The described conditions do not determine the proceedings in the stadium. For every competition or game, they influence the emotional reality in the stadium anew, and the outcome not only of the game, but also of the emotional atmosphere may differ significantly and for reasons unknown to the participants themselves. Thus, the legitimacy of emotions, the ritualistic aspects of the setting and the rules of conduct interact with the actual spontaneity of emotions, which remain incalculable to some extent.

When seen from a more abstract perspective, our article could also demonstrate that the sports stadium is a place with facets that can only be understood when contextualizing it with other societal developments, such as the 'civilizing' of the larger society. In turn, however, it also exhibits features that are unique to the stadium and constitute the specific make-up of this emotional niche. It is the interplay of both that makes the stadium such an interesting subject for sociological analyses (cf. Conclusion).

NOTES

1 The authors would like to thank Alexander Leistner and Lars Riedl for valuable comments, and Inga Ganzer and Louise Hughes for proof-reading the manuscript.
2 Several studies also emphasize another emotional aspect of the stadium: Quite often, the stadia themselves are emotionally charged places which fans connect to notions of 'home' and to their own biography, for example to childhood memories (e.g. Trujillo

and Krizek 1994, cf. Brown's Chapter 9 in this volume). In turn, changes that are being made to these stadia, such as renaming them after companies or rebuilding them to facilitate more VIP or commercial uses, are often disapproved of (e.g. Schroer 2008: 165, cf. Zinganel's Chapter 4 in this volume). These emotions towards stadia, however, will not be considered any further in the chapter.

3 The works of anthropologist Victor W. Turner show several similarities to this view, he describes how rituals can be the foundation for a sense of community he calls 'communitas' (see Turner 1974). Turner applied this idea, although only briefly, to youth movements such as 'hippies' and 'teeny boppers' (Turner 1989: 111) and other authors used it systematically for the analysis of sports (e.g. Zurcher 1972).

4 Quite similar observations are possible for pop and rock concerts, where proceedings can also easily be interpreted using Durkheim's description of rituals (for a summary see Schäfer 2010).

5 This quote has been translated into English for this publication, as have several other quotes from German books and articles.

6 Apart from these texts, more literature exists on emotional rules for competitors and players themselves, and also on the effects of crowds on team achievement (e.g. Bale 1989: 29ff., Bryan and Horton 1976: 4). But these effects on players and teams will not be focused on here.

REFERENCES

Alkemeyer, T. (2008) 'Fußball als Figurationsgeschehen. Über performative Gemeinschaften in modernen Gesellschaften', in G. Klein and M. Meuser (eds) *Ernste Spiele. Zur politischen Soziologie des Fußballs*, Bielefeld: transcript.

Bale, J. (1989) *Sports Geography*, London/New York: Spon.

—— (1993) 'The spatial development of the modern stadium', *International Review for the Sociology of Sport*, 28: 121–33.

—— (2005) 'Stadien als Grenzen und Überwachungsräume', in M. Marschik, R. Müllner, G. Spitaler and M. Zinganel (eds) *Das Stadion. Geschichte, Architektur, Politik, Ökonomie*, Wien: Turia+Kant.

Bette, K.-H. and Schimank, U. (2000) 'Sportevents. Eine Verschränkung von "erster" und "zweiter Moderne"', in W. Gebhardt, R. Hitzer and M. Pfadenhauer (eds) *Events. Soziologie des Außergewöhnlichen*, Opladen: Westdeutscher Verlag.

Bromberger, C. (1995) 'Football as world-view and as ritual', *French Cultural Studies*, 6: 293–311.

Bryan, C. and Horton, R. (1976) 'School athletics and fan aggression', *Educational Researcher*, 5: 2–11.

Cachay, K., Thiel, A., Riedl, L. and Wagner, C. (2005) *Global Player – Local Hero. Der Sportverein zwischen Spitzensport, Publikum und Vermarktung*, Bielefeld: Universität Bielefeld.

Collins, R. (2004) *Interaction Ritual Chains*, Princeton: Princeton University Press.

Dunning, E. (ed.) (1976) *The Sociology of Sport*, London: Cass.

—— (1986a) 'The dynamics of modern sport: Notes on achievement-striving and the social significance of sport', in N. Elias and E. Dunning (eds) *Quest for Excitement. Sport and leisure in the civilizing process*, Oxford/New York: Blackwell.

—— (1986b) 'Spectator violence at football matches: Towards a sociological explanation', in N. Elias and E. Dunning (eds) *Quest for Excitement. Sport and leisure in the civilizing process*, Oxford/New York: Blackwell.

Dunning, E., Murphy, P. and Williams, J. (1988) *The Roots of Football Hooliganism. A historical and sociological study*, London/New York: Routledge.

Dunning, E. and Rojek, C. (eds) (1992) *Sport and Leisure in the Civilizing Process*, Houndsmills: Macmillan.

Dunning, E. and Sheard, K. (2005) *Barbarians, Gentlemen And Players: A sociological study of the development of rugby*, London: Routledge.

Durkheim, E. (2001) *The Elementary Forms of Religious Life*, Oxford/New York: Oxford University Press.

Elias, N. (1986a) 'An essay on sport and violence', in N. Elias and E. Dunning (eds) *Quest for Excitement. Sport and leisure in the civilizing process*, Oxford/New York: Blackwell.

—— (1986b) 'The Genesis of Sport as a Sociological Problem', in N. Elias and E. Dunning (eds) *Quest for Excitement. Sport and leisure in the civilizing Process*, Oxford/New York: Blackwell.

—— (1986c) 'Introduction', in N. Elias and E. Dunning (eds) *Quest for Excitement. Sport and leisure in the civilizing process*, Oxford/New York: Blackwell.

—— (2000) *The Civilizing Process. Sociogenetic and psychogenetic investigations*, Oxford: Blackwell.

Elias, N. and Dunning, E. (1966) 'Dynamics of sport groups with special reference to football', *British Journal of Sociology*, 17: 388–402.

—— (1970) 'The Quest for excitement in unexciting societies', in G. Lüschen (ed.) *The Cross-Cultural Analysis of Sport and Games*, Champaign: Stipes.

—— (1984) *Sport im Zivilisationsprozeß. Studien zur Figurationssoziologie*, Münster: Lit.

—— (1986a) 'Dynamics of sport groups with special reference to football', in N. Elias and E. Dunning (eds) *Quest for Excitement. Sport and Leisure in the Civilizing Process*, Oxford/New York: Blackwell.

—— (1986b) 'Folk football in medieval and early modern Britain', in N. Elias and E. Dunning (eds) *Quest for Excitement. Sport and leisure in the civilizing process*, Oxford/New York: Blackwell.

—— (1986c) 'Leisure in the Spare-time Spectrum', in N. Elias and E. Dunning (eds) *Quest for Excitement. Sport and leisure in the civilizing process*, Oxford/New York: Blackwell.

—— (1986d) *Quest for Excitement. Sport and leisure in the civilizing process*, Oxford/New York: Blackwell.

Ferguson, J.D. (1981) 'Emotions in sport sociology', *International Review for the Sociology of Sport*, 16: 15–25.

Földesi, G.S. (1996) 'Social and demographic characteristics of Hungarian football fans and their motivations for attending matches', *International Review for the Sociology of Sport*, 31: 407–25.

Foucault, M. (1977) *Discipline and Punish: The birth of the prison*, New York: Vintage.

Friedenberg, E. (1967) 'Adolescence as a social problem', in H.S. Becker (ed.) *Social Problems: A modern approach*, New York: Wiley.

Gallmeier, C.P. (1987) 'Putting on the game face: The staging of emotions in professional hockey', *Sociology of Sport Journal*, 4: 347–62.

Hochschild, A.R. (1983) *The Managed Heart. Commercialization of human feeling*, Berkeley/Los Angeles/London: University of California Press.

Josuttis, M. (1996) '"Fußball ist unser Leben". Über implizite Religiosität auf dem Sportplatz', in K. Fechtner, L. Friedrichs, H. Grosse, I. Lukatis and S. Natrup (eds) *Religion wahrnehmen*, Marburg: diagonal.

Klein, C. and Schmidt-Lux, T. (2006) 'Ist Fußball Religion? Theoretische Perspektiven und Forschungsbefunde', in E. Thaler (ed.) *Fußball. Fremdsprachen. Forschung*, Aachen: Shaker.

Kopiez, R. (2002) 'Alles nur Gegröle? Kultische Elemente in Fußball-Fangesängen', in M. Herzog (ed.) *Fußball als Kulturphänomen. Kunst – Kult – Kommerz*, Stuttgart: Kohlhammer.

Leistner, A. and Schmidt-Lux, T. (2010) '"Ein schönes Spiel reicht noch nicht aus".

Fußballfans im Rausch', in Y. Niekrenz and S. Ganguin (eds) *Jugend und Rausch*, in press, Weinheim/München: Juventa.

Lewis, L.A. (ed.) (1992) *The Adoring Audience. Fan culture and popular media*, London/New York: Routledge.

Neilson, J. (1986) 'Dialogue with the city: the evolution of the baseball park', *Landscape*, 29: 39–47.

Prosser, M. (2002) ' "Fußballverzückung" beim Stadionbesuch. Zum rituell-festiven Charakter von Fußballveranstaltungen in Deutschland', in M. Herzog (ed.) *Fußball als Kulturphänomen. Kunst – Kult – Kommerz*, Stuttgart: Kohlhammer.

Riedl, L. (2006) *Spitzensport und Publikum. Überlegungen zu einer Theorie der Publikumsbildung*, Schorndorf: Hofmann.

Schäfer, M.S. (2010) 'Fans und Emotionen', in J. Roose and M.S. Schäfer and T. Schmidt-Lux (eds) *Fans. Soziologische Perspektiven*, Wiesbaden: Verlag für Sozialwissenschaften.

Schroer, M. (2008) 'Vom "Bolzplatz" zum "Fußballtempel". Was sagt die Architektur der neuen Fußballstadien über die Gesellschaft der Gegenwart aus?', in G. Klein and M. Meuser (eds) *Ernste Spiele. Zur politischen Soziologie des Fußballs*, Bielefeld: transcript.

Schwenzer, V. (2001) 'Fußball als kulturelles Ereignis: Eine ethnologische Untersuchung am Beispiel des 1. FC Union Berlin', *Jahrbuch für Europa- und Nordamerika-Studien*, 5: 87–115.

Stone, G.P. (1976) 'Wrestling – The great American passion play', in E. Dunning (ed.) *The Sociology of Sport*, London: Cass.

Taylor, I. (1976) ' "Football Mad": A speculative sociology of football hooliganism', in E. Dunning (ed.) *The Sociology of Sport*, London: Cass.

Trujillo, N. and Krizek, B. (1994) 'Emotionality in the stands and in the field: Expressing self through baseball', *Journal of Sport and Social Issues*, 18: 303–25.

Turner, V.W. (1974) *Dramas, Fields and Metaphors. Symbolic action in human society*, Ithaca: Cornell University Press.

—— (1989) *Das Ritual. Struktur und Anti-Struktur*, Frankfurt/New York: Campus.

Van Winkel, C. (2005) 'Tanz, Disziplin, Dichte und Tod. Die Masse im Stadion', in M. Marschik, R. Müllner, G. Spitaler and M. Zinganel (eds) *Das Stadion. Geschichte, Architektur, Politik, Ökonomie*, Wien: Turia+Kant.

Weber, M. (1993) *The Sociology of Religion*, Boston: Beacon.

Whannel, G. (1993) 'Sport and popular culture. The temporary triumph of process over product', *Innovation*, 6: 341–9.

Wohl, A. (1970) 'Competitive sport and its social functions', *International Review of Sport Sociology*, 5: 117–30.

Zurcher, L.A. (1972) 'The staging of emotion: A dramaturgical analysis', *Symbolic Interaction*, 5: 1–22.

Chapter 14: Heroes, Myths and Magic Moments

Religious Elements on the Sacred Ground[1]

Gunter Gebauer

Contrary to the general tendency in contemporary Western societies to divest the sacred of meaning, one sees an astonishing vitality of religious practices in football. In the Catholic regions of Europe such as southern Italy and Spain, one finds a close connection between the worship of saints and the veneration of exceptional football players. But not just there; the reverence for football heroes takes on religious dimensions in the protestant North as well. Football fans transform stadia into cathedrals where they perform roles and act in unison as a religious community. How is it possible for this kind of attitude to come into being?

INITIATION

Contrary to the deep-seated conviction among the fans of FC Barcelona, who believe themselves to belong to their club by birth, nobody is actually born a football fan. Rather, one becomes a fan of a particular club in a process that can be described as a 'second birth,' a process involving primarily men – in particular, fathers, older brothers, and sons (cf. Chapter 10).

The first time a child enters a football stadium, he is taken there by others. It is always the older ones that introduce the novice to the event; the fathers, older brothers, and good friends let the youngster come along into a world that was previously foreign to him. Within the interior of the stadium, they all become equals in the emotions of the game and the devotion of the fans to their team, in their collective arousal of enthusiasm – they form a brotherhood of initiates.[2] Thus, the distance is lessened between the sons and their fathers, who in the football arena become no more than older brothers. The brotherhood draws the initiate out of childhood; it takes him along into an arena ruled by very different values than those of the maternal world (cf. Chapter 13): combat, kicking, collision, but also the interaction among men and the virtuoso struggle for the ball. Initiation into the world of football means the recognition of growing up and the imminent arrival of manhood. Women are present here as well; they accompany the throngs of men or form their own groups of women who share their predilection for the life of rough sport, the battle on the field. Nor is the daughter who wants to be close to her father in his love for football any less welcome. All that counts is that the life in the stadium, with its emotions and values, is being introduced to a new member. Every spectator in the stadium wants the crowd of participants to increase; his desire, arising from a kind of 'oceanic feeling' (Freud 2001), is for the entire world to take part. It is a world one shares with others, joined together in enthusiasm for the same useless thing, for the completely senseless squandering of energy, without manners, ruled only by wild rituals.

It is an initiation into what, for the child, is a new world. In the stadium, it is as if all differences in age, in social standing, in profession, and in education were wiped away. Here, a brotherhood prevails whose members seek the greatest possible conformity to one another, in clothing, in determination, and in common defense against a second rival group – the other club – with whom they share the space of the stadium.

While childhood today is lived almost exclusively indoors, the football arena is one of the first places where the young initiate experiences not only the public sphere but also the masses: there, he is outside; the gazes of the many are directed toward the lawn at its center, illuminated by the bright light of the sun or of floodlights. The atmosphere is flush with expectation, sometimes even rambunctious, but never joyous. There is an underlying sense of gravitas, for much is at stake: points, victories. A serious, important matter is being negotiated publicly on the grassy field.

FASCINATION

From the moment when the starting whistle opens the game, the present is transformed. In a single moment, all else is forgotten, and the stadium becomes an almost unbearable place – the deafening, horrendous music from the loudspeakers, the crushing throng in the stands. Every detail of the game's events affects the spectators; every person involved is fascinated by the performance played out under the bright lights. The word *fascination* describes a situation in which one is pierced by the powerful impact of a phenomenon, as if by an arrow: the performance casts powerful beams at the spectators, captivating them with its mythic gaze, casting its spell on them as they watch it, transfixed.

The first description of spectators at a game comes from Augustine. In his case, it was the gladiator games in Rome: his friend Alypius had a pathological obsession with the 'cruel and bloodthirsty sport,' but had forbidden himself from going to the amphitheater (on ancient stadia see Chapter 2). One day, however, he was taken there by his friends, against his will.

> When they arrived at the arena, the place was seething with the lust for cruelty. They found seats as best they could and Alypius shut his eyes tightly, determined to have nothing to do with these atrocities. If only he had closed his

ears as well! For an incident in the fight drew a great roar from the crowd, and this thrilled him so deeply that he could not contain his curiosity. Whatever had caused the uproar, he was confident that, if he saw it, he would find it repulsive and remain master of himself. So he opened his eyes and his soul was stabbed with a wound more deadly than any which the gladiator, whom he was so anxious to see, had received in his body. [...] The din had pierced his ears and forced him to open his eyes, laying his soul open to receive the wound which struck it down. [...] When he saw the blood, it was as though he had drunk a deep draught of savage passion. Instead of turning away, he fixed his eyes upon the scene and drank in all its frenzy, unaware of what he was doing. He revelled in the wickedness of the fighting and was drunk with the fascination of the bloodshed. He was no longer the man who had come to the arena, but simply one of the crowd which he had joined, a fit companion for the friends who had brought him.

(Augustine 1961: 122)

In football, the game is not about life and death, but about the values that we not only accept, but also consider central to our culture. Although Augustine describes a game that to us may seem altogether foreign and bloodthirsty, we can learn from him how the fascination of passionate games played out in a stadium affects those who are present. As the spectators watch the game, it takes control of their will and their reason. All their thoughts outside the game are obliterated; their senses are strained to the limit; they are mesmerized. But the game does not turn them to stone; instead, its fascination lends them a kind of vitality, a joy, a degree of energy and excitement that typifies people in a state of euphoric abandonment.

THE CROWD IN THE ARENA

In football, the spectators find an arena in which all acts are rendered visible. Decisions about victory and defeat are made in the light of the public sphere – it is a drama of justice. The spectators want to see their team win, but they also want their triumph to be just. In their highly aroused emotional state, the spectators sense a connection to their players. They feel it physically when their players are fouled; when this happens, they, too, feel injured. When a striker meets his mark, the shot was directed by their own feet, they feel their own muscles twitch. They are the extension of their players' emotions, and their own feelings are conveyed in turn into the much larger body of the brotherhood as a whole, amplified there to mammoth proportions.

The watching crowd does things, however, that cannot be done on the field – a player has to accept a foul committed against him without complaining; he is not permitted to strike back, retaliate, or curse; he has to play on in a disciplined manner. The crowd takes over his emotional reaction. There is an emotional connection between players and spectators, creating a community of fundamentally different people. In the roaring, howling, cursing crowd, the repressed reactions of the players live on and are magnified exponentially, beyond all measure, carried further into the crude and barbarous. When the brotherhood hears its heroes cry out, it roars their pain and hurls their curses into the world. It gives its heroes a voice; it cries like Ajax before the walls of Troy, terrifying the enemy with its roar and intimidating them so that they think twice before attempting to perpetrate such injustices again. Or they shout down the referee when he calls a penalty kick so vociferously that he penalizes the other side with a penalty kick at the next opportunity. In the arena, there is only a spatial, but not an emotional separation between players and spectators. Rather, there is an exchange between the two. Sometimes the players are fascinated by their fans: the crowd transports them into ecstasy, into a state of delirium, of rapture, in which – when it all comes together – they are able to play magical football.

The fascination in the football arena causes the spectators to see the world differently, or to see a different world: it is a world of vision and adulation, at whose center stand the players; they act as heroes in a drama. In contrast to the theater, this arena's heroes call their own reality into existence. Here, also in contrast to theater, they are venerated for their deeds. Through the spectators' adulation, great players become idols.

An idol is an image; it outlives the real person and is larger than life. For a person of flesh and blood to become an idol, he must be adulated; he must be magnified by his adorers to larger-than-life-size. He is more than a role model; he is the very image around which the initiate orients his life.

HEROES

Like a drama, a football game shows heroes establishing a world order: the order that exists on the football field. But it also shows the futility of his heroic effort to maintain this order in perpetuity. Humans cannot compete with the gods. Their temporary successes lead ultimately to failure; it is this destiny that makes them mythical. A football hero is not doomed to a tragic fate, but he gets older with time and ends his career, becomes a coach or an agent, a sports commentator in popular sports magazines or on television, a tournament organizer, a club president, or (in the case of Franz Beckenbauer) all of the above.

Viewed as a drama, the football game takes shape around its hero; like the seigneur in the orders of knighthood, he is surrounded by vassals who cover his back and take care of the dirty work for him. They run, they toil, they commit fouls for their master; they are his lungs, his wall, his backup in emergency; they are there when needed, and they open up the space that he needs to realize his intentions. Credit for their accomplishments is given to their master.

At the center of every great team stands a seigneur, a 'playmaker,' who holds all the strings in his hands, a master surrounded by his faithful vassals: thus, there can be no Franz Beckenbauer without a *Katsche* Schwarzenbeck, no

Günter Netzer without a *Hacki* Wimmer (known as 'the running wonder' for his endurance). On the field, victory is achieved through the innumerable acts of an entire team, but at the center of all these acts is the seigneur, and around him is empty space. Even when surrounded by opposing players, he creates an alleyway for himself, with quick fakes to the left and right, and imperceptible movements of the ball that open up a space for him through a seemingly impenetrable mass. A dramatic hero like Zinedine Zidane opens up unimaginable free zones for himself – even when surrounded by three or four defenders as if by a wall. He has the capacity to create a kind of force field around himself and structure it in specific ways that no one else can anticipate. There is a video of Diego Maradona showing the path he follows from one end of the football field to the other: all the opposing players expect that he will pass the ball, dodge to one side, hook to the left or right, manoeuvre his strikers into position, so they all try to cut off these paths, position themselves in front of his teammates, cover the flanks. Maradona just runs straight ahead and shoots the ball into the goal.

When you see a player like that – one who structures all of the action on the field, anticipates many events in advance, and employs his actions in such a way that everyone does his bidding – you can understand why an almost magical power is attributed to him. His strength is not just in his pure physical power and energy, as embodied by Lothar Matthäus, but in his self-control coupled with his mastery of all the other players on the field. One does not see a hero like this taking off at a mad rush or trampling over his opponents; one sees him running to a specific place where he executes an intentional act that no one expected. His astonishing act is not the product of conscious planning; it is ignited by a spark – a sudden stroke of genius. At the same time, this demonstrates his domination over the others, on whom he imposes his will. The seigneur exercises his power without brute force, as the realization of his desire to establish structure and impose order; and when he does, it looks as though his opponents are actually playing for him. Beckenbauer shot a goal against the French national team by first running in the wrong direction and then, when no one followed, turning around in a split second and shooting the ball past the stunned defensive players into the empty goal. Everything a seigneur does is an expression of his self-evident and natural role, which makes his actions look easy and effortless. When such a player maintains this confident comportment as a public figure after the end of his football career, his gestures can sometimes take on the kind of relaxed ease and informality that used to be ascribed to members of the aristocracy – a manner that stands in marked contrast to the strained efforts at physical ease by some of the world's leading political and business figures.

THE COMEDIANS

While the heroic agents of order in the football drama withdraw into retirement as sports millionaires, the great comedians of the game – Helmut Rahn, Mané Garrincha, Reinhard Libuda, George Best – often see their careers end in tragedy.

Their role in football consists in mixing up the order that has been established in the game; they are virtuoso architects of turmoil, agents of mayhem and confusion; they run the opposing team's defenders in circles until they are dizzy, make fools of them, wreak pure chaos in the opposing team. Their brilliant acts express an obsessiveness that sometimes seems to be of supernatural, sometimes of animal origin. In contrast to the *shining, saintly heroes* of the football field, the comedians represent the dark, demonic side of the game. Their only real existence is on the field, and they only take the stage there in moments of overwhelming brilliance, when a switch inside them is thrown, when they are possessed by a force and suddenly rendered capable of acts that will be told of for decades to come. In interviews, they are barely capable of saying anything about themselves; their strength is not in articulation, but rather in their mute, fulminant action in the whirlwind of tumultuous events.

Their heroism reveals how the chaos of a life of abandon and personal anarchy gives rise to peak performance that can instantly paralyze the defenses of the best teams in the world. They are the folk heroes who manage suddenly to achieve grandiose things; they live the dream that is dreamed in every dissolute life: that of showing what incredible power and creativity resides within the wild, unrestrained individual who is crazy enough to abandon himself to his intoxication. The failure in personal life is the price they pay for their talents in football; but to their fans, this is only reason to love them all the more ardently. They appear destined to die young. Their deaths are moments of the deepest grief for an entire team: it is only then that the team grasps what genius has emerged from its midst, when they realize who lived among them, spending evenings in a corner bar in Essen or Dortmund, in a samba club in Rio, wasting his life away drinking, telling stories, and having affairs with women. Only the players will say that he had been destined to come to this tragic end; all the others know him as someone who had been endowed by the heavens with extraordinary talent, who had enthralled an entire nation.

With Garrincha, the greatest of all the tragicomic heroes, all the disadvantages he had inherited coming into the world became the basis for his fame: he was so small and delicate as a child that he was given the nickname 'little wren,' *garrincha*; his legs were strangely shaped, the left one bowed outward, the right one inward, the ideal anatomy for an outside wing player (Bellos 2004: 99). His contract had been incomprehensible to him; it did not matter to him that his dishonest club president had cheated him – he just wanted to play and make his fans happy. Comedian players do things that one simply doesn't do; they play with the ball, with their opponents, they do tricks and stunts, have fun on the playing field. Garrincha's dribbling was unpredictable; anthropologist José Sérgio Leite Lopes of the State University of Rio says of him: 'It sometimes happened that he would dribble toward his own goal. No one else did such things. He made us laugh' (Bellos 2004: 112). In Brazil, he was more popular than any other player, more beloved even than Pelé, the best and richest football player in the country who had even achieved political success as a government minister. His second nickname was 'alegrie do povo,' *joy of the people*. Fans dearly love a player who turns all his inherited disadvantages miraculously to his favor, and then has to watch it all melt away in his hands. After the end of his career, Garrincha became an alcoholic; his romances with women ended badly; he died in 1983 at the age of just 49. When the news of his death spread in Rio, there was a spontaneous gathering of 8,000 people in Maracana Stadium. The funeral of Garrincha, who had died in abject poverty, was followed by an entire population in mourning.

The heroes of football can be divided into players who are agents who create order and players who create disorder. A team's success depends crucially on the *playmaker*, the architect of the game; his failure will plunge his people and himself into the abyss. At the meeting of two great agents of order, it is decided which one is the greater, and which, despite his outstanding abilities, will go down in history among the great losers. In football, the old pattern still holds: Achilles or Hector, Caesar or Vercingetorix, Scipio or Hannibal. Just as in the ancient heroic epics and in military history, the greatest commanders on the football field are those who have achieved victory in their decisive battles – Fritz Walter, Pelé, Bobby Charlton, Franz Beckenbauer, Diego Maradona, Zinedine Zidane. The failed heroes are those who were abandoned by luck at the crucial moment – Ferenc Puskas (1954), Johan Cruyff (1974), Michel Platini (1982), and Roberto Baggio (1994). If an agent of disorder fails, his team may lack the rush of excitement and the humor, but this absence of pleasurable moments will not necessarily lead to defeat. There are lackluster victories based on nothing but hard work; a team can make the decisive goal by force or win in standard situations with a kick from a corner, a free kick, or a penalty kick. These victories bring satisfaction, but by no means excitement.

SAINTS AND THEIR COMMUNION WITH THE FAITHFUL

Football long ago entered a new stage; its 'heroic age' was transformed into a new kind of veneration. Fan communities have emerged that worship their heroes like saints. The action in the football arena is coming to resemble a religious ritual to an increasing degree. Football has become a heathen religion, as can be seen in the following incident.

In the year 1987, two miracles happened in Naples: the blood of the city's patron saint, San Gennaro, which had been preserved in congealed form in the Cathedral, mysteriously liquefied again as prophesied, and with Diego Maradona's S.S.C. Napoli surprised the nation by winning the Italian championship. The idea arose in the city that Maradona, who claimed to have won the 1986 World Cup with the aid of the 'hand of God,' was the reincarnation of San Gennaro. The religious followers who come to church to witness the ritual of the saint's blood differ from the fans in the stadium in composition and age, although there is a certain overlap; but what both groups share are similar forms of behavior in both places. The following details were related to me by Alain

Pons, a specialist on Neapolitan philosopher Giambattista Vico who was present for the blood miracle on invitation from the Bishop of Naples. According to Pons, long before the event, a huge mass of people had gathered in the church, particularly old women who sang and prayed, awaiting the foretold hour. As the time of the prophesied miracle approached, the religious excitement increased. From time to time, the ever more impatient believers were shown the ampoule with the blood. As no changes in the congealed blood appeared, the crowd began to grow even more restless. The hour passed without occurrence. The first lamentations and invectives began to be heard in their singing. When the blood remained congealed throughout the coming hours, the believers began to curse and hurl accusations at their saint, and finally they began to curse him. The congregation had lost control of itself: they had begun to spew blasphemies and sacrileges. Suddenly, the clotted blood liquefied. Their lamentations turned to prayers of thanksgiving and hymns of praise: the believers had been reconciled, saved, uplifted; Naples' future was secured.

The fans of a football team form a community of believers that is characterized by distinctively religious forms of behavior as well. The saints are *their* team's players, for whom they will make harrowing pilgrimages. They come to the stadia on night trains filled with singing fan club members, bearing crates of beer and chanting crude slogans. After their march through the town, they will finally enter the stadium and become who they really are in their 'fan block': there, they will be something great, a supremely powerful entity that each one of them perceives as a feeling of power mounting within himself. They will convey their strength to their players on the field through their single, superhuman voice.

Cultural theorists in general are blind to the religious engagement, the commitment to values, the feeling of duty and voluntary dedication within these communities; they see in their activities nothing more than mass spectacle. Much has been written on mass theory (cf. Canetti 1960; Freud 1988; Le Bon 1972): masses are docile and feminine, lacking their own will, devoid of boundaries, completely fixated on a leader who is a kind of idealized superego. Theories of mass culture emphasize the loss of self, the act of surrender to a more powerful will. For the communities of football, however, other theoretical instruments will have to be sought. There is certainly a top and bottom here as well: at the base of the quotidian world are the enthusiasts, the fans, the believers – at the top, separated from the community and the congregation are the saints: enthroned, inaccessible objects of veneration. But what most of the theories of the masses, from Le Bon to Moscovici, have to say about the experiences of the individual is strangely off the mark.

None of the participants in a football game is interested in negating his ego. Rather, the football fan wants *to feel*: to feel his own body and his own strength. This desire pushes him to expend his strength, to sing, cheer, drink, defame the enemy. They only appear to be self-abandonment, these acts of total overexertion. Yet the abandon, the sense of community, and the emotion are not the loss but the attainment of a new dimension of experiencing the self, a dimension that is unimaginable in everyday life. In the fans' own personal descriptions, they talk repeatedly about giving their all, putting up with everything, making sacrifices throughout the entire campaign. But they do not mean this as loss or depletion of the self; they mean that by giving their best, they create an entity of power and veneration that in turn fills them with deep inspiration. Further below, this idea will be explored in greater detail, but first I will turn to the cults of the football fans.

The first feature of fan communities that becomes apparent is their effort to establish unity. As with collective drinking, the singing of football hymns while carrying out identical choreographed movements has a unifying effect. English football fans reveal the religious character of the songs they sing very clearly. The most famous of all fan songs, *You'll never walk alone*, was sung after World War I during the English Cup Finals in Wembley Stadium in memory of all the fans who had died in the war.[3] When this hymn is sung in the stadium, the fans must adhere to a strict ritual order. They hold their scarves above their heads with both hands, and move them slowly back and forth like the swaying banners in a procession. Fans also maintain close contact with the saints. Fans of Marseille made a pilgrimage to the church of *Notre Dame de la Garde* prior to the finals of the UEFA Cup to light candles. Hamburg-based second division football club FC Sankt Pauli published a 'Fan Bible' entitled 'Faith, Love, Hope': whether consciously or not, they had made the divine virtues their slogan, which was then imprinted on fan products ranging from pennants to underwear, even on the Pauli garden gnome.

Football cults take on an almost irresistible power when they superimpose their forms over old local religions, as in Naples. After Naples won the Italian Championships, the words appeared on the walls of the city cemetery, 'What you have missed!' Overnight, a new inscription appeared: 'What do you know, anyhow!' (Dini 1994: 77). Journalists and fans love to borrow elements from the liturgy of Catholicism for their cult, often with an ironic wink of the eye. But the playful use of Christian rituals also expresses a distancing from religion; to the devotees, their cause is a gravely serious one; this can be seen in moments of defeat. Indeed the fans possess no other liturgical forms of expression than the Christian ones; they must draw on these for symbols and rituals that can be used to lend their cause a religious dimension.

THE SPACE OF THE FANS

In the stadium, the fans are in *their* space. It is a real and symbolic interior space; whoever finds himself within it belongs to the elect and finds himself on this side of the boundary that separates the sacred from the profane. In the interior space, there is a second subdivision into above and below, into the community of believers and the saints. It is usually overlooked, within this dichotomy – with the many unknown, insignificant believers on the one side and the few, exquisite stars on the other – what power the community of believers possesses. Blinded by the splendor of the holy ones, the fans at first appear unimportant minions. But the power that the saints possess is not of their own creation. All the symbolic powers invested in their bodies and all their actions they realize come from the activities of the congregation. This can be understood by reconstructing the mechanism that gives rise to religion. The process can be described best with reference to a theory that does not contain transcendent elements such as guilt, revelation, redemption, or resurrection. A theological construction in the narrower sense would be excessive in relation to the cult of sports and pop culture, and would produce a distorted view. Yet sports give rise to their own saints and religious experiences in collective social practices, in symbolic gestures, and in the ritual interactions within a community.

Figure 14.1a/b The 'saints' in the company of their followers.

The religious nature of the relation between the players and their supporters is expressed by the architecture of the stadium. As in the religious space of the cathedral, the central place of the sacred is separated from its mundane surroundings; no profane man has the right to transgress this borderline. The religious center of the stadium is the 'sacred ground'; in most stadia it is separated from the supporters by trenches and iron fences. Beyond its practical purpose of protecting the players from enemy attacks, this device has the symbolic function of dividing the stadium into two ritual spaces: the space of the holy actors and the space of the believers, who create faith in the religious activity through their actions. Physical contact is forbidden; the effective interaction between the supporters and the players has a spiritual character.

In the cathedral, the center of the sacred activity is elevated, whereas the playing field is situated on ground level, surrounded by the supporters who are elevated above it in the stands. This disposition calls to mind ancient religious events in natural settings: for example, a ceremony in a valley with the community seated on the slopes. This comparison clearly reveals that physical proximity is not important for the force of the religious event; what matters instead is the fact that the believers sense an extremely close and intimate contact with their saints. It is not important that both in the cathedral and in the stadium, the city's elite is seated closest to the event; this is an effect of social power. The driving force behind the religious events is the community of supporters in the cheap seats, far away from the altar and from the holy lawn.

There are certain conditions under which social processes take on a *religious life*. This term comes from Emile Durkheim (2008); it has the advantage of referring not to the beyond, but strictly to the intramundane world of social activity. In Durkheim's interpretation, the religious is created in *this* world. What seems supernatural in religion is actually created by the society in which the believer lives. Altogether normal people bring into being the idea of something higher in this world.

> The division of the world into two areas, the one comprising all that is sacred, the other all that is profane – this is the trait that characterizes religious thinking; the beliefs, the myths, the dogmas, the legends are either representations or systems of representation that express the nature of the sacred things, the effects and capabilities attributed to them, their history, and the relationships they have to each other and to the profane things.
>
> (Colpe 1990: 28f.)

Durkheim affirms the basic structural distinction between the sacred and the profane, and asserts that the distinction between these two categories is *absolute*. For him, there exists no other case in the history of humanity in which two categories of things stand in such radical opposition as in this one.

The basic principle of Durkheim's theory is that religion is lent its specific forms and characteristics by the society that practices it: first, through the structure of the society, second through the performance of collective acts, through common, physical ritual acts (cf. Chapter 13). Durkheim himself speaks of 'collective acts' or 'collective life,' but what he means is more than just acts that a number of people carry out simultaneously. For society to give rise to a religious community, a special form of social cohesion must emerge. A community has its origins in particular changes that occur within the normal social relationships between individuals, infusing these relationships with emotions and meanings that lift them far beyond their quotidian contexts. The changes occur spontaneously and locally in specific material environments; they take place in actions with a ritualized character that happen at set points in time and are repeated cyclically at typical locations such as cathedrals and stadia, and that are carried out voluntarily by individuals in collective movements (cf. Conclusion).

THE RITUAL OF SANCTIFICATION

In the French discussion, it is a familiar idea that ritually repeated collective movements allow an *inner form*, a belief, and religious feelings to emerge. This was first formulated by Pascal, who said that by following the imperative of 'kneel and pray' in ritual physical practice, belief in God would result (Pascal 2007: 69). The belief results from the physical movements: namely, by lending the body a specific outer form that evokes an inner attitude – in other words, precisely the opposite of the way one normally imagines religious belief to arise. 'Practical belief,' said Bourdieu, 'is [...] a state of the body' (Bourdieu 1980: 68). The first step in creating the religious life is the transformation of formerly normal members of society into a community united by common acts and feelings, deeper relationships, commonality of activities and goals, and a feeling of solidarity: a spontaneous, informal social union associated with a sense of shared obligation and commitment, infused with affective and symbolic meanings – precisely like those found in football.

Every society develops ideal conceptions of itself. The activity of the social imagination is one of the mechanisms by which a society perpetuates itself through an unceasing process of self-renewal. Particularly religious communities take on this task: from within their midst, there emerge ideal conceptions of how society *ought to be*. With the aid of common actions, these communities display all the characteristics that should ideally correspond to the society as a whole; they demonstrate, according to Durkheim 'everything that is essential in society [...] because the idea of society is the soul of religion' (Durkheim 2008: 314f.). Through its imaginative and performative activities, the community of believers adopts a prominent position and a unique meaning in its society.

From this perspective, the remarkably important role of religion for society becomes clear. Religion heightens a society's emotions and increases its cohesion; to put it more succinctly, as social existence is intensified, it begins to approach religion. This idea can be generalized beyond Durkheim as well: one can posit that football communities each conceive their own concept – and the corresponding qualities – of an ideal society, that they embody this concept in their performances, and reveal it in their specific religious practice.

When a community of football is capable of elevating its idea of society to the level of a religious phenomenon, this serves as an unmistakable indication of its social efficacy: its power has impressed the community's members – who helped to produce it – so deeply that they believe in it fervently. Their belief is what functions as the source of religious life, and opens up access to the domain of the sacred. Membership in such a community is experienced as a distinction. Not everyone can belong to it; only those who it has taken in, and on whom it has imposed particular demands for their behavior within the community. It cannot be assumed that the individuals understand the mechanisms by which the sacred is created; but one can assume that they recognize the power of the community and that they submit themselves to it willingly for their duration of the congregation in the stadium.

REMEMBERING BY RETELLING

The heroes and saints of football live on through the telling and retelling of past games. Spectators and journalists are linked to them through the telling and retelling of all the events that are worthy of remembrance. The football myths consolidate everything that ever achieved the heights of greatness in football: great games, great teams, and great athletes. By harking back to this glorious past, current events are elevated and lent meaning. All those who participate in these myths find themselves in a world of passions; they are connoisseurs and aficionados of their country's football tradition. In the world of football, there is no objective memory, just emotionally charged memory.

The heroes are both remote and close enough to touch. They become irreal through the act of retelling: narrated images, monuments, icons. The tellers of the myths have an affective relationship to them: they are *their* heroes, created by them, taken in to their lives, and woven into the fabric of their own histories.

Unlike politicians and generals, great football players are not commemorated in monuments, but live on like the heroes of antiquity and the medieval age in mythic stories perpetuated by specialists in narrative and vivid description.[4] A mythical narrative never ends; it is woven into an endless fabric of a multitude of similar stories told by many different people. It creates a space in which many different temporal realities exist simultaneously. 'Earlier' and 'later,' 'older' and 'younger' are not points on a timeline but events that appear alongside one another, simultaneously: Uwe Seeler alongside Lothar Matthäus, Diego Maradona alongside Lionel Messi, Sepp Meier alongside Oliver Kahn, or Paul Gascoigne alongside Wayne Rooney. The players of the past look no older than those of the present, no less athletic, no less well-trained – there is no age in epic space. The work of memory is a dynamic process of temporal adaptation; it shows the past games at the same speed as the present ones (although they were actually much slower). Their images are repeatedly revised; the new players are adapted to the catalog of apparently eternal virtues. Each retelling is a repetition of the original narrative, a renewing reintegration into the respective present. This unceasing dynamic of remembering, of retelling the past is the hallmark of myth; here, the golden times are never really old.

Myths describe an agonal world. Those involved in them are almost exclusively the warrior class – not the ruling class or those who have to provide for the society's material wellbeing, and not warrior nobility – not King Arthur, but his knights. Since the nineteenth century, the middle classes have sought the greatness that the bourgeois world did not provide in the context of brave deeds, courage, daring, and generosity. It is the brave one who goes to war; he is free from lowly tasks. It is incorrect to claim that there can be no more mythic stories in the bourgeois age. The more the bourgeois age becomes aware that it is an age of struggle, that life today consists essentially of struggle – that religious benefices and patrimonial favors are a thing of the past – the more accurately mythic narratives will be able to express the reality of the living situation today.

GREATNESS

Translating normal middle-class existence into the life of an omnipotent hero is the basic principle of successful trivial literature. But in contrast to the novel, sport has the decisive advantage that it possesses a kernel of reality: there exists this extraordinary reality and a community that believes in its existence. The stories told in sports are not pure fantasies; individuals who were previously powerless really *are* elevated; they really *do* win fame and fortune by their own strength and are thereby allowed to play a role in society that is otherwise closed off to them. The mythic character of their narratives results from the fact that their objective is to attain power and that the power attained is rooted in superior natural abilities. The powerful are lifted out of the quotidian world, but they remain connected to it by their origins. The middle-class Franz Beckenbauer rises to become a *genius*, the working-class Berti Vogts a *world champion* through hard work; Jürgen Klinsmann, a baker by trade, becomes an entrepreneurial, cosmopolitan team captain; and David Beckham, born into a lower middle-class home in the London suburbs, an international pop star (cf. Chapter 15). In the memory of football, the famous players are elevated to ideal images of what the average male citizen desires for himself in his own everyday life: they attain a broad sphere of action and an unlimited power to act that has long ceased to exist. The principle of the modern mythic narrative in football is the reinterpretation of the increased power that technical and economic progress actually has brought to society and the individual as the power of the individual person. This reinterpretation through retelling is by no means a pure illusion but rather a view of the current situation from a positive, optimistic perspective: the average citizen has, in the grand scheme of things, a relatively limited sphere of action, but on the other hand, much greater technical and economic power than ever before. The telling of stories about championships and goals revolves around the effort to perpetuate the power of the great players, to protect them from transience.

Sporting events are not experienced only in terms of their sensual presence, but also from the perspective of their value for future memory. Tales of unforgettable games and great players immortalize important moments of fleeting events. When one recalls these games of decades past, they appear to incorporate the quintessence of their age, in all its sensual fullness. The myths of football are simultaneously stories of our lives, of our own past. They allow us to bring important moments of our life stories into the present, moment by moment, image by image. Through their linkage with the events of our lives, the mythic stories of football games take on a meaning that goes far beyond that of the games themselves. Because we interweave our life stories with the stories of football, football becomes part of our lives (cf. Hornby 2000). When the important moments of our life take place in football, our life consists, in significant part, of football. As personal memories and experiences are always connected to places, football stadia are to be seen not just as breathtaking architectural structures. Through their ritual and communal occupancy they are highly relevant to individual biographies.

NOTES

1 Translated from the German by Deborah Anne Bowen.
2 In his famous autobiographic novel *Fever Pitch*, Nick Hornby describes such an initiation. The author tells a story about an 11-year-old boy (himself) who followed his father one day to Highbury, the home of Arsenal FC. When the novice saw the huge stadium bowl filled with the number of inhabitants of a middle size town for the first time, he was inexplicably bewitched. Fascinated by the experience of the crowds, the fan's rituals and the stadium's atmosphere, he 'fell in love with football as [he] was later to fall in love with women: suddenly, inexplicably, uncritically, giving no thought to the pain it would bring' (Hornby 2000: 15).
3 The song is a prime example of the effusive emotionality that may initially appear to contradict the fans' toughness, 'When you walk through a storm, hold your head up high and don't be afraid of the dark./ At the end of the storm, there's a golden sky and a sweet silver song of a lark [...].'
4 Specialists in this mode of narration are found in many places: in the stadia, in pubs, in workplaces, in newspapers, on the radio, on television; their stories flow together into the same circular narrative. What the professional epic storytellers of the mass media absorb has almost always been told previously, and is already presorted into good and evil, acceptance and rejection, etc.

REFERENCES

Augustine (1961) Confessions, edited by R.S. Pine-Coffin, Penguin Classics, Book 6, London: Penguin Books.
Bellos, A. (2004) *Futebol. Fußball. Die brasilianische Kunst des Lebens*, Berlin: Edition TIAMAT.
Bourdieu, P. (1980) *The Logic of Practice*, Stanford: Stanford University Press.
Canetti, E. (1960) *Masse und Macht*, Hamburg: Claassen.
Colpe, C. (1990) *Über das Heilige. Versuch, seiner Verkennung kritisch vorzubeugen*, Frankfurt am Main: A. Hain.

Dini, V. (1994) 'Maradona, héro napolitain', *Actes de la recherche en sciences sociales*, 103: 75–8.

Durkheim, E. (2008) *The Elementary Forms of Religious Life*, Oxford: Oxford University Press.

Freud, S. (1988) *Massenpsychologie und Ich-Analyse*, Frankfurt am Main: Fischer.

Freud, S. (2001) *Das Unbehagen in der Kultur und andere kulturtheoretische Schriften*, Frankfurt am Main: Fischer.

Hornby, N. (2000) *Fever Pitch*, Harmondsworth: Penguin.

Le Bon, G. (1972) *Psychologie der Massen*, Stuttgart: Alfred Kröner Verlag.

Pascal, B. (2007) *Pensées*, Sioux Falls: Nuvision Publications.

Chapter 15: Beckhamania

Promoting Post-modern Celebrities beyond the Stadium[1]

Johannes John

EPILOGUE AS PROLOGUE

By now the story can be written from its end. He is said to have cried when England manager Steve McLaren did not call him up for the 'Three Lions' in August 2006. Were there tears when he was recalled in May 2007? We do not know. When he earned his 100th cap on 26 March 2008 against France, some might have preferred the '99' as a symbol of incompletion. His transfer from Real Madrid via Hollywood to Los Angeles Galaxy in July 2007 was considered by many to be consistent with his previous career, as was signing, on loan, with AC Milan in the 2008/09 winter break; increasingly, the term 'travelling circus' began to be used. First pictures from Milan showed his spouse Victoria on the VIP stand of the Giuseppe Meazza stadium, others showed huge advertising signs for underwear displayed on buildings. All this leads directly away from the football pitch, and right to the heart of our subject.

NOT BECKHAM BUT 'BECKHAMANIA'

No pictures are necessary to introduce him: everyone will have one in his or her mind's eye as soon as the name comes up; though it might be interesting to see which image from which period is the preferred one. The once clear separation between public representation and the commonly defined sphere of personal privacy is not only obsolete and out-of-date, it does not even seem to have existed: we have learned about the location and circumstances of his sons' conceptions, about his choice of underwear and his obsession with scrupulously keeping the cans of drinks in order in the fridge (*Spiegel Online* 2006b). Interestingly, that old-fashioned division between the public image and the private self, resembling a Russian *matryoshka*, is usually invoked when the image conveyed by the media reaches a stage of crisis or is about to crumble. But that is by the way.

This is not about the person or the personality David Beckham but about the phenomenon sometimes referred to as 'Beckhamania', the media hype unleashed by and around him. Which is why hagiographic florilegia like *David Beckham Talking* (Stevenson 2004) will be not be scrutinized here – regardless of all the 'sensational new material' and 'previously unseen photographs' announced on the cover of *My World* (Freeman 2000), not least, in order to avoid the danger of self-set traps. But more about that later.

Furthermore, this text, which started to mature during the World Cup 2006 did not need to be rejected in light of Euro 2008, but has simply been extended, since the setting was the same in both instances: which role in the drama would be reserved for David Beckham this time? That of a bright, shining light and undisputed superstar, or – on the other side of the dramatic spectrum – that of tragic hero, a failure, perhaps even a villain (on the distinction between heroes and tragic heroes in football cf. Chapter 14 in this volume). Or – and this might have been the most calamitous of all options – that of inconspicuous hanger-on. The upshot of 2006: one-and-a-half strokes of genius that decided the matches against Paraguay and Ecuador, substitution in the last 16 and in the quarterfinals: David Beckham, visibly less than fit, was not able to leave a mark, indeed *his* mark, on the England team or on the tournament. Which calls to mind the words of an English journalist who, while watching the 2006 World Cup opener on 9 June at my house, saw this tournament as Beckham's last chance to immortalize himself as a *footballer*, or alternatively 'just being remembered for being famous'. A very apt phrase with a latent tautological subtext.

DAVID BECKHAM – AN APPROACH IN SEVERAL ATTEMPTS

You may be familiar with the joke in which someone approaches a crowd of people on the street, asks what all the commotion is about, only to receive the reply: 'No idea. The last person who knew left five minutes ago...' An initial thesis would be that this is how it seems with David Beckham, once you take the term 'field' studies literally in the search for reasons for his immense popularity and take a closer look at his merits as a football player.

A comparison with Anna Kournikova – the Russian tennis player whose fame similarly goes far beyond her sporting achievements in spite of her never having won a tournament – is certainly unfair; between 1996 and 2003, Beckham, playing for Manchester United, has won the League six times, the F.A. Cup three times and, on that memorable night of 26 May 1999, the UEFA Champions League once.

However, comparable success with the England national team, captained by David Beckham from November 2000 to July 2006, has eluded him, or, to put it another way: he too has failed to help end four decades of titleless misery for the motherland of football. Even worse: specifically Beckham's career in the jersey with the three lions seems – beyond spite and prejudice – inevitably linked in collective memory with two significant failures: the red card received after a foul against the Argentinian Diego Simeone in the last 16 of the 1998 World Cup in France, which turned the then 23-year-old, considered to be a major world talent, into the scapegoat for the exit of the English team in the eyes of the English public, and two missed penalties during Euro 2004 in Portugal, the first one of which paved the road to defeat in the opening match against France, the second one cementing England's reputation of being able to win everything in football – except a penalty shootout.

There is no lack of critical English voices accompanying the development of Beckham the football player, such as the author Julian Barnes, who said in August 2005:

> He is a player of unbelievable potential, which he has never fully realized. He does not tackle, has lost his rhythm and never uses his left foot anymore. Instead, and to his own satisfaction, he has fully developed into a brand name and a money machine – in his own interest and that of others.
>
> (Barnes 2005: 16)[2]

And the *Observer*, which drily noted before the World Cup in Germany that never before was there such a gap between a player's talent and his level of fame (cf. Honigstein 2006: 29).

But to be fair one has to make distinctions. Although 'Beckhamania' is a global phenomenon, it is viewed differently in different parts of the world. In Germany, David Beckham is more or less seen as a glamorous and somewhat exotic member of the international jet set, news about whom can be found in the gossip columns and thus away from the football ground. I spoke to an English colleague, however, on 25 June 2006, the day of the Ecuador match, who, when asked for her spontaneous thoughts on David Beckham answered 'he scored some marvellous goals' – among which she surely would have included the late equalizer against Greece which paved the way for the England team to the 2002 World Cup in Japan/Korea. It is significant and noteworthy that the adjective of choice was 'marvellous' and not – as might be assumed – 'important', since 'marvellous' suggests an aesthetic element as well as a purely sporting one. Confronted with the words of Harald Irnberger, who in 2005 called Beckham 'a sort of Lady Di of football', the incarnation of mediocrity and who posed the question 'Why do the media pay so much attention to a substantially unimportant figure?' (Irnberger 2005: 157)[3] she conceded these judgements in a polite English way, only then to remark: 'but he showed what a football player can be!'

To understand what is meant by that, a brief look at the sociological, socio-economic, and political background of sport in the late 1980s is necessary, without which – and this is a second thesis – the 'Beckhamania' of the 1990s, prefigured by structurally similar mass phenomena like the 'Beatlemania' of the swinging sixties, cannot be properly understood. Two aspects – a national, genuine British one, on the one hand, and an international one, noticeable all over Europe, on the other – seem to be of special significance here.

To begin with the latter aspect: with the introduction of an increasing number of private television channels in the mid-1980s the amount of airtime available – of which sport and football in particular cornered a significant amount – multiplied dramatically. A result of this was airtime that had to be filled – after all the length of a football match, usually 90, occasionally 120 minutes, remained unchanged. This led to an explosion of transmitted images, a topic that I shall address later, accompanied almost automatically by forms of medial presentation focusing on a more personalized reporting style, or, more precisely, on the concept of stardom with all its known ingredients: the swing between providing an object of identification and the principle of an unbridgeable distance between star and audience, as well as the cycles of build-up followed by destruction. A side effect of these developments has been that 'secondary' personnel like pre-senters and commentators have mutated into 'stars' or 'celebrities'. Channels governed by public law (like the BBC in the UK or ARD and ZDF in Germany) lost out to the competition of commercial channels, meaning that now a surplus of time *and* money became part of the game, thus placing football, the people's game, in a significantly different if not wholly new kind of sociological focus. In short: football became acceptable to those parts of society for which the game previously held no interest, or at most a rudimentary one, watching only major events. Football here explicitly encompasses the full media package, including hours and hours of pre- and post-game shows (cf. Chapter 5).

As an *English* phenomenon, the conditions that made Beckhamania possible must be traced back to the events of 29 May 1985, the night when clashes between fans of Liverpool FC and Juventus and the ensuing panic led to the death of 39 people at the European Cup final at the Heysel Stadium in Brussels. These events, without doubt a low point in the history of international football, not only led to years of isolation for English football, when club teams were excluded from European competition; English football also became synonymous with hooliganism, an excessive propensity towards violence. This seemed to be confirmed by the Hillsborough catastrophe on 15 April 1989, when 96 people died and 730 were injured at an FA Cup semi-final between Liverpool and Not-tingham Forest, though – as is common knowledge now – this tragedy had nothing to do with hooliganism, but rather was entirely due to a break-down in security measures that were insufficient and ill-conceived in the first place (cf. Chapter 1).

At precisely this moment, when the image of English football seemed to have reached its nadir, the 1990 World Cup marked a decisive turning point, a truly 'iconic turn' that has entered into the collective memory in the form of a highly significant snapshot in time. I refer, of course, to Paul Gascoigne's tears following England's elimination by Germany in the semi-finals, needless to say in a penalty shootout (Figure 15.1). This was not only significant because a man in a typical man's world was unashamed of his tears, but also because 'Gazza' rep-resented the epitome of so-called 'lad culture': a line of tradition which under-stood football as a specific expression of British machismo, as an integral part of

Figure 15.1
Paul Gascoigne of
England bursts into tears
after defeat in the World
Cup semi-final against
West Germany at the
Stadio Delle Alpi in Turin,
1990.

a world based around beer and booze, fast cars and bad women, from where it was only a short distance to rowdiness and bullying.

The creation of movements in the early 1990s by important and increasingly influential parts of English fan culture to rid themselves and English football *in toto* from this image can be seen as an act of purification and of taking stock: supporters' associations, fanzines, most famously *When Saturday Comes*, which evolved from the English punk scene, and initiatives like *Philosophy Football* emerged. The enormous acclaim for Nick Hornby's *Fever Pitch* may also be considered part of these developments, since Hornby's approach was groundbreaking, insofar as he re-introduced football not just as a simple, mostly male leisure activity or mildly smiled-upon mania, but as something which could not only strongly shape biographies but was also capable of developing a metaphorical quality transcending the events on the pitch. In other words: through Nick Hornby and authors like Tim Parks in England and Italy, Javier Marias and the South American Eduardo Galeano in Spain, F.C. Delius, Thomas Brussig or Klaus Theweleit in Germany, Péter Esterházy in Hungary, and many others elsewhere, football suddenly developed a 'literariness' which made it attractive and acceptable in intellectual circles (where following football might previously have been considered a guilty pleasure). Parallel to this, football also gained increasing attention in non-fiction literature and became the subject of serious, i.e. professional, historical and sociological scholarship, allowing a most gratifying and productive rapprochement between sports and arts pages in newspapers: an overcoming of boundaries which has extended the playing field from stadium to news stand to book shop.

These developments formed the backdrop as well as the breeding ground on which 'Product David Beckham', in appearance and demeanour the very opposite of a 'bad boy', could, from the mid-1990s, become attractive and demonstrate 'what a football player can be'. Even more so, since there was a whole new target group to be discovered and served: the number of women attending matches and developing a general interest in the game and those who played it had increased significantly in the wake of Gazza's tears. Another group of fans and consumers was added to this when David Robert Joseph Beckham, born on 2 May 1975 into a lower middle class home in the London suburb of Chingford and since 1993 under contract as a professional football player with Manchester United, married Victoria Caroline Adams, known as Posh Spice, member of the Spice Girls and thus a widely popular teenage idol, on 4 July 1999. This was an act of symbolic symbiosis, which finally made him an integral part of pop culture and created a new label: the footballer as pop star – an obvious label that nevertheless may deserve a caveat.

BECKHAMANIA, OR: MONEY MAKES THE BALL GO ROUND

Out of the polyphony of attempts to define 'pop' here is one, which, if not with scholarly precision, does so in a serious way, taking its cue from Nik Cohn:

> Pop: pure surface, beautiful semblance, glorious hollow-sounding trash and nothing else. On occasion trivial myths blown up to bursting-point, a play with bubbles, shimmery and glimmery, nothing but balmy air below the film. Lots of bubble-blowing silly billys in this corral of infantilism, precocious faces and adolescent old-age wisdom, a coterie one only leaves with a loss of innocence. And who cares about pop stars that have lost their innocence? Only grouchy old critics.
>
> This infantile autism by the way does not contradict the fact that the pop star ultimately is a public and publicly created persona – though of course he

eventually sees himself almost always as someone 'totally different' from the image created by clever management. But whatever is actually concealed behind this persona ultimately is only of interest to the star's confessor, his dentist, baker or hair dresser. As distinct as one has to project oneself in this business, preferably with at least one particular quirk, or several: any kind of lapse into individuality, any personal facet would be an ugly scratch on a spotless façade. That's a contradiction, a double bind even, you object? Yes, but one that is usually countervailed by excessive damages for pain and suffering.

That's cynical, you say? But of course! Which introduces a further criterion: pop is cynical and deeply so. That does not mean that the whole circus is not governed by certain rules and regulations. Only these are not categories like 'honesty', 'veracity' or 'authenticity'. The values of pop carry strict sell-by dates and only the fluctuation of fashions remains permanent.

(John 1998: 20f.)[4]

Another 'snapshot' to illustrate this: an internet search for the name 'Beckham' in combination with 'Bilder' (images) in June 2006 turned up 20 photographs on the first page, of which only three clearly showed a scene from a football match; altogether, eight at least showed Beckham in his football gear. The other 12 would not give the uninitiated – should there be such a person left out there – any clue as to Beckham's actual profession: on the second page the result is even more decisive 16–2!

All of this illustrates the title of this chapter precisely and in the true sense of the word. The stadium is no longer the primary location for the creation of the 'Beckham' brand – photo studios and agencies who feed the 'images' created there into the media machine play at least an equal part in the gigantic mechanism of distribution and multiplication which has turned David Beckham into a universal icon, 'the first global pop star in studs' (Honigstein 2006: 29). A flood of images that have – and this is also a result of the transgressions outlined above – long since reached youth media and the glossy pages of lifestyle and fashion magazines, in which advertising and journalistic contributions often are hard to tell apart at the best of times. This ultimately means that it is no longer the stadium which is David Beckham's genuine workplace: it is rather a stage besides others, on which his market value, fixed for good, as promotion icon is validated here and there or – to use stock exchange terminology – is adjusted upwards or downwards: be it in Madrid, Milan, Los Angeles or perhaps some time soon in Britain again.

In spite of this I have avoided the term 'star' – which Peter Sloterdijk (2006: 71) distinguishes from the image and the notion of the (classical) 'hero' – in the title of this chapter and instead have used 'celebrity', a distinction which is important to Diedrich Diederichsen as well, thus stating a significant flattening and deflating of concepts and terminology nowadays comparable to the use of language among the 'facebook generation' when speaking of 'friendship' instead of 'incidental contacting' or similarly of 'friends' instead of 'virtual communication partners':

> During the last ten to fifteen years we have been able to witness the slow wreckage of the good old system of superstars. The Superstar has been replaced by the celebrity. The Superstar signified something, the celebrity nothing but himself; not himself as a person, that is, but as a brand. The Superstar was worshipped, people wanted to subject themselves to him or be like him; the celebrity on the other hand meets with indifferent recognition, but cannot be removed from the day to day conversations (just as little as time or the alphabet). The Superstar has history, during which he developed his substance, the general, reverent and public dimension of a personality that remained identifiable and individual; the celebrity reproduces by reduplication. Everyone could choose a Superstar, nobody can escape the celebrity.
>
>   The Superstar was typically a specialist in one form of media; the celebrity, on the contrary, is characterized by his ability to jump from one milieu to another while triumphantly remaining true to his brand: his face. The structurally changed public of cable television and the internet supports him; it serves as his meta-milieu.
>
> (Diederichsen 2004: 17)[5]

Franz Beckenbauer, the Kaiser. Gerd Müller, the Bomber. Maradona, the Hand of God: 'legends' all of them, manifest and cast in stone in set formulas (cf. Chapter 14). In contrast, it is remarkable in the case of 'Beckhamania' that the acquired image – that attributed role which, in its recognisability, anchors it in the public consciousness while at the same time acting as a cage or a bind – has been replaced by the orchestration of *several* images, alternating visuals that render the quest for identity and authenticity as outmoded, just as old fashioned as the bourgeois demand for evidence of an 'accomplishment' to justify such popularity – one thinks here of a non-entity such as Paris Hilton, ennobled to 'pop icon' in spite of everything. Julie Burchill touches on this when in her book *Burchill on Beckham* she asks whether he is a complete fool, extremely clever or just a lucky devil (as quoted in Irnberger 2005: 159). This should not prevent us from at least asking the right questions, but in order to do so, we must address the current discourse.

The extent to which these discourses were hopelessly at odds was demonstrated when David Beckham joined Real Madrid in July 2003 for a transfer fee of 37.5 million euro – by no means the largest ever such fee, but only because of the vagaries of the market. The move faced opposition from many sides. The sporting argument went that Real already had good players on the right side and did not need Beckham. The psychological objection was that Zidane and Beckham would not get along. Someone like Beckham is too expensive: this was the economic aspect. Or there was the ethical complaint about the immorality of paying that kind of money for a football player. And everyone who considers David Beckham to be stupid and hopelessly overrated raises matters of taste, but argues in conspicuously close proximity to the lines of reasoning of an intellectual

Figure 15.2
David Beckham leaves
the field after the
exhibition game Los
Angeles Galaxy vs. FC
Barcelona at the Rose
Bowl Stadium in
Pasadena, California,
2009.

discourse which in its attitude of superiority runs the danger of degrading the
object of its epistemic interest without actually understanding it. Of course, when
Victoria Beckham admits to never having read a book because she does not have
the time, when the couple flashes the accessories of the well-to-do in a way
which in its nouveau riche swank easily falls below every adjustable level of
embarrassment, when he gets a new tattoo in which her name is spelled wrongly
in Hindi, or when he lets on that he does not understand his six-year-old son's
maths homework – somebody enters a shop at 11.45 and leaves at 12.15: how
long has he been in there? – he by choice subjects himself to a kind of mockery,
which, beyond pure denunciation, is certainly understandable.

But these attempts to reach the kernel, in order to divine the sense of it all – honest and well-schooled in a number of western traditions as they may be – fall hopelessly behind the aesthetic credo of Andy Warhol, who declared the surface to be the message with no intrinsic 'meaning' to be found either behind the mirror or in some other hidden depths. If polarization is an important aspect of pop culture, here we have to deal with a levelling counterweight which is not only characteristic of much of postmodern aesthetics but may also be at the core of 'Beckhamania': design determines consciousness. Categories like 'good' or 'bad' become irrelevant, the important thing is to remain in the public eye – even if only for Warhol's famous 15 minutes. Besides which: it's all just a game, which nowadays translates as 'hedonistic society'. This also forms the core of the concept of metrosexuality as defined by Mark Simpson in 1994. Along with superstars like Robbie Williams, David Beckham is considered the paradigmatic representative of this concept which avoids conformity with a strictly male role model, in order to play – and only play – with other models and orientation, from androgyny to homosexuality, without accepting them as a 'real' identity; there will be no 'coming out'. Thus the male body, until now of interest to the advertising industry only in the field of personal hygiene, becomes a surface on which a diversity of fashions and styling from make-up to manicure can be projected.

None of these images create the impression of David Beckham *actually* being a samurai, or a member of a street gang, a punk, a rocker or a knight. The staging of these pictures is obvious, there is never a doubt that we are dealing with a pose – note, not a mask. In only one profession is that kind of permanent change of attire the norm: the model. Closely related to this – we are in the age of globalization after all – is an equally playful exchangeability of locations and time periods: today Tokyo, tomorrow New York, here an allusion to the Japanese Empire, there one to the European Middle Ages. Anything goes, everything is pretty.

Furthermore: were one to analyse these images more closely with an approach schooled in art history, one would notice a consistent aura of unspoilt distance and other-worldliness. Many of these photos display conspicuously solipsistic, almost autistic gestures. Not only does no-one else usually share the picture: the gaze, if it is directed at the viewer at all, seems strangely veiled, seems directed inward, and remains introverted, even when directed into the distance. This is underlined by the positioning of the hands, which often seek contact with the body, thus demonstratively making it the dominating focus; a contact that, at the same time, may be seen as a symbolic simulation of the touch which admirers of an idol more or less secretly desire. It is these careful stagings which have turned David Beckham – and this is a purely phenomenological, not a value judgment – into *the* icon of a narcissistic decade, a term that fits the 1990s for a variety of reasons.

To chastize David Beckham by calling him a chameleon because of this, or to compare him to Woody Allen's *Zelig*, a character who could easily adjust to all changes in time and life, seems wrong, because it underestimates the creative potential of the braintrust which uses the David Beckham *brand* quite consciously and calculatedly as a trend setter. Moving the discussion at this point to the subject of money, from the stadium into the vicinity of banks and other financial institutions, may not be very original, but it is completely unavoidable.

The question as to what is being advertised here becomes at once superfluous and can at the same time be framed precisely, even if it revolves around a blank space – remembered as being famous – because David Beckham stands for nothing else but David Beckham, who or whatever that may be. The term 'brand' can be taken literally here, since David Beckham is one of the few athletes that not only have their own lines of products created but also have them distributed under their own logo: a privilege he shares with greats like Tiger Woods or Michael Jordan, whose number 23 he astutely picked after his move to Spain.

Transfers of the Beckham dimension are no longer possible unless embedded into a concomitant merchandizing campaign. The deal was financed by Real to a large extent through the sale of Beckham jerseys, a common practice nowadays in global football. To make it work the club had to specifically target East Asian markets from China via Japan to Thailand, though the promotional tour the team had to undertake seriously undermined the preparation for the upcoming season at a time when a team is supposed to lay the foundation for the next 11 months. A high price to pay and a vicious circle, which probably played a large part in the failure of the concept of galactic *Heldenfußball*, or heroic football (cf. Biermann 2004, cf. Chapter 14 in this volume).

It is indisputably difficult and demands much analytical endeavour to distinguish in the chamber of public noise, in which an enormous amount of information floats anonymously and unchecked, between the source of a sound and its echo, something of which Goethe was already aware when he had Mephisto say in *Faust*, *Walpurgisnacht*: 'Du glaubst zu schieben und du wirst geschoben' ('You believe that you push and you are pushed,' Goethe 1986: verse 4117). This does not free the scholar from the obligation to take familiar contemporary conventions of speech at their word and to expose them as what they are: mostly ideologemes of the superstructure created at the drawing board. The precept 'to reinvent oneself daily' – which must surely overtax every normal person after a very short time – in this context mostly means to take one's money to the hairdresser and the make-up artist (not that we begrudge anyone the pleasure to feel like a new person with a new haircut). To resume the cynical thread mentioned above: The purpose of the cleverly fuelled 'Beckhamania', with all its fluctuating fashions, trends and images, is first and foremost to create new stimuli for consumption, because the Beckham brand will only remain profitable at its current astronomical levels – one hears of an annual income of more than 20 million euro – when the clientele can never obtain 'his' or 'her' Beckham once and for all, but – one thinks of the introduction of home and away kits – must newly deck itself out each spring and fall season, in Summer and in Winter. To this we now turn.

THE OCCUPATION OF BODIES: CONSPIRATIVE FINALE

In November 1998 the following report, largely unnoticed by the public, appeared in the sports pages of the *Süddeutsche Zeitung*:

> The International Volleyball Federation (FIVB) at the women's world
> championship in Japan has fined five teams $3,000 for wearing 'loose and
> baggy' shirts. In the preliminary round, Brazil, Bulgaria, Croatia, Italy and Russia
> had not conformed to regulations, the federation announced. On the other
> hand, the Cubans, who appeared in skintight one-piece suits, together with
> four other teams, were lauded for 'world class outfits.' The dress code is
> checked by a committee, and the federation has emphatically rejected the
> accusation of being sexist. The new rules, which demand jerseys to be skimpier,
> shorter and tighter, also apply to men and give volleyball 'an attractive image,
> stressing the most important values of the sport: power and speed.'
>
> (*Süddeutsche Zeitung* 1998: 56)[6]

This does not describe an option, not a recommendation but a diktat, which may truly be termed a form of terrorism. Athletes, especially women beach volleyball players, learned their lesson, and when *Der Spiegel* published a long report about the new sport first staged at the 1996 Atlanta Olympic Games under the headline 'Lots of bottoms' (Der Spiegel 1996), this reflected a tendency towards sexualization, in this case nuditization, which, in accord with other sectors of public life, has now also fully taken hold in sport (cf. Chapter 11).

Whoever nowadays researches celebrity websites on the internet, in this case nude celebs, will not only be linked to sites of actresses and models, but will also be directed, with one mouseclick, to those of musicians and athletes. In other words, the demands placed by a certain segment of the public on a celebrity includes, as a matter of course, his or her body, specifically the naked body, as a price of fame, so to speak. Although there are significant differences to be noted between the (merely) exposed (male) and the naked female body.

A few observations can be made. Should a female athlete succumb to the pressure of putting her bare skin on the market, quite literally in this case, she basically has three options. The exposure can refer strictly to her discipline, something that often makes no sense and might well have unintended comical results. Cultural and artistic traditions suggest another mode of presentation, that of modelling antique sculptures, as was done by the shot putter Astrid Kumbernuß and the speed skater Annie Friesinger. In these cases the athletic body, even in a state of disclosure, still appeared 'veiled', with the mental image of antique sculptures acting as a foil in the eye of the beholder; another speed skater, Franziska Schenk, and the discus thrower Lars Riedel actually had their bodies painted with glossy paint to create an actual additional foil. The third option is that of the 'classic' pin-up; such pictures are supposed to be 'aesthetic' and 'tasteful', terms denoting sanctioned limitations and taboos, though these are fluctuating and need to be negotiated and tested in each instance. As yet, the only more or less unacceptable exception is the pornographic pose, as reactions to the photo spread of the Norwegian skier Ingvild Engesland have demonstrated.

Gunter Gebauer has pointed out the social element of this erotic interest especially in times of an excessive cult of the body: 'Even in the nude people differ, there is no equality of the nude. Never before has social inequality reached that far, even into what is most natural in human beings. Everybody has the body one deserves' (Gebauer 1997: 285).[7] Physical fitness has moved from being a recipe for individual well-being to becoming an expected social norm, a sporting value that links successful achievement with a well-trained body (Caysa 1997: 9), and this is also reflected in other fields of public life, as the basis for perseverance in professional life. The body thus becomes a merciless benchmark for the extent to which somebody proves adept to the pressure to perform in a competitive climate no longer limited to public life: the body not only needs to be permanently toughened, more importantly, it has to be presented.

Even more significant to me seems the economical component of this accessing of the body, which makes the concept of an area of privacy and intimacy appear like a quaint relic of the twentieth century. In July 1997 the monthly magazine *Max* presented a picture of the German long-jumper Susanne Tiedtke-Greene. The promise on the cover – 'Miss Track-and-Field unveiled' – remained fulfilled and unfulfilled at the same time, since remnants of clothing shrouded her breasts and genitals. The picture can still be found on the Internet, yet *without* the information given next to it in the original, which listed the companies that had provided shoes, shorts and armband. The artist's monogram, which used to give a painting the signature of singularity and distinctiveness, has been superseded by product placement, by brand names that have a tendency towards global ubiquity.

Figure 15.3
The body as occupied territory for sponsors' marks: UK sprinter Linford Christie wearing PUMA contact lenses, 1996.

The next logical step, the placement of the logo straight on the skin of the 'advertising medium', had already been taken, as demonstrated during the 1995 World Athletics Championships in Gothenburg by a Reebok tattoo on the thigh of the African runner Maria Mutola and the Puma logo on the chests of sprinters Colin Jackson and Linford Christie, the latter of whom also adorned his eyes with contact lenses with the sponsor logo at a press conference (Figure 15.4). Acts of colonisation, doubtlessly: the body as occupied territory on which sponsors mark their claims in a symbolic act. One is reminded of the brand used to mark horses or cattle in Marlboro country, or of board games in which pins mark the appropriation of real estate. Or, naturally, of Kafka's *In the Penal Colony*.

What does all this have to do with David Beckham and 'Beckhamania'? On this point, one final thesis which stands aloof from sinister conspiracy theories by its sheer obviousness: flanked and supported by a media revolution in the form of private television and the internet in the last couple of decades, an interested (because profiting) industry has conducted an aggressive campaign towards the occupation of our bodies, which has taken possession of large parts of the body's surface – and will not stop there. What in football began with accessories such as flags that can be waved and put aside, and jerseys that one puts on and later takes off again, soon reached, referring back to atavistic customs like war paint, the skin, from which the paint can still be washed off. By then sport had, of course, in the form of doping, reached *into* the body and its metabolic processes and had found its imitators in fitness studios – and not only there. The perforation of the body surface with longer lasting, tendentially irreversible marks in the form of piercings and tattoos is a comparatively new mass phenomenon. And the form in which the march into the inner body is already in progress may be illustrated by the example of the footballer Djibril Cissé, whose body was transformed in a commercial by his supplier Adidas – citing models of machine men – into a bolide, a fighting machine. Marcello Lippi, coach of the *squadra azzurra*, called his player Daniele de Rossi, sent off in the match against the USA during the 2006 World Cup, a 'fantastic guy' who nevertheless should 'have his computer chip changed' (*Spiegel Online* 2006b). It is with exactly that, the implantation of computer chips below the skin, that RFID (Radio Frequency Identification) technology has for some time now been concerned.

This occupation of the body as potential advertising space has to be prepared, has to be playfully exercised and rendered harmless in order to achieve mass compatibility. Nobody should be prevented from viewing Denis Rodman as a loopy kind of monster or David Beckham as the contemporary incarnation of some sort of British spleen. But you can also interpret 'Beckhamania' in its substance as an experiment, the subject of which is to test, innovatively and by proxy, the threshold and limit of our willingness to accept the occupation and manipulation of our bodies, and in the process to extend those limits further, bit by bit.

And the consequences? These are to be observed in urban life already. The extent to which technology and industry have taken possession of large parts of our orifices, thus separating us from the outside world and its sensual experience, especially the acoustic one, is hard to overlook and creates a whole new range of potential risks and accidents: collisions with passers-by whose far-away look is fixed on the display of their mobile phones and not on oncoming traffic, which could and should be avoided. Similarly resistant to outside signals are underground travellers, cyclists or fully-wired joggers attached to their personal music players: autistic monads in a nutrient acoustic solution, in their own way just as enraptured, self-involved and self-sufficient as David Beckham in his best moments. From there it is only a small step, not a forcibly constructed one, it seems to me, to the vision of a human being sitting in his or her room in front of a monitor in the belief of 'experiencing' something of this world through screen and loudspeaker. Not only the individual but also the sociopolitical implications of this placement have been precisely captured by Birgit Vanderbeke, who characterizes this cross-linked, fully transparent and permanently controllable *homo ludens* in the following way:

> As long as they, however many, stay at their computers, in their houses and thus away from each other, [...] in their close-circuited electronic systems they remain antisocial, usually overweight by the way, and isolated, but because of that harmless all the same.
>
> (Vanderbecke 2005: 61)[8]

Where will it all lead? Thankfully, it is not my task to answer that question here. In 2006 David Beckham's (footballing) successor had already been crowned, although Wayne Rooney seems determined to carry on in the more conventional English working-class tradition. Which decidedly differs from the job profile for young German professional footballers, Mehmet Scholl's heirs, as outlined by Rolf Heßbrügge, football writer for the German youth magazine *Bravo-Sport* in 2002:

> Very important: he needs a trendy haircut, preferably with gel. Combined with a face suitable for a boy group. He should be nice and relaxed. A little bit extravagant – but not too much. Preferably he plays for a big club. And, really important: he has to score goals.
>
> (Vielberg 2002)

That, at least, has not yet been completely sidelined.

EPILOGUE AS EPILOGUE

The 'galactic' plan Real Madrid followed early in the first decade of the new century failed. It seemed (though later chroniclers will be better placed to judge) as if in subsequent years those teams would dominate that promoted teamwork and perfect organization rather than a couple of (pop) stars; of course, teams like Manchester United, FC Barcelona and Chelsea FC consisted almost exclusively of superstars too, yet too old to enjoy the status of a pop star: possibly an indication that the trend towards being a 'pop-star' or a 'celebrity' is not necessarily inevitable, but reversible – at least partially or periodically. Now that Real Madrid has bought Christiano Ronaldo, Kaká and Karim Benzema for altogether 200 million euros, the season 2009/10 appears to mark the renaissance of the *Galaktikos* as well as a return to an emphasis on pop stars, even though Ronaldo has recently and tellingly been labelled as 'poster boy' (Gertz 2009). Whether or not this attempt will meet with success is one question; whether such success is desirable, another one.

NOTES

1 I have once again to thank Sybille Frank and Silke Steets, not only for inviting me to give this lecture – which I did on 5 July 2006 at the Darmstadt University of Technology – but equally for their generous hospitality. The lecture has been revised for printing and in the process, unfortunately, has had to be shortened with the loss of its numerous illustrations. I am grateful to Dr Claus Melchior for important suggestions and, above all, for his invaluable help with the translation of this piece. For helpful assistance I would also like to thank Caroline Kelly, Dr. Christopher Krebs and Stefan Erhardt.
2 Translation from German: Johannes John.
3 Translation from German: Johannes John.
4 Translation from German: Johannes John.
5 Translation from German: Johannes John.
6 Translation from German: Johannes John.
7 Translation from German: Johannes John.
8 Translation from German: Johannes John.

REFERENCES

Barnes, J. (2005) 'Niemand glaubt Blair', *Falter*, 31: 16.
Biermann, C. (2004) 'Vision vom gemeinsamen Spiel', *Süddeutsche Zeitung*, 13/14 November, p. 41.
Caysa, V. (ed.) (1997) *Sportphilosophie*, Leipzig: Reclam.
Der Spiegel (1996) *Jede Menge Hintern*, 32: 170–3.
Diederichsen, D. (2004) 'Der Promi ist eine Mikrobe', *taz*, 16 January, p. 17.
Freeman, D. (2000) *David Beckham, My World, Photography*, London: Hodder & Stoughton.
Gebauer, G. (1997) 'Von der Körpertechnologisierung zur Körpershow', in V. Caysa (ed.) *Sportphilosophie*, Leipzig: Reclam.
Gertz, H. (2009) 'Helden haben ihren Preis', *Süddeutsche Zeitung*, 18/19 July.
Goethe, J.W. (1986) *Sämtliche Werke nach Epochen seines Schaffens*, Münchner Ausgabe, vol. 6.1, edited by V. Lange, München: Carl Hanser.
Honigstein, R. (2006) 'Eine Kluft, groß wie der Grand Canyon', *Süddeutsche Zeitung*, 23 June, p. 29.
Irnberger, H. (2005) *Die Mannschaft ohne Eigenschaften. Fußball im Netz der Globalisierung*, Salzburg/Wien: Otto Müller Verlag.
John, J. (1998) 'Fußball und Pop – Oder: Ist Mehmet Scholl ein Popstar und wenn ja, warum nicht?', *Der Tödliche Paß. Zeitschrift zur näheren Betrachtung des Fußballspiels*, 12: 20–1.
Sloterdjik, P. (2006) 'Ein Team von Hermaphroditen', *Der Spiegel*, 23: 70–3.
Spiegel Online (2006a) *Beckhams Ticks: Coladosen dürfen nur paarweise in den Kühlschrank*, Online. Available www.spiegel.de/panorama/0,1518,409584,00.html (accessed 9 April 2009).

Spiegel Online (2006b) *Die besten WM-Sprüche: Systemabsturz*. Online. Available www.spiegel.de/panorama/0,1518,425554,00.html (accessed 15 March 2009).

Stevenson, J. (ed.) (2004) *David Beckham Talking*, Berlin: Schwarzkopf & Schwarzkopf.

Süddeutsche Zeitung (1998) *Ausgebeulte Trikots. Volleyballerinnen bei WM bestraft*, 7/8 November, p. 56.

Vanderbecke, B. (2005) *Sweet Sixteen*, Frankfurt/Main: S. Fischer.

Vielberg, U. (2002) 'Scholls Erben verzweifelt gesucht', *Welt am Sonntag*, 29 Dezember, Online. Available www.welt.de/print-wams/article111268/Scholls_Erben_verzweifelt_gesucht.html (accessed 6 October 2009).

Conclusion

The Stadium – Lens and Refuge

Sybille Frank and Silke Steets

Football is more than a game and the stadium is not just any type of building. The preceding chapters have given us diverse insights into events in and around the stadium. It has become clear that football stadia are ideal for socio-diagnostic analyses: social trends are condensed within them, as if under a magnifying glass. At the same time, football stadia also function as places of refuge, since behaviour possible inside their gates is not (or no longer) acceptable outside them. In this concluding chapter, we first refer to the findings of the chapters of this book in the light of this particular double-sided nature of the stadium. Subsequently, we expand on our thesis outlined in the introduction, namely, that the cause of this double-sided nature can be found in the very specific spatiality and materiality of the stadium. What constitutes the built and social space of the stadium in all phases of its history is its introversion and clear structural demarcation from the outside world, the spatial separation between active participants and spectators, the direction of the spectators' gazes onto a central point, and the spatial process by which the crowds are made visible and reflexively conscious of themselves.

THE STADIUM AS LENS

The potential of the football stadium to provide us with social insights can be explained by reference to the field of architectural sociology: Emile Durkheim (1951: 313) argues that materialities such as technical artefacts, transport routes and buildings represent 'social facts' just as much as do the moral and legal principles of a society. By social facts, Durkheim means *collective* forms of thinking, believing and acting, in tangible contrast to, and independent of, the actions of, the individual. Even when there is a societal conflict about interpretation, sovereignty and moral rules, as well as about the form of buildings, their reality is always the result and expression of social consensus and is thus a mirror of society (cf. Introduction to this volume). More than this: by collectively giving its buildings a 'character', a social form to be decoded symbolically, society identifies with and reassures itself of its own identity (cf. Halbwachs 1938). Social and spatial orders therefore directly refer to each other.

This is also true of football stadia. The parallels between social and built structures were addressed in the contributions by King, Kratzmüller and Schulke. Anthony King considers the latest prototype, the 'New European Stadium', to be a post-modern construction embodying the power of global and opaque capital flows that are difficult to localize, a fact he establishes on the basis of apparently weightless roof constructions and apparently transparent façades. While Bettina Kratzmüller sees the social order of the ancient city states reflected in the spatial division of ancient stadia, Hans-Jürgen Schulke shows how the development of competitive sport in modern industrial and mass society brought about the construction of a specific form of building, the modern stadium. Against this background, and that of the recently observed return of mass events to the inner city's public spaces – as in the example of Public Viewing – Schulke sees current stadia as being faced with a challenge: what will their future be like when the spectator experience of football returns to the place of its Middle Ages origins: on the streets and squares of the inner cities? Michael Zinganel's view of the future of stadia is similarly critical. In order to remain profitable in the long term, a much greater flexibilization of this vast urban building type, both structurally and spatially, will be essential.

The most important reason for the continuing popularity of stadia, however, is the growing worldwide demand for the medial transmission of what it is that takes place *in* football stadia. Television cameras, with their constant switching between long shots, slow motion replays and close-ups, present a fragmented space and connect the stadium with the outside world. The potential and crisis-ridden nature of this medially construed space in the global event society of today is illustrated by Angelika Schnell, the astonishing absence of such a construction in the special case of a war situation is examined by Bruno Arich-Gerz. The image of the football stadium as conveyed by the media is also the starting point for Christian Banse's reflections. Any African or South American footballer who makes it into an English, Spanish, French, Italian or German stadium has arrived at the centre of European society: the stadium becomes a place of longing.

The two case studies from Manchester deal with the meaning of places in the global here and now. From different theoretical perspectives, both Tim Edensor and Steve Millington as well as Adam Brown conclude that stadia, and those places around stadia created by perceptions, memories and ritual practices experienced on match day, are barely interchangeable. Football stadia are places that evoke a very particular emotional intensity, best summed up by the terms 'topophilia' (home ground) and 'topophobia' (away grounds) (cf. Bale 1993: 64ff., cf. Bachelard 1957).

THE STADIUM AS REFUGE

The emotional intensity of the football stadium is accompanied by strong masculine codes. The stadium is a space connected beyond cultural boundaries with rituals of physical strength, manly brotherhood, heterosexual camaraderie, heroism (cf. Gerbauer's Chapter 14) and with solidarity. These codes are so strong and definite that they allow men to experience themselves *as men* and to reassure themselves of their masculinity (cf. Bromberger's Chapter 10), even when they demonstrate behaviour commonly seen as unmanly: in the stadium, men are allowed to cry, to hug each other and show emotions (cf. Schäfer's and Roose's Chapter 13) or – in the case of the global pop star David Beckham – to utilize the body in a post-modern dalliance with gender identities, without, for example, being suspected of being gay (cf. John's Chapter 15).

This unambiguity of the heteronormative manly world of the football stadium can pose a problem for anyone who is different from this role model, such as women or gay men. They feel the normative power of this space, when they search for their own gender role, their (gay or heterosexual) womanhood or gay manhood as football players or as passionate fans (cf. Chapter 11). Conversely, however, the stadium, as a clearly heterosexual and male-coded space, also allows institutionalized gender orders to be tested in an emancipatory way. Women in the fan areas of the Ararat Stadium in Tehran bravely adapt male forms of behaviour: they cheer and shout, are cheeky and spur their team on (cf. Chapter 12). By discarding 'typically female' characteristics such as restraint and subordination and by behaving in a 'manly' way, they performatively question established ideas of manhood and womanhood in the stadium.

Corinna Assmann and Silke Gülker's study of women's football in Iran also clearly shows that football stadia can be places of public, but unpunished, dissidence in totalitarian states. This is underlined by a case, not dissimilar to the Iranian example, which was observed in the Soviet Union by historian Robert Edelman between 1930 and 1950. Edelman, who examined the fan rivalry between Dinamo Moscow – a Soviet sports club, founded in 1923 by the secret police – and Spartak Moscow (founded 1935) – a club independent of the state and therefore loved by many workers – signified being a Spartak fan as 'a small way of saying "No"', and referred to the Armenian anthropologist Levon Abramian:

> In a Communist country [...] the football club you supported was a community to which you yourself chose to belong. The regime did not send you to support a club [...] It might be your only chance to choose a community, and, also, in that community you could express yourself as you wished.
>
> (Edelman 2002: 1444)

In the highly competitive games between Dinamo and Spartak Moscow 'you could hear from the stands "kill the cops" [*bei militsiia*] or "kill the soldiers" [*bei koniushek*, literally, the grooms]' (Edelman 2002: 1455), pronouncements that would have provoked punishment outside the stadium. In the GDR in the 1980s, a follower of the workers' club Chemie Leipzig had a similar stadium experience:

> The football pitch was a fascinating field of experimentation for one's own behaviour and the reactions of the state. [...] Here [in the stadium], songs were chanted with fervour, with texts that would have landed you in the nick if you had said them on the street. German rhymes were set to melodies by Western pop groups, about being confined in the zone and the NVA [National People's Army], which insulted the police or GDR football in the worst possible way. It went as far as verbal death threats and was overflowing with 'originality' and 'wit'. Expressions such as 'Red pig' or 'Reds out!' etc., which referred to the colours on the pitch, were nothing if not ambiguous.
>
> (Schneider 1999: 70)

THE STADIUM AS LENS AND REFUGE: HETEROTOPIA

Summing up, it can be said that stadia, and the way they are built and used, always reveal something about the condition of a society. Social, cultural and economic trends are condensed within, as under a magnifying glass. At the same time, they are more than just a concentrated image of society. Because spaces are created in stadia, through which social structures such as gender orders, behavioural codes or power relationships are performatively questioned, they are places that are potentially critical in relation to the respective society, albeit in different ways: in the rational, civilized and strictly regulated society of (Western) modernity they are places where excitement is released; in countries in which the political system has traces of totalitarianism, they can be places of dissidence and, in the confusion of war, places of a brutal prison order (cf. Hachleitner 2005). Michel Foucault calls such places 'heterotopias'. By this he means

> real places – places that do exist and that are formed in the very founding of society – which are something like counter-sites, a kind of effectively enacted utopia in which [...] all the other real sites that can be found within the culture, are simultaneously represented, contested, and inverted. Places of this kind are outside of all places, even though it may be possible to indicate their location in reality.
>
> (Foucault 1986: 24)

Based on Foucault, stadia can be described as heterotopias, as places of compression (lens) and as 'contre-emplacements' (refuge). But what are the characteristics of stadia that make them become such places? We suppose that the reason for this is to be found in the specific spatiality and materiality of the stadium through which gazes are focused, actions are put in the limelight and crowds are celebrated and controlled.

GAZE-DIRECTING REGIMES, CROWDS AND ISOLATION

Stadia have always been material structures built with the intention of focusing the gaze of the many spectators to their centre, the pitch (and, in recently built stadia, to the video cube located above the pitch), thereby creating a highly representational and power-laden space in which socio-cultural trends or political messages could be successfully staged and atmospherically promoted. At the same time, stadia enable crowds to experience themselves physically, visually and acoustically *as crowds* so that individuals, released from social norms within the protection of the crowds, may perform acts that would be judged as socially retrograde or even delinquent outside the stadium. However, there are serious differences between the stadia of antiquity and those of today.

The arena of antiquity

According to Michel Foucault, ancient society was 'a civilization of spectacle' (Foucault 1979: 216). For him it was the architecture of the temples, theatres and circuses that most clearly reflected the curiosity of this civilization. On the one hand they were constructed in such a way that they centred the gaze of the crowds onto the altar or stage, thus providing 'to a multitude of men the inspection of a small number of objects' (N.H. Julius 1831, quoted in Foucault 1979: 216). On the other hand they were built so that the people in the tiers could perceive each other physically and visually, and fill each other with enthusiasm: on the stone seats of the stands, arranged as close to each other as possible, the crowd could melt into a 'single great body' while watching together (Foucault 1979: 216). Correspondingly, Foucault sums up the social function of the arena of antiquity as follows: 'With spectacle, there was a predominance of public life, the intensity of festivals, sensual proximity. In these rituals in which blood flowed, society found new vigour' (Foucault 1979: 216). This vigour is illustrated in a report by Augustine about a Christian,

> who went to the Colosseum to test his faith. The Christian initially kept his head turned away from the violent show taking place in the arena below, praying for inner strength; slowly, as though a vice twisted his head, he began to look and succumbed to the spectacle, its bloody images entrancing him until he shouted and cheered like the mass of people around him. In the visual prison constructed in the pagan world, the Christian will weakened, then surrendered to images.
>
> (Sennett 1994: 101, cf. Chapter 14)

The architecture of the cauldron-like arenas of antiquity were laid out for the unfolding of precisely this power of the images upon which the gazes were centred, and the crowds, which became loudly excitable about the event and whipped the individual along as if in a whirlpool.

Figure 16.1
G.B. Piranesi, Coliseum,
1756.

The modern stadium

After cathedrals and churches had replaced stadia as architectures of assembly in the Middle Ages, stadia returned to Europe in the course of secularization in the late eighteenth century (Figure 16.2). From there, conveyed by the standards of international associations such as the International Olympic Committee (IOC, founded in the late nineteenth century) or Fédération Internationale de Football Association (FIFA, established in the early twentieth century), they gradually spread across the entire globe. However, these stadia had little in common with the arenas of antiquity: instead of seated tiers they were surrounded by stands,

Figure 16.2
Paris, celebration of the confederation, 1790.

which were often less steep and also, due to the presence of running tracks, at a remove from the rectangular field in the middle (Figure 3.1). But just as in ancient arenas they, too, directed the gaze of the crowds towards the centre. They also had clear demarcations between the inside and outside and separated the active participants from the spectators.

Following Elias Canetti (1973) the Dutch art theorist Camiel van Winkel sees in modern stadia a prototypical venue for the physical confrontation between crowds and architecture (van Winkel 2005). Whereas it is in the nature of the crowds to want to grow, stadia are 'pre-existing vessels' (Canetti 1973: 21), with the primary function of limiting crowds. In this way, an antagonism emerges between the crowds and architecture which, for van Winkel, is illustrated by the numerous, literally boundary-breaking catastrophes in the history of the modern stadium: because the spectator in the terraces of the modern stadium could move much more freely than in the ancient arenas with arranged seating, they were more susceptible to critical confrontations between the crowds and architecture. Sudden occurrences of exit panic (Lima 1964, with 300 deaths), false alarm (Teresina 1973, four deaths), hooligan violence (Heysel 1985, 39 deaths), sudden hailstorm (Kathmandu, 1988, 80 deaths) or fatal logistics (Hillsborough/Sheffield 1989, 96 deaths) became the cause of collapsing stands, fire or the destruction of installations.

In all of these cases, the extreme density of people becomes a problem. As discourses about hooliganism show (Elias and Dunning 1986), the precarious nature of the encounters between crowds and architecture moves further into the foreground in modern times and extends beyond the theories of Elias and Dunning referred to in the introduction to this book. According to them, the football stadium must be interpreted as a place that provides an opportunity for the communal acting-out of strong emotions, which would otherwise be suppressed in a modern society that demands rationality and self-control. From Elias' and Dunning's perspective, stadia generally have a stabilizing effect on social coexistence since the acting-out of excitement here 'does not disturb and endanger the relative orderliness of social life as the serious type of excitement is liable to do' (Elias and Dunning 1986: 71). However, as modern stadia must be considered from this perspective as places of freedom and of peaceful, regulated competition, they only enable a collective 'release of emotion' within certain boundaries of intensity: in stadia, the norms of mainstream society which can be reflected on, in contrast to ancient society, as strict demarcations between playfulness and seriousness, are always present. If one applies Elias' and Dunning's theory to the stadium, bloody confrontations in the stands and on the pitch, or even deaths, must be regarded as inconceivable and intolerable in the highly civilized, recreational competitive culture of modern times. When playfulness turns into life-threatening seriousness, the modern stadium becomes a place for discourses about the necessity of disciplining the crowds as Canetti described it.

The panopticon

The most comprehensive examination of the emergence of architectures for the surveillance and disciplining of crowds in modern times is that of Michel Foucault. According to Foucault, public life and the community no longer stand at the centre of modern society as they did in the ancient society of the spectacle, but instead it is the state and the individual that do so. The relationships between the latter are, according to Foucault, regulated in a form 'that is the exact reverse of the spectacle' (Foucault 1979: 216): since the modern state is dependent upon being able to control the activities of the individual, in order to guarantee the smooth intertwining of functions and thus its survival, the present times have to solve the problem of how '[t]o procure for a small number, or even for a single individual, the instantaneous view of a great multitude' (N.H. Julius 1831, quoted in Foucault 1979: 216).

The epitome of a modern architecture constructed 'to avoid the inconveniences of over-large assemblies' (Foucault 1979: 210) was, for Foucault, the panopticon conceived by Jeremy Bentham (1748–1832). Like the ancient Roman arena (Figure 16.1) the panopticon (Figure 16.3) is a building that is sealed off from the outside world. In its centre – where the playing field was situated in the arena of antiquity, upon which all gazes were directed – a huge tower soars. The stone rotunda surrounding the tower, corresponding to the position of the ancient seating areas, is a ring-shaped building consisting of individual cells, in each of which a prisoner sits. The cells are separated from each other by thick walls but have glass walls facing the tower and the outside, so that each prisoner is back-lit in his cell. On the tower's highest storey there is a warder. At this height, the tower, which is otherwise solid and blocks the prisoners' views into the other cells, is glazed all around (in the more recent example of the tower displayed in Figure 16.3 the stone façade is disrupted by windows). The walls within

Figure 16.3
Inside one of the prison buildings at Presidio Modelo, Isla de la Juventud, Cuba, 2005 (Creative Commons by-nc-sa 3.0, Photography: Friman).

the tower are constructed so that no back-lighting occurs here, which means that the prisoners cannot see the warder. Foucault summarizes the power relations between prisoner and warder, which are determined in this structural arrangement by the difference between seeing and being seen, as follows: 'in the peripheric ring, one is totally seen, without ever seeing; in the central tower, one sees everything without ever being seen. [...] From the point of view of the guardian, [the crowd] is replaced by a multiplicity that can be numbered and supervised; from the point of view of the inmates, by a sequestered and observed solitude' (Foucault 1979: 202, 201).

Since the permanent visibility of the tower imprints on the consciousness of the prisoners the possibility of being seen at any time by the warder, their surveillance ultimately becomes, according to Foucault, superfluous: the knowledge of their visibility makes the prisoners control their own behaviour. While the arena of antiquity was, for Foucault, the structural-spatial expression of the ancient society of the spectacle, the panopticon, which 'automatizes and disindividualizes power' and replaced the 'collective effect' of the ancient arena 'by a collection of separated individuals' (Foucault 1979: 202, 201), is for him the material expression of the modern 'society [...] of surveillance' (Foucault 1979: 217). It is a society in which, '[p]ower has its principle not so much in a person as in a certain concerted distribution of bodies, surfaces, lights, gazes' (Foucault 1979: 202).

THE FOOTBALL ARENAS OF TODAY

Built space

In sum, the arenas of antiquity were built, according to Foucault, in order to 'render accessible to a multitude of men the inspection of a small number of objects' (N.H. Julius 1831, quoted in Foucault 1979: 216) as well as to merge the individual into the crowds. As demonstrated, the modern stadia built between the late eighteenth century and the 1980s also followed this principle structurally. The modern panopticon, in contrast, was built in order '[t]o procure for a small number, or even for a single individual, the instantaneous view of a great multitude' (N.H. Julius 1831, quoted in Foucault 1979: 216) and to *prevent* the merging of the individual into the crowds. Our theory in relation to the structural form of the contemporary stadium is that its materiality as well as the gaze-directing regime and the spatial arrangement of the stands, represent a combination of both structural principles (cf. Bale 2005). According to the German architectural firm agn Niederberghaus & Partner, specialists in stadium construction, the newer arenas offer a combination of 'a real cauldron-like atmosphere and a very close fan feeling with modern comfort and the highest standards of safety.'[1]

On the one hand, the football arenas that have been built since the 1990s are, like the ancient arenas and modern stadia before them, also characterized by the direction of the spectators' gaze towards the centre of the building. There, as before, a spectacle takes place, which captivates the crowds. The football match produces – as once in ancient dramas or gladiator battles – new heroes again and again and still releases tremendous emotions among the crowd in the stands. In today's football arenas, the stands are usually built more steeply than in modern times and, in the absence of the running track, once characteristic of many multifunctional stadia, they again directly adjoin the pitch, just as in antiquity. This not only means that active participants and spectators are as near as possible to each other, but also that the people in the stands become more intensively aware of the other spectators, visually and acoustically. The roofing of today's stadia intensifies the cauldron-like effect, which was characteristic of the ancient arena, a fact increasingly exploited by the organisers of rock concerts and other mass events. The return to the structural qualities of the ancient architectures of assembly is also apparent in the naming of numerous stadia in recent years: since 2005, the German *Bundesliga* team Bayern Munich no longer plays in the Olympia*stadion*, but in the Allianz *Arena*.

On the other hand, the restructuring of stadia since the 1990s, following the stadium catastrophes such as those at Hillsborough or Heysel, can be described as a process of the gradual entry of the panoptical principle into today's football arenas. First – in contrast to the stone seating areas of ancient arenas or the terraces of modern stadia which required the crowd to move together as closely as possible – installed in the stands of contemporary stadia is the plastic seat (Figure 1.3). It positions people at defined distances to each other and thus transforms the mass of the crowd into a 'multiplicity that can be numbered and supervised' (Foucault 1979: 201). Accordingly, Anthony King in this book (cf. Chapter 1) attributes the individual plastic seat with a behaviour-normalizing and disciplinary power (cf. Brown 1998: 58ff.). It is no coincidence that complicated fan choreographies, the lighting of Bengal fireworks or outbreaks of violence in today's arenas only take place in the protecting confines of the few terrace places. However, the Mexican Wave, which depends upon a precisely timed interaction of seated individuals, is not only enactable in, but also characteristic of, the seated areas.

Second, today's football stadia are highly supervised spaces. This is demonstrated by numerous surveillance cameras which observe the crowd from countless perspectives from the stands and roofs of the stadium. The control rooms of the security staff who evaluate the pictures are situated in a narrow glazed ring that encompasses the entire rotunda of the stadium and which separates the upper tiers of the arena from the lower ones (Figure 1.5). Here is also where the hugely expensive separate cubicles of the business and VIP lounges can be found (Figure 3.2). And so the glazed viewing platform of the tower at the centre of the panopticon has been transformed into an all-round glazed area in the stands of today's stadia which not only allows 'supervisors' and 'warders' but also higher-ranking social groups to see without being seen. Correspondingly, the 'traditional fans', banned to the narrow terraces of the stadium with their club flags, trumpets and fan paraphernalia, complain about being watched not only by security staff but also by the business and lifestyle audience, for which they seem to provide an entertaining atmospheric background from their secluded private rooms (Hasselbauer 2007).

By this, the structural-spatial development of the latest generation of football arena points to the fact that the ambivalent relationship between crowds and architecture – which, according to Canetti, has been constitutive for the modern stadium as a building – is increasingly subjected to a differentiated form of control. Van Winkel describes this process as a progressive encompassment and disciplining of the crowds. 'If it were possible to watch a speeded up video tape of the history of modern stadium construction what one would see is one long-drawn-out and continuous encapsulation of the crowd' (van Winkel 2000: 33). John Bale (2005) adds the aspect of demarcation to this diagnosis. Sports stadia, according to Bale, are examples of the growing segmentation of spaces in modernity, with the goal of increasing the power and control over these spaces. Bale makes this clear in a comparison between the stadia of the early twentieth century and the all-seater stadia of today:

> In the former, we see how the spectators group themselves freely and without
> separating demarcations around the playing area and how the different groups
> mix together. In the modern stadium, in contrast, we see the individualised
> visitors on their numbered seats, where each one is identifiable, both by the
> computerised ticket and by the knowledge that we receive from those
> comprehensive surveillance methods that are common in modern sports
> venues.
>
> (Bale 2005: 39)

A catastrophe like that at Hillsborough in 1989 seems just as inconceivable in the newest stadia as it would be to shout 'Kill the Cops!' nowadays and still manage to remain unidentified and unpunished. In sum, it certainly is no coincidence that, with the restructuring of modern stadia to all-seater facilities, FIFA and UEFA have been using *spatial* measures to make stadia safer and more profitable spaces, confronting the tradition of the terraces which made individual acts unattributable to concrete persons.

However, if someone wanted to film every single spectator in a full, 40,000-seat football stadium for only one second, they would need 666 minutes to do so. With a match duration of 90 minutes, the task of checking and evaluating the camera pictures would have to be divided among eight people. This very simple calculation shows how incomplete the protection provided by surveillance cameras and a few security personnel must necessarily remain.

Foucault has pointed to the fact that an architecture that aims to discipline the crowds is not only dependent on the separation of the crowds into single individuals to provide the warder with 'the instantaneous view of a great multitude' (N.H. Julius 1831, quoted in Foucault 1979: 216) but also on representing the power of the gaze of the (permanently invisible) warder structurally in order to make his or her *power* permanently visible. Only the permanent presence of the tower, the physical incarnation of the possibility of being seen without being able to see, ultimately makes the prisoners control their own behaviour. But how can today's football arenas display their disciplinary power completely when the control centres of contemporary arenas have wandered to the stands so that the structural proof of surveillance is no longer visible at the spot to which the spectators' gazes are being directed?

Medial and social space: the society of control

In the middle of today's arena, roughly at the height of the panoptic tower's viewing platform and therefore located at the centre of the once disciplinary power, is the video cube. Where the panopticon tower symbolized the ubiquity of the disciplining gaze of the invisible warder, the video cube, surveying the pitch, embodies the ubiquity of the television cameras and therefore, the media. The ability of the cube to present both bird's-eye perspectives of the event, as well as close-ups of players and spectators, displays, on the one hand, the omnipotence of the panoptic view as it suggests both overview and proximity simultaneously. On the other hand, the video cube creates a strange transparency of the panoptic situation: the pictures displayed allow the audience both to see and 'control' whether and when they are actually being watched or not.

When people see themselves on the cube they generally react with enthusiasm: being caught on camera is not considered threatening. Quite the opposite: the visibility of an individual on the video cube guarantees that he or she gets a double appearance in their gleeful act of sticking out from the crowd. In the first instance, the fan suddenly becomes visible to others in the stadium: the individuals exposed here can contact and react to each other. Additionally, however, the stadium's spectators are exhibited in precisely that medium and on that surface usually reserved for the heroes of the game, thus guaranteeing the transfer of their own image outside the stadium and onto television screens. As the intermediary of inside and outside, the video cube brings the entire enclosed space of the stadium into question.

From one viewpoint, this constellation removes the threatening nature of the central structure of the panopticon: imagine a warder who has lost sight of the prisoners not only because he or she had to give up the central surveillance position to the media but also because all the prisoners are suddenly standing simultaneously at their windows, trying to draw the attention of the (TV or journalists') cameras. However, from another, the panoptic situation in today's arenas is strengthened by the fact that part of the disciplinary work has been delegated to the television cameras and has therefore become more subtle. It is a power structure, created by gazes, which is comparable with commercial internet portals such as the publicly visible, diary-type microblog portal Twitter, or Facebook, which offers personal profile pages: a self-exposure that is half voluntary, half produced by the pressure of the social environment, which ignores the fact, or hazards the consequences, that not only friends but also 'overseers' such as a future boss or a state institution can access personal pages on the internet, and gain information about personal preferences, social networks or events.

Like Twitter or Facebook, today's stadia therefore embody the promise of being part of a *community of exposure*, which constitutes itself by being seen by others. But, as in the panopticon, surveillance and control is both disguised and omnipresent: 'under the surface of images, one invests bodies in depth' (Foucault 1979: 217).

These phenomena can be further explained with reference to a reconsideration of Foucault's theory by French philosopher Gilles Deleuze (1990). Deleuze argues that the modern disciplinary society has been succeeded by a new societal formation: the society of control. According to Deleuze, we are 'in a generalized crisis in relation to all the environments of enclosure – prison, hospital, factory, school, family',[2] the structural prototype of which Foucault had found in the panopticon. These disciplining milieus, dependent on the permanence of (state) institutions, have been replaced by 'ultrarapid forms of free-floating control'. For Deleuze, the computer 'that tracks each person's position – licit or illicit – and effects a universal modulation' is thus the symbol of the new society of control.

In the society of control, the forms of exercising power have become more flexible, while remaining continuous and limitless, and the structures of power have receded from view, while remaining omnipresent – as has been demonstrated in this volume with reference to the use of computerized TV and surveillance cameras, electronic ticket sales systems and databases of football hooligans known to the police. The new control mechanisms are compared by Deleuze to a mole's burrow, which invisibly undercuts all earlier disciplining institutions. Like a gas, the control mechanisms also traverse the psyche of subjects who now not only *control* themselves, but also *optimize* themselves as commodities for the market (cf. Bröckling 2007) – as illustrated by spectators posing in front of the video cube in gaudy costumes and makeup. For Deleuze, where people in disciplinary societies were individualized, today's control mechanisms produce 'dividual' individuals. The society of control is thus characterized by 'the brashest rivalry [...], an excellent motivational force that opposes individuals against one another and runs through each, dividing each within'.

Deleuze delegated to future research the task of investigating the motivations of individuals who devote themselves to the 'joys of marketing'. However, this analysis of the contemporary football arena suggests that the self-disciplining and self-marketing of individuals is realized by the individuals' aspiration to draw attention to themselves, often in the form of aggressive attempts to appeal to the camera and thereby *attract* its gaze. Through the entry of television into the stadium, the arena of today celebrates not only the crowds but also the individual. It promises him or her the chance to be looked at by the crowd of other individuals and to have prevailed against them. In the stadium, the individual can thus, by means of his or her presence, be both part of a crowd as well as deliberately stick out from it. Either directly or via the media, s/he can establish contact or interact with the spectators present, with the absent television viewers and with the heroes on the pitch. It is as if the panopticon cells were replaced by individual showrooms and the tower disguised by a glass mirrored from the outside:

the one-time centre of power reflects its images back to the individuals who pose in front of the mirrored glass. Thus, by exposing themselves they reduce the disciplining power to absurdity while simultaneously making use of it and enforcing it.

Spatially and architecturally, we can observe a few new trends that mirror these developments: first, there is the growing popularity of ephemeral stadia, erected as *temporary* party zones that can be quickly dismantled. Here, the people no longer go to the stadium, but rather the mediatized stadium comes to them, becoming more and more flexible. However, the impression of control by the confinement of bodies in an enclosed, static structure only *seems* to be annulled by the provisional and temporary nature of the ephemeral event architecture. In fact, it can be interpreted as a new expression of the Deleuzian society of control.

Second, current stadia appear in many respects to be much more *open* than their historical predecessors: this is manifest in the glass façades or those that mirror the events in the stadium to the outside world as medial interfaces. The ubiquity of the television cameras and the stadium's video cube have made these into transmission media that reach well beyond the boundaries of the building, as well as the city, region, nation and continent in which the stadium stands. Because today's stadia are safer than their modern predecessors, more and more, though not all, social groups are represented as spectators. However, each social group is allocated their own particular place in the stands according to their social status, just as in the ancient arena – a distribution organized nowadays by means of pricing policies. By this, the arena of today mirrors the social order of society as a whole, right up to its mechanisms of exclusion.

THE STADIUM OF THE FUTURE

Against the background of the above analysis of the built, social (and medial) space of ancient, modern and current (football) stadia, how will the future development of the stadium look? Based on his concept of the generational development of stadia, the architect Rod Sheard (2000, 2005, cf. introduction to this volume) identified two essential trends for the building's future. First, he predicts that stadia will revert to being built increasingly in city centres – namely as urban event architectures alongside cinemas and shopping malls – and, second, that they will integrate the increasing digitalization and medialization of the game of football architecturally, in order to eliminate the competition from television and the internet.

Sheard explains the prospective return of the stadium to the inner cities with the help of an economic argument. If the large structure of the football stadium is to be profitable, it must be opened up to other functions such as living, going out and shopping: 'The modern stadia of the future will be all about the facilities that are packed into and around them and the effects these facilities have on their local environment' (Sheard 2000: 51). A diversification of functions would mean that stadium buildings could be used for more than just 20 large events a year, but in addition for many other occasions, from family celebrations in the attached restaurant to visits to the fan shop. But in the course of the rediscovery and festivalization of the urban (Häußermann and Siebel 1993), this can only succeed, as Sheard rightly says, if football, together with its buildings, returns to the place with the largest profit margins: the metropolitan centres.

It is also conceivable – as predicted by Schulke in Chapter 3 – that football will return as a spectator event to the city centres in the form of Public Viewing, but not in the form of the stadium, which, as a large built structure, needs enormous mass logistics, which can be organized more easily outside the centre. John Bale points out that the negative effects of the new developments in stadium construction, particularly on the neighbourhood, namely spill-over effects such as traffic congestion, crowding and hooliganism, could not be removed (cf. Bale 2000).

Concerning Sheard's second point: in order to make the visit to the stadium competitive in the face of the medially transmitted football consumption on television and the internet in the living room at home, stadia must become more comfortable and weather-proof in future. In addition, it is conceivable that each seat will be equipped with the necessary electronic devices so that – just as in front of the television or computer screen at home – disputed or celebrated scenes of the play can be recapitulated individually and in slow motion, statistics on the state of play, ball possession and players' running performance can be accessed and tactical formations can be studied. The collective gaze of the spectator, which is actually what characterizes the stadium, whether on the pitch or the video cube, will be radically individualized in this scenario. The visitor to the stadium becomes autistic and collective emotions are barely imaginable, a danger that is also recognized by Sheard. 'Sport is all about the passion of watching an event. Future stadia are therefore all about not losing that passion' (2000: 51). How this can be achieved, however, is left open by Sheard.

Against the background of the insights collected in this book, we conclude that future stadia must also be orientated towards their genuine fundamental principles, regardless of their size, their location, or the societal form they (are supposed to) represent: (1) the clear separation from the outside world – as such they also turn their backs on the city, (2) the focusing of the gaze of all spectators towards the centre, (3) a built structure through which the crowds are made visible and become reflexively conscious of themselves and (4) the staging of actions – not only of players but also of spectators who try to stand out from the crowd and are therefore dependent on its presence – in the spotlight. It is the interplay between these factors that differentiates the stadium as a building type from other material and social spaces with which it is often compared (such as living rooms, public squares, cathedrals or television studios).

The objective of this book has been to highlight association football as a space-constituting, sociocultural practice, and to investigate the connection between this practice, its spaces and the built environment, that is, the stadium.

We have paid particular attention to current trends and the latest developments, which can also lead us to systematic blind spots. While we – as here in the conclusion – discuss how gaze-directing regimes and the relationship between the crowds and architecture in the new arenas change, it is easy to forget that there is a world of football beyond the *Premier League*, *Primera División*, *Ligue 1*, *Serie A* and *Bundesliga*, which takes place in other stadia entirely. These are the football pitches with unroofed terraces of the third, fourth and fifth divisions, in which much of that being increasingly forced out of present arenas by the growing control of the crowds, continues to exist – in all of its positive as well as negative aspects. Newspapers continue to report instances of racism, hooliganism, violence and sexism in the lower leagues, but also write about a non-commercialized fan presence and self-determination. Beyond the established disciplining mechanisms of the new arenas, the refuge character of the stadium lives on. It would be useful to examine how this is changing, or to what extent it is comparable with modern stadia. For example, what does being a man or a woman mean in these stadia? What value is placed on heroes there and how are they made?

We have suggested that the built and socio-spatial alterations of a specific building type indicate the formation of its respective society. In concluding, we might ask why it is that stadia existed in antiquity and in modern times, but not in the Middle Ages, and why stadia were replaced for a while as architectures of mass assembly by cathedrals and other religious buildings.[3] Our hypothesis is that stadia are buildings in which profoundly worldly practices, often resembling religious rituals, are performed. As architectures of mass assembly, cathedrals and stadia are buildings with an aural quality where the gaze of those present is directed towards a central point, which is either the altar, or the pitch. Both building types are extraordinary: They mark a clear structural boundary to the outside world and, here as there, communities are reinforced by means of ritual actions. Yet how does the spatial structure of stadia and cathedrals differ? In cathedrals, the crowds are dedicated to the reverence of something beyond the building, that is, 'a Higher Being' or 'an Other Presence'. In stadiums, however, the architecture reveals the crowds not only to their adored heroes, physically present on the pitch, and in the centre, but also *to themselves*. In this they can find both delight and danger.

NOTES

1 www.baunetz.de/meldungen/Meldungen-Stadion_in_Aachen_eingeweiht_814216. html, accessed 24 August 2009.
2 For all subsequent quotations cf. www.nadir.org/nadir/archiv/netzkritik/societyofcontrol. html, accessed 9 December 2009.
3 Regrettably, the book *The New Cathedrals* by R.C. Trumpbour (2007) is, despite the title, not very helpful with regard to this question: The book focuses on modern American stadia as secular buildings. Its title refers to the skyline of cities, arguing that stadia have 'supplanted the ancient cathedral as the most visible and recognizable structure in many communities' (Trumpbour 2007: 2, cf. Bale 1993).

REFERENCES

Bachelard, G. (1957) *La Poétique de l'Espace*, Paris: Presses Universitaires de France.

Bale, J. (1993) *Sport, Space, and the City*, London/New York: Routledge.

Bale, J. (2000) 'The changing face of football: Stadiums and communities', in J. Garland, D. Malcolm and M. Rowe (eds) *The Future of Football: Challenges for the twenty-first century*, London et al.: Frank Cass.

Bale, J. (2005) 'Stadien als Grenzen und Überwachungsräume', in M. Marschik, R. Müllner, G. Spitaler and M. Zinganel (eds) *Das Stadion. Geschichte, Architektur, Politik, Ökonomie*, Wien: Turia+Kant.

Bröckling, U. (2007) *Das unternehmerische Selbst. Soziologie einer Subjektivierungsform*, Frankfurt am Main: Suhrkamp.

Brown, A. (1998) 'United we stand: Some problems with fan democracy', in A. Brown (ed.) *Fanatics! Power, identity and fandom in football*, London/New York: Routledge.

Canetti, E. (1973) *Crowds and Power*, London: Penguin Books.

Deleuze, G. (1990) *Society of Control*. Online. Available www.nadir.org/nadir/archiv/netzkritik/societyofcontrol.html (accessed 12 December 2009).

Durkheim, E. (1951) *Suicide, a Study in Sociology*, Glencoe: Free Press.

Durkheim, E. (1961) *Die Regeln der soziologischen Methode*, Darmstadt: Luchterhand.

Edelman, R. (2002) 'A small way of saying "no": Moscow working men, Spartak soccer, and the communist party, 1900–1945', *The American Historical Review*, 107: 1441–73.

Elias, N. and Dunning, E. (1986) *Quest for Excitement: Sport and leisure in the civilizing process*, Oxford: Blackwell.

Foucault, M. (1979) *Discipline and Punish. The birth of the prison*, New York: Vintage Books.

Foucault, M. (1986) 'Of other spaces', *diacritics* 16(1): 22–7.

Hachleitner, B. (2005) 'Das Stadion als Gefängnis', in M. Marschik, R. Müllner, G. Spitaler and M. Zinganel (eds) *Das Stadion. Geschichte, Architektur, Politik, Ökonomie*, Vienna: Turia+Kant.

Halbwachs, M. (1938) *Morphologie Sociale*, Paris: A. Colin.

Hasselbauer, T. (2007) 'Architektur gegen Fan. Miese Laune in neuen Arenen', *die tageszeitung*, 4 December.

Häußermann, H. and Siebel, W. (1993) (eds) *Festivalisierung der Stadtpolitik. Stadtentwicklung durch große Projekte*, Opladen: Westdeutscher Verlag.

Schneider, R. (1999) 'Chemie', in C. Remath and R. Schneider (eds) *Haare auf Krawall. Jugendsubkultur in Leipzig 1980 bis 1991*, Leipzig: Connewitzer Verlagsgesellschaft.

Sennet, R. (1994) *Flesh and Stone. The body and the city in Western civilization*. New York/London.

Sheard, R. (2000) '"Enhance the passion of watching the event": Interview with HOK+LOBB', in M. Provoost and Nederlands Architectuurinstituut (eds) *The Stadium: The architecture of mass sport*, Rotterdam: NAi Publishers.

Sheard, R. (2005) *The Stadium. Architecture for the new global culture*, Berkeley: Periplus Editions.

Trumpbour, R.C. (2007) *The New Cathedrals. Politics and media in the history of stadium construction*, New York: Syracuse University Press.

van Winkel, C. (2000) 'Dance, discipline, density and death', in M. Provoost and Nederlands Architectuurinstituut (eds) *The Stadium: The architecture of mass sport*, Rotterdam: NAi Publishers.

Index